INEQUALITY

OXFORD ETHICS SERIES
Series Editor: Derek Parfit, All Souls College, Oxford

THE LIMITS OF MORALITY
Shelly Kagan

PERFECTIONISM
Thomas Hurka

INEQUALITY
Larry S. Temkin

MORALITY, MORTALITY, Volume I
Death and Whom to Save from It
F. M. Kamm

INEQUALITY

Larry S. Temkin

New York   Oxford
OXFORD UNIVERSITY PRESS
1993

Oxford University Press

Oxford   New York   Toronto
Delhi   Bombay   Calcutta   Madras   Karachi
Kuala Lumpur   Singapore   Hong Kong   Tokyo
Nairobi   Dar es Salaam   Cape Town
Melbourne   Auckland   Madrid

and associated companies in
Berlin   Ibadan

Published by Oxford University Press, Inc.
200 Madison Avenue, New York, New York 10016

Oxford is a registered trademark of Oxford University Press

Library of Congress Cataloging-in-Publication Data
Temkin, Larry S.
Inequality / Larry S. Temkin
p.   cm. — (Oxford ethics series)
Includes bibliographical references and index.
ISBN 0-19-507860-8
1. Equality.   I. Title.   II. Series
HM146.T45   1993   305—dc20   92-9497

2 4 6 8 9 7 5 3 1

Printed in the United States of America
on acid-free paper

To my family, especially Meg

Preface

In 1977 two chance conversations changed the direction of my philosophical life. First, a fellow graduate student at Princeton, Milton Wachsberg, convinced me to attend a course taught by someone I had never heard of. The course, given by Derek Parfit, covered much of the seminal work later developed in *Reasons and Persons*, and I found it fascinating. Later, Eileen O'Neill and I were discussing our readiness for the next year's job market. Eileen wasn't worried; she was going to France for the year to study at the Sorbonne. What a brilliant idea! Perhaps I could take a year off and study at Oxford with Parfit.

Three days later I ran into Parfit at the copy machine in 1879 Hall. I asked if he was going to be at Oxford the following year. "Why?" he answered. "Were you thinking of coming to study with me?" I indicated that I was, without, of course, elaborating on my idea's recent origin. Though he hardly knew me, Parfit immediately and warmly replied, "I think that would be a marvelous idea." I arrived in Oxford the following summer.

Having gained an extra year for research, I decided to treat myself to some philosophical fun. Before turning to my dissertation, I would write up some criticisms of Parfit's work regarding future generations. I ended up writing a fifty-page paper that included a twenty-five page "aside" entitled "Reflections on Equality." Parfit's response was strong and wholly unexpected: to forget about my previous plans and write a thesis on inequality. I followed his advice, never imagining that I would still be working on the topic 13 years later. Nor could I have known, though I sometimes let myself dream, that I might one day publish a book on inequality with Oxford University Press, whose flag I used to gaze at from my Little Clarendon Street flat as I wrote out my initial thoughts on inequality.

Much has happened in the intervening years, and there are many who have aided in this book's production. But first let me record my debt to my philosophical teachers. At the University of Wisconsin, I had many dedicated teachers who first sparked, and then fanned, my interest in philosophy: Robert Hambourger, Zane Parks, Marcus Singer, Fred Dretske, and, especially, Dennis Stampe. In graduate school I learned from many, including Michael Frede, Gilbert Harman, David Lewis, Thomas Nagel, Tim Scanlon, and Margaret Wilson. At Oxford I profited from a seminar given jointly by John Mackie and John McDowell, and another given by Ronald Dworkin, Parfit, and Amartya Sen. In addition, I was stimulated by the Oxford Moral Philosophy Discussion Group, whose members included

Dworkin, Philippa Foot, Ray Frey, Jonathan Glover, James Griffin, Richard Hare, Joseph Raz, Parfit, and Sen.

In writing this book I have received substantial financial support and leave time from Rice University. I am particularly indebted to Dean Allen Matusow for his patient and continuing support of this on- (and on and on) going project. I am also grateful to the National Humanities Center, where I spent a delightful year of research in 1984–85. In addition, I would like to thank the Danforth Foundation, which funded me throughout graduate school.

Portions of chapters 2, 7, 8, and 9 have appeared elsewhere. I am grateful to the editors of *Philosophy and Public Affairs*, Yale University Press, and Cambridge University Press for their permission to publish the relevant material here. Sue Brod and Minranda Robinson helped prepare this manuscript. Beto Zuniga spent hours improving my diagrams, and Nancy Hogan helped with the bibliography and index. To these, and to the people at Oxford University Press who worked so diligently on this book, many thanks.

Over the years I have benefitted from the ideas of many students, colleagues, and lecture audiences in the United States and Europe. It would be hopeless to try to acknowledge them all here, but three groups deserve special mention: first, Grahame Lock and his colleagues, who recently afforded me the opportunity to present and discuss significant portions of this work at a series of lectures at the University of Leiden and the Instituut voor Politicologie at the Katholieke Universiteit in the Netherlands; second, my colleagues in the Rice Center for the Study of Institutions and Values Reading Group on Rationality and Equality, especially Bill Nelson and Peter Mieszkowski; and third, my departmental colleagues, past and present, who have provided me with as collegial, supportive, and pleasant an intellectual environment as one could ever ask for. Tristram Engelhardt, Donald Morrison, George Sher, Sonja Sullivan, and Kenneth Waters all have my appreciation, with special thanks to Baruch Brody, Steven Crowell, Dick Grandy, Konstantin Kolenda, and Mark Kulstad.

Larry Lohmann and William Rued commented on an early draft of chapter 2. Michael Bayles, Jonathan Dancy, John O'Connor, Bill Rowe, and members of the Triangle Circle Ethics Group in Chapel Hill offered useful comments on chapter 9. In addition, I have profited from helpful discussions with James Griffin, and from James Ward Smith's reader's report on my dissertation.

Thomas Nagel's comments about chapter 2 motivated the writing of chapter 9, and influenced chapter 10. Beyond that, his writings have been a fertile source of ideas. Unfortunately, his recent book, *Equality and Partiality*, appeared after this book was already undergoing final revisions; thus, I have not been able to relate my work to his. Tim Scanlon has shaped my thinking in various ways. I am indebted to his seminar on social and political philosophy, to his excellent writings, to several useful conversations, and especially to his astute written comments on my dissertation.

Several economists were particularly helpful. Amartya Sen provided many excellent comments on early drafts, and his book, *On Economic Inequality*, was easily my most useful resource. Tyler Cowen sent extensive comments on many drafts, as did John Broome, whose criticisms were forceful and troubling. Although I was unable to pursue them all, I am very grateful for Cowen and Broome's numerous suggestions as to ways of further developing my views in connection with the economics literature.

More specific debts are recorded in my footnotes. In addition, other relevant works are indicated in the bibliography, along with a sampling of the philosophical and economics literature on inequality. To all those who have taken the time to give me their comments, criticisms, and encouragement but who are not acknowledged here or in my footnotes, I offer my apologies and heartfelt gratitude. Similarly, I apologize to all those who have written important work on inequality that I have not cited, or worse, who have written relevant work of which I was unaware during this book's writing. The literature on inequality is vast, and I have not been able to survey it completely.

Shelly Kagan deserves separate mention. His thirty-six pages of single-spaced comments were as acute as any I received. Though I am sure I have not adequately responded to all of his worries, there are many places where his comments illuminated my thinking, clarified my exposition, and saved me from error.

Derek Parfit has been mentioned before, but it would be impossible to exaggerate his influence on this work. Morally and politically, I had been concerned about inequality as long as I could remember. But it was not until reading Parfit that I was first stimulated to examine inequality seriously. Moreover, it was Parfit who encouraged me to develop my views on this topic—no small point, since, looking back, my initial "Reflections on Equality" was unbelievably crude and ill-formed. Parfit has been an extraordinary source of rich ideas and penetrating criticisms, and he has had a profound influence on this book's development and content. In addition, he has been an inexhaustible source of inspiration and encouragement, for which I am deeply grateful.

Let me end with a few personal remarks. My children, Daniel, Andrea, and Rebecca, have lived under this book's shadow for as long as they have been alive. Though they didn't really understand why they couldn't play in my study while I worked on my book, they were remarkably patient and forgiving when I kicked them out. And while I dared not admit it at the time, their interruptions brought joy and welcome relief, even though they slowed my progress some. My parents, Blair and Leah, have been an unfailing source of financial and emotional assistance. They have also been my best, and most important, teachers. Almost every significant lesson that I have learned in life I learned from them. Finally, my greatest debt, by far, is to my wife, Meg, who has provided me with essential and unwavering support. She deserves much more thanks than I can ever give her here.

Houston, Texas   *L.S.T.*
May, 1992

Contents

INEQUALITY

1

Introduction

Equality has long been among the most potent of human ideals, and it continues to play a prominent role in political argument. Views about equality inform much of the debate about such wide-ranging issues as racism, sexism, obligations to the poor or handicapped, relations between developed and underdeveloped countries, and the justification of competing political, economic, and ideological systems.

Most philosophical discussions of equality have focused on two questions: Is equality really desirable? And what kind of equality should we seek—that is, insofar as we are egalitarians, should we want equality of opportunity, primary goods, need satisfaction, welfare, or what? These are important questions. But I shall be asking a third question. When is one situation *worse* than another regarding inequality? There are two reasons for addressing this question. First, it can be of little practical consequence that one regards inequality as bad—as many do[1]—unless one is generally able to determine if one situation's inequality is worse than another's. Second, and more fundamental, I believe it is only by addressing this question that one can begin to understand the nature and complexity of the notion of inequality. It is toward that end this book is written.

1.1 Overview of the Book

I begin this chapter with a brief overview of the book. I then present some preliminary comments that help clarify and explain this book's methodological approach, terminology, and background assumptions.

In chapter 2, I begin my examination of how we judge one situation's inequality to be worse than another's. By considering various judgments we make, together with others we might make, I show there are many different plausible positions underlying and influencing our egalitarian judgments. I do not claim these positions are equally appealing. But I argue that each represents elements of our thinking that are not easily dismissed. The considerations presented illustrate that the notion of inequality is surprisingly complex.

---

1. In claiming that many regard inequality as bad, I am not claiming they think equality is the only, or even most important, moral ideal. I am merely claiming equality is one ideal, among others, about which they care.

3

In chapter 3, I consider inequality in complex situations. I consider how in-creases and decreases in different group levels affect inequality, and also how different kinds of transfers between groups affect inequality. I also assess a position widely held among economists, the Pigou-Dalton condition. This chapter corrobo-rates chapter 2's results, answers many questions to which chapter 2 naturally gives rise, helps guard against mistaken conclusions to which some might otherwise be drawn, and offers fresh insights into the nature of inequality.

In chapter 4, I address two topics relevant to the proper focus of egalitarian concern. I begin by considering and rejecting an average principle of equality, and a proportional average principle. This discussion supports this book's methodologi-cal approach. I next consider whether certain egalitarian comparisons should focus on how people compare relative to the best-off person or, like Rawls, on how they compare relative to the best-off group. I ultimately reject the Rawlsian analogy, in ways that have implications for Rawls's approach elsewhere as well.

In chapter 5, I consider several approaches for measuring inequality. I begin by examining the standard statistical measures of inequality economists offered. I argue there are significant correlations between the statistical measures and our earlier results. I next consider Atkinson's measure of inequality. I argue that my work illuminates both the strengths and weaknesses of his measure. I then consider an intersection approach suggested by Amartya Sen. After noting several problems facing an intersection approach, I offer my own proposal for how best to capture a complex notion like inequality. I conclude this chapter by suggesting that my posi-tion is compatible with the rejection of additive separability, and hence with the important hermeneutic and gestalt point[2] that the nature or value of the whole need not merely be equal to the sum of its parts.

In chapter 6, I consider whether inequality matters more in a poor society than in a rich one. Although this is a topic about which there has been much confusion, I argue it is one of the few significant questions about inequality to which a (fairly!) clear answer can be given. I then consider how best to capture the correct answer in a measure of inequality. In doing this, I argue against the standard approach incorporated in many economists' measures.

In chapter 7, I consider how, if at all, variations in population size affect in-equality. Here, too, I argue against the standard view of most economists and others, according to which proportional size variations do not affect inequality. I note certain controversial implications of my view and various ways one might respond to them. My discussion suggests that our moral ideals may have to share certain formal, or structural, features not generally recognized. In addition, I argue that we need a new model for understanding our moral ideals and the role they play in our all-things-considered judgments.

In chapter 8, I consider three different views one might hold regarding the proper unit of egalitarian concern. Roughly, on these views inequality should be measured by comparing *simultaneous*, or overlapping, segments of people's lives—for example, one might directly compare the current lives of aged A and youthful

---

2. The point is an ancient one. For example, it was already made by Plato in the *Protagoras*. Still, among its most forceful contemporary exponents are followers of the hermeneutic and gestalt traditions.

B; *corresponding* segments of people's lives—aged A's youth, with B's youth; or complete lives—A's and B's lives taken as complete wholes.[3] I argue that each of these views is plausible in some cases, and implausible in others. I also note that the issue has important practical implications.

In chapter 9, I consider a view that underlies the thinking of many non-egalitarians. Roughly, the view is that one situation cannot be better or worse than another if there is no one for whom it is better or worse. On this view, decreases in inequality are not morally desirable if they *solely* result from losses to the better-off, and similarly, increases in inequality are not morally objectionable if they solely result from gains to the better-off.[4] Thus, it is argued, equality is not intrinsically desirable nor is inequality intrinsically undesirable. In discussing the view in question, I argue that it is extremely powerful, widely accepted, and underlies numerous arguments in philosophy and economics. Nevertheless, I argue that the position should probably be rejected, and in any event does not support the particular conclusions for which it has been invoked. My discussion illustrates the importance of thinking more clearly and carefully about our theory, or theories, of the good.

In my concluding chapter, I summarize the previous ones, consider whether inequality is complex or inconsistent, suggest some possible practical implications, and comment a final time on my theoretical approach.

In addressing these topics, I present and develop a new way of thinking about inequality. The common view is that the notion of inequality is simple,[5] holistic, and essentially distributive. The considerations I present suggest that this view is thoroughly misguided—that in fact the notion of inequality is complex, individualistic, and essentially comparative. What I mean by these claims will become evident as the book unfolds.

Because this book's approach is so different from much of what has been thought on this topic, I expect the reader will initially greet many of my claims with a healthy measure of skepticism. Still, I believe the approach is a promising one with many advantages. Mostly, I believe it offers the prospect of a coherent, systematic, non-ad hoc method for accommodating, explaining, and ultimately guiding our egalitarian judgments.

Finally, although I think most of the arguments that have been offered against equality can be refuted, let me emphasize that this book is neither a defense of, nor an attack on, the ideal of equality. I do not address the question of whether one

3. These views were suggested by Dennis McKerlie, in his fascinating article "Equality and Time," *Ethics* 99 (1989): 475-91.

4. Naturally, if the losses or gains to the better-off are accompanied by corresponding gains or losses to the worse-off, it is another matter, as the view in question would not apply then.

5. People have thought there are complicated issues *connected* with inequality, such as whether inequality is truly undesirable and, if so, with respect to what (income, resources, primary goods, welfare, opportunity, or whatever). Still, most have thought the notion of inequality *itself* is rather simple. We *all* know what equality is, it has been thought: that's where everybody has the same amount of x (for whatever x we are interested in). Similarly, we *all* know what inequality is: that's where some have more x than others. What could be simpler? Thus, I think it has commonly been assumed that once we determine with respect to what, if anything, we should care about inequality, it will be relatively easy to determine which of two distributions is worse regarding inequality. Some economists have recognized this is mistaken, but as we will see not even they have realized just how complex inequality is.

should care about inequality, or the question of how much one should care about inequality. It seems to me that until one understands the notion these questions are premature.

1.2 Preliminary Comments

In this section I present a lengthy set of preliminary comments. Unfortunately, experience has taught me that there is great confusion about inequality, and an immediate, almost visceral, temptation to reject any claim not in accord with one's pretheoretical views. Therefore, to forestall unnecessary misunderstandings, let me explain my methodological approach, terminology, and background assumptions. In addition, let me comment on the scope of my claims, lest I be misunderstood as addressing issues that are beyond this book's purview.

I begin with methodological remarks. Throughout this work there is argument at the level of principles. Some of this is technical, and much is abstract and theoretical. But significant attention is also paid to actual and hypothetical egalitarian judgments[6]—egalitarian intuitions, if one likes—and these may range from initial, tentative judgments to considered, final judgments. In fact, throughout this work alternative positions are derived from, and assessed in terms of their ability to account for, people's egalitarian judgments.

Some may think this book pays too much attention to identifying and capturing the many nuances of our egalitarian judgments. And perhaps it does. But in this work I follow Sidgwick in regarding our moral judgments—at the levels of both particular intuitions and underlying principles—as providing the starting place from which moral theory should proceed. More generally, my guiding methodological approach is the Sidgwickian one of seeking a coherent, systematic, and non-ad hoc method of accommodating and explaining both our pretheoretical egalitarian judgments and our firm considered ones. Moreover, the method sought should offer a plausible and principled way of assessing—and, where appropriate, revising— people's egalitarian judgments (again, at the levels of both particular intuitions and underlying principles).[7]

There are serious questions about my methodological approach. The most important concern the normative status of this approach's results. What claims can our results make on our allegiance? Is such an approach self-justifying and, if not, why

6. In this context, a "hypothetical" judgment is one there is reason to think egalitarians would, or might, make were they asked to judge the situation in question. An "actual" judgment is one we know some egalitarians make.

7. In pursuing my Sidgwickian methodology I frequently proceed in ways reminiscent of Rawls's method of equilibrium. For example, at times I move from judgments to principles, and at times from principles to judgments. Moreover, both judgments and principles are assessed in terms of their intrinsic plausibility, their implications for each other, their "fit" within the overall theory, and any other relevant factors. Similarities between my approach and Rawls's are not coincidental. In part, they stem from my being influenced by Rawls as well as Sidgwick, and in part, I suspect they stem from Rawls's view of reflective equilibrium itself being one of the many places where Sidgwick influenced Rawls's thinking. Cf. Henry Sidgwick's *The Methods Of Ethics*, 7th ed. (Macmillan, 1907), as well as John Rawls's *A Theory of Justice* (Harvard University Press, 1971).

should we believe our results correspond with the truth about morality, if there is such a thing, rather than merely cohering with most of our initial beliefs? I do not want to minimize the importance of such questions, which will be familiar to most of this book's readers. Neither do I want to try to answer them, which would require another book. Instead, let me simply assert what I believe to be true.

The problems with Sidgwick's approach suggest we must be wary of the normative status of our results. They may even cast doubt on the approach's appropriateness for certain tasks in moral theory. Nevertheless, I believe such an approach is appropriate, and even necessary, for achieving the aim of a book like this. We cannot hope to understand the notion of inequality, without paying careful attention to people's judgments regarding inequality.[8]

Let me next turn to issues of terminology. The set of issues that most philosophers cast in the terminology of *equality*, most economists cast in the terminology of *inequality*. The issues are the same, but there are two ways of talking about them. Thus the egalitarian's concern to promote equality just is the concern to reduce inequality. Still, on this point, I think the economists' terminology is more perspicuous, and for the most part, except in quotations or where it would be awkward to do so, I employ the terminology of *inequality*. In a concession to standard philosophical usage, however, I refer later to several principles of *equality*. Nevertheless, as fleshed out, these principles tell us how bad a situation's *inequality* is.

More terminology. Egalitarians come in many stripes. Too many I'm afraid. Therefore, to avoid confusion, let me be clear about what I mean by an egalitarian, and what this work will be focusing on. Although there may be many differences between them, as I use the term an *egalitarian* is anyone who attaches *some* value to equality *itself*. That is, an egalitarian is anyone who cares *at all* about equality *over and above the extent it promotes other ideals*.[9] So, equality needn't be the only ideal the egalitarian values, or even the ideal she values most. Still, throughout this book, when I consider what an egalitarian might say about a situation I shall be considering what one might say about it *insofar as one cares about (in)equality*. That is, I shall be considering situations in terms of but one respect—inequality—in which they can be better or worse.[10]

8. At least this much seems right about Wittgenstein's oft quoted—and oft misunderstood—insight that "meaning is use." To understand the ideal of equality, we have to know what egalitarians *mean* by it, and to do this we must see how they *use* the notions of equality and inequality. (See Ludwig Wittgenstein's *Philosophical Investigations*, trans. by G. E. M. Anscombe [Macmillan, 1953].)

9. There is a long tradition in philosophy according to which one would make my point by saying that an egalitarian is anyone who thinks equality is *intrinsically*, and not merely *extrinsically*, good. I think this terminology is useful, but often misleading. Many think that if an ideal is intrinsically good, then to the extent one situation is better than another regarding that ideal it must, *to that same extent*, be better all things considered. I think this is mistaken, for a variety of reasons, some of which are given in chapters 5 and 7. Still, on my view an egalitarian is someone who thinks equality is not merely extrinsically good, that is, insofar as it promotes some other good. Correspondingly, one might say that on my view equality is intrinsically valuable in the sense that there are cases where its value is not merely derivable from, or supervenient on, other values or ideals.

10. For some readers it may help to think about such situations by imagining, contrary to fact, that equality were their only moral concern. That is, by asking themselves how they would judge such situations *if* equality were the only thing they valued. Although some readers may find this too

It is important to bear the foregoing in mind, since the names "equality" and "egalitarianism" are, for a variety of reasons, often associated with positions having nothing to do with equality per se. Thus, for example, many who think of themselves as egalitarians, because they favor transfers from the better-off to the worse-off, are in fact *humanitarians*.[11] They favor equality *solely* as a means to helping the worse-off, and given the choice between redistribution from the better-off to the worse-off, and identical gains for the worse-off with equal, or even greater, gains for the better-off, they would see no reason to favor the former over the latter. Such people are not "egalitarians" as I use the term, and in my view are no more (or less) deserving of the name than utilitarians who favor transfers from better-off to worse-off on all and only those occasions that maximize utility (though to be sure humanitarians would approve many "inefficient" transfers that utilitarians would condemn). Similarly, some think of themselves as egalitarians because they favor a system of socialized medicine guaranteeing the poor access to quality health care. But such people are not egalitarians in my sense if their concerns would be satisfied by a system in which the poor had access to quality care, but the rich had even greater access to much better care.

Of course, people can use terms how they see fit, and obviously insofar as people *mean* by "equality" and "egalitarianism" positions like the foregoing, this book will not address their concerns. But it addresses the concerns of those who are egalitarians in my sense—*genuine* egalitarians, if I dare say so!—and that is an important task. (See my subsequent discussion, and also chapters 6 and 9, for related comments.)

Still more terminology. Throughout this book, I employ diagrams of the sort shown in diagram 1.1. In doing so, I often refer to the alternatives represented as "worlds." This terminology has several advantages, but since it is nonstandard English, let me stress that my use of "world" is generally synonymous with "outcome," "situation," "alternative," or in some cases, "society." So, for example, in asking whether A's world is better than B's regarding inequality, I am asking whether the outcome, situation, alternative, or society represented by A is better than that represented by B.

Let me next explain how to interpret my diagrams. A and B in diagram 1.1 represent alternative outcomes, each containing two groups. The column heights represent how well off people are,[12] the widths represent the number in each group.

---

implausible a position to take seriously, I find it helps focus my attention in illuminating ways. Also, although I think inequality's complexity makes it hard to assess outcomes only in that one respect, I don't see the intelligibility of doing so as inherently more problematic than that of assessing outcomes solely in terms of utility or maximin (practices that are readily understandable and familiar to most of this book's readers). See my subsequent discussion.

11. Or perhaps *extended humanitarians*, as I define the term in chapter 9. Extended humanitarianism is an important and prevalent position, which is often conflated with egalitarianism. But, as I will argue in chapter 9, it is not plausibly regarded as an egalitarian position. Derek Parfit has an important discussion of this kind of a position, which he dubs "the Priority View," in his unpublished manuscript "On Giving Priority to the Worse-off" (1989). (In some ways I like Parfit's terminology better than mine, but since I have been employing my terminology for many years, I have found it too hard, psychologically, to change now. As the old joke goes, "extended humanitarianism" may be an ugly name, but its *my* name.)

12. For our purposes this will generally be in terms of welfare but, as will be discussed, it could be

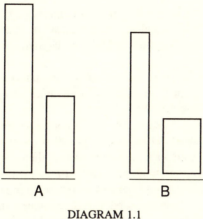

DIAGRAM 1.1

Unless noted otherwise, groups are assumed to be at a level where life is worth living. As drawn, A and B both represent situations with the same number of people, and where the better-off group is "significantly" better off than the worse-off group. However, both the levels and the sizes of the better- and worse-off groups vary from A to B.

In general, I shall leave my diagrams' details unspecified. Readers may wish to supply such details for themselves; for example, to think of A's and B's populations as about the size of the United States's and as about as well off as some of the United States's better- and worse-off members. Finally, let me observe that my diagrams are drawn as rectangular boxes mainly for reasons of simplicity and aesthetic appeal. Since this may naturally suggest that my diagrams' bases represent the zero level for welfare—the level below which life ceases to be worth living—let me note that, except in chapter 6, few, if any, of my arguments depend on the zero level. More important, I believe this book's substantive conclusions do not depend on our being able to establish the zero level. Thus, in most cases I might have drawn my diagrams without bases (perhaps with vertical dotted lines toward their bottoms indicating our ignorance of the zero level's location); but doing so would have been unnecessarily complicated and distracting.[13]

---

in terms of most any dimension with which one is concerned. For example, the column heights could represent levels of income, opportunity, primary goods, need satisfaction, and so on.

13. Technically, my point might be put as follows. Given this book's purposes it does not hurt—and in fact is often easier and useful—to assume a *ratio-scale* for welfare, according to which it makes sense to say that one person is twice as well off as another. Most of my claims, however, only depend on our having an *interval-scale*, according to which ratios between numbers representing how well off people are make no sense, but the ratios of differences between such numbers do. Whereas ratio-scales depend on a meaningful zero level, interval-scales do not. Standard examples of ratio-scales are those we use for length, where it makes sense to say that one object is twice as long as another and it doesn't matter whether we measure the length in inches or centimeters. Standard examples of interval-scales are those used for temperature. So, as Amartya Sen observes, "the gap between 100° Centigrade and 90° Centigrade is recorded as twice that between 90°C and 85°C no matter whether we express these temperatures in Centigrade or Fahrenheit (in which they correspond respectively to 212°F, 194°F and 185°F), but the ratio of the temperatures themselves will vary according to the scale chosen"

Next let me comment on my use of such diagrams. My diagrams are abstract and highly simplified. Still, though one must be careful in drawing general conclusions from such simplified diagrams, I think my diagrams are both appropriate and sufficient for my purposes.

Unfortunately, over the years I have found some philosophers react negatively to my diagrams. For example, one reaction I sometimes hear is, put crudely, "What do *boxes* have to do with ethics!?!"

I find such reactions perplexing, but let me not try to give a full defense of the use of "boxes" here. Instead, let me just request that those who find my diagrams disconcerting please keep an open mind to my *use* of them. My diagrams are neither a substitute for argument, nor some new kind of argument. They merely represent visually facts that would otherwise have to be presented in cumbersome prose. My diagrams may not be worth a thousand words, but they can, I think, be a useful shorthand if we do not allow ourselves to be misled by them, or put off by their unfamiliarity in the moral realm. Readers who find my diagrams problematic are encouraged to focus on the situations they represent and to substitute in their thinking about these issues a fleshy verbal description for the abstract pictorial one.

Throughout this work I shall mainly discuss inequality of *welfare*.[14] This does not affect my arguments. Analogous arguments could be made in terms of inequality of income, opportunity, primary goods, need satisfaction, or whatever. This is not to say the reasons for caring about welfare inequality are the same as those for caring about other kinds of inequality. Only that whatever *kind* of inequality one might care about, call it inequality of x, analogous considerations will be relevant for assessing whether the *inequality* of x is better in one situation or another.[15]

(*On Economic Inequality* [Clarendon Press, 1973], p. 4). Thus, if in the text I used an example with three people at levels 800, 600, and 400, respectively, it would usually only be important that we have an interval-scale for welfare, so, for instance, we could meaningfully claim the gap between the third person and the first was twice that between the third and the second. On the other hand, it will not generally hurt if the reader implicitly assumes that we have a ratio-scale, and so thinks, for instance, that the third person is only half as well off as the first.

14. In this book I leave the term "welfare" largely undefined. In the literature the notion of welfare is frequently used interchangeably with such notions as utility, well-being, or quality of life, but some would argue that these notions are not the same. For example, Amartya Sen argues that *utility*—which might be understood in terms of happiness, desire fulfillment, or choice—is only one component of *well-being*. More specifically, Sen argues that well-being involves an irreducible duality of what he calls "well-being freedom" and what he calls "achievements of well being." For simplicity I ignore such distinctions, important as they are in their own right. Although most of my examples are naturally cast and interpreted in terms of utility, my central claims are neutral between competing views of welfare. One might say they apply to welfare *as such*, whatever that ultimately involves. See Sen's "Well-being, Agency and Freedom: The Dewey Lectures 1984," *Journal of Philosophy* (1985): 169-221. See also James Griffin's *Well-Being: Its Meaning, Measurement, and Moral Importance* (Oxford University Press, 1987) for an extended and important discussion of well-being.

15. One might say I am focusing on that portion of one's concern about inequality of x which makes the concern an *egalitarian* one. It is the notion of *inequality* I am elucidating, not the notion of x. It might help in this respect to consider the difference between a consequentialist and an egalitarian concern for x. Presumably both the consequentialist and the egalitarian care about x in a certain way, but the former wants to *maximize* x, the latter to *equalize* it. Moreover, this is so whatever x's nature. Roughly, then, this book tries to illuminate what is involved in improving a situation's *inequality* regarding x. The answer to this question is, I think, largely (I won't say wholly) independent of x.

Besides focusing on different kinds of inequality, versions of egalitarianism may differ in their underlying nature or structure. For example, a *person-affecting* version would condemn inequality only insofar as it adversely affects people. An *impersonal* version would condemn inequality even if there were no one for whom it was worse. Such a view would enable one to compare any outcomes regarding inequality, including outcomes at different times or with different people.[16] Similarly, on a *teleological* version inequality is primarily relevant to assessing outcomes, and any outcomes might be compared, even if their inequality were unavoidable and no one were responsible for it. On a *deontological* version inequality is primarily relevant to assessing agents or actions, so unavoidable inequality for which no one is responsible might not matter morally. On the last-named version inequality's importance is not that it makes an outcome better or worse *per se*, but that in certain situations we have moral reasons to reduce or remove inequality, reasons that are not simply derivative from other moral ideals.

Characterizing and assessing the many possible versions of egalitarianism would be an interesting and important task. But doing this adequately would require a book by itself and would carry us far afield from the central concerns of *this* book.[17] Regrettably, then, I shall not *directly* address which version of egalitarianism is most plausible. However, I have views on the matter, and some of my claims have a bearing on the issue (see especially chapters 7 and 9). In any event, this book's task is to illuminate the notion of inequality. Fortunately, much progress can be made toward understanding inequality without settling—or getting bogged down in!—the difficult issues surrounding the different versions of egalitarianism noted above.

For the purposes of discussion it will be useful to focus on a single egalitarian

---

To the reader convinced at the outset that this approach is mistaken, I beg your patience. I believe that by the book's end (and hopefully long before that!) you will find my approach useful and revealing, even if you ultimately decide that in certain respects it is misleading, mistaken, or incomplete.

16. It is worth emphasizing that my terminology here and later is mainly intended to be *suggestive* of possible egalitarian positions, not definitive of such positions. Nor am I trying to offer anything like a complete taxonomy of alternative positions. For example, I realize one might usefully distinguish between narrow and wide person-affecting principles, where the latter but not the former would enable us to compare outcomes with different people. (See part 4 of Derek Parfit's *Reasons and Persons* [Oxford University Press, 1984], esp. chap. 18.) I also realize one might distinguish different senses of impersonality. For example, one might hold that a position is impersonal in one sense if it implies that a situation could be good or bad period without meaning that it is good or bad for *particular* people. On the other hand, a position is impersonal in a second and different sense, if it denies the view that nothing can be good period unless it is good for people. I am here using "impersonal" in the second sense. Notice, for example, a wide person-affecting principle would be impersonal in the first sense, but not the second. Finally, let me acknowledge that some versions of teleological or deontological egalitarianism might be characterized differently than those in the text.

17. Derek Parfit is pursuing this task in his manuscript "On Giving Priority." Some relevant considerations are contained in my "Intransitivity and the Mere Addition Paradox," *Philosophy and Public Affairs* 16 (1987): 138–87; my "Intergenerational Inequality," in *Philosophy, Politics, and Society*, 6th series, ed. by Peter Laslett and James Fishkin (Yale University Press, 1992), pp. 169–205; and my "Harmful Goods, Harmless Bads," in *Value, Welfare and Morality*, ed. by R. G. Frey and Christopher Morris (Cambridge University Press), forthcoming.

position, rather than to vacillate between several. I shall focus on a position that might be characterized as an impersonal teleological view. As suggested already, on such a view inequality is relevant to assessing outcomes. It is a feature of situations that makes outcomes (pro tanto) morally objectionable. Roughly, on this view, undeserved[18] inequality is always objectionable; whether or not it is unavoidable, any one is responsible for it, there is anyone for whom it is worse, or it involves different people, societies, places, or times.

I focus on this version of egalitarianism for several reasons. First, in holding that undeserved inequality is always objectionable, it is a fairly "pure" or "extreme" egalitarian position. This makes it controversial, but it also makes it the clearest position to discuss.

Second, focusing on the "extreme" position reveals many core components shared by different egalitarian positions. Moreover, I think once we have clarified the "extreme" position, we can see how modifying that position's assumptions would affect our results for other, less "extreme," positions. Thus, although this book is not strictly *neutral* between egalitarian positions, I think many of its main claims are generalizable and, importantly, that it provides a blueprint for illuminating alternative positions.[19]

Finally, let me confess a strong attraction toward an impersonal teleological view. Though controversial, I think it may be the most defensible egalitarian position. This is not to say such a view is plausible as an *all-things-considered* position, only that it is more defensible than alternative views *insofar as one is an egalitarian* (see further for more on this distinction). Unfortunately, as already noted, I cannot defend this view here.

Unless noted otherwise, I shall assume for each of this book's examples that the better-off are not responsible for their situation's inequality, either directly, through exploitation of the worse-off, or indirectly, through unwillingness to share their good fortune. This would be so, for instance, if the inequality were due to unavoidable and irremediable differences in health. This assumption is in keeping with my focus on an impersonal teleological view of inequality. In addition, because our concern with my examples regards their inequality, this assumption helps ensure that our judgments about them are as free as possible from the disturbing influence of other moral factors. Still, let me note that this assumption, though useful, is not necessary for my claims.

---

18. The reason for this qualification will be explained later.

19. For example, on a deontological view my central question, When is one situation worse than another regarding inequality? has little relevance, at least *as stated*. However, on a deontological view we have reason to reduce inequality, at least in some contexts, by raising people up if we can. Suppose, then, there were several people we could raise up. How are we to decide the relative strengths of their egalitarian claims? In other words, if we could bring about one situation, by raising some people, or another situation, by raising others, which course of action ought we to do? Other things equal, which would best satisfy people's competing egalitarian claims or, as some might put it, which situation are there stronger egalitarian reasons to promote? This would be my book's central question on a deontological view, and though it slightly varies from mine, and has different implications for inequality's scope, I submit that analogous considerations would be relevant to answering the two questions.

Some people think the issue of responsibility is crucial to the moral character of the question we are asking.[20] For example, some would deny that inequality is morally objectionable if no one could do anything to alleviate it, or if no one is responsible for producing or failing to prevent it. Such views would significantly alter inequality's scope and require one to reject the simplifying (and purifying) assumption noted previously, but they do not alter the force of my claims. Specifically, even if one thinks inequality only matters in certain cases—say, those cases people are responsible for—I think this book's main claims will apply to those cases, whatever they are.

Some readers are surprised about the extent to which this book is concerned with justice and fairness. Indeed, one person suggested that this book is more about justice and fairness than about inequality. This may be a terminological issue, but I find such reactions puzzling. I believe the book *is* about inequality, but to be about inequality it must *also* be about justice and fairness. On my view inequality is a subtopic of the more general—and even more complex—topics of justice and fairness. Specifically, concern about inequality is that portion of our concern about justice and fairness that focuses on how people fare relative to others. Thus, I think there is an intimate connection between people's views about inequality and certain of their views about justice and fairness. In particular, I believe egalitarians have the deep and (for them) compelling view that it is bad—unjust and unfair—for some to be worse off than others through no fault of their own.[21] Unfortunately, as we shall see, it is one matter to note that egalitarians have such a view, and quite another to unpack what it involves.

A few words about injustice. Some think a situation cannot be unjust unless something could have been done to prevent or improve that situation. More generally, some regard the concept of natural injustice as bogus. I maintain it is a natural injustice that some are born blind whereas others are not, though it may be more appropriate to say it is a natural unfairness rather than a natural injustice. This is a point I do not want to go into, as it would carry me far off my present path. However, the difference between these positions is, at least

20. Here, and later, my discussion is intended to convey some sensitivity to the many views one might hold on the issue of responsibility. However I know that my remarks blur the differences between many positions. Lest the reader be misled by my textual remarks I note the following: some might hold people responsible for (1) what they "directly" cause, create, or produce; (2) what they "indirectly" cause by "omissions" or by failing to prevent; (3) situations they can alleviate even if they didn't "directly" or "indirectly" cause those situations; or (4) situations that would not have occurred but for their direct or indirect influence on the course of events. And of course these are only *very* rough sketches, and but a few of the many positions one might hold regarding responsibility.

Fortunately, for my purposes it is not necessary to adjudicate between the many different views of responsibility. While such issues are fundamentally important, they are the subject matter of many other books, not this one.

21. Throughout this book I use the expression "through no fault of their own," as shorthand for the expression "through no fault or choice of their own." Thus, "fault" need not mean moral fault. It might include any instance of voluntary choice or responsibility. For example, it might be A's own "fault" that he is worse off than B, if the inequality between them resulted from A's voluntarily choosing a certain life-style or making large sacrifices for his children. In such cases it is arguable that A "deserves" his lot in life and is not worse off than B through no fault of his own. See my further discussion of related points.

for some writers, largely terminological. Even if one wants to say, with Rawls or Nozick, that an *injustice* has been suffered only where there is a perpetrator of the injustice, we can still recognize that a situation is such that if someone *had* deliberately brought it about, she would have been perpetrating an injustice. This tells us something about the situation. It tells us that if the situation were such that we *could* do something to improve it, we should, or, more accurately, there would at least be some (prima facie) reason to do so. (Rawls would, I think, agree with this, though perhaps Nozick would not.)

The preceding comment is relevant to our point regarding the issue of responsibility and the moral character of our question.[22] Some believe that if one person is worse off than another as a result of natural circumstances, and if nobody could do anything to alleviate the situation, the situation is not *unjust* and there is nothing *morally* objectionable about it. They might admit the situation is *unfortunate*, perhaps even *tragic*, but they deny that the language of morality applies to such situations. Like Aristotle, they might claim that morality is a guide to practical action. Accordingly, they would view claims to the effect that the situation is *bad*, or that the one person *ought* not to be worse off than the other, as purely *evaluative* rather than *moral*—perhaps as claims about what we want to be the case, rather than as claims about what we have (moral) reason to do.[23]

Such usage of the terminology of "morality" is prevalent, perhaps even dominant. I find this unfortunate. I want to say there are victims of natural injustice, and that it is bad for one person to be worse off than another even if it is nobody's fault. I don't mean by this that natural injustice is bad in exactly the same sense in which agents, or acts, can be morally bad. Rather, it is bad in the sense in which natural disasters that cause suffering are bad. But I contend this is bad in a way that is morally relevant, and I think such usage should be acceptable to anyone who regards consequentialist considerations as at least relevant to moral deliberations. Still, let me not argue this here or insist on the terminological point. To my mind the crucial question is not whether we call instances of natural and irremediable inequality *morally* objectionable *injustices*, but whether such instances are "bad" in such a way that if we *could* do something about them, we should; that is, would we have some (prima facie) moral reason to alleviate the inequality if it *were* possible for us to do so?

As I have suggested, I think some who reject the notion of natural injustices would nonetheless agree that it *would* be morally objectionable to disregard such occurrences *if* we could alleviate them. As indicated, I think the difference between their position and mine is largely terminological. On the other hand, some believe that it would not be morally objectionable to disregard such occurrences, even if we could alleviate them. The difference between their position and mine is substantive.

22. I am grateful to Thomas Scanlon and Amartya Sen for calling my attention to this issue and the importance of clarifying the terminological and substantive points discussed here and later.

23. See Gilbert Harman's "Moral Relativism Defended," *Philosophical Review* 84 (1975): 3–22, for an example of this kind of position—though Harman's motivation differs in important ways from that of some who hold such a position.

Still, though such people will have different views than I do about inequality's scope, unless they are simply nonegalitarians—that is, as long as they agree inequality is genuinely objectionable in some cases, say, those we produce—this book's arguments should be relevant to their views.

Let me next note a related point. In chapter 2 I introduce a notion of individual *complaints* and consider who has a complaint regarding inequality. I find this terminology natural, plausible, and useful. But some think the notion of complaint is intimately bound up with there being a person or institution responsible for the situation against whom the complaint can be legitimately lodged. They think complaints about something for which no one is responsible and about which nothing can be done are silly at best and perhaps irrational. According to such a view we might describe the situation of those suffering from irremediable natural misfortune using the language of pathos, or perhaps even tragedy, but not the language of complaints.[24]

I do not share such linguistic sensibilities. But to those who do, I would again urge that for my purposes the crucial issue is whether there *would* be egalitarian reason to improve someone's situation if we *could*. If so, then the person has an egalitarian complaint in my *technical* use of the term. Naturally, those who find my usage grating may think about the relation in other, more linguistically sensitive, terms. On the other hand, as before, some may hold there is no reason for complaint in cases of irremediable natural "injustice" because there is nothing morally objectionable about such cases and, as noted, they may hold this for substantive reasons. To those holding such a position I repeat my earlier assertion. Unless they are simply nonegalitarians, this book's main claims should apply to their views.

In sum, on the view adopted in this book—the "extreme" view of the impartial teleological egalitarian—one should care about natural, as well as social, inequalities. However, even if one cared only about certain social inequalities, most of the same considerations would apply. (My own view is that most concern about social inequality must ultimately ride piggyback on concern about natural inequality. It is difficult to see why social inequality would be bad per se if natural inequality were not.)

Throughout this work, I shall be considering how situations compare *regarding inequality*. I am not interested in how they compare regarding *other* ideals, or in how they compare *all things considered*. This is an important point I shall stress again in section 2.1. It is also a controversial point, deserving of special note.

Many will be puzzled, if not entirely put off, by a starting point that presumes to treat inequality in isolation from other ideals. Some will see my starting point as ruling out one of the economists' standard approaches to inequality, Atkinson's approach, which neither treats nor admits the possibility of treating equality separately. Some will see my starting point as ignoring the insight—championed by the hermeneutic and gestalt traditions—that (often) the part/whole relation is a complex one of mutual interdependence such that the whole may be different from the sum of its parts, and the parts, in turn, may not be fully understandable except in relation

---

24. This view was suggested to me by Amartya Sen, who found the terminology of complaints interesting and suggestive, but linguistically grating for the reasons suggested.

to each other and the whole.[25] Some will see my starting point as limiting my inquiry's scope to a small subset of egalitarian positions.

Having acknowledged these views let me briefly comment on each. First, though I think it unfortunate that my starting point may puzzle or alienate Atkinson's followers, this is not a shortcoming of my approach. To the contrary, I think my approach is only in tension with Atkinson's precisely where his approach is most dubious. Thus, as I argue in chapter 5, despite its popularity and many strengths, Atkinson's approach has important shortcomings. In addition, my approach helps illuminate both the strengths and weaknesses of Atkinson's approach, and is compatible with the former.

Second, although the analytic method often overlooks insights of the hermeneutic and gestalt traditions, as I sketch in chapter 5, this book's focused approach is compatible with the interdependence of the part/whole relation.[26] Moreover, even if my results ultimately need revision in light of further reflection about the whole of morality, I think a focused approach has been, and can continue to be, an important step in clarifying our moral thinking.[27]

Third, it is arguable that some egalitarian concerns are inextricably linked with other factors. For example, one might claim that a judge's concern about equality before the law is only fully understandable in terms of a particular legal system and the judge's institutional role within that system, or that a citizen's democratic concern about political equality is only understandable in terms of the nature and

25. The idea is that equality is but one part of the whole of morality along with other "parts" like utility, justice, freedom, and perfection, and the suggestion would be that none of the different "parts" of morality could be fully understood in isolation from each other and the whole. In addition, the "whole" of morality would have to take account of virtue, duty, rights-based, and consequentialist elements, and would itself have to be seen as part of the larger whole of practical rationality (which, no doubt, would in turn have to be seen as part of other, still larger, wholes).

26. By the "focused approach" I simply mean the approach of focusing, so far as possible, on a particular notion or ideal, independently of others, so as to get as clear as possible about what that notion or ideal itself involves.

27. Classical utilitarians were mistaken in believing, and hence proceeding as if, utility is all that matters. But their insights regarding the nature of utility illuminate that ideal, and are of lasting value even for those who only see utility as one part of the whole of morality.

Similarly, although neither Rawls nor his critics believe social justice constitutes the whole of morality, or even the whole of the subject of justice, the restricted focus of *A Theory of Justice* did not preclude Rawls from significantly advancing the level of debate on, and hence our understanding of, the nature and foundations of social justice. (Recall Rawls's explicit acknowledgment that he is concerned with "the way in which the major social institutions distribute fundamental rights and duties and determine the division of advantages from social cooperation," and hence that "the scope of . . . [his] inquiry is limited in two ways." First, he does "not consider the justice of institutions generally, nor except in passing the justice of the law of nations and of relations between states." Second, for the most part he restricts his attention to "the principles of justice that would regulate a well-ordered society" (see *A Theory of Justice*, pp. 7 and 8).

The point, of course, is not to suggest that the analogy between my approach and the classical utilitarians' or Rawls's is perfect, or that this book will enhance our understanding of inequality to the same extent as the classical utilitarians and Rawls enhanced our understanding of utility and social justice, respectively; it is only that the reader not be too quick to dismiss our focused inquiry. Whatever our inquiry's shortcomings, it may still yield substantial progress in our understanding of inequality. Such a possibility cannot be ruled out in advance, and that is all I ask the reader to grant me for now.

foundations of democracy. I confess, I am not sure if such positions are, in the end, best regarded as "genuinely" egalitarian, or if, perhaps, they are egalitarian in a derivative sense. Moreover, I suspect that insofar as such positions *are* egalitarian, this work's results apply to them. But let me not insist on these points. Instead, following Rawls, let me acknowledge that my inquiry's scope is limited and that I am concerned with a special class of egalitarian problems.[28]

My aim is not to elucidate every egalitarian question or concern. My aim is to elucidate the notion of inequality as it is used in evaluating alternative distributions;[29] and this can, I think, be achieved by treating inequality as (largely) separable from other moral factors. Thus, even if some egalitarian positions cannot be illuminated via my approach, the position I am interested in can be. Such a position is, at least, *one* important egalitarian position—perhaps even the most fundamental.

The preceding remarks are offered as temporizing assertions. Their defense must await the book's exposition.[30]

I am concerned with inequality from a *moral* perspective. This is why my question is not, When is there *more* inequality in one situation than another? but rather, When is one situation *worse* than another regarding inequality? I realize that approaching inequality as a *normative* rather than purely *descriptive* notion raises some tricky questions regarding my treatment of inequality separately from other ideals (a topic I shall say more about, though still not enough, in chapter 5).[31] Nevertheless this is a book in normative theory; and there are good reasons to think some situations might be *worse* than others regarding inequality, though in a descriptive sense they have *less* inequality.

For example, I think egalitarians are not committed to the view that deserved inequalities—if there are any—are as bad as undeserved ones.[32] In fact, I think deserved inequalities are not bad *at all*. Rather, what is objectionable is some being worse off than others *through no fault of their own*. Thus, although there may be more inequality in one situation than in another, that needn't be *worse* if the lesser inequality is deserved but the greater is not. Correspondingly, for each of this book's examples I shall assume that people are equally skilled, hardworking, morally worthy, and so forth, so that those who are worse off than others are so through no fault of their own.

It is, of course, extremely difficult to decide when people *are* worse off than others through no fault of their own. Some think this is nearly always the case,

28. After acknowledging that his inquiry's scope is limited (see the previous note) Rawls wrote, "I am concerned with a special case of the problem of justice" (*A Theory of Justice*, p. 7).

29. Actually, as will already be evident from this introduction, this is only a rough approximation of my aim. But it is adequate for these purposes.

30. In the end, I believe this book vindicates my approach, but that it also partially vindicates the view that we cannot *fully* understand inequality in isolation from other factors. For relevant considerations see chapters 5 and 7. Also, see note 16 in chapter 10, where I directly address this point.

31. In different ways, this point has been conveyed to me by John Broome, Shelly Kagan, Thomas Scanlon, and Amartya Sen.

32. Another reason I couch my question in normative rather than purely descriptive terms is presented obliquely in section 2.3. See, in particular, my discussion of why a maximin principle of equality might yield a "better and better" ordering of the sequence of worlds introduced in section 2.2.

others, almost never the case. Fortunately, one need not decide this issue[33] in order to recognize that only undeserved inequalities are bad.

Finally, I remind the reader that this book's aim is not to convince people of the truth or falsity of egalitarianism. It is to *understand* it. I want to elucidate the notion of inequality.[34] Once we have determined what an egalitarian view is, we will be in a better position to assess whether we should be motivated by egalitarian concerns, and if so, to what extent.[35]

33. Which involves, among other things, the mare's nest of free will.

34. As noted earlier, not in all its usages, but in a fundamentally important one.

35. Of course, our inquiry may reveal that there is no single "egalitarian view." There may be many such views that are more or less compatible. Also, our assessment of egalitarian concerns need not be all or nothing. We may decide some egalitarian concerns matter, but not others. Similarly, we may decide that although some egalitarian concerns are themselves implausible, we should give weight to other concerns that are like them in certain important respects.

2

Inequality: A Complex Notion

When is one situation *worse* than another regarding inequality? In some cases the answer to this question can be easily given. We know, for instance, that among equally deserving people a situation where some are worse off than others is worse than one where everyone is equal, in terms of inequality. We also know that among equally deserving people the inequality in a situation would be worse if the gaps between the better- and worse-off were large, than if they were small. Consider, however, a situation where many are better-off, and a few are worse-off. How would the inequality in such a situation compare with the inequality in a situation where a few are better-off and many are worse-off? How would both of these compare with a situation where the better- and worse-off groups were equal in size? It is questions such as these that I shall be addressing in this chapter. As we shall see, these are complicated questions, and ones to which several plausible but conflicting answers might be given.

2.1 Individual Complaints

My main aim is to consider our judgments about how situations compare regarding inequality. However, there is another, more particular kind of judgment it will help to consider first. This kind of judgment is about how bad the inequality in a situation is from the standpoint of particular individuals in that situation.

Such judgments can be made using the terminology of "complaints." Thus, for any situation where some people are better off than others, we can say that the best-off have nothing to complain about while the worst-off have the most to complain about. (Here, and in what follows, I often drop the locution "regarding inequality." Henceforth all references to complaints are to be understood as complaints regarding inequality, unless stated otherwise.)

To say that the best-off have nothing to complain about is in no way to impugn their moral sensibilities. They may be just as concerned about the inequality in their world as anyone else. Nor is it to deny that, insofar as one is concerned about inequality, one might have a complaint *about* them being as well off as they are. It is only to recognize that, because they are at least as well off as every other member of their world, *they* have nothing about which to complain. Similarly, to say that the worst-off have a complaint is not to make any claim at all as to whether they will *in fact* complain (they may not). It is only to recognize that it is bad (unjust or unfair) for them to be worse off than the other members of their world through no fault of their own.[1]

For any world, then, in which some are worse off than others, two questions arise. Who is it that has a complaint? And, how should we compare the seriousness of different people's complaints? To the first question there seem to be two natural but competing answers, neither of which can be easily dismissed.

According to the first answer, only those *worse off than the average* have a complaint. This answer might be defended as follows. In a world of n equally deserving people the fairest distribution would be for each person to receive one nth of the total, since among equally deserving people a fair share is an *equal* share. Those who receive less than one nth of the total would thus have a complaint, since they are receiving *less* than their fair share. Moreover, they are the only people who have a complaint, since those who receive one nth or more of the total are *already* receiving their fair share or *more* than their fair share. But in a world of n people one nth of the total welfare is the average level of welfare. Hence, all and only those below the average have a complaint.[2]

---

1. Thomas Scanlon has wondered whether the *personal* character of complaints biases our thinking toward the individualistic and, if so, whether it filters out some objections to inequality *per se*. I take it Scanlon's worry is that there may be holistic objections to inequality that cannot be adequately understood in terms of individual complaints. Scanlon may be right. If we focus exclusively on individual complaints, we may fail to note holistic objections to inequality—if there are any. But, as Scanlon would no doubt agree, this is no argument against thinking about inequality in terms of individual complaints. At most it is a reminder that any account of inequality in terms of individual complaints may be incomplete.

Also, let me add the following four comments. First, it is *extremely* natural and plausible to think about different individuals having more or less to complain about regarding inequality and, once we recognize this, it is also natural and plausible to think about a situation's inequality in terms of how its different individuals fare regarding inequality. I would deny, therefore, that the personal character of complaints *biases* our thinking toward the individualistic, and suggest instead that the naturalness of thinking about inequality in terms of complaints *reflects* the fact that so much of our thinking about inequality *is* individualistic.

Second, I would deny that only holistic objections can be objections to inequality *per se*. More specifically, I think objections to inequality that are based on individual complaints *are* objections to inequality *per se*, but they are individualistic objections rather than holistic ones. (I think Scanlon might agree. His worry was only that the individualistic approach might filter out *some* objections to inequality *per se*, such as holistic ones.)

Third, as implied already, nothing in my discussion *precludes* the possibility of thinking about inequality holistically, or in any other way that doesn't focus on individual complaints. For anything I have said so far focusing on individual complaints is *one* natural and plausible way of thinking about inequality; there may be others. Thus, thinking about inequality in terms of complaints needn't filter out, at least not in the sense of rule out, some objections to inequality *per se* (holistic or otherwise). Of course, we may ultimately decide that an individualistic account of inequality is sufficiently adequate that we can dispense entirely with thinking about inequality holistically. But this would be a vindication of the individualistic approach, not a criticism of it.

Finally, I find Scanlon's worry slightly ironic. My own view is that in the past a holistic approach to inequality has so dominated people's thinking that the possibility of understanding inequality individualistically has been almost completely overlooked.

2. The reader will note that the argument in the text supports a view that would compare people's actual levels with the level they would be at were the welfare in their world equally distributed. Strictly

There seems to be a connection in our thinking between our notion of luck and our notion of who has a complaint. Thus, we tend to think that someone can appropriately complain about something, s, only if she has been unlucky with respect to s. If, for instance, someone has guessed seven out of ten coin tosses correctly, then she is lucky to have done as well as she did, and we will tend to think that she has no cause for complaint. Similarly, we will tend to think that someone who guesses correctly five out of ten times will have no cause for complaint. A complaint from such a person would amount to a complaint about the fact that she has not been lucky; but while one can *hope* to be lucky, it doesn't seem that one can legitimately *complain* about not being lucky. Finally, if someone *has* been unlucky and guessed correctly only three out of ten times, then we will think that she *does* have a cause for complaint; and in general, the more unlucky she has been, the more we will think she has to complain about.

But notice, whether we regard someone as having been unlucky with respect to s depends upon how she fares relative to the average person with respect to s. In our world, for instance, we regard as unlucky someone who only guesses four out of ten coin tosses correctly. However, if our world were different, and the average number of correct guesses was three out of ten instead of five out of ten, then we would no longer regard such a person as unlucky.

This way of thinking might be summed up as follows. Whatever someone is complaining about, the lament, Why me?! will tend to ring hollow if she is at or above the average in the relevant respect, because it will seem that she has not, after all, been unlucky. It will meet with a sympathetic response, however, if she is below average in the relevant respect. It seems, then, that in a world of equally deserving people someone who has less than the average level of welfare has been treated unkindly by Fate. Because she has received less than she would have if the welfare in her world had been distributed equally, it seems she has not been treated (by Fate) as the equal of her peers but has, as it were, been treated as *less* than the equal of her peers. She will have a complaint, therefore, and one that is a complaint regarding inequality.[3]

---

speaking, the latter level corresponds to a hypothetical average level, which may, but probably would not, equal their world's *actual* average level. That is, depending on how one unpacks the relevant—and tricky—counterfactual regarding the level people would be at "were the welfare in their world equally distributed," one might think that if everyone received an equal share the total and average levels of welfare might be either greater or less than they are in the actual world. Correspondingly, one might think someone better off than the actual average might have a complaint regarding inequality, if one thought—say, in accordance with diminishing marginal welfare of resources—they were worse off than the average person would be were everyone treated fairly and equally. By the same token, one might think someone worse off than the actual average might not have a complaint regarding inequality, if one thought—say, because of increasing returns to scale—they were better off than the average person would be were everyone treated fairly and equally. In what follows I shall ignore such complications—which depend, in part, on exactly what one thinks would be involved in treating everyone fairly and equally—and proceed as if people should be compared with the actual average. This does not affect the substance of my theoretical claims, though it would presumably make a difference for their practical application.

3. An important reminder. Readers may wish to reconsider chapter 1's remarks about natural injustice and complaints if they find this example troubling, either because of my talk about Fate, or because they think the notion of "complaint" is inappropriate in such contexts. I maintain that even if there is no entity

One case where the intuitions I have been discussing seem to be operative is in the way we think about those who accidentally discover a fortune in mineral deposits on land bought for farming or development. Given that such a person is much richer than her world's average member, most people think that such a person is *lucky* to be as rich as she is. Although she may not be the world's richest person, most would contend that she has *already* received more than her fair share of the wealth, and hence that she has *nothing* to complain about regarding her wealth. In fact, while we may not begrudge her her good fortune, most would probably contend that, regarding inequality, it is bad (unjust or unfair) for her to be as rich as she is. This is because such a person seems to have been treated (by Fate) as *more* than the equal of her peers and, regarding inequality, it would seem bad for any person to receive (even from Fate) more than equal treatment.

In the case of wealth, then, whether we regard someone as having a complaint regarding inequality may seem to depend upon how she fares relative to the average

---

Fate who is responsible for someone's being unlucky (as presumably there is not) and against whom that person has a complaint, it is still bad for someone to be unlucky in matters of serious importance. To see that it *is* bad for someone to be unlucky, one only needs to recognize that if there *were* a Fate or God who had intentionally brought about the "unlucky" person's misfortune, He would have been perpetrating an injustice, and the person would have a complaint against Him. This leads me to want to say that the unlucky person has been the victim of a natural, or cosmic injustice; and to indicate the "badness" of her situation by saying that she has a "complaint."

I realize that some religious people think we could never have a just complaint about God's treatment of us, that He could treat us any way He wanted without being guilty of treating us unjustly or acting wrongly. Some think this in virtue of God's status as our creator, others in virtue of God's status as omnipotent (recall God's response to Job's questioning of his apparently unjust predicament, "Where wast thou when I laid the foundations of the earth?" in Job 38:4). I reject the view in question. Even if God, in virtue of His infinite wisdom and goodness never *does* act unjustly, I believe there are ways He *could* act toward us that would be unjust and wrong. I shall not pursue this point. Instead, let me remind the reader who is worried about this particular example that I offer other examples and reasons supporting the conclusion that there is a natural and plausible way of thinking according to which it is those worse off than the average who have a complaint regarding inequality.

One other point. It may seem I am assuming all levels of welfare are alterable, or at least metaphysically contingent. For example, it may seem that Mary would have no grounds for complaint about Fate making her worse off than another, if there is no way that *she* could have been better off. Perhaps one would think this if Mary suffered from a genetically based handicap, and one also thought that those genes were essential to her identity. (Cf. Derek Parfit's discussion of the Non-Identity Problem in *Reasons and Persons* [Oxford University Press, 1984].) In fact, my own view is that Mary would have a complaint regarding inequality. That is, I think the egalitarian could regard Mary's being worse off than others through no fault of her own as bad (unjust or unfair) even if, by hypothesis, Mary is as well off as *she* could be. To my mind such a situation can still be cause for appropriate concern or regret. We can still feel the force of the claim that Mary's situation is such that if we *could* do something to improve it, we should. (Neither fate, nor we, could escape the charge of acting unjustly simply by creating people, or animals, whose undeserved sufferings are essential components of their identity.)

Having noted this point let me set it aside. Though the issues it raises are interesting and important (some of which I shall address, indirectly, in chapter 9), it affects the scope of my claims, but not their content. That is, this work's arguments and results are compatible with both the view that all (undeserved) inequalities are bad, and the view that only metaphysically contingent inequalities are bad. Indeed, as indicated in chapter 1, this work's central arguments and results are compatible with numerous interpretations and variations of these positions—for example, the view that only *certain* metaphysically contingent inequalities are bad, say, those socially produced.

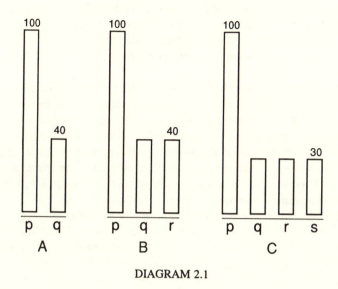

DIAGRAM 2.1

member of her world, and not on how she fares relative to the best-off member of her world. The case of welfare would seem to be analogous to the case of wealth.

Let us now turn to the second answer to the question of who has a complaint. According to this answer, *all but the very best-off* have a complaint. A defense of this answer may be made with the aid of diagram 2.1.[4]

In A, we may judge that q has a complaint because, among equally deserving people, we think it is bad (unjust or unfair) for one person to be at q's level while another is at p's. In B, for instance, it may seem that q would have just as much to complain about as in A, since she is not better off than she was in A, and since p is no worse off than she was in A. True, in B there is another who is as poorly off relative to p as q is. However, that doesn't lessen the injustice of q's being worse off than p—it only makes it the case that instead of there being one instance of injustice there are two!

Consider C. From q's perspective, C's inequality might appear worse than A's, since p is just as well off as she was in A, while q is worse off. More particularly, it appears that q's complaint would be larger in C than in A, since it is worse to be at level 30 while another is at level 100, than it is to be at level 40 while another is at level 100. Again, the presence in C of r and s may not seem to lessen the injustice of q's being worse off than p through no fault of her own; their presence only makes it the case that instead of there being one person with a larger complaint than q had

4. Throughout this book, it will often be easiest if I assign numbers to the different levels represented in my diagrams. This naturally suggests that the bottoms of these diagrams represent the zero level of welfare—the point at which life ceases to be worth living. Although presumably there *is* such a zero level, there are large disagreements about where that level is. Let me note, therefore, that nowhere in this book do my theoretical results depend upon our being able to determine the zero level precisely.

in A, there are three. But note, in C, q fares better relative to the average than she did in A. (She is 17.5 units worse off than the average rather than 30, and has 63 percent of the average rather than 57 percent.) Hence, the view that q would have a larger complaint indicates that we determine q's complaint by comparing her to p, and not to the average.

Extended, such reasoning may lead one to conclude that all but the very best-off have a complaint. Applied to the sort of example considered earlier, this reasoning suggests that even if we admit that *relatively speaking* the second best-off person has "nothing" to complain about, when we focus on the individual comparison between the best-off person and that person it will appear to be unfair or unjust for the one to be worse off than the other through no fault of her own. So, even the second best-off person will have a complaint, though her complaint may be small, both in absolute terms, and relative to the complaints of others.

Because the intuitions opposing this position are powerful, let me further illustrate the intuition that all but the very best-off have a complaint. Most regard the Millian claim that it is better to be a dissatisfied Socrates than a satisfied pig as an instance of the more general and equally true claim that it is better to be a dissatisfied human than a contented animal. The dissatisfaction would have to be pretty abject indeed, before most people would prefer to become a contented pig, or mouse, or frog. Yet we *don't* believe that the blind, crippled, or poor have nothing to complain about regarding inequality. This is because we compare them not to *all* the beings in the world, but to beings better off than they.[5]

This way of thinking has a long history. For instance, in medieval times people worried about the following question: Why doesn't man have a right to complain about his imperfections; about the fact that God created him *flawed* as a *man*, rather than pure as an angel or more like God Himself? Although the theologians and philosophers who regarded this as a serious question agreed that man was better off

---

5. One might contend that we are concerned with inequalities within our species but not inequalities between species because we feel responsible for the former but not the latter. For instance, it might be claimed that it is simply not our fault that pigs are brutes, whereas it is our fault that blacks fare worse than whites. Though true, this claim fails to explain the point in question. In my examples, I have assumed that the better-off are not responsible for the lot of the worse-off, yet I believe that egalitarians would be offended by the inequality in such worlds. Although we are no more responsible for the fact that someone was born deaf, dumb, or blind, than for the fact that pigs are brutes, it still strikes us as bad that such a person should be worse off than others through no fault of her own.

It might be claimed that cross-species comparisons are unintelligible, so that no sense can be made of the claim that human beings are "better off" than pigs or mice. Whether or not this is the case, most people *think* humans are better off than the other animals, and thinking this does not lead them to the conclusion that the worst-off members of our species have nothing about which to complain.

Similarly, although there are sophisticated philosophical reasons to believe that a pig, unlike a deaf or blind person, couldn't have ever led the life of a healthy human, I don't believe that these reasons—which concern deep issues in the metaphysics of personal identity and natural kinds—govern our commonsense intuitions on these matters. To the contrary, our cultural tradition is rich with myths, fairy tales, and other folklore that readily allow for the possibility of humans turning into animals and vice versa without loss of personal identity.

It appears, therefore, that the commonsense view that the blind, crippled, and poor have a complaint regarding inequality—despite their being better off than most animals—does implicitly involve the notion that all but the best-off have a complaint.

than other animals, they still wondered why it should not be regarded as unfair that man, through no fault of his own, should be saddled with imperfections, while others, such as the angels, were better off. This reveals the intuition that all but the very best-off have something about which to complain.

This intuition may also be involved in the way many think about America's poor. Considering the gross differences existing in America, most contend that the average poor person in America has something to complain about regarding inequality. Most would admit, however, that the average poor person in America is better off than most of the people alive today (the masses of India, China, Pakistan, and so on). This latter fact does not make us think that the average poor person in America has nothing about which to complain. Instead, it forces us to acknowledge that there are people with even more to complain about than she; and that there are even greater inequalities in the world than those existing in the United States alone. This seems to be another case where we think that all but the very best-off have something about which to complain. (Note. An alternative explanation of this last example is possible. It might be contended that America's inequality is a matter of social injustice, and that where social justice is concerned one's complaints are naturally about, and directed toward, one's own society. It might seem, therefore, that America's poor have a complaint because, relative to the other members of *their society*, they are badly off. This explanation would not apply to the other examples. This is because where natural, or cosmic, injustice is concerned it is as if one is addressing one's complaint to God, and the relevant community for comparison when complaining to God is the whole of His creation.)

On the question of *who* has a complaint, then, there appear to be two plausible answers: those below the average and all but the very best-off. Let us next consider the question of how we assess the seriousness, or size, of someone's complaint.

To this question there seem to be *three* plausible answers. The first two parallel the division in our thinking about who has a complaint. Thus we might think that the size of someone's complaint will depend upon how she compares with either *the average member of her world*, or *the best-off member of her world*. These two ways of regarding the size of someone's complaint correspond to two natural ways of viewing an unequal world: as a deviation from the situation that would have obtained if the welfare had been distributed equally, and as a deviation from the situation in which each person is as well off as the best-off person. On both views it would be natural to determine the size of someone's complaint by comparing her level to the level at which she would cease to have a complaint. On the first view, this would be the average level of her world—the level she would be at if Fate had treated each person equally. On the second view, it would be the level of the best-off person—the level at which she would no longer be worse off than another.

There is a third way of measuring the size of someone's complaint. This way accepts the view that all but the very best-off have a complaint, but contends that the size of someone's complaint depends not on how she fares relative to the best-off person but on how she fares relative to *all of the others who are better off than she.*

This view might be defended as follows. It is bad for someone to be worse off than another through no fault of her own. This is why any person who is in such a position will have a complaint. But if it is bad to be worse off than one person through no fault of your own, it should be even worse to be worse off than two people through no fault of your own. And, in general, the more people there are who are better off than someone (and the larger the gap between them), the more that person should have to complain about regarding inequality. Therefore, to determine the size of someone's complaint one must compare her level to those of *all* who are better off than she, and not only to the level of the very best-off person.

Although this third way of regarding the size of someone's complaint may seem less natural than the first two, it does not seem less plausible. Indeed, it is arguable that this position captures certain of the most plausible features of the first two views, while avoiding their most implausible features.[6]

Let us summarize the argument so far. Our notion of inequality allows us to focus on particular individuals and make judgments about whether, and the extent to which, they have a complaint regarding inequality. There is, however, a division in our thinking concerning who has a complaint and how we determine the magnitude of a complaint. Specifically, one might plausibly maintain that only those below the average have a complaint and the size of their complaint depends upon (1) how they fare relative to the average—henceforth, I shall call this the *relative to the average view* of complaints. Alternatively, one may claim that all but the best-off have a complaint and the size of their complaint depends either upon (2) how they fare relative to the best-off person—henceforth the *relative to the best-off person view* of complaints—or upon (3) how they fare relative to all those better off than they—henceforth, the *relative to all those better off* view of complaints.

A further question arises as to how we actually measure the size of someone's complaint on any of the three views just stated. In this chapter, I assume that someone's complaint can be measured by subtracting her level of welfare from the level of the best-off person, or the level of the average person, or the levels of all those better off than she, depending upon the view of complaints in question. So, for example, if she is at level 100, and the best-off person is at level 175, she will have a complaint of 75 on the relative to the best-off person view of complaints. In fact this way of measuring complaints is too simple because, as we shall see in chapter 6, the figures arrived at in this way need supplementing to reflect the fact that inequality matters more at low levels than at high levels (so, someone 100 units worse off than the best-off person would have more to complain about if she were at level 200 than if she were at level 2,000). Still, for the purposes of this chapter it will be easier

---

6. Shelly Kagan suggests there may be four ways of regarding the size of individual complaints rather than three. He writes (in correspondence) "if the thought that 'there are others better off than me' gets divided into two variants depending on whether the complaint is increased by multiple offenders: i.e. I have a complaint relative to the best-off versus I have a complaint relative to all better off than me—then why not something similar for the 'relative to the average' view? Maybe my complaint is increased as more and more people are above the average (it is one thing if only one lucky stiff is up there: that is a fluke; it is worse if every joker but me is above average)." I confess, I do not find the fourth view suggested by Kagan as appealing as the three argued for in the text. Still, some variation of it may be plausible. If so, then the notion of inequality is even more complex than I claim.

The Sequence

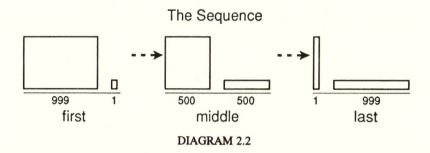

| 999 | 1 | | 500 | 500 | | 1 | 999 |
| first | | | middle | | | last | |

DIAGRAM 2.2

to make the simplifying assumption that complaints can be measured in the manner suggested. This assumption does not affect my main conclusions.

2.2 The Sequence

We are now in a position to consider our general judgments about how situations compare regarding inequality. In order to explore the reasoning underlying and influencing such judgments I shall be looking at a group of artificially simple worlds, which I shall refer to as the *Sequence*. This consists of 999 outcomes, or *worlds*, each containing two groups of people, the better-off and the worse-off. The level of the better-off group is the same in each world with each member of that group being equally well off. Similarly for the worst-off groups. In addition, in each world the total size of the population is 1,000, but the ratio between the two groups steadily changes. In the first world there are 999 people better-off and 1 person worse-off, in the second 998 better-off and 2 worse-off, and so on. By the last world 1 person is better-off and 999 are worse-off.[7] The first, middle, and last worlds of the Sequence are represented in diagram 2.2.

For each world of the Sequence, I shall retain the assumptions that the members of that world are equally skilled, hardworking, morally worthy, and so forth, and that the better-off are not responsible for the plight of the worse-off. Although these assumptions help keep our judgments about the Sequence free from the disturbing influence of certain nonegalitarian ideals, there *are* still morally significant differences between the worlds of the Sequence other than differences in their patterns of inequality. Consider, for example, the first world of the Sequence, where there are 999 people in the better-off group, and the last world, where there are 999 people

7. I first had the idea to compare the worlds of the Sequence from an unpublished article of Derek Parfit's on overpopulation ("Overpopulation," 1976). In his article, Parfit suggested that given a world whose pattern of distribution resembled an early member of the Sequence, there would be another world whose pattern resembled a later member of the Sequence that was equivalent to it regarding inequality. I found this suggestion—which struck me as both plausible and implausible—to be extremely interesting, and began to consider how the worlds of the Sequence compare regarding inequality. This led, initially, to the writing of an early version of the following discussion and, ultimately, to the writing of this book.

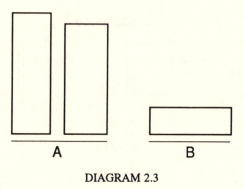

DIAGRAM 2.3

in the worse-off group. The first world is better than the last in terms of both total and average utility. Given this difference, it might be claimed that "all things considered" the first world is better than the last. This may be so. But in this book I am *not* interested in how the worlds of the Sequence compare "all things considered." I am only interested in how they compare *regarding inequality*. This distinction can be made by looking at diagram 2.3.

We may think that "all things considered" A is better than B, since everybody in A is better off than everybody in B, and since A's inequality may strike us as relatively slight. Nevertheless, regarding inequality, B is obviously better than A, since B represents a perfectly equal situation whereas A does not.[8]

I emphasize this point because the Sequence's worlds are getting progressively worse in terms of both total and average utility. This is an unavoidable feature of the Sequence, but one that should not mislead us as long as we are careful to bear in mind the question in which we are interested. Fortunately, most people, or at least most philosophers, are already used to distinguishing between utilitarian and egalitarian considerations. This lessens the chance of our being seriously misled by the Sequence's variation in utility.

Despite the foregoing, many readers are surprised that I ask them to compare situations that differ so regarding utility. Some, especially economists, think the Sequence confuses matters in avoidable—and objectionable—ways. Strictly speaking, they are right. But unfortunately there is *no* way of drawing my diagrams which is not confusing in *some* respects, and ultimately I think the Sequence is the least objectionable way of addressing my concerns. I shall not try to defend this position, but let me note the following.

I want to consider how, if at all, changing the number, or ratio, of better- and worse-off affects inequality. But in order to vary the sizes of the better- and worse-off groups while holding utility constant, one must either change the size of the gaps

8. Here, as elsewhere, I retain the assumption that the inequalities are undeserved. (Henceforth, I shall drop this tag.) Also, throughout this book, when I say that A is better than B regarding inequality, I mean that A's inequality is not as bad as B's.

between the better- and worse-off or the population's total size. The former brings egalitarian considerations into conflict with those about perfectionism or maximin. In addition, it makes it difficult, if not impossible, to tell how much our egalitarian judgments are actually being influenced by changes in the sizes of the better- and worse-off groups, rather than in the gaps between them. On the other hand, the latter raises a host of complicated issues I shall detail in chapter 7. In either case, I think one would ultimately face difficulties graver than the Sequence's.

Finally, let me conclude this section by acknowledging that there is a danger in looking at neatly divided worlds in that some of the conclusions reached may not be generalizable to the real world. However, here too, I think if we are careful we should be able to prevent that feature of the Sequence from leading us astray. (The issue of how our egalitarian judgments might change in situations more complex than the Sequence will be addressed in chapter 3.)

2.3 Orderings of the Sequence

There are five judgments about the Sequence I would like to consider: namely, that the worlds are (1) getting better and better, (2) getting worse and worse, (3) first getting worse then getting better, (4) first getting better then getting worse, and (5) all equivalent. As we shall see, though these judgments conflict, most can be plausibly supported. (Here, and in what follows, I have [often] dropped the locution *regarding inequality*. Throughout this book comparisons are regarding inequality unless stated otherwise.)

Better and Better

When one first considers the Sequence one might judge that the worlds are getting *better and better*, partly because as the Sequence progresses it appears to be less and less the case that a single person or small group is being especially victimized by the situation. In the *first* world, for instance, it is as if the entire burden of the inequality is borne by the one, lone member of the worse-off "group." Given that that person is worse off than *every other* member of her world, it may seem both that she has a very large complaint, and that the inequality is especially offensive. By contrast, the last world's inequality may seem relatively inoffensive. In *that* world each member of the worse-off group is as well off as *all* but *one* of the other members of her world. Hence, in that world it may seem as if nobody has much to complain about regarding inequality.

This view is plausible, and it expresses itself in the way we react to the actions of bullies or tyrants. Consider, for example, the case of a prison warden who, for nonsecurity reasons, likes to remind his prisoners that he is the boss. Suppose that without provocation, this warden regularly suspended the exercise and visitation privileges of each person whose last name began with a letter from A through L. Although undoubtedly we would find such behavior objectionable, I believe that in a certain sense we would find it even more objectionable if the warden selected one or two inmates and regularly prevented them from exercising or having any visitors.

Whereas in the one case it seems neither right nor fair that half the inmates should have their privileges suspended, in the other case it would seem especially unfair that one or two individuals alone have to bear the brunt of the warden's irrational behavior.

This same feeling influences our thinking about the abuses of a genuine political tyrant, although in such cases it is more likely that our egalitarian notions will be tempered by our utilitarian ones. If the head of a government decrees that a certain portion of the population is to be mistreated in a wide variety of humiliating ways, from a utilitarian standpoint we may well hope that it is a small portion of the population that is so mistreated. Nevertheless, from an egalitarian standpoint we may well find the decree most offensive if it applies to only a small segment of the population. This is because from an egalitarian standpoint it may seem particularly unfair for one small group to bear the brunt of the injustice in its world; and it may seem especially galling that the vast majority of the population should be leading normal happy lives, while one small segment of it gets "crushed beneath the heel of oppression."

One way of putting my point is as follows. I think that certain of our egalitarian intuitions are especially attuned to instances of invidious or capricious discrimination where a particular person or small group is *singled* out for discriminatory treatment. In fact, I think it is the *singling out* in this way of an individual or small group that is the paradigmatic case of where we judge a (harmful) discrimination to be grossly unjust or unfair. This is not to say, of course, that all things considered we should always prefer the mistreatment of a large portion of the population to the mistreatment of a small portion of the population. It is only to suggest that we might prefer this from the standpoint of (at least certain elements of) our notion of inequality. (Whether we would actually prefer the mistreatment of a large group to the mistreatment of a small group, all things considered, would presumably depend upon of what the mistreatment consisted. All things considered, we must be glad that Hitler only ordered the mass murder of the Jews, Gypsies, and homosexuals, and not of all the occupied peoples, and this is surely so even if [one element of] the notion of inequality conflicts with this judgment. It might have been better, however, if he had made all of the occupied peoples shave their heads and wear yellow armbands, instead of just humiliating and dehumanizing the Jews in that manner.)[9]

I suspect that this element of our egalitarian thinking may be one of the reasons why it has taken us so long to recognize the pervading discrimination against women in our society. Even though women were (and still are) being treated very differently than men, half of the population was being treated in the same way. Because of this, and because of the fact that our egalitarian intuitions are especially attuned to discrimination against individuals and small groups, it was easy for both

9. Unfortunately, this example is not completely pure. Part of the reason we might think it would have been better if all of the occupied people had to shave their heads and wear yellow armbands is that we might think that would have lessened the humiliation and dehumanization accompanying those practices. My position is that even if this were *not* so, it still might have been better if Hitler had made more people shave their heads and wear yellow armbands. In this case our egalitarian concerns may be sufficiently strong to outweigh the competing concerns of other ideals such as utility.

men and women to realize that women were being treated differently and yet fail to recognize that women were actually being *discriminated* against.

Having seen that certain elements of our thinking support the "better and better" ordering, let us next try to get clearer about what those elements involve.

One principle which might seem relevant here is the *maximin* principle of justice. Roughly, this principle states that a society's political, social, and economic institutions are just if they maximize the average level of the worst-off group.[10] In one form or another many philosophers have come to advocate a maximin principle of justice, and one can see why. There is strong appeal to the view that just as it would be right for a mother to devote most of her effort and resources to her neediest child, so it would be right for a society to devote most of *its* effort and resources to its neediest members. This view is captured by the maximin principle, a principle that, in essence, maintains that it would be unjust for society to benefit the "haves" if instead it could benefit the "have nots."[11]

Now strictly speaking a Rawlsian version of the maximin principle is not relevant to our discussion. The main reason for this is simply that it has been offered as a principle of *justice, not* as a principle of equality. Consider diagram 2.4. Assuming the people are equally deserving, an egalitarian will regard B's inequality as worse than A's. In chapter 9 we shall consider a position—extended humanitarianism—that would deny this. But as we shall see, though extended humanitarianism is often conflated with egalitarianism, and is a plausible position in its own right, it is not plausible as an *egalitarian* position. Surely, insofar as one cares about *inequality*, one should find B's situation, where some are *much* worse off than others, more objectionable than A's, where everyone is almost equally well-off.

But note, according to Rawls a society's principles and institutions would be better, and not *unjust*, if they were altered to improve the lot of the worst-off group. This is so even if in order to effect a small improvement the lot of the best-off had to be improved immensely. In particular, according to Rawls's maximin principle a society's institutions would be more just if they were altered so as to transform the

---

10. More accurately, the maximin principle of justice focuses on the expectations of the representative member of the worst-off group. But the formulation given in the text is simpler and sufficient for our present purposes.

11. I think the view suggested in the text helps explain much of maximin's appeal, I certainly do not claim it explains *all* of maximin's appeal.

Tim Scanlon reminds me that there is a disanalogy between the mother example and maximin, since on maximin it is not enough that society devote *most* of its effort and resources to its neediest members; rather it must, in essence, devote *all* of its effort and resources to its neediest members—at least up to the point where the expectations of the average member of the worst-off group are maximized. Scanlon is right. But I think the disanalogy he points to may support my view about the basic appeal underlying maximin, since I think many believe maximin is too strong precisely at the point in question. That is, I think most would hold it is one thing to claim a mother should devote *most* of her effort and resources to her neediest child, something quite different, and implausible, to claim she must, in essence, devote *all* of her effort and resources to her neediest child. Similarly, I suspect most of maximin's proponents actually accept a "weak" version as most plausible, according to which society should devote most, but not all, of its effort and resources to its neediest members.

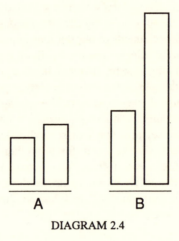

DIAGRAM 2.4

society from one like A to one like B.[12] Thus, as indicated, the maximin principle of justice is *not* a plausible principle of *equality*, for whether or not such an alteration in a society's institutions would make that society more *just*, it would certainly not make it better regarding inequality.[13]

Interestingly, many would agree with Rawls's ranking of B over A, but for very different reasons. Some might prefer B to A for perfectionist reasons, others for reasons of utility or efficiency. Those are *not* Rawls's reasons. Rawls would be willing to accept losses in perfection or utility, just as we have seen he would accept losses in equality. His concern is not with perfection, utility, or equality, but with *justice* in his sense of the term.

It should now be clear why I claimed that Rawls's maximin principle is not *itself* relevant to our discussion. Still, the *spirit* of that principle is relevant. The maximin principle of justice is a very demanding principle. It requires us to assist the "have nots" rather than the "haves" even if we could assist the "haves" more easily and efficiently than the "have nots," and even if the "haves" are only "haves" relative to the "have nots."[14] It follows, therefore, that for the maximin principle to be as attractive as a survey of the literature

12. This is most evident, on Rawls's view, if we assume that B involves the pattern of inequality that, of those achievable, makes the worst-off as well off as possible.

13. It might be contended that even if the maximin principle is not a plausible principle of equality, it, or something like it, is the closest thing to an egalitarian principle that could plausibly be adopted. Put differently, it might be contended that although the maximin principle does not capture what the egalitarian *does* care about, it, or something like it, captures what the sensible egalitarian *should* care about. The kind of reasoning that might lead someone to make such a claim will be considered, and rejected, in chapter 9.

14. One might say that Rawls has given us a theory that expresses a concern for "relative poverty" or "relative deprivation of primary goods" rather than for "absolute poverty" or "absolute deprivation of primary goods." In this respect his position is more like "extended humanitarianism" (see chapter 9) than "pure" humanitarianism, which mainly focuses on relieving misery or suffering. (I trust my use of "relative deprivation" is clear here and will not be confused with W. G. Runciman's rather different usage in his important *Relative Deprivation and Social Justice* [Routledge and Kegan Paul, 1966].)

reveals it to be, it must be capturing and expressing a deep and powerful element of our thought. Surely, though, what the maximin principle of justice seems to be capturing and expressing is the fact that our moral sensibilities are especially attuned to the lot of the worst-off. But if this is so, then it appears that a plausible principle of equality would be a maximin principle of equality. That is, the same basic concern for the worst-off that supports a maximin principle of justice would also seem to support a maximin principle of equality.

One way my point might be interpreted is as follows.[15] Concern for the worst-off is essentially adjectival, or parasitical. It is a special concern for the situation or complaint of the worst-off regarding _____, so that any determinate concern for the worst-off rides piggyback on some other particular value about which we care and with which we fill in the blank. Thus, we can plug in the view that absolute levels of utility or welfare matter and generate a (Rawlsian) maximin principle that reflects special concern for the worst-off's welfare levels. Or we can plug in the view that inequality matters and generate a maximin principle of equality that reflects special concern for the gaps between the worst-off and others. Similarly for other values. On this view Rawls's difference principle is best understood *not* as a compromise between equality and utility, as some have suggested, but as a result of taking a concern for welfare and adjectivally modifying it with a concern for the worst-off. Also, this view supports the claim that a maximin principle of equality should be as plausible as a Rawlsian maximin principle, because each is a modification of an independently plausible value, and there is nothing about "special concern for the situation or complaint of the worst-off" that intrinsically favors piggybacking this on one value rather than another.

At this point one might object that even if a maximin principle of equality is plausible, it is not plausible as a principle of "pure" equality. That is, someone might claim that just as Rawls's difference principle does not plausibly express the position of someone whose *sole* concern is utility or welfare but instead expresses a compromise of sorts between a concern about utility and a special concern about the worst-off, so a maximin principle of equality does not plausibly express the position of someone whose *sole* concern is equality but instead expresses a compromise of sorts between a concern about equality and a special concern about the worst-off. On this view then, *insofar as one is an egalitarian*—that is, insofar as one judges outcomes *as if* equality were the *only* thing one cared about—one should not be influenced by a maximin principle, even a maximin principle of equality.

This objection has force, but it is unclear how telling it is. One might argue that insofar as a maximin principle of equality is plausible it is just that—a plausible principle *of equality*. One might claim that the distinguishing feature of egalitarianism is that it ranks outcomes not by how people fare in absolute terms, but by how people fare in relative terms. More specifically, one might argue that a principle is *egalitarian* as long as it ranks outcomes according to the size of the gaps between the better- and worse-off, but that the egalitarian may take various views regarding the manner and extent to which different gaps matter. On this view a maximin

---

15. Both this paragraph and the following one are paraphrased from points Shelly Kagan made in correspondence.

principle of equality will be essentially egalitarian, or at least distinctively or "sufficiently" egalitarian to warrant consideration in this work, as long as it ranks outcomes in terms of how the worst-off fare regarding *equality*—that is, in terms of how the worst-off fare relative to others—rather than in terms of how the worst-off fare regarding some other value. Finally, it is worth recalling that our initial question was not "when is there *more* inequality in one situation than another," but "when is one situation *worse* than another *regarding inequality*." In answering this question one can, I think, plausibly claim that a maximin principle of equality underlies and influences our egalitarian judgments.[16]

One version of the maximin principle of equality might be stated as follows. How bad a world is regarding inequality will depend upon how badly the worst-off group in that world fares regarding inequality; so, if the average level of complaint of the worst-off group is larger in one of two worlds, that is the world that is worse. *If* the level of complaint of the worst-off group is the same in both worlds, then that world will be better whose worst-off group is smallest; if the two worst-off groups are the same size, then the next worst-off groups are similarly compared, and so forth.

Notice the second clause of this principle comes into play *only* if the worst-off groups fare the same in two worlds. This is important, for depending upon which view of complaints one adopts, the magnitude of the worst-off group's complaint may decrease as the size of the better-off group decreases or the size of the worse-off group increases. In such cases the first clause of the maximin principle would tell us the situation was improving and the second clause would not apply. Intuitively, then, the maximin principle of equality would first have us maximize the relative position of the worst-off group and then minimize the size of that group, as long as we were not thereby increasing the complaint of the remaining members of the worst-off group. It would then have us do the same thing for the next worst-off group (as long as this did not increase the complaints of those in the worst-off group), and so on, until all of the groups were as well off and as small as they could be.

We can now see one reason why the "better and better" ordering seems plausible. In accordance with certain plausible positions the members of the worst-off group have less and less to complain about as the Sequence progresses. This is true on both the "relative to all those better off" and the "relative to the average" views of complaints (since as the ratio between the better- and worse-off groups decreases, the members of the worst-off group fare better and better with respect both to the number of people who are better off than they [by a certain amount], and to the average). Therefore, insofar as we accept a maximin principle of equality there will be reason to think that the Sequence is getting better and better. And intuitively, I

---

16. It is not implausible for an egalitarian to hold that A's *inequality* is *worse* than B's because A's worst-off have larger complaints than B's *regarding equality*, and one might hold this even if in some sense there was *more* inequality in B than A. On the other hand one could not plausibly hold that A's *inequality* is worse than B's because, say, there is less *utility* in A than B. The former is plausible as an *egalitarian* judgment—that is, as a judgment about the goodness of how people fare relative to each other in that situation—in a way the latter is clearly not.

think the maximin principle of equality should be at least as plausible as a principle of equality as the maximin principle of justice is as a principle of justice.

It is worth noting that the advocate of the maximin principle of equality is concerned not with the sum total of complaints but with the *distribution* of those complaints. Specifically, she wants the inequality to be distributed in such a way that the "load" that each member of the worst-off group has to "bear" is as small as possible. Therefore, she would say, not implausibly, that regarding inequality a world where many have small complaints might be preferable to a world where a few have large complaints. (An extreme example. In one world 1,000,000 people each have a complaint of 1. In another, 1 person has a complaint of 900,000. The maximin principle would say, quite plausibly, that regarding inequality the first is vastly preferable to the second.)

Let me emphasize that in suggesting that a maximin principle would be a plausible principle of equality, I am not suggesting that such a principle would adequately capture the whole of our notion of equality. In focusing on the worst-off group and (to a large extent) ignoring the lot of the rest of society, a maximin principle of equality is too crude to serve as a complete principle of equality, just as the maximin principle of justice is too crude to serve as a complete principle of justice. Still, it must be recognized that like a maximin principle of justice, a maximin principle of equality expresses a deep and powerful element of our thinking, one that, when combined with other plausible elements,[17] will support the judgment that the Sequence is getting better and better.

There is another line of thought supporting the "better and better" ordering. To illustrate it, let me temporarily drop my usual assumption that the better-off are not responsible for the plight of the worse-off through an unwillingness to share their good fortune. Specifically, let me temporarily assume that the members of the Sequence can redistribute their welfare the way money can be redistributed. On this assumption there may seem to be no excuse for the inequality in the earlier worlds. If a redistribution of welfare took place, the better-off would hardly lose anything and the worse-off would gain a tremendous amount. Hence, the inequality in those worlds may seem particularly offensive as there seems to be virtually nothing gained by it. In the middle worlds, on the other hand, a redistribution of welfare would "cost" a lot. A large number would have to sacrifice a great deal to achieve equality. In those worlds we could understand the reluctance of the better-off to redistribute, and while we might think it would be good if they were to do this voluntarily, we might not think they were morally *required* to do this. In those worlds, then, the inequality might strike us as more excusable, and hence less disturbing, than the inequality in the earlier worlds. In the end worlds, a redistribution of welfare would involve a tremendous loss in the quality of life for some, with virtually no gain in the quality of life of those thus "benefited." Therefore, of all the Sequence's worlds the inequality might seem

---

17. It is important to recognize that the maximin principle of equality does not *itself* support this ordering; it does this only when combined with the views of measuring complaints in question. As we shall see, and as the reader may have already surmised, the maximin principle will support a different ordering of the Sequence when combined with the view that the size of someone's complaint depends upon how she fares relative to the best-off person.

least offensive in the end worlds, since in those worlds the "cost" of the inequality might seem smallest and the "gain" highest.

So, on the assumption that welfare is redistributable, the inequality may seem less and less offensive as the Sequence progresses. However, even without that assumption we might react to the Sequence in the manner suggested. If we drop that assumption we may no longer regard the inequality in the earlier worlds as inexcusable; still, the unavoidability of the inequality in those worlds may do nothing to lessen the feeling that it is so "pointless and unnecessary." We still feel that Fate has been especially unkind to the worse-off; and we still fully recognize that a situation of complete equality would have obtained *if only* each better-off person had received a tiny bit less welfare, and *if only* "the extra table scraps" of welfare had gone to the worse-off. Therefore, with or without the assumption the earlier worlds' inequality may strike us as especially gratuitous and, hence, as especially regrettable.

This position might be summed up as follows. Whether or not anything could be done about it, it will offend egalitarians for some to be badly off (struggling to survive) while others are well off (living lives of ease and comfort). But from one perspective, at least, we will be most offended if just a few are badly off while the vast majority are well off, since the inequality then seems particularly gratuitous. Thus, in accordance with this way of thinking, it will seem that the Sequence is getting better and better.[18]

18. Thomas Scanlon has questioned whether our reactions to such cases correspond to the inequality's "gratuitousness" or to the effect of "the norm" that is at work in such cases. Let me suggest two reasons for favoring the former over the latter.

First, consider the Sequence's first and last worlds. In both worlds "the norm" is for everybody, but one, to be perfectly equal. So how does appeal to the norm explain the intuition that the first world's inequality is especially offensive, whereas the last world's hardly matters? One might stress that in the first world "the norm" is for everybody, but one, to be perfectly equal *and* very well off, whereas in the last "the norm" is for everybody, but one, to be perfectly equal and *not* very well off. Moreover, in the first the unequal person is much *worse* off than the norm, whereas in the second he is much *better* off. Such statements accurately characterize the Sequence's first and last worlds, but they don't explain *why* it is worse if the norm is for most to be well off, with one person worse off, than if the norm is for most to be not well off, with one person better off. In other words, we need an explanation as to *why* deviations from the norm bother us in some cases but not others. Naturally, I think appeal to the inequality's (relative) gratuitousness helps explain our reaction to such cases in a way that appeal to the norms themselves do not.

Second, appeals to "the norm" can be tricky and I am not sure how, if at all, they are supposed to be relevant to the egalitarian's claims. Suppose, for example, an egalitarian criticized a society like the first world of the Sequence on the grounds that its inequality was so "pointless and unnecessary." Could one undercut the egalitarian's charge by arguing that the inequality to which he objected was "the norm" in that society, that in fact, as long as that society had ever existed (a very long time, let us assume) inequality of such a kind had obtained? I think the egalitarian might plausibly reply that it didn't matter whether the inequality was "the norm" or not; it was nonetheless gratuitous and, hence, especially offensive.

In sum, I am suspicious of appeals to "the norm." Even if they play *some* role in explaining our thinking, I doubt that it is the effect of "the norm" *rather than* a notion like gratuitousness that explains the reactions discussed in the text. I might add that here, as elsewhere, I am not wedded to my terminology. I find the term "gratuitousness" useful for describing certain egalitarian sentiments, but it is the sentiments that matter, not the term itself.

To summarize the discussion of this ordering. Several plausible elements support the judgment that the Sequence is getting better and better. In accordance with either the view that someone's complaint depends upon how she fares relative to all those better off than she, or the view that someone's complaint depends upon how she fares relative to the average, a maximin principle of equality would support such a judgment. In addition, such a judgment might seem plausible because the inequality seems less and less gratuitous as the Sequence progresses. There are, then, three different positions supporting the "better and better" ordering. Although these positions yield the same judgments about simple split-level cases, they represent different (combinations of) views. Correspondingly, as we shall see in chapter 3, in more complicated cases the judgments they yield may often diverge.

Worse and Worse

I would next like to suggest that certain elements of our thinking support the judgment that the Sequence is getting not better and better, but *worse and worse*. Let me begin by illustrating an example where these intuitions were, I think, at work. In the late 1960s and early 1970s, critics of the worldwide distribution pattern of wealth (henceforth "liberals") liked to point out how the United States compared with much of the rest of the world. The following comparison is the sort that was perhaps most often made: "In 1970 the national *per capita* income of the U.S. was $4,760. In that same year, half of the world's population lived in countries with national *per capita* income of less than $175.[19]

The liberal might also have tried to sway her audience with more specific country-to-country comparisons. These comparisons were almost always between the United States and a much poorer country with a very large population. Typically, the liberal would be (implicitly) asking her audience whether it really seemed equitable that the national per capita income of its country ($4,760) should be so much higher than the national per capita income of China ($160) with its 800,000,000 inhabitants, or of India ($110) with its 550,000,000 inhabitants, or of Pakistan ($100) with its 129,000,000 inhabitants.

Now it is understandable why liberals would introduce such statistics into popular debate; such statistics are both attention, and sympathy, grabbers. However, one might wonder why the liberal would choose to compare the United States to India, or China, or Pakistan, when she might have compared the United States to a much smaller, but equally poor country, such as Sri Lanka, Haiti, or Tanzania. Why was the liberal so anxious to inform her audience that half the world's population lived in countries with a national per capita income of less than $175, when instead she could have emphasized that the 5 million people in Haiti lived in a country with a national per capita income of only $110?

19. These figures, as well as the other national per capita income figures cited below were taken from A. B. Atkinson's book *The Economics of Inequality* (Clarendon Press, 1975), pp. 238–39. Atkinson implicitly makes this comparison himself, when, after presenting a table giving the 1970 national per capita incomes of a number of countries (with the United States heading the list at $4,760), he writes that "it should be stressed, for example, that in 1970 half of the world's population lived in countries with *per capita* income of less than $175" (p. 239).

There are, I think, several answers to these questions. One obvious answer is that the liberal was appealing to her audience's humanitarian instincts, by drawing attention to the vast numbers of people who fare poorly. Another answer is that the liberal was appealing to her audience's utilitarian instincts, by drawing attention to a great source of disutility, and the vast potential for increasing utility by helping the needy masses. Such answers partially explain the liberal's comparisons but do not, I think, fully explain them. The liberal did not simply point out that there were masses of people faring poorly whose utility could be greatly improved. Rather she emphasized the *comparison* between the vast numbers who were poorly off and those in the United States who were best off. I suggest that *one* reason she did this is because she recognized that such comparisons could awaken the egalitarian instincts of even the most insensitive and complacent members of an audience, and convince an audience that there was a tremendous amount of *inequality* in the world. That is, implicit in the liberal's choice of comparisons is recognition of the fact that while, regarding inequality, we would undoubtedly be dismayed to learn that 5 million Haitians fare miserably compared with the average citizen of the U.S., we would be *outraged* to learn that this was the basic situation not merely for 5 million people, but for 1.5 billion people—half the population of the world!

This point may seem obvious; but given our earlier results it is not unimportant. It suggests that as long as the gap between the "haves" and the "have nots" is approximately the same, certain of our egalitarian intuitions will be particularly offended if there are *more* people worse off relative to the best-off than if there are fewer. These egalitarian intuitions would support the judgment that the Sequence is getting worse and worse.

In addition to emphasizing the extent of the inequality in the present distribution, liberals contended that worldwide inequality was worsening. It was pointed out in this regard that the rate of population growth of the underdeveloped countries was increasing exponentially, while the rate of population growth of the developed countries was slowing down. What the liberal was drawing her audience's attention to, of course, was the fact that the ratio of better- to worse-off people was decreasing. Presumably she did this at least partly because she recognized that in accordance with certain of our egalitarian intuitions we would regard the situation as becoming worse and worse as the proportion of the developed countries shrank and the proportion of the underdeveloped countries swelled.[20] Again, such intuitions would support the judgment that the Sequence is getting worse and worse.

Another example where such intuitions seem operative is a Marxian analysis of

---

20. I do not deny that the liberal may *also* have been appealing to other sentiments by stressing the exponential growth of the underdeveloped countries relative to the developed countries. She may have been implicitly appealing to humanitarian concerns on the assumption that the growing population would lower the welfare level of the have nots. For that matter, she may have been implicitly appealing to self-interested concerns on the assumption that the growing population would lower the welfare level of the haves. Here, as elsewhere, the problem with real-world examples is that they involve many different elements that are not easily distinguishable. Still, I am convinced that *one* reason the liberal stressed such a factor was because of the way it affected and heightened certain of our egalitarian intuitions. Or, more modestly, I am convinced that one effect of the liberal's stressing such factors was to heighten certain egalitarian intuitions as discussed in the text.

the advance of capitalism. Roughly, on a Marxian analysis natural inequalities between people—those owing to initial differences in environment and natural endowment—are greatly increased under capitalism as the (necessary) accumulation of capital results in wealth (and power) becoming increasingly concentrated in the hands of an ever shrinking capitalist class. So, on a Marxian view, as capitalism advances more and more people who may initially fare well under capitalism are squeezed out of the ranks of the bourgeoisie into the ranks of the proletariat; hence fewer and fewer people come to reap the benefits of capitalism.

Now whatever one thinks of its ultimate accuracy, it must be admitted that as stories go a Marxian analysis of capitalism exerts a strong pull on one's egalitarian intuitions. Specifically, I think egalitarians would find the (Marxian) advance of capitalism increasingly objectionable for (at least) two reasons: first, because the rich become richer and the poor (at least relatively) poorer; and second, because the ranks of the worse-off swell and the ranks of the better-off shrink. It is the latter point that concerns us here. It suggests that certain egalitarian intuitions will be increasingly offended as more and more people are worse off relative to the better-off. These intuitions, which are particularly elicited and aroused by a Marxian story of the advance of capitalism, would support the judgment that the Sequence is getting worse and worse.

Note, as with my "liberal" example, I am not suggesting that our responses to a Marxian story can be fully understood in egalitarian terms. On a Marxian view the advance of capitalism would be objectionable for *many* reasons, concerning utility, humanitarianism, and exploitation, among others. Still, it is no accident that in many people's thinking Marxism is deeply entwined with egalitarianism, for a substantial element of a Marxian critique is that capitalism is fundamentally, and increasingly, antiegalitarian. I have emphasized one respect in which this is so; there may, of course, be others that need not concern us here.

Finally, let me briefly mention one other example. If one asks an audience to think of the worst periods of inequality in human history—as I have many times over the years—one finds one of the most common responses to be that of medieval Europe. But the common conception of medieval Europe involves a few (kings, queens, and noblemen) living in the lap of luxury while the vast majority (peasants and serfs) struggle to survive. Such a situation resembles one of the last worlds of the Sequence, rather than one of the first or middle worlds. And although here, as elsewhere, I think people's intuitive responses may be partly influenced by non-egalitarian factors as well as various different egalitarian factors, I think *one* reason so many think of medieval Europe as among the worst periods of inequality is that the number of worse-off is so large relative to the fortunate few who are well off. On reflection, then, I believe there are certain powerful egalitarian intuitions that influence people's judgment about medieval Europe and that would also support the judgment that the Sequence is getting worse and worse.

One question the foregoing discussion raises is whether the egalitarian is centrally concerned about the *absolute* numbers of worse-off, or about the *relative number* (the ratio) of worse-off to better-off. Sometimes the discussion implies one interpretation, sometimes the other, and sometimes it is (purposely) ambiguous. This is an important question, but one we can set aside for now as the relevant positions are extensionally equivalent regarding the worlds of the Sequence. Considerations for answering this question will be assessed in chapter 6.

We have suggested that certain elements of the egalitarian's thinking would support the "worse and worse" ordering. Let us next try to determine what these elements involve. One principle that seems relevant is what I shall refer to as the *additive principle* of equality. According to this principle a world's inequality is measured by summing up each of the complaints that its individuals have, and the larger that sum is, the worse the inequality is.

An additive principle involves two natural and plausible assumptions: (1) given any two situations, the best situation with respect to some factor f will be the one in which the *most* f obtains if f is something desirable (pleasure, happiness, equality), and the one in which the *least* f obtains if f is something undesirable (pain, misery, inequality); and (2) to determine how much f obtains in a situation one needs only determine the magnitude of the individual instances of f obtaining and then sum them together.

Because this *kind* of principle is—understandably enough—associated with utilitarianism, let me point out that it is not its additive aspect that most people object to about utilitarianism. Most utilitarians accept three claims: the best world is that world which is best regarding utility; the best world regarding utility is that world which has the most utility; and the world with the most utility is the world in which the sum total of individual utilities is greatest. Where people usually disagree with utilitarianism is not with its additive aspect, contained in the second and third claims, but with its assumption, contained in the first claim, that utility is all that matters.

So, like the maximin principle, an additive principle of equality represents certain plausible positions. It captures the view that it is bad for one person to be in such a position that she has a complaint, and the corresponding view that it should be even worse if, in addition to the first person with her complaint, there is a second person who has a complaint. Like the maximin principle, the additive principle does not *itself* yield an ordering of the Sequence. However, when combined with the "relative to the best-off person" view of complaints, it supports the judgment that the Sequence is getting worse and worse. After all, on that view more and more people will have a complaint of a certain constant amount as the Sequence progresses, and according to the additive principle the more people there are with a given amount to complain about, the worse the situation is regarding inequality[21]

Another view supports the "worse and worse" ordering. Because the main elements of this view have already been examined, I can be brief. Earlier I noted how the maximin principle of equality could be combined with either of two plausible views about complaints to support the "better and better" ordering. However, when combined with the "relative to the best-off person" view, the maximin principle will yield the "worse and worse" ordering. This is because on this view of complaints the worst-off groups fare the same throughout the Sequence, and, according to the most plausible version of the maximin principle of equality, if the worst-off groups

---

21. I shall consider below the ordering that the additive principle supports when combined with either of the other two ways of measuring complaints.

fare the same in two worlds, that world will be best whose worst-off group is smallest.[22] Thus, there is a second set of plausible views that combine to support the "worse and worse" ordering.

There is yet another position supporting the "worse and worse" ordering. One might arrive at this position by reasoning as follows. Despite its appeal, the maximin principle is less plausible when applied to more realistic worlds where people are spread out over a continuum of welfare levels. This is because no matter what level is chosen to separate the worst-off group from the rest of society, it seems implausible that we should be genuinely concerned with the complaints of the people at that level, but shouldn't be concerned at all (except in the case of ties) with the complaints of those who are just above that level. We may thus decide that the ever-so-slightly better-off people should be included in the worst-off group, but then the same reasoning would lead us to include the people who are ever-so-slightly better off than *they*, and so on.

What such reasoning suggests is not that there is no significant difference between those with large complaints and those with small complaints, but rather that it is implausible to contend that the complaints of the one group should matter but that the complaints of the other group should not (except in the case of ties). Thus, an additive principle might seem preferable to a maximin principle insofar as it is concerned with the complaints of *all* those who have a complaint, and not just with the complaints of some arbitrarily selected worst-off group. Yet a maximin principle might seem preferable to an additive principle insofar as it is concerned with the *distribution* rather than merely the sum total of complaints. This suggests that a principle that plausibly combined these two elements would have great appeal.

Here is one such principle: we measure a world's inequality by adding together people's complaints, after first attaching extra weight to them in such a way that the larger someone's complaint is the more weight is attached to it. Let us call this the *weighted additive* principle of equality.[23] Such a principle gives expression to both the view that we should be especially concerned with the worst-off and the view that we should be concerned with all complaints. It would thus give us a way of capturing the intuition that a world in which 40 people have complaints of 200 would be worse than a world in which 5 people have complaints of 205, and 200 people have complaints of 40. This is, I believe, a plausible intuition, but one that neither the additive principle nor the maximin principle captures.[24]

Like the additive principle and the maximin principle, the weighted additive

22. I shall say more about why I think the most plausible version of the maximin principle has the feature in question in my discussion of the "all equivalent" ordering.

23. Note, in arriving at our weighted additive principle, the weighting function we employ to attach extra weight to large complaints may or may not itself be additive. It might, for example, be multiplicative, logarithmic, or something much more complicated.

24. Let me emphasize that although an example of this sort illustrates the plausibility of the kind of position in question, it does *not* establish the *implausibility* of the other positions. Just as it is easy to construct examples where this kind of position will seem most plausible, it is also easy to construct examples where the other positions will seem most plausible. This will become clearer in chapters 3 and 5.

principle appears to be a plausible principle of equality. Combined with the "relative to the best-off person" view of complaints, such a principle supports the "worse and worse" ordering. This is because no matter how the individual complaints are weighted, since the complaints are nonnegative, n + 1 weighted complaints will always be larger than n weighted complaints.

To sum up the discussion of this ordering. The additive principle, the maximin principle, and the weighted additive principle each combine with the "relative to the best-off person" view of complaints to yield the "worse and worse" ordering. As with the positions discussed in connection with the last ordering, it is important to bear in mind that although these different positions yield the same judgment about the Sequence, the judgments they yield will often, in more realistic cases, disagree.

First Worse, Then Better

We have seen that certain plausible positions support the "better and better" ordering, and that others support the "worse and worse" ordering. Still others support the judgment that the Sequence *first gets worse, then gets better.*

It is easy to be drawn to such an ordering by reasoning as follows. In the first world of the Sequence everyone is perfectly equal except, regrettably, for one, single, isolated individual. In that world, then, the worse-off "group" represents an ever-so-slight perturbation in an otherwise perfectly homogeneous system. Therefore, because in the first world there is just a slight deviation from absolute equality, that world may seem nearly perfect regarding inequality. In the second world there are two people who are not at the level of everyone else. The deviation from a state of absolute equality has become more pronounced; hence that world may seem worse than the first. As the Sequence progresses this pattern continues for a while. The deviations from absolute equality become larger, and as they do the Sequence appears to be getting worse and worse. After the midpoint, however, the deviations from absolute equality begin to get smaller, as the better-off group comes to represent a perturbation in the system. By the end world there is once again just an ever-so-slight deviation from absolute equality. Everyone is perfectly equal except, regrettably, for one, single, isolated individual. Like the first world, therefore, that world may appear almost perfect regarding inequality. In sum, because it seems almost tautological that the less a situation deviates from absolute equality the better it is regarding inequality, it seems natural and plausible to judge that the Sequence first gets worse, then gets better.

Implicit in such reasoning is an intuitive notion as to how the deviation from a state of absolute equality should be measured. Let me give some content to this intuitive notion. Suppose that the best-off person in the last world (l) of the Sequence has 100 units of welfare, and that each of the worse-off people have 80 units. We would then say that l deviates from a state of perfect equality by a mere 20 units of welfare, since if the best-off person had 20 less units l would be a perfectly equal world. Now l also deviates from (infinitely) many other perfectly equal situations. For instance, l deviates from the situation where everybody is at level 100 by 19,980 units of welfare. This, however, does *not* (and should not) lead us to conclude that there is really a large deviation from absolute equality in 1.

The point here is that, in determining how much a given world deviates from absolute equality, it seems reasonable to compare that world with the closest possible world that is perfectly equal (where r will be closer to s than to t, if the total number of units that have to be added to and/or subtracted from the various members of r to transform r into s is less than the total number of units that would be involved in transforming r into t). Now it can easily be shown that for any world w, the closest possible world to w that is perfectly equal will be that world where everybody is at w's median level.[25] Thus, on the reasoning under discussion inequality could be measured by determining the amount of deviation from the median.

Applied to the Sequence, it is easy to determine that this reasoning would yield an ordering corresponding to a symmetrical hump. Each of the various "reciprocal" worlds—that is, the first and last, and more generally nth and nth last worlds—are equivalent, with the first and last worlds being the best and the middle world the worst. Naturally, in realistic cases a society's median level (roughly, the level of the person below and above which there are the same number of people) will almost never be the same as the level of either the best-off person or the average person, hence the amount of deviation from the median will *not* generally be the same as the amount of deviation from either the best-off person or the average person.

Another line of thought supports the "worse, then better" ordering. In the first world of the Sequence only *one* person has a complaint, so as large as that complaint may be that world's inequality may not seem too bad. Specifically, it may not seem as bad as the second world's inequality, where it may seem that *two* people have almost as much to complain about as the one person had in the first world. And these two worlds' inequality may not seem *nearly* as bad as the middle world's inequality. In the middle world, it may seem *both* that a large number have a complaint (half of the population), *and* that the magnitude of their complaints will be large (they are, after all, worse off than half the population through no fault of their own). In the last world, on the other hand, the situation may seem analogous to, though the reverse of, the one obtaining in the first. Although almost everyone has *something* to complain about, it may seem that the size of their complaints will be virtually negligible. Hence, as with the first world, the inequality may not seem too bad.

Such reasoning involves two by now familiar elements: the view that the size of

25. Basically the median level of welfare is that level where there are the same number of people at or above it, as at or below it. If there are an odd number of people in a society, then the median level will simply be the level of the middle person. If there are an even number of people, then the median level will be the arithmetic average of the two "middle" people; so if there are 100 people and the level of welfare of the 50th person is 500 and the level of the 51st person is 600 then the median level will be 550. (Actually, it is easy to show that when the population of world w is even, there may be many perfectly equal worlds that are equally close to w. Specifically, any world where everyone is at one of the levels ranging from the one "middle" person to the other "middle" person would be equally close to w. So, in the example given, any world where everyone is at the same level ranging from 500 to 600 would be equally close to the world in question.)

someone's complaint depends upon how she fares relative to all those better off than she, and the additive principle of equality. According to the "relative to all those better off" view of complaints the size of individual complaints will decrease as the Sequence progresses, as there will be fewer and fewer better off than those who have a complaint. According to the additive principle, how bad a world is will depend upon both the magnitude *and* the number of complaints. Combined, these views support the judgment that, regarding inequality, the middle worlds, where a fairly large number have fairly large complaints, will be worse than either the initial worlds, where just a few have very large complaints, or the end worlds, where many have very small complaints. Indeed, on the view assumed here, according to which the size of someone's complaint is measured by summing up the difference between her level and that of each person better off than she, it is a simple task to verify that the combination of views I have been discussing will support the judgment that the Sequence first gets worse, then better.

Similar reasoning would lead one to expect that the additive principle would also support the "worse, then better" ordering when combined with the "relative to the average" view of complaints. As the Sequence progresses the situation changes from there being a few much worse off than the average to there being many only a little worse off than the average. So, by combining the two views in question, it might seem that the middle worlds, where a fairly large number have fairly large complaints, will be worse than either the initial worlds, where just a few have very large complaints, or the end worlds, where many have very small complaints. And it is easy to verify that the "worse, then better" ordering is yielded by these views, if one makes the assumption that how bad it is for someone to deviate from the average can be measured by taking the difference between her level of welfare and that of the average person.

The foregoing is slightly oversimplified. On the "relative to the average" view of complaints it might seem that deviations *above* the average should be regarded as bad as well as deviations *below* the average. This is because, as noted earlier, on the intuitions underlying the relative to the average view of complaints anyone receiving more than the average will appear to be receiving *more* than her fair share. Such a person will seem to have been treated (by Fate) as *more* than the equal of her peers and, regarding inequality, just as it would seem bad for any person to receive (even from Fate) *less* than equal treatment, so it would seem bad for any person to receive *more* than equal treatment.

Using the terminology of *complaints*, it might be said that although those above the average do not have a complaint, *we* have a complaint about them being as well off as they are. Correspondingly, on the additive principle we would measure inequality by adding up all of the complaints of those below the average and all of our complaints about those above the average. In essence, then, because on the relative to the average view of complaints deviation from the average in either direction is bad, on the additive principle the worse of two worlds would be that one in which the total deviation from the average was greatest. Although this complicates the overall view, it would not change the ordering, or the basic reasoning underlying it. After all, in the first world only *1* person deviates below the average by a very large amount while the other 999 barely deviate above the average. Thus the inequality in that world may not strike us as nearly as bad as the inequality in the middle world, where half the population is much *worse* off than the average and half is much *better* off than the average. The last world is analogous to the first, as *1* person deviates above the average by a very large amount, while the other 999 barely deviate below the average. Hence the inequality in that world, like the inequality in the first, may not seem particularly bad.

The preceding raises a general worry about my book's presentation and focus. I have suggested that we can measure inequality (primarily) as a function of those who have complaints regarding inequality. But, it might be urged, equality is a symmetrical relation. If we think it is bad for A to be worse off than B, then we should think it is equally bad for B to be better off than A. Correspondingly, if A has a complaint vis-à-vis B, then following the suggestion given above one might claim that even if *B* has no complaint vis-à-vis A, *we* have a complaint *about* B's position vis-à-vis A. Such reasoning suggests that on the intuitions underlying the "relative to the best-off person" view we should count both the complaints of the worse-off relative to the best-off, and *our* complaints about how the best-off fares relative to the worse-off. Similarly, on the intuitions underlying the "relative to all those better off" view, we should count both the complaints of the worse-off relative to all those better off, and *our* complaints about how the better-off fare relative to each person worse off.

The above view has some plausibility, but I am not sure it dictates a revision in my claims or approach. Let me grant that equality is symmetrical in the manner in question, that the egalitarian who objects to A's being worse off than B equally objects to B's being better off than A. Even so, these seem to be just two alternative ways of describing the same thing: namely, the egalitarian's basic objection to the inequality between A and B. If, for example, we have already measured the egalitarian's objection to the inequality between A and B in terms of A's complaint regarding B, it is not clear that we must *also* measure the egalitarian's objection to the inequality between A and B in terms of our complaint about B's position regarding A. Such a move may simply involve double counting and may, in any event, be unnecessarily complicated and otiose. Thus, although I think there is reason to invoke the conception of *our* complaints about those better off than the average given the basic intuitions underlying the relative to the average view of complaints, and while doing this will often affect the orderings generated by that view,[26] it is not clear that we should invoke the conception of our complaints about the position of the best-off relative to those worse off, or about the positions of the better-off relative to all those worse off, given the basic intuitions underlying the relative to the best-off person and the relative to all those better off views of complaints (and given that we are already measuring individual complaints of the worse-off in accordance with those views). Moreover, it is even less clear that adding *our* complaints about the relative positions of the best- or better-off to the worse-off's complaints would affect the orderings generated by

26. Although it doesn't happen to do this in the case of the Sequence discussed previously, it will in many other cases.

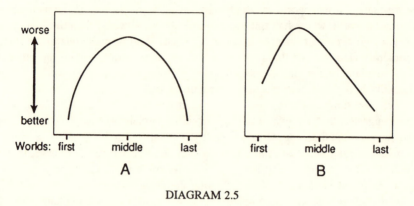

DIAGRAM 2.5

the views in question and, hence, that there would be any point in doing so. In sum, I tentatively conclude that for most of inequality's aspects focusing on individual complaints is sufficient, and that we only need to consider *our* complaints about the better-off on the relative to the average view. Naturally, if I am mistaken about this my arguments and results must be revised accordingly, perhaps reflecting even further inequality's complexity.

Returning to the main argument, we saw above that the additive principle would support the "worse, then better" ordering when combined with either the "relative to all those better off" or the "relative to the average" view of complaints. In addition, the *weighted* additive principle, in any plausible version, would support the "worse, then better" ordering when combined with either of those views of complaints. But whereas the additive principle would combine with the "relative to all those better off" and the "relative to the average" views of complaints to yield an ordering of the Sequence corresponding to a *symmetrical curve* (like A of diagram 2.5), the weighted additive principle would combine with those views to yield a *skewed* curve (like B of diagram 2.5). That is, on the weighted additive principle the Sequence would first get worse and then get better, but the various "reciprocal" worlds would not be equivalent (for n < 500 the nth world would be worse than the nth last world), and the worst world would not be the middle world but an earlier world. The extent to which the curve would be skewed would depend on the exact weighting system employed by the weighted additive principle. If larger complaints receive lots of extra weight, it will be greatly skewed; if they only receive a little extra weight, it will only be slightly skewed.[27]

To sum up the discussion of this ordering. Several different positions support the judgment that the Sequence first gets worse, then gets better. The view that a world's inequality can be determined by considering how much that world deviates

27. If the weighting scheme were extreme enough, the weighted additive principle would support the "better and better" ordering when combined with the two views of complaints in question. However, such a weighting scheme would implausibly imply that to be worse off than 999 people is not merely *somewhat* worse than being worse off than 998, it is at least twice as bad. Given any plausible system of weighting, the "worse, then better" ordering results.

from a state of absolute equality would support such an ordering; so would both the additive principle and the weighted additive principle when combined with either the "relative to all those better off" or the "relative to the average" view of complaints. As usual, because each of these positions represents different (combinations of) elements of our thinking, the judgments they yield about more realistic situations will often disagree.

First Better, Then Worse

By now it may seem that there are *bound* to be several plausible positions supporting the judgment that the Sequence *first gets better, then gets worse*. However, if there *are* such elements, I am not aware of them. (One position that may initially seem to support such an ordering is considered, and rejected, in appendix A.)

All Equivalent

Do any plausible views support the judgment that the Sequence's worlds are *all equivalent*? One principle that would support this ordering when combined with the "relative to the best-off person" view of complaints would be a maximin principle of equality that lacked the tie-breaking clause that if the worst-off groups in two worlds fare the same, then that world will be best whose worst-off group is smallest.

I believe that the version of the maximin principle with the tie-breaking clause is more plausible than the version without it. However, it might be charged that it is the latter version that actually captures our *maximin* views, and that the former version just represents an *ad hoc* attempt to reconcile our maximin views with certain other views. I think this charge cannot be sustained, and shall briefly suggest why.

The claim that we are especially concerned about the worst-off group is misleading, insofar as it suggests a concern on our part about the *group itself* as opposed to the *members* of that group. We do not have a special concern for some real or abstract entity, "the worst-off group." What we have is a special concern for the worst-off members of our world, and it is *this* concern that the maximin principle expresses.[28] But surely, insofar as we are especially concerned with the worst-off members of our world, we would want to raise as many of them as possible above their present level, as long as by doing that we were not increasing the others' complaints. This suggests that of the two competing versions it is indeed the one first considered that accurately expresses our maximin views. Thus one must look elsewhere to support the judgment that the Sequence's worlds are all equivalent.

One line of reasoning supporting this ordering can be illustrated with the following example. Suppose there were three Greek city-states, A, B, and C. Suppose that

28. This claim is significant. Also controversial. It reflects the *individualistic position* that individuals, rather than groups or societies, are the proper objects of moral concern. The individualistic position opposes the *holistic one*, which maintains that groups or societies may also be the proper objects of moral concern. The implications and relative merits of these positions will receive further attention in many of the following chapters.

in A any foreigner could be enslaved and treated in any manner whatsoever, whereas in both B *and* C only adult male foreigners could be enslaved and only if they were properly clothed, sheltered, and fed. Now, even without knowing how many people were enslaved in each of these societies, there are two senses in which one could plausibly claim that B was better than A and equivalent to C with respect to slavery. One might mean by such a claim that the kind of slavery in B—how well the slaves fare—is the same as the kind of slavery in C, and better than the kind of slavery in A. One might also mean by such a claim that the principles and institutions responsible for the systems of slavery in the societies are equally unjust in B and C, and even more unjust in A. In this second sense, our judgment about how bad the societies are with respect to slavery would not depend upon the number of people affected by the principles and institutions in question; for our judgments would be, as it were, judgments about the "character" of those societies. Thus, just as we would not regard one judge who solicited and accepted bribes in each of her cases as less corrupt than another who did the same, merely because she tried fewer cases, so we would not regard society B as less unjust than society C, merely because (being located in a less densely populated area) its members had captured fewer slaves.

These considerations suggest two ways in which the worlds of the Sequence might plausibly be regarded as equivalent. First, because on the "relative to the best-off person" view of complaints the members of the worse-off groups fare the same throughout the Sequence, it may seem that the *kind* of inequality is the same throughout the Sequence and, hence, that in that sense each of the worlds is equivalent. Second, if one adopts the "relative to the best-off person" view of complaints, *and* if one thinks of the worlds of the Sequence as representing societies whose principles and institutions are responsible for the *kind* of inequality in those worlds but not the number of people who are in the better- and worse-off groups, then one might regard each of those worlds as equivalent, in the sense that insofar as the inequality in those worlds is concerned each of those societies—that is, the principles and institutions governing them—would be equally unjust. (Note, as used here, to say two societies are more or less unjust is not equivalent to saying that they are more or less objectionable because of the extent to which they are unequal; rather it is to say that they are more or less objectionable because of the way in which their principles and institutions promote or prevent inequality.)

Now the first sense in which the worlds might be regarded as equivalent merely illustrates what we have known all along—that the gap between the better- and worse-off groups is constant throughout the Sequence. Knowing that the worlds of the Sequence are all equivalent in *this* sense would give us no reason to regard them as equally desirable from a moral perspective in the absence of an argument that how good a society is regarding inequality depends solely on the size of the gaps between the better- and worse-off groups. However, the second sense in which the worlds might be regarded as equivalent is, I believe, a substantive one. It expresses the view that there is a sense in which two societies can be equally unjust, though things may be worse in one than the other.[29] I believe, therefore, that it *can* be

---

29. It is, I think, one of the great, but too often overlooked, strengths of Rawls's theory of justice that it accommodates this view, along with the analogous view that one society might be less just than another

plausibly claimed that the Sequence's worlds are equivalent regarding inequality. However, this is more plausible where *social* justice is concerned than where natural or cosmic justice is concerned.

Consider again slaveholding societies B and C, and suppose they are equally populous. If 10 percent of B's population are slaves, and 60 percent of C's population are slaves, then even though B and C may be equally unjust as far as *social* justice is concerned, C will seem worse than B as far as *natural* justice is concerned, since the slaves in B and C are the victims of the same kind of injustice, and since there are *more* victims of injustice in C than in B. The case of inequality is more complicated than that of slavery, since we may think that the kind of inequality changes as the ratios between the better- and worse-off groups shift; still, as far as natural justice is concerned, it seems that a change in the ratios between the better- and worse-off groups should have some affect on a situation's inequality.

There may be a different kind of position supporting this ordering. One may think that the Sequence's worlds are all equivalent, not in the sense that they are *exactly* as good as each other, but in the sense that one cannot choose between them. On this view a change in the ratios between the better- and worse-off groups may affect a world's inequality, but not in a way that permits one to say whether the world has gotten better or worse. One might be driven to such a position as either a compromise between, or a skeptical result of, the numerous conflicting views already discussed. Looking at the Sequence we find that different intuitions lead us to judge that it is getting better and better, worse and worse, and first worse and then better. This may lead us to conclude that we cannot compare the Sequence's worlds regarding inequality, that our notion of inequality is complex and incomplete, a notion that allows us to make *some* inequality judgments but not others.

The idea here might be put as follows. When we consider our notion of inequality it may seem that there are various *aspects* involved in that notion. In comparing two worlds these aspects may, as they do with respect to the Sequence, conflict. When this happens it may seem that we cannot judge which of the worlds is better regarding inequality. Perhaps the best we can do is point out that in terms of *certain* aspects of inequality the one world is better, whereas in terms of *other* aspects the other is.

It is an important question whether or not such reasoning ultimately supports the judgment that the worlds of the Sequence are equivalent—at least in the sense that one cannot choose between them. However, I do not wish to pursue this question now.[30] In this chapter I am not trying to determine what the most plausible compromise between some or all of our egalitarian judgments would be (if there even *is* such a compromise to be found). I am interested in trying to determine what our egalitarian views actually are. My question, then, is whether there are any independently plausible elements of our thinking that would support the judgment that the Sequence's worlds are all equivalent regarding inequality. The only such element I

though in absolute terms its members (*including* those in the worst-off group) fare better. This tremendously important point has, I think, profound implications. (See part 3 of my "Intransitivity and the Mere Addition Paradox," *Philosophy and Public Affairs* 16 [1987]: especially pp. 173-79.)

30. I shall be returning to it, albeit indirectly, in sections 3 and 4 of chapter 5.

am aware of, is the one according to which the worlds would be regarded as equivalent *if* the "relative to the best-off person" view of complaints was adopted, and *if* the worlds of the Sequence represented societies whose principles and institutions were responsible for the size of the gaps between the better- and worse-off groups, but not the number of people in those groups.

2.4 Concluding Remarks

In this chapter I have been examining the question of how we judge one situation to be worse than another regarding inequality. I have suggested that a number of plausible positions might influence our egalitarian judgments. Specifically, I have suggested that the additive, weighted additive, and maximin principles could each be combined with the relative to the average, the relative to the best-off person, and the relative to the all those better off views of complaints, to yield a judgment about how good or bad a situation is regarding inequality. I have also suggested that in accordance with certain other plausible views, we might judge a situation's inequality in terms of either how gratuitous it appears to be, or how much it deviates from a state of absolute equality. Finally, I have suggested that we may judge how good or bad a society is regarding inequality in terms of the principles and institutions of that society responsible for the inequality.

In all then, I claimed there were (at least) twelve different aspects or positions underlying or influencing our egalitarian judgments (there may be more). In illustrating my claims I showed how different orderings of the Sequence would be supported by different aspects. Diagram 2.6 sums up the relevant results. Note, the concern about social inequality will only rank the Sequence's worlds equivalent given certain assumptions discussed in the text. With different assumptions the concern about social inequality might support any ordering of the Sequence.

I have not offered a final judgment about how the Sequence's worlds compare regarding inequality. I shall return to this in chapter 10 when I discuss practical implications. For now, my concern with the Sequence has been solely to help illustrate inequality's complexity. Also, I have not attached any special importance to the extent of agreement, or lack thereof, which the different positions have regarding the Sequence. To the contrary, as I have emphasized throughout, and shall illustrate in the following chapters, positions that agree, or disagree, regarding the Sequence may disagree, or agree, in other cases.

In suggesting that many different positions underlie and influence egalitarian judgments, I am *not* suggesting that each of these positions is equally appealing much less that everyone will find them so. But I do think that each represents certain plausible views that cannot easily be dismissed. Because these views often conflict, it may be possible, for each of the positions discussed, to construct examples where the judgment yielded by that position seems implausible. This does *not* show that the various positions are not plausible, nor does it show that they are not involved in people's egalitarian judgments. What it shows is that each position does not *itself* underlie each such judgment.

I have focused in this chapter on what happens to our egalitarian judgments

Aspects of Inequality	Orderings of the Sequence				
	Better and Better	Worse and Worse	First Worse then Better	First Better then Worse	All Equivalent
MP & AVE :	X				
MP & BOP :		X			
MP & ATBO :	X				
AP & AVE :			X		
AP & BOP :		X			
AP & ATBO :			X		
WAP & AVE :			X		
WAP & BOP :		X			
WAP & ATBO :			X		
Deviation :			X		
Gratuitousness :	X				
Social Inequality :					X

MP = Maximin Principle of Equality
AP = Additive Principle of Equality
WAP = Weighted Additive Principle of Equality
AVE = Relative to the Average View of Complaints
BOP = Relative to the Best-Off Person View of Complaints
ATBO = Relative to the All Those Better Off View of Complaints

DIAGRAM 2.6

when the levels between the better- and worse-off groups remain the same, but the ratios between those groups vary. Questions still needing to be explored are: what happens to our egalitarian judgments in cases involving more than two groups; how are our egalitarian judgments affected by variations in group levels, by transfers between groups, or by variations involving nonhomogeneous groups; does inequality matter more in a poor society than in a rich one; and is inequality affected by a population's size? These questions, and others, will be addressed later. As we shall see, although these questions concern important elements of the egalitarian's thinking, their answers do not affect the main results of this chapter.[31]

One conclusion this chapter suggests that the *non*egalitarian might readily em-

31. As we shall see in chapter 3, it may be that some of our initial judgments about which egalitarian positions seem *most* plausible will have to be revised when we consider situations more complicated than the Sequence. However, even in more complex situations, it remains true that each position discussed represents elements that cannot easily be dismissed; elements that will influence our judgments about those situations, and that will often conflict with one another.

brace can be put as follows. Upon examination, the notion of inequality turns out to involve a hodgepodge of different and often conflicting positions. Moreover, and more important, many of these positions are fundamentally incompatible, resting as they do on contrary views. It simply cannot be true, for instance, *both* that everybody but the best-off person has a complaint *and* that only those below the average have a complaint. Nor can it be true that the size of someone's complaint should be measured by comparing her to the average, *and* by comparing her to the best-off person, *and* by comparing her to all those better off than she. The notion of inequality may thus be largely inconsistent and severely limited. Although it may permit certain rather trivial judgments, such as the judgments that an equal world is better than an unequal one, and that "other things being equal" large gaps between people are worse than small ones, in many, and perhaps most, realistic cases, one cannot compare situations regarding inequality.

Understandably, the egalitarian might try to resist this conclusion. As indicated in the discussion of the last ordering, she might contend that each of the positions presented in this chapter represents a different *aspect* of inequality, and she might insist that what the conflict between these aspects illustrates is just how complex and multifaceted that notion truly is. What we need, it might be claimed, is to arrive at a measure of inequality that accurately captures each of the aspects involved in that notion, according them each their due weight. Such a measure would give us a way of accurately comparing many, though perhaps not all, situations regarding inequality.

In chapter 10 I shall return to the question of whether inequality is inconsistent, and if so what that implies about egalitarianism. But as this book's concern is with elucidating egalitarianism, not defending it, in the intervening chapters I simply assume the egalitarian can defend the position that the notion of inequality is complex, multifaceted, and partially incomplete, rather than largely inconsistent and severely limited. Either way, however, I think many of our commonsense egalitarian judgments will have to be revised.[32]

---

32. I shall say more about the manner in which our egalitarian judgments will have to be revised in chapter 10, when I discuss some of this work's practical implications.

3

Inequality in Complex Situations

In chapter 2 I considered how the simple, split-level worlds of the Sequence compare regarding inequality. In this chapter, I shall examine situations involving four groups rather than two. In doing this, I shall consider how our egalitarian judgments would be affected by simple increases or decreases in different group levels, and by various transfers *between* groups. Examining these more complex situations both corroborates some of our earlier results and helps safeguard us from drawing mistaken or misleading conclusions based on those results. In addition, it provides fresh insights into the nature of inequality and new slants on some of the insights already gained.

As before, I shall employ diagrams to represent the different situations and to help elicit judgments concerning them. I shall mainly focus on what the aspects uncovered in chapter 2 imply about the situations, without attempting further to explain or justify those aspects. However, in appendix A, I consider several new factors that might also be thought relevant to the situations discussed.

3.1 Poll Results and Aspects: A Striking Correlation

In this section and the next, I shall refer to the results of a poll taken at the National Humanities Center in the fall of 1984. Basically the poll contained a series of diagrams, including a *Standard* situation, S (diagram 3.1), and variations of it.[1] S represents a situation, or world, evenly divided into four groups by three gaps of the same size. So, the third group is better off than the fourth by the same amount that the second is better off than the third and that the first is better off than the second. The variations of S involved increasing and decreasing the levels of S's groups. More specifically, each group was moved, in turn, to levels ranging from being even better off than S's best-off group, through the levels of each of S's other groups, to being even worse off than S's worst-off group.

Focusing on two diagrams at a time, respondents were asked to indicate how the situations represented by those diagrams compared *regarding inequal-*

1. Note, my poll's diagrams were originally drawn with sloped tops of the sort described in section 4.2. For reasons of clarity and simplicity, I have redrawn them here so as to match the format of the other diagrams presented to this point. This does not affect my results. For as appendix B implies, each of my claims regarding the poll could be made in terms of the original diagrams.

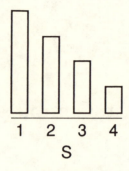

DIAGRAM 3.1

ity.[2] Their choice of possible responses is given in diagram 3.2: specifically, for each A and B to be compared, respondents were to indicate if A's inequality could be characterized by choices a through k. My interest was in determining how increases or decreases in different group levels might affect people's pre-theoretical judgments about a situation's inequality. Correspondingly, although respondents knew I was a philosopher writing on inequality, they were not informed of the nature of my work or the results arrived at considering the Sequence. Unfortunately, only ten of the forty who received the poll completed it. However, they represented diverse fields, including medicine and biology, American history, Russian history, literary criticism, English literature, classics, medieval architecture, anthropology, and philosophy.

A few caveats are in order. First, methodological questions might be raised about the wording of any poll, including (perhaps especially) mine. Second, despite the diversity of the respondents, fellows of the National Humanities Center are not necessarily representative of the "average person in the street." Third, ten respondents constitute too small a sample from which to draw statistically significant conclusions. Fourth, I am focusing on the poll responses that seem most illuminating—and supportive of my views! Not all of the poll's responses fit so clearly with our other results. Finally, little follows about what people *should* believe from what they actually believe.

So, in what follows, I am *not* appealing to the poll to demonstrate convincingly what most people believe regarding inequality, much less what they should believe. Rather, I am presenting certain results I found interesting and suggestive. Mostly, the poll enables me to fruitfully and concretely introduce certain claims I would otherwise have to make at a more abstract, theoretical level.

One striking feature of the poll's results was the range of answers given to different questions. Consider diagram 3.3. In A, S's fourth group has been lowered so the gap between it and the third group is twice what it was before. In B, S's third

2. Naturally, in keeping with this work's approach the instructions stressed the importance of trying, so far as possible, to convey purely one's egalitarian responses. Thus, people were instructed to set aside their "all-things-considered" judgments and indicate what they would say about the situations in terms of but one respect, inequality; that is, *as if* equality were the *only* thing about which they cared.

a. definitely worse and unequivocally so
b. definitely worse though they felt some slight pull in the other direction
c. somewhat worse and unequivocally so
d. somewhat worse though they felt some pull in the other direction
e. about the same as the inequality in the other
f. somewhat better though they felt some pull in the other direction
g. somewhat better and unequivocally so
h. definitely better though they felt some slight pull in the other direction
i. definitely better and unequivocally so
j. they have no feelings about the comparison at all
k. other (please indicate)

DIAGRAM 3.2

group has been raised to the level of the first. In C and D, S's first group has been lowered to the levels of the fourth and third groups, respectively. Here, and elsewhere, diagrams have been drawn to ensure consistent presentations in the patterns of inequality. For example, in B the positions of the second and third groups were switched, so as not to visually divert attention from the relevant fact that after the third group has been raised the pattern of inequality involves two groups at the first group's level and one group each at the second and fourth levels.

Poll respondents were asked to compare three cases: S with A (case I), C with D (case II), and S with B (case III). Their answers appear in diagram 3.4, where a–k correspond to the alternatives noted in diagram 3.2. For each pair of situations, the

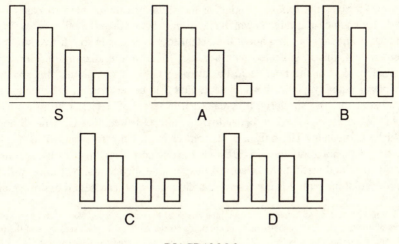

DIAGRAM 3.3

	a	b	c	d	e	f	g	h	i	j	k
I (S,A):	0	0	0	0	0	0	2	0	8	0	0
II (C,D):	3	1	3	1	1	0	0	1	0	0	0
III (S,B):	1	1	1	0	1	2	1	0	1	1	0

DIAGRAM 3.4

alternatives marked indicate how respondents thought the inequality in the first situation (S, C, or S) compared with that in the second (A, D, or B). As the chart indicates, there was marked variation in the range of answers given for these cases.

In case I, there was complete agreement that S was unequivocally better than A regarding inequality. There was *some* disagreement about *how much* better it was, but not a lot, as eight judged it definitely better, whereas only two judged it somewhat better. In case II, there was general agreement C was not better than D—only one person thought otherwise—but there was much divergence about their exact relation. Although most (eight) agreed that C was worse than D, they were evenly split as to whether it was "definitely" worse or "somewhat" worse. Moreover, while six thought C was unequivocally worse than D, four thought otherwise. In case III, we have the democrat's nightmare. Ten people express nine different positions, ranging from one extreme to the other. Viewing this from the outside, one naturally sympathizes with the person who marked that she or he had no feelings about this comparison, as well as the person who gave no answer at all.

The responses to cases I–III buttress the claim that inequality is a complex notion. In addition, they *appear* to provide further, indirect, support for the claims of chapter 2.[3] Consider diagram 3.5. For each of chapter 2's relevant aspects, diagram 3.5 gives the *ordinal* ranking of the situations represented by cases I–III. That is, for each case it tells us which situation is better than the other according to each aspect but says nothing about the extent to which this is so.[4] If two situations are equivalent, this is indicated with a *T*. So, for example, diagram 3.5 illustrates that combined with the relative to the average view of complaints, the maximin principle of equality yields the judgments that S is better than A, C better than D, and S better than B. Similarly, it reveals that in terms of deviation from a state of absolute equality, S would be better than A, and D better than C, while S and B would be equivalent. The only aspect from chapter 2 not represented in diagram 3.5—as it does not apply to such cases—is the one corresponding to our concern for the principles and institutions of society responsible for inequality. (Since our concern for social inequality is not relevant, unless stated otherwise, all ensuing claims

3. I emphasize the word "appear" to remind the reader of the caveats noted earlier, and hence of the dangers of drawing any firm conclusions from my poll's results. Still, as we shall see, some of the poll's results are so striking that it is hard not to be impressed by the correlations they suggest vis-à-vis our other results.

4. For example, in case II, D is only better than C according to MP & BOP in virtue of the tie-breaking clause of maximin noted in chapter 2.

	Case I (S,A)	Case II (C,D)	Case III (S,B)
MP & AVE :	S	C	S
MP & BOP :	S	D	B
MP & ATBO :	S	D	S
AP & AVE :	S	D	T
AP & BOP :	S	D	B
AP & ATBO :	S	T	T
WAP & AVE :	S	D	T v S
WAP & BOP :	S	D	B
WAP & ATBO :	S	D	S
Deviation :	S	D	T
Gratuitousness :	S	C	S

MP = Maximin Principle of Equality
AP = Additive Principle of Equality
WAP = Weighted Additive Principle of Equality
AVE = Relative to the Average View of Complaints
BOP = Relative to the Best-Off Person View of Complaints
ATBO = Relative to the All Those Better Off View of Complaints
T = Tie

DIAGRAM 3.5

about chapter 2's aspects—for example, that S is better than A according to *each* of chapter 2's aspects—apply *only* to diagram 3.5's aspects.)

A word about the disjunct in case III. As noted in chapter 2, there are different ways a weighted additive principle might weight large complaints when combined with a relative to the average view of complaints. If being above the average counts as much as being below the average, then S and B would probably be judged equivalent on the view in question. On the other hand, if being below the average counts for more, then S would be better than B.[5] The details of this need not concern us here, nor, more generally, the details of how one determines the ranking of different alternatives according to the different aspects. For the most part, the reasoning and calculations underlying the rankings presented are fairly straightforward, but tedious.[6]

5. There is no disjunct in cases I and II, as both methods of weighting complaints agree in those cases. That is, combined with the relative to the average principle the weighted additive principle would judge S was better than A, and D better than C, *whichever* plausible method of weighting one adopted.

6. To rank outcomes like those of diagram 3.3, it is easiest if one assumes there is one person in each group and assigns an appropriate level to each person. Such an assumption greatly simplifies one's calculations, and does not affect one's ordinal rankings.

Diagram 3.5 does not tell us how much, if at all, people care about the different aspects. Nevertheless, I believe it sheds light on the variation noted in diagram 3.4. In case I, there was complete agreement that S was unequivocally better than A. Correspondingly, as diagram 3.5 shows, S is better than A according to *each* of chapter 2's aspects. In case II, most agreed that D was better than C, but there was variation in the strength and purity of this judgment. Correspondingly, eight of eleven aspects agree that D is better than C, but two aspects yield the reverse judgment, and one deems them equivalent. In case III, there was great disagreement about how S compares with B. Correspondingly, there is tremendous divergence among the aspects. Depending on one's view of WAP, either S would be better than B on five aspects, equivalent on three, and worse on three, or S would be better than B on four aspects, equivalent on four, and worse on three. It seems, then, chapter 2's aspects can account for the variation in diagram 3.4. All one needs to bear in

---

For example, assume S has four people at levels 1,000, 800, 600, and 400, respectively, and A has four people at levels 1,000, 800, 600, and 200, respectively. Then to compare S with A in terms of MP & AVE one can simply measure the size of the gap between the average person and the worst-off person in each outcome to see that S will be better than A, since $(700 - 400) = 300 < (650 - 200) = 450$. Similarly, to compare S with A in terms of MP & BOP one can simply measure the size of the gaps between the best-off and the worst-off to see that S will be better than A, since $(1,000 - 400) = 600 < (1,000 - 200) = 800$, while to compare S with A in terms of MP & ATBO one can measure the gaps between the worst-off and all those better off to see that S will be better than A, since $(1,000 - 400) + (800 - 400) + (600 - 400) = 1,200 < (1,000 - 200) + (800 - 200) + (600 - 200) = 1,800$.

Analogously, it is a simple matter to calculate how outcomes will compare on AP & AVE, AP & BOP, AP & ATBO, and Deviation. For example, to compare S with A in terms of AP & BOP one can measure the gaps between each person and the best-off to see that S will be better than A, since $(1,000 - 800) + (1,000 - 600) + (1,000 - 400) = 1,200 < (1,000 - 800) + (1,000 - 600) + (1,000 - 200) = 1,400$. (Recall that Deviation simply measures the total deviation from the median. Also, recall that to measure a situation regarding AP & AVE one must decide whether on the relative to the average view of complaints deviations above the average should count as well deviations below the average. I assumed they should in my examples.)

There are two cases where ranking outcomes is nontrivial. First, in the absence of a determinate function for how much (extra) to weight the largest complaints and/or those of the worst-off, there is no simple algorithm for comparing outcomes according to aspects involving WAP in those cases where the worst-off individual and/or the largest complaint is in the outcome with the smallest sum total of (relevant) complaints. In such cases I either used my judgment to rank the better outcome, if I thought such a ranking was fairly uncontroversial, or I indicated how the ranking would depend on one's weighting scheme.

Second, it is unclear how best to compare situations regarding gratuitousness. For the purposes of this chapter, I measured gratuitousness by dividing the average level of those better off than the average by the average and then subtracting that number from the number arrived at by dividing the average by the average level of those worse off than the average. Intuitively, the latter number represented the relative "cost" of the inequality to those worse off and the former the relative "gain" from the inequality for those better off. The larger the relative "cost" and the smaller the relative "gain"—and hence the larger the size of the relative "cost" minus the relative "gain"—the more gratuitous, and thus worse, the inequality. For example, on this formula S would be better than A according to Gratuitousness, since S's gratuitousness, $(700/500) - (900/700) = \sim.11$, would be better (less) than A's, $(650/400) - (900/650) = \sim.24$.

Note, as will become clearer in chapter 6, the above approaches for measuring inequality's aspects are somewhat oversimplified. However, they have various advantages, not the least of which is that they are easy to apply and, more important, they yield plausible rankings for this chapter's outcomes. Correspondingly, though they must ultimately be revised in light of chapter 6, they are suitable for our present purposes.

mind is that (at the intuitive level) different people may be influenced by different aspects, and to greater and lesser extents.

Initially, many find the variation in diagram 3.4 and especially the great dis-agreement about case III, surprising. This is because too little attention has been paid to comparing situations regarding inequality. More specifically, comparisons have tended to focus on certain obvious "paradigm" cases involving perfect equality versus inequality, or small gaps between the better- and worse-off versus large ones. Because there is general agreement about such cases, people have naturally sup-posed that inequality is a simple notion and, more particularly, that most others assess inequality the same way they do (though they may *care* about it more or less). Clearly, on such a view one would neither expect, nor could one easily account for, the sort of variation found in diagram 3.4.

Unfortunately, the "paradigm" cases are very misleading. Like case I, they are cases about which *each* of chapter 2's aspects concur. Correspondingly, agreement about such cases may obscure the fact that different people are actually responding to different features of the situations in assessing their inequality. That this is so is suggested by chapter 2's theoretical arguments, together with the empirical re-sponses given to cases II and III.

Once one recognizes inequality's complexity, the variation in diagram 3.4 is no longer surprising. To the contrary, depending on how much people care about the different aspects, one might expect greater or lesser agreement about situations roughly to parallel greater or lesser agreement among aspects.

On the view that inequality is a simple notion, someone who holds that one situation is definitely and unequivocally worse than another will be tempted to dismiss the opposite view as absurd, badly mistaken, or, at best, confused. Indeed, the temptation will be to assume that anyone holding the opposite view has misun-derstood the issue, that whatever she is comparing the situations in terms of, it isn't inequality. (Naturally, the holder of such a view will have the same temptation regarding *her* position.) This temptation should be resisted. To be sure, sometimes people are mistaken in the factors to which they appeal. But in general the lesson suggested by the Sequence, together with cases like I–III, is that we will make more progress in our understanding of inequality once we recognize that substantive disagreements may reflect not stupidity or misunderstanding, but the complex na-ture of inequality.

Considered by itself, it is tempting to conclude that the results of case III tell us more about academics than about inequality. Thus, the cynic might claim that *when-ever* one asks ten academics a question of value one should expect ten different answers. On this view the real surprise about case III is that two people actually agreed! This view is engaging, but it is also silly. Case I shows that agreement *is* possible. We need an explanation of why this is so in some cases but not others.

The stubborn cynic might persist. She might admit that sometimes there is agreement and sometimes not, but contend this is accidental, having little or nothing to do with the notion of inequality. Diagram 3.5 belies this position, and in any event I do not find it plausible. Suppose I had asked people to compare cases I–III regarding utility instead of inequality. In all three cases there would have been agreement of the sort in case I. That is, while there might be some disagreement whether the situations were "definitely" better, or merely "somewhat" better, there would be complete accord that regarding (both total and average) utility, S, D, and B are unequivocally better than A, C, and S, respectively. This is no accident. Utility is a relatively clear and straightforward notion that yields clear and straightforward judgments in most cases of the sort described. The situation is otherwise regarding inequality. In some cases it permits clear and straightforward judgments. But in others it does not.

To conclude this section let me note one other respect in which diagram 3.5 supports certain claims of chapter 2. In chapter 2, I stated that since the aspects express different positions, those agreeing in their judgments about the Sequence may disagree about more realistic situations. Similarly, I contended that aspects disagreeing about the Sequence may in turn agree about other situations. Diagram 3.5 confirms the latter point and partially illustrates the former. The aspects that disagree regarding the Sequence agree regarding case I. On the other hand, some aspects that agree regarding the Sequence (and case I) disagree regarding cases II or III. For example, Gratuitousness agrees with MP & AVE and MP & ATBO regarding the Sequence, but not regarding case II. Similarly, the measures that agree with AP & ATBO regarding the Sequence[7] disagree with it regarding case II. Finally, whereas WAP & ATBO agrees with AP & AVE and Deviation for all the other cases so far discussed, it disagrees with them about case III.

I have not shown that all the aspects agreeing about the Sequence disagree about other cases. But this is so for some aspects, and since each aspect represents a distinct position there is good reason to think it is so for all. In any event, since each aspect represents different (combinations of) views, each is capable of underlying and influencing our egalitarian judgments in its own manner. Correspondingly, each must be assessed in its own terms and given its due weight. The importance of this will be discussed further in chapter 5.

3.2 How Increases in Group Levels Affect Inequality

Let us next consider more systematically how increases in group levels affect inequality.

Suppose one had a nondivisible good with which one could improve the lot of some, but not all, members of society. To avoid irrelevant complications, suppose further that the good was like manna from heaven in the sense that it came with "no strings attached"—that is, no one produced it, owned it, deserved it, and so on. It seems clear that an egalitarian's first choice would be for the good to go to those worst-off, her second choice would be for the good to go to those next worst-off, and so on. Her last choice would be for the good to go to those best-off. Surely, improving the lot of those *already* better off than everybody else would only worsen the situation regarding inequality (however much it might improve it in other respects, regarding perfectionism or utility, for example).

7. Namely, AP & AVE, WAP & AVE, WAP & ATBO, and Deviation.

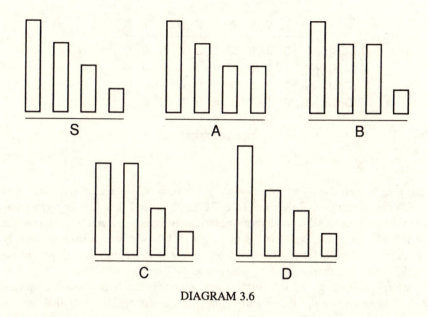

DIAGRAM 3.6

The *relative* ranking of the alternatives seems clear. Less clear, in some cases, is how raising a group actually affects inequality. For example, to know that raising the third group is preferable to raising the second is not yet to know whether either move is desirable. Let us next consider what respondents to my poll thought about some such cases, together with what chapter 2's aspects imply.

Diagram 3.6 illustrates the results of raising the different groups in S one level. So, in A the fourth group has been raised to the level of the third, in B the third group has been raised to the level of the second, in C the second group has been raised to the level of the first, and in D the first group has been raised one level higher, so the gap between them and the second group is twice what it was before.

Poll respondents were asked to compare four cases: A with S (case I), B with S (case II), C with S (case III), and D with S (case IV). Their answers appear on diagram 3.7 where, as before, a–k correspond to the alternatives noted in diagram 3.2. As in diagram 3.4, for each pair of situations the alternatives marked indicate how respondents thought the inequality in the first situation (A, B, C, or D) compared with that in the second (S).

As diagram 3.7 illustrates, there was strong agreement about case I. Eight respondents agreed A is unequivocally better than S regarding inequality, including six who thought it was "definitely" better. Interestingly, the one person who thought S was better than A marked that it was "definitely and unequivocally" so. I shall say more about this response later. Case II yielded far less agreement. Though six thought B was better than S, three thought otherwise, and one thought them equivalent. More significantly, while eight felt at least

	a	b	c	d	e	f	g	h	i	j	k
I (A,S):	1	0	0	0	1	0	2	0	6	0	0
II (B,S):	1	1	1	0	1	2	1	2	1	0	0
III (C,S):	2	1	3	2	0	1	0	0	1	0	0
IV (D,S):	8	0	1	1	0	0	0	0	0	0	0

DIAGRAM 3.7

some pull toward the view that B was better than S, eight also felt some pull in the other direction.[8] Regarding case III, eight agreed that C was worse than S, but there was significant divergence within this general position. Moreover, five felt at least some pull toward the view that S was worse than C. Finally, case IV elicited virtual agreement. All ten respondents agreed that D was worse than S, with nine marking it as "unequivocally" so.

Before proceeding, let me briefly note a correlation between the empirical results just noted and the theoretical claim made at the beginning of this section. Put roughly, my poll's "typical" respondent believes that, regarding S's inequality, raising the fourth, third, second, and first groups one level would be, respectively, clearly and significantly better, somewhat better overall though in some respects worse, worse overall though in some respects better, and clearly and significantly worse. These results are consistent with the claim that an egalitarian's first choice would be for a nondivisible good to go to those worst-off, her second choice would be for the good to go to the next worst-off, and so on. Thus, taken collectively, the results in diagram 3.7 express the *relative* ranking noted earlier. They also reveal more than this, as we shall soon see.

As with diagram 3.5, diagram 3.8 gives the ordinal ranking of the situations represented by cases I–IV for each of chapter 2's relevant aspects. For example, it illustrates that combined with the relative to the best-off person view of complaints, the additive principle of equality would yield the judgments that A is better than S, S better than B, C better than S, and S better than D. The question marks in case II stem from the fact that the weighted additive principle gives expression both to certain intuitions underlying the additive principle and to certain intuitions underlying the maximin principle. Insofar as it does the former, WAP & AVE and WAP & ATBO will tend to yield the judgment that B is better than S (just as AP & AVE and AP & ATBO do). Insofar as it does the latter, WAP & AVE and WAP & ATBO will tend to yield the judgment

8. As the reader can infer, I count someone who regards two situations as equivalent (or "about the same") as pulled in both directions. So, the five responses directly entailing a pull in each direction, together with the one ranking the situations equivalent, indicate six respondents pulled in each direction. Combined with the two who thought B unequivocally better than S, and the two who thought B unequivocally worse, those six account for each view having eight pulled toward it despite there only being ten responses.

	Case I (A,S)	Case II (B,S)	Case III (C,S)	Case IV (D,S)
MP & AVE :	A	S	S	S
MP & BOP :	A	B	C	S
MP & ATBO :	A	S	S	S
AP & AVE :	A	B	S	S
AP & BOP :	A	S	C	S
AP & ATBO :	A	B	S	S
WAP & AVE :	A	?	S	S
WAP & BOP :	A	B	C	S
WAP & ATBO :	A	?	S	S
Deviation :	A	B	S	S
Gratuitousness :	A	S	S	S

MP = Maximin Principle of Equality
AP = Additive Principle of Equality
WAP = Weighted Additive Principle of Equality
AVE = Relative to the Average View of Complaints
BOP = Relative to the Best-Off Person View of Complaints
ATBO = Relative to the All Those Better Off View of Complaints

DIAGRAM 3.8

that S is better than B (just as MP & AVE and MP & ATBO do). The issue still to be decided is how much extra weight is to be given large complaints on WAP. Until that issue is resolved, it is an open question how S and B compare on the views under discussion.

Diagram 3.8 dovetails nicely with diagram 3.7. In case I, A is better than S according to *each* of chapter 2's aspects. Correspondingly, eight of ten respondents agreed that A was unequivocally better than S. In case II, five aspects yield the judgment that B is better than S, four yield the reverse judgment, and two express a tendency in both directions. Correspondingly, though most thought B was better than S, eight felt pulled in each direction. In case III, S is better than C according to eight aspects, while C is better than S according to three. Correspondingly, eight respondents thought S was better than C, though five felt some pull toward the reverse ranking. Finally, in case IV, S is better than D according to every aspect. Correspondingly, every respondent agreed with that ranking, with nine marking it unequivocally so.

The "fit" between diagrams 3.8 and 3.7 is not perfect, but it is striking. With few exceptions one can account for the results noted in diagram 3.7 solely by appeal to chapter 2's theoretical results, together with the assumption that, at the intuitive level, people are influenced by different aspects to different

degrees. To an extent, then, the poll's empirical results and chapter 2's theoretical results are mutually supportive. The implications of the latter suggest
that the poll has (largely) succeeded in eliciting people's egalitarian judgments.
In turn, the former seems to provide further support—however weak[9]—for the
claims of chapter 2.

One person who indicated that S was better than D felt some pull in the other
direction. The ambivalence noted is puzzling, since S is better than D according to
every aspect of chapter 2. Even more puzzling was the response that A was definitely and unequivocally worse than S. Clearly this response cannot be accounted
for in terms of chapter 2's aspects, each of which implies that A is better than S. Do
these responses show that chapter 2's results must be revised or further supplemented? Perhaps, but probably not. Both responses were unique, and on reflection
they seem idiosyncratic and implausible. Further considerations relevant to assessing these responses are given in appendix A where I discuss, and reject, several
positions one might think support them. Ultimately then, although we must remain
open to the possibility that inequality is even *more* complex than so far realized, I
see *no* respect in which raising the worst-off group to the level of the next worst-off
group would *worsen* inequality. Similarly, it seems clear that, by itself, improving
the lot of those who are *already* better off than everyone else could only worsen
inequality, not improve it.[10]

At the end of the preceding section I noted how the aspects that disagree about
the Sequence agree about other cases, whereas the aspects that agree about the
Sequence may disagree about other cases. Although I do not wish to belabor the
point, the reader may have noticed I did not mention the aspects yielding the "worse
and worse" ordering of the Sequence: AP & BOP, MP & BOP, and WAP & BOP.
Those aspects not only agree about the Sequence, they agree about each of the cases
discussed in section 3.1. Still, as diagram 3.8 illustrates, they do not agree in all
cases. In case II, for instance, AP & BOP's judgment differs from that of MP &
BOP and WAP & BOP's.

A final point. Some believe that the relative to the best-off person view of
complaints is the least plausible of the three views of complaints. Some even doubt
whether anyone actually subscribes to BOP. But consider again diagrams 3.7 and
3.8. Regarding case III, eight agreed that S is better than C, but five felt at least
some pull in the other direction. Notice, however, that the *only* aspects supporting
the judgment that C is better than S are those involving BOP. This suggests that
insofar as one is pulled toward the view that C is better than S—and half of the
respondents were—one is (probably) being influenced by BOP. Thus, it seems clear
that BOP is not a view one can simply dismiss. This point will take on even greater
force in the following section.

---

9. Bearing in mind the methodological problems noted earlier, we must remain wary of attaching too
much weight to our poll's results. With only ten respondents from a select population sample, we must
continue to look at our results as mainly suggestive, however striking.

10. On a person-affecting or deontological view of inequality one might be able to hold that
improving the lot of the best-off doesn't *worsen* inequality, but not that it *improves* inequality. Hence, it
seems clear that the person who judged S better than D but felt some pull in the other direction was being
pulled by *nonegalitarian* factors.

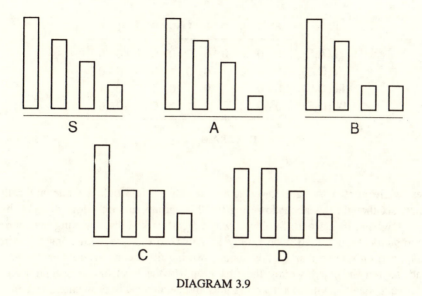

DIAGRAM 3.9

3.3 How Decreases in Group Levels Affect Inequality

Let us next consider how decreases in group levels affect inequality.

Suppose an undeserved and nondivisible misfortune was destined to befall some, but not all, members of society. If one could not prevent the misfortune but could direct it, then an egalitarian's first choice would be to direct it toward those best-off, her second choice would be to direct it toward those next best-off, and so on. Her last choice would be for the misfortune to befall the worst-off.

As before, the *relative* ranking of the alternatives seems clear, while less clear, in some cases, is how lowering a group actually affects inequality. Let us again consider what my poll respondents thought about some such cases, together with what chapter 2's aspects might imply.

Diagram 3.9 illustrates the results of lowering S's different groups one level. In A, the fourth group has been lowered so the gap between them and the third group is twice what it was before, in B, the third group has been lowered to the level of the fourth, in C, the second group has been lowered to the the level of the third, and in D, the first group has been lowered to the level of the second.

Poll respondents were asked to compare four cases: A with S (case I), B with S (case II), C with S (case III), and D with S (case IV). Their answers appear in diagram 3.10, where a–k again correspond to the alternatives noted in diagram 3.2. As before, for each pair of situations the alternatives marked indicate how respondents thought the inequality in the first situation (A, B, C, or D) compared with that in the second (S).

All ten respondents thought lowering the worst-off group one level would worsen the inequality. Eight thought lowering the third group one level would worsen the inequality, and six thought this about lowering the second group. More-

	a	b	c	d	e	f	g	h	i	j	k
I (A,S):	8	0	2	0	0	0	0	0	0	0	0
II (B,S):	3	1	3	1	0	0	1	0	1	0	0
III (C,S):	3	0	1	2	0	1	0	0	2	0	1
IV (D,S):	0	0	0	0	0	1	1	0	8	0	0

DIAGRAM 3.10

over, while all ten thought lowering the fourth group would be unequivocally worse, six thought this about lowering the third group, and only four thought this about lowering the second. Similarly, while eight marked that lowering the fourth group would be definitely worse, only four marked this about lowering the third group, and only three marked this about lowering the second group. On the other hand, all ten thought lowering the first group to the level of the second would improve inequality, with nine marking it as an unequivocal improvement, and eight marking it as a definite improvement. There is a distinct pattern to the progression of these responses, apparent even to the eye in viewing diagram 3.10. The pattern is consistent with, and (presumably) expresses, the relative ranking already noted—that is, the egalitarian's first choice would be for an undeserved and nondivisible misfortune to befall the best-off, her second choice would be for the misfortune to befall those next best-off, and so on.

Now consider diagram 3.11. As in diagram 3.8, the question marks in case II reflect the fact that the weighted additive principle gives expression both to certain intuitions underlying the additive principle *and* to certain intuitions underlying the maximin principle. Insofar as it does the former, WAP & AVE and WAP & ATBO will tend to judge S better than B; insofar as it does the latter, they will tend toward the reverse judgment.

Diagram 3.11 suggests a natural and plausible account for the relative ranking noted earlier. If, in fact, the aspects noted in chapter 2 underlie the notion of inequality, there is good reason for the egalitarian to care least about misfortune befalling the best-off and most about misfortune befalling the worst-off. As S's first, second, third, and fourth groups are lowered one level, respectively, the aspects yielding the judgment that the situation has worsened go from zero, to three, to seven (with two question marks), to eleven.[11]

---

11. I am not claiming the sheer number of aspects supporting each judgment always carries the day. Also relevant will be the weight each aspect deserves, as well as the strength of the judgment each aspect yields. However, when these factors are appropriately considered, I think the extent to which the aspects' judgments vary will remain a significant part of the explanation for why we regard situations as we do. Similarly, I am not claiming appeal to the different aspects is the *only* way of accounting for the relative rankings discussed in this section and the last. To the contrary, a few aspects would yield these relative rankings by themselves. However, those aspects cannot, by themselves, account for many of inequality's other features. In other words, while other explanations are available, I believe the best explanation of the rankings in question will run, at least in large part, along the line suggested.

	Case I (A,S)	Case II (B,S)	Case III (C,S)	Case IV (D,S)
MP & AVE :	S	B	C	D
MP & BOP :	S	S	S	D
MP & ATBO :	S	B	C	D
AP & AVE :	S	S	C	D
AP & BOP :	S	S	S	D
AP & ATBO :	S	S	C	D
WAP & AVE :	S	?	C	D
WAP & BOP :	S	S	S	D
WAP & ATBO :	S	?	C	D
Deviation :	S	S	C	D
Gratuitousness :	S	S	C	D

MP = Maximin Principle of Equality

AP = Additive Principle of Equality

WAP = Weighted Additive Principle of Equality

AVE = Relative to the Average View of Complaints

BOP = Relative to the Best-Off Person View of Complaints

ATBO = Relative to the All Those Better Off View of Complaints

DIAGRAM 3.11

In addition to the relative rankings, diagram 3.11 can account for most of the empirical results recorded in diagram 3.10. It can explain the virtual unanimity regarding cases I and IV, and the general, but not complete, agreement regarding case II. However, case III is different. On the basis of what the aspects reveal, we would expect general agreement that C is better than S. After all, eight aspects yield that judgment, only three yield the reverse judgment. However, most thought C was worse than S. What, if anything, does this tell us? Several suggestions are possible.

First, one might claim I am mistaken about the nature of inequality. The extreme version of this claim would reject the very approach taken in this book, and attempt to account for case II, and all the other cases discussed, in an entirely different way. Not surprisingly, I am less that enthusiastic about this claim and feel the many arguments contained in this book militate against it. Alternatively, one might accept my general approach but argue that I've overlooked certain important aspects or that some of my aspects should be rejected or revised. It seems to me likely that this is true and should be pursued regardless of case III. However, I am suspicious whether a more plausible and complete list of aspects will accommodate the empirical responses given in case III. It would, of course, be easy to condense our list of aspects or supplement them to ensure that they fit the responses to case III. The problem is to do this in a plausible way that doesn't ignore other responses to which we may be even more attached.

Second, it might be claimed that the conflict between diagrams 3.11 and 3.10 is more apparent than real. Diagram 3.11 merely reveals the *ordinal* ranking of the different situations. It tells us which situation is better according to each aspect, but nothing about *how much* better it is. It is possible, therefore, that in the respects in which C is better than S it is only *slightly* better, whereas in the respects in which S is better than C it is *much* better. If this were so, diagrams 3.11 and 3.10 would not be incompatible. One could account for why six respondents thought S was better than C, while five felt at least some pull in the other direction.

This line is promising and, as we shall see in chapter 5, the general point is important. However, in the end, it is not plausible regarding case III. When one actually does the relevant calculations for each of the measures, it appears that the extent to which S is better than C on the aspects yielding that ranking is not significantly greater than the extent to which C is better than S on the aspects yielding that ranking.

Third, there is another way diagrams 3.11 and 3.10 might be compatible. In chapter 2, I argued for the plausibility of each aspect presented. I did not argue that each aspect was equally plausible. There may be good reason to attach more weight to some aspects than others.[12] If the aspects involving the relative to the best-off person view of complaints deserved "sufficient" weight relative to the others, this would account for the results in question.

Unfortunately, there are two problems with this position. First, if one grants sufficient weight to those aspects involving BOP to account for the empirical responses in case III, it is not clear one could still plausibly account for the empirical responses in many of the other cases discussed. Second, and more important, it is not clear that the aspects involving BOP *should* be granted more weight than the other aspects, but even if they should, it does not seem that, other things equal, they should be granted *so* much more weight as to enable them to outweigh *all* the other aspects combined.[13]

The problems with the other positions naturally suggest a fourth. Perhaps the conflict between diagrams 3.11 and 3.10 simply illustrates one of those cases in which theoretical considerations condemn, and force us to revise, certain of our pretheoretical judgments.

Considering diagram 3.10 it is easy to be misled. Not only are there strong nonegalitarian reasons for preferring S to C but, regarding inequality, the respects in which C is worse than S are patent, while those in which C is better are more obscure. After all, lowering the second group clearly worsens its position relative to the best-off, without improving the *actual* positions of the third and fourth groups. Hence, it is perhaps not so surprising that people might initially judge S better than C. On reflection, though, once we recognize the different aspects of inequality and

12. See chapter 5.
13. The "other things equal" clause reflects the insight of the second position noted. Clearly a few aspects could be weighted so as to outweigh all others combined in cases where one situation is *much* better (or worse) regarding the few aspects and only *slightly* worse (or better) regarding the others. But, of course, depending on the extent of the differences in question, this might be so even if the few aspects mattered *less* than the others, and were weighted accordingly.

what they imply, we realize that C is better than S, even though in some respects it is worse.

Together, diagrams 3.10 and 3.11 further confirm our view that BOP cannot simply be dismissed. Given the empirical responses to case III, it seems clear that BOP influences people's egalitarian judgments and, in some cases, at least, to a large extent. The question is whether it sometimes influences our judgments more than it should.

I believe the aspects involving BOP are important. We *may* even want to count them more than the other aspects. However, I do not believe they should count *so* much more as to justify the judgment that S's inequality is better than C's. Instead, I would suggest that in case III BOP's aspects are *salient* in the psychologists' sense of the term—that is, for the sort of reasons implied already, they "disproportionally engage [our] attention and accordingly disproportionally affect [our] judgments."[14] Ultimately, then, I believe many will have to revise their pretheoretical judgments about situations like case III. But I suspect the required revision may not be too hard. Even at the purely intuitive level, three of ten respondents felt C was better than S, two others felt pulled in that direction, and one had no feeling about the comparison. In light of the theoretical considerations diagram 3.11 reflects, I suspect most would come to believe that C's inequality is better than S's.

Before leaving this topic, one possible revision of the aspects is worth special mention. Some people distinguish between different methods of altering a situation's distribution. They claim that insofar as a method involves *benefits* to the less fortunate it is morally desirable, but insofar as it involves *losses* to the more fortunate it is *not* desirable (and may be undesirable). This position has great plausibility for our all-things-considered judgments. But some apply it further. They insist there is *no* respect in which *merely* lowering people could (morally) improve a situation. On this view, lowering the better-off to the level of the worse-off might, in some purely descriptive sense, reduce inequality, but in *no way* would it make the situation *better*—that is, not even regarding inequality.

I suspect most who endorse this view are simply nonegalitarians. Some may think of themselves as egalitarians, but in fact be influenced by another position— which I call *extended humanitarianism*—that often overlaps with egalitarianism and may be mistaken for it. As noted earlier, I shall discuss extended humanitarianism and its attractions in chapter 9. My present interest is the view that a significant version of *egalitarianism* could be compatible with the position I have just sketched. On this view concern about inequality is concern not merely that inequality be removed, but that it be removed *in a certain way* so as to *benefit* the worse-off, where this further concern is *not* due to our concern about *other* ideals or values—for example, rights, freedom, utility, or duty—but to our concern for inequality itself. One way of capturing this view—which may be the view of certain

---

14. Shelley E. Taylor, "The Availability Bias in Social Perception and Interaction," (in *Judgment under Uncertainty: Heuristics and Biases*, ed. D. Kahneman, P. Slovic, and A. Tversky (Cambridge University Press, 1982), p. 192. The topic of salience has been much discussed by perceptual and social psychologists. See, for example, works by Fiske, McArthur, Nisbett, L. Ross, S. E. Taylor, and A. Tversky (full citations are given in the Bibliography).

person-affecting or deontological egalitarians—would be to restrict the scope of chapter 2's aspects. For example, they might apply in cases where people are benefited, and in cases where the worse-off suffer, but not in cases where the better-off suffer (without the worse-off benefiting).

As stated, such a position could not account for the diversity of responses in case III, or for the responses in case IV. However, variations of the pure position are possible that compromise between it and the observed responses, including the telling fact that almost all thought that lowering the first group *would* definitely and unequivocally improve the situation's inequality. Such variations might involve restricting the scope of some aspects but not others, or lessening the impact of certain aspects in certain kinds of cases. For example, the aspects involving BOP might be significant in all cases, but the other aspects might lose much of their significance in cases where the better-off suffered without the worse-off benefiting. Such a view could account not only for the empirical responses of case III, but for all the other empirical responses so far noted (including those of diagrams 3.4 and 3.7, as well as those of diagram 3.10).

I have presented the foregoing in some depth, not because it handles case III's responses, but because it exemplifies an extremely important position regarding certain values. On both the pure view, and the compromise view, inequality would be *essentially comparative* not merely in the sense that it would be concerned with how people compare, but in the sense that how good or bad a situation was regarding inequality would depend on the alternatives with which it was compared, and *not* solely on the intrinsic, or internal, features of that situation. So, for example, a situation's inequality might be good if it resulted from benefits to those previously worse off, but bad if it resulted from losses to those previously better off—and this might be so *completely independently* of the many other respects in which such changes would be good or bad. Unfortunately, as interesting and important as this position is for moral philosophy, its details and implications are enormously complex, and it would take at least another book to address them adequately. I have begun the task elsewhere but cannot pursue it here.[15] In the end, I think this is not the most plausible way of responding to case III.

---

15. A major problem with essentially comparative views is that they threaten the transitivity of our all-things-considered judgments. Suppose, for example, that inequality's scope is restricted, so that it is relevant for comparing some outcomes but not others. (This would be like the claim that Rawls's maximin principle is not suited for comparing certain kinds of cases where different numbers of people are involved, or the claim that Parfit's principle of beneficence, Q, is plausible for comparing cases where the same people or number of people are involved, but not for comparing cases where different numbers are involved. See sections 144 and 125 of Derek Parfit's *Reasons and Persons* [Oxford University Press, 1984].) Then A, B, and C might be three alternatives such that given its restrictive scope inequality is only relevant in comparing A and C. It could then be the cases that, all things considered, A is better than B, and B better than C, yet C better than A. This is because even if C is worse than A in terms of the relevant factors for comparing A with B, and B with C, the extent to which this is so might be outweighed by the extent to which C might be better than A regarding inequality. Similarly, if how good a situation is regarding inequality depends on the alternative with which it is compared, then in essence the factors that are relevant and significant for comparing A with B may be different that those that are relevant and significant for comparing B with C, or A with C, and if this is so there is no reason to suppose inequality rankings will be transitive. Specifically, it might be the case

Some of the aspects that seem least plausible when considering the Sequence may seem more plausible when considering other situations. For many, I suspect this is the case for the aspects involving BOP. By the same token, some of the aspects which seem most plausible when considering the Sequence may seem less plausible in other situations. Let me end this section by briefly supporting this claim. Similar points might have been raised in section 3.2, and will be argued for in more detail in the following section.

In presenting the Sequence, one of the most popular aspects is the one that measures deviation from a state of absolute equality. Indeed, many considering the Sequence have suggested we could dispense with the other aspects and make do with that one. However, it is easy to see that Deviation alone cannot capture the relative rankings discussed in either this section or the previous one. According to Deviation, lowering the fourth group in S would *not* be worse than lowering the third, as each would equally affect the total deviation from a state of absolute equality. Similarly, lowering the first group would not be better than lowering the second. Now I take it to be a *firm* feature of the egalitarian's thinking that it would be best if an undeserved (and unavoidable) misfortune befell the best-off, second best if it befell those next best-off, and so on. This tells us something important. It tells us that Deviation captures only one part of the egalitarian's concern.

A similar point could be made regarding AP & AVE, AP & BOP, and Gratuitousness. For all their plausibility in other cases, each of these aspects is indifferent between lowering the fourth group and lowering the third. Does this mean each of these aspects should be rejected? No. Inequality is a complex notion. In different cases different aspects will seem more or less plausible.

3.4 How Direct Transfers Affect Inequality: The Pigou-Dalton Condition

Let us next consider how transfers *between* groups affect inequality. Suppose, contrary to fact, that welfare—like money—was directly transferable.[16] How would the egalitarian view transfers from one group to another?

In discussing economic inequality many economists endorse the Pigou-Dalton condition, *PD*, which holds roughly that, other things equal, transfers from

---

that in terms of the factors that are relevant and significant for making each pairwise comparison, A's inequality is good if its alternative is B, yet poor if its alternative is C, while C's inequality is good if its alternative is A, yet poor if its alternative is B. In such a case, A would be better than B, and B better than C, yet C would be better than A, regarding inequality. But then if A, B, and C are equivalent or nearly equivalent in other respects, it is plausible to think inequality's intransitivity will carry over into our all-things-considered judgments. That is, in terms of each of the factors that are relevant and significant for making each comparison, it may be that A is better than B, and B better than C, yet C better than A. For further explication and defense of these claims and a deeper examination of the complex issues they raise see my "Intransitivity and the Mere Addition Paradox," *Philosophy and Public Affairs* 16 (1987): 138–87.

16. This assumption is useful for our present purposes, but of course only certain *sources* of welfare—not welfare itself—are transferable. In the next section we consider how transfers affect inequality when this assumption is removed or altered.

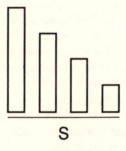

S

DIAGRAM 3.12

rich to poor decrease inequality, whereas transfers from poor to rich increase inequality.[17] PD has great plausibility and can be extended beyond discussions of economic inequality. For example, it seems clear that if one assumes one-for-one transfers of welfare—so the transferee gains one unit for each unit lost by the transferer—then transfers from the better- to the worse-off improve inequality, whereas transfers from the worse- to the better-off worsen it. (In section 3.5, we shall consider what happens if we drop the assumption that transfers are one-for-one.) Analogously, the spirit of PD would apply to primary goods, opportunity, need satisfaction, or whatever.

Consider again the Standard situation, S (diagram 3.12). Suppose n units were to be transferred from one group in S to another. Surely an egalitarian's first choice would be for the transfer to go from the first group to the fourth. Her last choice would be for the transfer to go from the fourth group to the first. These judgments are uncontroversial. Other judgments are less obvious but, in general, it seems intuitively clear that the egalitarian will want transfers to go from the "highest" possible group to the "lowest" possible group.

This intuitive claim can be derived from (a corollary of) the Pigou-Dalton condition. Suppose we could transfer n units of welfare from the first group to either the third or fourth. According to PD, transferring n units from the first group to the third would improve inequality, so too would transferring n units from the third group to the fourth. It follows that the inequality would be better if the n units were first transferred to the third group and then transferred to the fourth, than if it were simply transferred to the third. But the distribution resulting from the two transfers is exactly the distribution resulting from the direct transfer of n units from the first group to the fourth. Hence, PD implies that it would be better to transfer the welfare to the fourth group rather than the third. Similar reasoning could be adduced to show that according to PD an egalitarian's preference ranking about transfers in S should be for welfare to be transferred *from* the first, second, third, and fourth groups, respectively, and *to* the fourth, third, second, and first groups, respectively.

The foregoing conclusion should sound familiar. It parallels precisely some of our earlier results. In sections 3.2 and 3.3, we saw that the worse off a group was

17. This condition was first advocated by A. C. Pigou, *Wealth and Welfare* (Macmillan, 1912), p. 24, and Hugh Dalton, in "The Measurement of Inequality of Incomes," *Economic Journal* 30 (1920): 351.

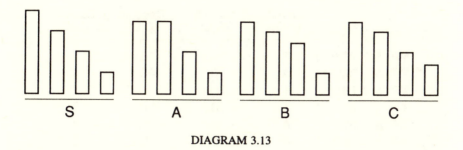

DIAGRAM 3.13

the more an egalitarian would object to group losses and the more she would approve group gains. Combined, these results yield the same relative ranking of transfers as the Pigou-Dalton condition. Thus, since together chapter 2's aspects can account for the relative rankings of sections 3.2 and 3.3, they can also account for PD's relative rankings. Given PD's plausibility, this adds further support to the judgments yielded by chapter 2's aspects.

Let us consider a few specific cases, depicted in diagram 3.13. A involves a transfer from the first group in S to the second, removing the gap between them. B and C involve the same size transfer from the first group to the third and fourth groups, respectively. Diagram 3.14 illustrates what chapter 2's aspects imply about such transfers.

In case I, six aspects rank A better than S, while five rank them equivalent. In case II, ten aspects rank B better than S, although two do this only in virtue of maximin's tie-breaking clause. One aspect ranks S better. In case III, all eleven aspects rank C better than S. In case IV, eight aspects rank C better than B, three rank them equivalent.

Though poll respondents were not asked to assess these cases, I believe the foregoing results correspond with how many would react to such situations. Regarding case I, I think many would feel a certain indifference about one-for-one transfers between the best-off and others who are *already* better off than most, but that on reflection most would agree with the Pigou-Dalton condition that such a transfer would improve inequality, even if not a lot. Similarly, though in case II there might be a slight temptation to regard B as worse than S, as the lot of the worst-off could seemingly be improved at relatively little cost to the better-off, most would agree that one-for-one transfers between the best-off and others who are worse off than most would definitely improve inequality. Finally, regarding cases III and IV, surely almost all would agree that one-for-one transfers from the first group to the fourth would unequivocally improve inequality and would be even better than similar transfers from the first group to the third.

Cases like I and IV help buttress the point made at the end of the last section. As noted, in considering the Sequence some are tempted to claim that inequality can be captured by Deviation alone. But Deviation is indifferent between S and A, and also between B and C. Given the overall implausibility of these judgments, Deviation is best regarded as only one aspect of inequality, albeit an important one. By

	Case I (A,S)	Case II (B,S)	Case III (C,S)	Case IV (B,C)
MP & AVE :	T	B(t)	C	C
MP & BOP :	A	B	C	C
MP & ATBO :	T	B(t)	C	C
AP & AVE :	T	B	C	T
AP & BOP :	A	B	C	T
AP & ATBO :	A	B	C	C
WAP & AVE :	A	B	C	C
WAP & BOP :	A	B	C	C
WAP & ATBO :	A	B	C	C
Deviation :	T	B	C	T
Gratuitousness :	T	S	C	C

MP = Maximin Principle of Equality
AP = Additive Principle of Equality
WAP = Weighted Additive Principle of Equality
AVE = Relative to the Average View of Complaints
BOP = Relative to the Best-Off Person View of Complaints
ATBO = Relative to the All Those Better Off View of Complaints
T = Tie
B(t) = B is judged better than S, but only in virtue of
Maximin's tie-breaking clause

DIAGRAM 3.14

the same token, AP & AVE and AP & BOP yield the same judgment as Deviation
about B and C. So neither they alone, nor some combination of them and Deviation,
fully captures the notion of inequality. Similarly, for MP & AVE, MP & ATBO, AP
& AVE, and Gratuitousness, each of which yields the same judgment as Deviation
about S and A.

Next consider diagram 3.15. As in diagram 3.13, A involves a transfer from the
first group in S to the second, removing the gap between them. B and C involve
similar transfers from the second and third to the third and fourth groups, respectively.

How do A, B, and C compare regarding inequality? It is not immediately clear.
In some respects A seems best, in others B, in still others C. This is not surprising
given our earlier results. Focusing on the groups welfare has been transferred *from*,
A would clearly be the best and C the worst. But focusing on the groups welfare has
been transferred *to*, C would be the best and A the worst.[18] Moreover, each of the

18. See sections 3.2 and 3.3 for a defense of these claims.

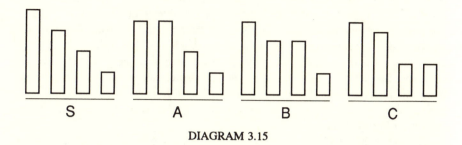

DIAGRAM 3.15

competing judgments is supported by different aspects—the first by MP & BOP, AP & BOP, and WAP & BOP; the second by AP & AVE, and Deviation; and the third by MP & AVE, MP & ATBO, WAP & ATBO, and Gratuitousness. (WAP & AVE would support B or C depending on the system of weighting employed.)

Considering diagram 3.15, some may be indifferent between A, B, and C. Correspondingly, some may be most drawn to AP & ATBO's judgment that A, B, and C are equivalent regarding inequality. However, even if one finds AP & ATBO's judgment more plausible than that of the other aspects, one must be careful to be clear why this is so.

One reason one might be indifferent between A, B, and C is one *might* believe that AP & ATBO is the *only* plausible aspect of inequality,[19] and hence believe that A, B, and C are exactly as good as each other in terms of inequality. On this view, one should feel no pull toward the claim that B is better than A in virtue of the fact that B's total deviation from a state of absolute equality is smaller than A's. Nor should one be swayed to the opposite view by the fact that the gaps between the worse-off and the best-off are as large or larger in B than in A and there are *more* people who are worse off than the best-off. Nor, for that matter, should it make any difference that relative to both the average and the best-off, the worst-off fare better in C than in B. Suffice it to say, I find such a view implausible. It will not do justice to this book's earlier results, or people's actual reactions to A, B, and C.

There is another reason one might be indifferent between A, B, and C. One might feel the force of other aspects besides AP & ATBO, but believe they *exactly* balance off against each other. On this view, though A, B, and C differ in certain respects, all things considered they are equivalent (regarding inequality). This view is also implausible. Among other things, it suggests a degree of precision in these matters highly unlikely to be warranted.[20]

Alternatively, one may feel indifferent between A, B, and C not because one regards them as equivalent, but because the countervailing influences of the different aspects leave one unable to choose between them. Such indifference may or

19. Some philosophers have been drawn to such a view when considering the Sequence.

20. Recall Aristotle's sage warning, "that in every subject . . . [one must look] for only so much precision as its subject matter permits" (*Nicomachean Ethics*, book 1, chapter 3). The importance of this for the notion of inequality will become clearer, especially in chapter 5.

may not be due to lack of knowledge or indecision. Thus, further consideration of the relative importance of inequality's aspects may reveal a ranking of A, B, and C one is currently unable to make. On the other hand the notion of inequality may be incomplete, so there may not be a complete ranking of alternatives. In that case indifference between A, B, and C might fully and accurately reflect how they compare. Specifically, they might be neither better nor worse than each other, without their being *exactly equally as good*. The difference between complete and incomplete concepts, and the likelihood that inequality is incomplete, will be discussed further in chapter 5.

Diagram's like 3.15 can be revealing. It is hard to believe one should be *completely* neutral between transfers in S from the first group to the second, the second to the third, or the third to the fourth, in the sense that one should regard such transfers as *exactly equally as good*. Yet one may feel unable to choose between A, B, and C regarding inequality. If this is so, this may tell us something important about the notion of inequality; namely that it is incomplete—one that permits some rankings, but not others. On the other hand, one may believe A, B, and C can be ranked. If so, this may reveal important insights about how much one cares about the different aspects in relation to each other. For example, someone who ranks B best probably weighs AP & AVE or Deviation more than the other aspects, while someone who ranks A best probably most weighs the aspects involving BOP.[21]

My own view is that C is probably best. Perhaps this is simply because *more* aspects support that judgment than any other, but perhaps not. One way of thinking about such alternatives is to consider what would be involved in transforming A, B, and C into S. Each move would involve transferring n units from some members of a group to other members of that group, but the groups in question would be the best-off, average, and worst-off groups, respectively. Of these, I think the third move would be most offensive. Although it would benefit some who (initially) fare as poorly as anyone else, I find it especially galling that it would do so only by making even worse off others who were *already* as poorly off or worse off than *every other* person.[22] This reaction suggests that I may be particularly influenced by a principle like MP. Similarly, though I am largely indifferent between the first move and the second, I think the former would be slightly worse than the latter because it would improve the lot of some who were *already* as well or better off than *every other* person. This suggests that the aspects involving BOP may influence me more than AP & AVE and Deviation.

It is, of course, not important what I think about A, B, and C. The important point is that, in addition to providing further evidence for the complexity of inequality, our reactions to diagrams like 3.15 can reveal further insights into the notion of inequality.[23]

21. However, one might believe AP & ATBO is the most important aspect, but that B (or A) is best because AP & AVE or Deviation (or those aspects involving BOP) are more important than any of inequality's *other* aspects.

22. Of course, it would be even *more* galling if some of the worst-off were lowered to benefit the best-off!

23. But note, while diagrams like 3.15 may help us see which of inequality's aspects matter most to us, as should be clear by now one must be careful not to draw general conclusions too quickly from a

3.5 How Indirect Transfers Affect Inequality

In section 3.4, we discussed how transfers would affect inequality on the simplifying assumption that welfare could be transferred directly. But, of course, welfare itself cannot be transferred, only some of its means or sources. Therefore, let us next consider what happens if we remove or alter our simplifying assumption.

It is wellknown that for many reasons—including physical, psychological, social, and economic factors—transfers of the sources of welfare will be correlated to varying degrees with changes in welfare. For example, transfers of income from rich to poor may increase the latter's welfare by more than it decreases the former's, whereas transfers from the healthy to the severely handicapped may decrease the former's welfare by more than it increases the latter's. Now for our purposes it remains convenient to speak of "transfers of welfare," rather than the more cumbersome "transfers of some of the sources of welfare." However, in doing this it is useful to distinguish between three different kinds of transfers. Specifically, let us say a transfer of welfare is:

1. *Efficient* if the underlying transfer of sources of welfare increases the welfare of those benefited by the transfer by more than it decreases the welfare of those worsened by the transfer.
2. *Even* if the underlying transfer of sources of welfare increases the welfare of those benefited by the same amount as it decreases the welfare of those worsened.
3. *Inefficient* if the underlying transfer of sources of welfare increases the welfare of those benefited by less than it decreases the welfare of those worsened.

Applying these criteria to the previous examples, the transfers from rich to poor and from the healthy to the handicapped would involve efficient and inefficient transfers of welfare, respectively. Likewise, on these criteria our earlier examples—which assumed direct one-for-one transfers of welfare—involved even transfers.[24]

Let us now consider how, if at all, egalitarian judgments about transfers would depend on the kind of transfer in question. Consider diagram 3.16. S is the familiar Standard situation. A, B, and C represent the result of efficient transfers from S's best-off group, to the second, third, and fourth groups, respectively. As drawn, each transfer involves the best-off losing n units, and the beneficiaries gaining 2n units, where 4n is the size of the gaps between adjacent groups. So, for example, the move from S to A lowers the best-off group n units, raises the second group 2n units, and reduces the gap between them from 4n units to n units. Correspondingly, the gaps

---

few examples. As note 21 recognizes, the aspects one most cares about may not be reflected in some comparisons if the relevant alternatives do not significantly differ regarding those aspects. Moreover, different aspects may merit different weight in different circumstances. Hence, one must be sure to vary one's examples so as to provide a true test of the way the different aspects matter in relation to each other. I return to these issues in chapter 5.

24. Strictly speaking, this claim involves regarding welfare itself as a special instance of the "sources of welfare." This would not be inappropriate on the assumption in question.

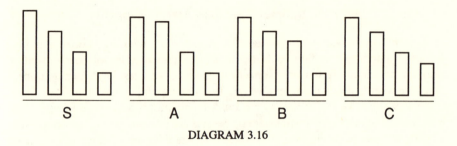

DIAGRAM 3.16

between the best-off group and the other groups are decreased by n units, while those between the second group and the other groups are increased by 2n units.

How do A and B compare regarding inequality? A and B are basically equivalent according to five of chapter 2's aspects: specifically, MP & AVE, MP & BOP, MP & ATBO, AP & BOP, and WAP & BOP.[25] On the other hand, B is better than A according to chapter 2's other aspects: AP & AVE, AP & ATBO, WAP & AVE, WAP & ATBO, Deviation, and Gratuitousness. This suggests that while in some respects the egalitarian may feel indifferent between an efficient transfer from S's best-off group to the second group, and a similar transfer to the third group, in other respects the latter will be preferable to the former. The net effect should be an egalitarian preference for the efficient transfer to the third group rather than the second.

Next compare B with C. B and C are equivalent according to AP & AVE, AP & BOP, Deviation, and Gratuitousness. On the other hand, B is worse than C according to chapter 2's other aspects: MP & AVE, MP & BOP, MP & ATBO, AP & ATBO, WAP & AVE, WAP & BOP, and WAP & ATBO. This suggests that although in some respects the egalitarian may be indifferent between an efficient transfer from the best-off group to the third group, and a similar transfer to the worst-off group, taking all the relevant aspects into consideration the latter is preferable.

Next consider A and C. A and C are equivalent according to AP & BOP. So, insofar as one compares each person with the best-off person, there may seem nothing to choose between an efficient transfer from the best-off group to the second group, and a similar transfer to the worst-off group. However, A is worse than C according to each of chapter 2's other aspects. This suggests that of the two transfers, the egalitarian would prefer the one to the worst-off group.

I believe the foregoing corresponds with, and explains, how most egalitarians would respond to the alternatives discussed. In certain respects one may feel indifferent between A and B, B and C, and (even, in one respect) A and C. But ultimately, most egalitarians would agree not only that C is better than A—which seems patently clear even to the eye—but that C is better than B, which in turn is

25. I say "basically equivalent," because in fact B will be slightly better than A according to the principles involving MP, but only in virtue of maximin's tie-breaking clause. Similarly, B will be slightly better than A according to WAP & BOP, but not significantly so.

better than A. That is, whatever the merits of an efficient transfer from the best-off group to the second group, a similar transfer to the third group would be even better, and to the fourth group better still.

These results should not be surprising. In section 3.4 we noted that most egalitarians accept the Pigou-Dalton condition (PD), according to which one-for-one transfers from the better- to the worse-off improve inequality. We also noted how chapter 2's results can account for PD's plausibility. But notice, according to PD, B is better than A, C better than B, and C better than A, since B, C, and C would result from A, B, and A, respectively, via the direct one-for-one transfer (of 2n units) from a better-off group to a worse-off group (specifically, from the second, third, and second groups, to the third, fourth, and fourth groups, respectively.)

In section 3.4 I claimed, while discussing even transfers, that in general the egalitarian will want transfers to go from the "highest" possible group to the "lowest" possible group. Reflection on cases like the preceding one reveals that the claim also holds for efficient and inefficient transfers. This is exactly what we should have expected given sections 3.2 and 3.3, where we saw that for any situation involving better- and worse-off groups, the worse off a group is the more an egalitarian would object to group losses and the more she would approve of group gains.[26] Of course, this does not mean that any transfer between "further apart" groups will be preferable to any transfer between "closer" groups. For example, a small transfer between the top and bottom groups may not be preferable to a significant transfer between two middle groups. But for any transfer involving the loss of n units for some, and the gain of p units for others, the egalitarian will want the "highest" possible group to suffer the loss, and the "lowest" possible group to receive the gain, and this will be so whatever the sizes of n and p and, hence, whatever kind of transfer is involved.[27]

This result is general and important, but relative in nature. It tells us nothing about when a given transfer improves inequality. For example, knowing it would be better for an efficient transfer to go from the first group to the fourth, rather than to the second, we know C is better than A in diagram 3.16. But this does not yet tell us whether either transfer would be an improvement regarding inequality, that is, whether C or A is better than S.

Consider again diagram 3.16. Comparing C with S, it is evident C is better regarding inequality. The efficient transfer from the best-off to the worst-off leaves the gap between the second and third groups unchanged, while reducing the gaps between each of the other groups. This would appear to be a clear and unequivocal improvement regarding inequality and, in fact, it would be endorsed by *all* of chapter 2's aspects.

Comparing A with S the situation is rather different. A seems better in some respects, worse in others. For example, while the efficient transfer from the best-off

---

26. Note, for our purposes "better- and worse-off" are relative, not absolute, notions. So, an egalitarian may object more to lowering the worse-off in one possible situation than the better-off in another possible situation, even though in absolute terms those "better-off" might be worse off than those "worse-off."

27. The transfer will be efficient if n < p, even if n = p, and inefficient if n > p.

group to the second group reduces the gaps between the best-off group and all the others, it increases the gaps between the second group and the third and fourth groups.[28] Moreover, as drawn, the decreases between the first group and the third and fourth groups are only half the size of the increases between the second group and those groups (n units to 2n units). In terms of chapter 2's aspects, A is better than S according to MP & BOP, AP & BOP, WAP & BOP, and AP & ATBO. In addition, A *may* be better on WAP & ATBO (depending on the precise system of weighting employed by WAP). On the other hand, S may be better than A according to WAP & ATBO, and will be better according to each of the other aspects, specifically, MP & AVE, MP & ATBO, AP & AVE, WAP & AVE, Deviation, and Gratuitousness. Thus, it is by no means clear that, all things considered, A is better than S regarding inequality. To the contrary, it is likely S is better (though, of course, whether this is so will ultimately depend on how much the different aspects matter, and the strength of the judgments yielded by those aspects).

The foregoing suggests that whether a given transfer would improve inequality does not depend solely on whether those "gaining" are less well off than those "losing." Nor does it depend solely on the *kind* of transfer involved. In some cases, at least, one must take account of both the relative levels of the groups involved *and* the kind of transfer in question. Indeed, reflection reveals that even that is not enough, as ultimately the egalitarian's judgment must often turn on the *extent* to which a transfer is efficient or inefficient.

Let us expand on these remarks. In section 3.3, we saw that lowering S's first group to the level of the second would improve inequality according to each of chapter 2's aspects.[29] In section 3.2, we saw that, all things considered, raising the second group to the level of the first would worsen inequality (although three aspects would approve such a move, these would almost certainly be outweighed by the eight aspects opposing it). This suggests that insofar as a transfer lowers the first group toward the initial level of the second it will improve S's inequality, whereas insofar as it raises the second group toward the initial level of the first it will worsen S's inequality.

But notice, raising the second group to the level of the first can be seen as a limiting case of an efficient transfer: although strictly speaking there has been no *transfer*, we might say such a case is a "perfectly efficient transfer," since the second group not only gains more than the first group loses, it gains some without the first group losing anything! Similarly, lowering the first group to the level of the second can be seen as a limiting case of an inefficient transfer. This suggests that transfers between the first two groups will improve inequality if they are "sufficiently" inefficient, but worsen inequality if they are "sufficiently" efficient. Can we

---

28. The gap between the third and fourth groups will remain unchanged, and hence will presumably not affect our judgment about the relative merits of A and S.

29. That is, according to every aspect relevant to judging such a situation. The aspect reflecting our concern for social justice will be silent about this, and each of this section's other cases, in the absence of knowledge about the principles and institutions that might be responsible for the kind of inequality obtaining. Henceforth I omit this qualifying remark, but it applies to all my claims about what "each" of chapter 2's aspects imply.

say more? We can. But we must resist the natural temptation to simply remove the qualifier "sufficiently."

In section 3.4, we saw that an even transfer removing the gap between the first two groups in S would improve inequality. More particularly, we noted that none of chapter 2's aspects would condemn such a transfer while five would approve it.[30] This indicates that the extent to which raising the second group toward the initial level of the first tends to worsen S's inequality is not as significant, proportionally, as the extent to which lowering the first group toward the initial level of the second tends to improve S's inequality. Thus, there is good reason for the egalitarian to approve *any* inefficient transfer reducing or removing the gap between the first two groups.[31] On the other hand, there is also good reason to suppose *not all* efficient transfers will worsen inequality. After all, if the even transfer of 100 units from the first group to the second improved inequality by reducing the gap between them, it is highly unlikely that a *slightly* efficient transfer whereby the first group lost 99 units and the second group gained 101 would suddenly worsen it. But, of course, as our earlier observations suggest, it is very likely S's inequality would be worsened by an *extremely* efficient transfer whereby the first group lost 1 unit and the second group gained 199 units. It appears, then, that the egalitarian's judgments about efficient transfers between the first two groups will shift depending on just how efficient those transfers are. Naturally, the general range during which the shift occurs (there is unlikely to be a precise point) will be a function both of how the judgments yielded by the different aspects vary in such cases, and how much the different aspects matter.

Similar considerations could be presented to assess how different kinds of transfers between different groups would affect inequality. I shall not pursue the many possibilities here. However, let me observe that the case of transfers between S's third and fourth groups interestingly, but not surprisingly, mirrors the one just presented. As before, even transfers will be approved insofar as they reduce the gap between the third and fourth groups, but all efficient transfers will be approved, instead of inefficient ones. Similarly, whether an inefficient transfer is condemned or not will depend on how inefficient it is. Very inefficient transfers will be condemned, slightly inefficient transfers will be approved, and somewhere between the two extremes the judgments will shift. Underlying these judgments is the fact that insofar as a transfer lowers the third group toward the initial level of the fourth it will worsen S's inequality, but the extent to which it does this is not as significant, proportionally, as the extent to which the fourth group's being raised toward the initial level of the third improves it.

Let us sum up our discussion. We have seen that for any particular kind of transfer of any particular size the egalitarian will prefer the transfer to go from the "highest"

30. As the reader can infer, or may recollect, six aspects would be indifferent about such a move.

31. One can view the inefficient transfer as a two-step process. First, for every unit gained by the second group a unit is lost by the first group. This constitutes an even exchange, which, as we have seen, would be approved by some of inequality's aspects and condemned by none. Second, as the transfer is inefficient, there would be an additional lowering of the first group toward the second. This, as we have seen, would be approved by each of chapter 2's aspects. Thus, the net effect would be for each aspect to approve such a transfer.

possible group to the "lowest" possible group. We have also seen that not all transfers from the better- to the worse-off improve inequality. Whether a particular transfer improves inequality can depend on the relative levels of those between whom the transfer occurs, on the kind of transfer involved and, in some cases, on the extent to which a transfer is efficient or inefficient. So, for example, in a situation like S, the egalitarian will approve any even transfer between a better- and worse-off group that reduces or removes the gap between them. Similarly, the egalitarian will approve any inefficient transfer from the first group to the second, and any efficient transfer from the third group to the fourth. On the other hand, although the egalitarian will approve some efficient transfers between the first and second groups, and some inefficient transfers between the third and fourth groups, this will only be so if the transfers are "sufficiently moderate." So, whereas a particularly efficient transfer might be approved if it occurred between the third group and the fourth—and even more so if it occurred between the first or second group and the fourth—it might be condemned if it occurred between the first group and the second.

3.6 Revisiting the Pigou-Dalton Condition

In this section I want to comment on several implications of the foregoing, especially in connection with the Pigou-Dalton condition. But first, let me note one way the Pigou-Dalton condition will need to be revised independently of the foregoing.

As noted in section 3.4, many economists have felt that any plausible measure of inequality should meet the Pigou-Dalton condition, according to which any transfer from the worse- to the better-off would, ceteris paribus, worsen inequality. Most seem to have implicitly assumed this equivalent to the view that any transfer from the better- to the worse-off would, ceteris paribus, improve inequality.[32] But it is easy to see that, strictly speaking, the latter position is implausible and not equivalent to the former one.

Consider a simple two-person case of economic inequality, where A has $100,000 and B $50,000. A transfer of $50,000 from B to A would, as PD implies, worsen the economic inequality. However, a transfer of $50,000 from A to B would not improve the inequality. The inequality would be just as bad after such a transfer as before it, only now B would have the $100,000 and A the $50,000. Similarly, a transfer of $100,000 from A to B would worsen the economic inequality, not improve it, as the gap between the better- and worse-off would go from $50,000 to $150,000. Of course, as a result of the transfer the better- and worse-off would shift from A and B, respectively, to B and A, respectively, but this would not, by itself, make the inequality better.[33]

32. For example, in *On Economic Inequality* (Clarendon Press, 1973) A. K. Sen introduces the Pigou-Dalton condition in terms of transfers from the worse- to better-off, but he thereafter discusses it in terms of transfers from the better- to worse-off. Thus, to cite one case, he writes "as far as the Pigou-Dalton condition is concerned, both the coefficient of variation and the Gini coefficient, pass the test, i.e., a transfer from a richer person to a poorer person always reduces the value of both" (p. 31). (See p. 27, where PD is introduced, and pp. 31–32 and 35 where it is subsequently referred to.)

33. I take it my point here is fairly obvious and needs no elaboration. However, let me acknowledge

The preceding illustrates that, contrary to what many have assumed, one cannot simply move from the claim that transfers from the worse- to the better-off worsen inequality to the claim that transfers from the better- to the worse-off improve inequality. Some qualification of the latter is necessary. This is why, in discussing transfers from the better- to the worse-off, I (often) inserted the qualification that the transfers "reduce or remove the gap between them." PD would approve transfers from the better- to worse-off up to the point where the gap between them has been removed. Beyond that point such transfers involve the (further) lowering of some to benefit others who are (now) better off than they, and that is to be condemned according to PD.

In fairness to the economists who did not explicitly acknowledge this qualification, let us observe that most were implicitly assuming conditions under which such a qualification would be otiose. Most were discussing income inequality, and income, unlike welfare, is naturally thought of as directly and incrementally transferrable—that is, dollar for dollar, or perhaps penny for penny. Consequently, insofar as economists implicitly assumed transfers from rich to poor were to be incremental—one dollar or penny at a time, as it were—there would have been no need for this qualification. The spirit of PD would approve such transfers exactly up to the point where the gap between the better- and worse-off was removed, after which any further transfers would be from a poorer person to a richer one, in violation of PD. Still, money can be transferred in lump sums, and not all goods are incremental. Thus, to generalize the Pigou-Dalton condition to cover transfers from the better- to worse-off, one must restrict one's claims to transfers that reduce or remove the gaps between them.

Though technically necessary, the above restriction will not, I think, substantially affect people's views about PD's scope. However, our earlier discussion suggests that PD's scope must also be restricted in more significant and far-reaching ways. Not all transfers from the better- to the worse-off will improve inequality, even if they reduce or remove the gaps between them. As we have seen, a highly efficient transfer between two well-off groups may worsen inequality, even if the "gainers" are worse off than the "losers." Similarly, not all transfers from the worse- to the better-off will worsen inequality. Highly efficient transfers between two poorly off groups may improve inequality, even if the "gainers" are better off than the "losers."[34]

Unfortunately, there is no simple way of qualifying PD so it accurately indicates all and only those transfers that improve (or worsen) inequality. However, on reflection it seems not only that PD needs serious modification, but that such modification lies within the spirit of PD itself. In essence, the spirit of PD seems to be that, other things equal, increasing the gap between two groups worsens inequality, whereas decreasing the gap improves it. But then, if the consequence of altering the

---

that the qualification "by itself" is important, as among other things it enables me to ignore how we should regard inequality between people over time. This interesting, and surprisingly difficult, question is addressed in chapter 8.

34. This is a corollary of the observed fact that highly inefficient transfers between two poorly off groups may worsen inequality, even if the "gainers" are worse off than the "losers."

gap between A and B is that the gaps between A and B and *other* groups are also altered, it seems that in accordance with PD's spirit the net effect of such a transfer would depend, at least in part, on both the size and number of *all* the different increases and decreases. In any event, as we saw, there are reasons the egalitarian should accept such a view. Hence, PD should be revised accordingly.

Most economists seem to have been unaware of PD's serious limitations. Let me briefly note several factors that may help explain this. First, as observed previously, most economists considered models of economic inequality where transfers were even, that is, one-for-one. And, as we saw in section 3.4, together inequality's aspects support PD for even transfers. Second, when discussing inequality people often focus on comparing two particular groups, ignoring how those groups compare with others. And it is true that if A and B were the only groups in a world and A were better off than B, then any transfer from B to A would worsen inequality and any transfer from A to B would improve it, as long as the transfer merely reduced or removed the gaps between them. So, for the kinds of cases often considered PD *is* plausible and does not need revision. Moreover, even in complex situations involving uneven transfers, PD as it is normally presented often holds. Thus, it is perhaps not surprising that PD's limitations have not generally been recognized. Still, on reflection, they are both apparent and significant.

The foregoing has practical, as well as theoretical, implications. Consider, the following example. Mr. and Mrs. Gelt have amassed a sizable fortune, enabling them to amply provide for their children and grandchildren. As a result, though their descendants are not as well off as the Gelts, they are much better off than most— both in terms of wealth and the quality of their lives. To maximize what their heirs receive the Gelts decide, correctly, to begin disbursing their estate slowly but steadily over a period of years. Given the U.S. Tax Code,[35] this significantly affects how much of the estate actually ends up in their heirs' hands, rather than the government's.[36] If we set aside how the government or heirs would use the money, how, if at all, will the Gelt's decision affect inequality?

Assume the disbursement of the Gelts' estate involves a long sequence of even

35. Internal Revenue Code of 1986, as Amended.

36. For the sake of this example, assume the following. The Gelts have an $8,000,000 estate whose value is increasing at the rate of 7.5 percent per year, after taxes. Their personal expenditures total $150,000 a year, and they want their estate to eventually be divided equally between four children and twelve grandchildren. If, after twenty years, the Gelts pass away without having disbursed any of their estate their estate's value will be $27,000,000, half of which will go to the government for inheritance taxes. The remainder, divided equally between their 16 heirs, will be approximately $844,000 each. However, the Tax Code permits the Gelts to each give $10,000 a year in assets to each heir, tax free. If they do this, and their heirs let the assets continue to grow at 7.5 percent per year, the net value of the combined assets will still be $27,000,000 after twenty years. But now if the Gelts pass away over half their assets will have been disbursed tax free, with only $12,000,000 remaining subject to the inheritance tax. As a result, while each heir will "only" receive approximately $380,000 in strict inheritance, the value of their individual nest eggs will have grown to $930,000. Hence, each heir ends up with over $1,300,000 if the Gelts take advantage of what the Tax Code permits. In sum, on the assumptions of this example, the Gelts' sixteen heirs *each* gain over $450,000 if the estate is disbursed over twenty years. This is certainly a significant figure at the levels in question. (Perhaps if someone had $100,000,000 another half million would make little difference to the quality of their life.)

transfers of wealth. Since, by hypothesis, each of these transfers goes from a richer to a poorer person, the egalitarian should approve these transfers *if* she is concerned about equality of *wealth*. However, suppose she is concerned about equality of *welfare*. In accordance with the diminishing marginal utility of wealth there is good reason to believe the transfers of welfare will be efficient rather than even. Indeed, the loss in quality of life for the Gelts may be insignificant, or even nonexistent, while their heirs may significantly benefit from the transfers of wealth.[37] Thus, the Gelts' heirs, who are already much better off than most and who, by assumption, have already been handed so much "on a silver platter," stand to gain even more by the Gelts' actions, and they stand to gain much more than the Gelts themselves lose. This may be good in many respects, but it would not, I think, be good regarding equality of welfare.

Though oversimplified, this example illustrates both the plausibility and a practical implication of our earlier results. The U.S. Tax Code provides strong incentive for the wealthy to disburse their estates over many years rather than all at once, at death. In the past, advocates of the relevant provisions of the code might have argued for them partly on egalitarian grounds. Because the transfers encouraged by the code would often go from the richer, better-off, to the poorer, less well-off, it might have been urged, in accordance with PD, that this would clearly and unequivocally improve the situation's inequality. But I think many would be suspicious of the claim that, as Rockefeller began disbursing his millions to his children, this improved inequality. A common intuitive reaction would be that Rockefeller's disbursement worsened inequality, as it merely resulted in several people being much better off than most, rather than just one. Our arguments can support this intuitive reaction because they show that while even transfers of wealth may improve inequality of *wealth*, they may worsen inequality of *welfare*.[38] Thus, certain transfers

---

37. Since the bulk of the Gelts' estate will continue to grow as they slowly disburse some assets, their net value may increase during the period of transfers. See, for example, the previous note, where even with dispursal the Gelts' estate would grow from $8,000,000 to over $12,000,000 after twenty years. Moreover, the Gelt's may be transferring assets that have no effect on their income or life-style. Indeed, the quality of the Gelt's lives may increase as they derive great satisfaction from the way their actions will provide for their heirs. And of course the Gelt's heirs might significantly benefit from simply investing the money—freeing up more of their own salaries for life's little pleasantries, and easing their minds about their future financial security.

38. It has long been recognized that promoting equality of one kind may entail permitting, or even requiring, inequality of another. For example, equality of primary goods may lead to inequality of need satisfaction, equality of need satisfaction may require inequality of income or wealth, equality of income or wealth may require inequality of opportunity, and so on.

An interesting article making this sort of point is John Schaar's "Equality of Opportunity and Beyond," in *Nomos IX: Equality*, ed. R. Pennock and J. Chapman (Atherton Press, 1967), pp. 228–49. Schaar argues pointedly that, by itself, equality of opportunity would do little to improve many of societies most pernicious inequalities. For example, instead of reducing the huge gap between, say, physicians and ditchdiggers, it might merely change the demographic composition of those groups. Indeed, Schaar suggests genuine equality of opportunity would not merely preserve society's underlying patterns of inequality, it would worsen them. Schaar's argument shows that equality of opportunity need not promote, and may even interfere with, other kinds of equality that deeply concern us—for example, equality of income, primary goods, need satisfaction, or welfare.

One can see, then, this book's considerations are no substitute for those presented in support of

encouraged by the Tax Code are precisely the kind for which PD needs revision. Correspondingly, insofar as one cares about inequality of welfare, one will find the code needs revision.

We have seen how focusing on cases involving even transfers can be misleading, as the desirability of transfers can be a complicated matter when they are not one-for-one. We have also seen this can have practical implications.[39] Fortunately, this book's theoretical considerations can plausibly account for both the much discussed cases of even transfers, and the less discussed—but perhaps more common—cases of efficient and inefficient transfers.

Some deny that there is any respect in which an efficient transfer could be bad, or an inefficient transfer good. Their objection may rest on definitional grounds. As they use the words "efficient" and "inefficient," this section's claims *could not* be true. So based, their objection is trivial and may be ignored. Their objection may also be based on substantive grounds, most notably utilitarian ones. So based, their objection has considerable force, but must, I think, ultimately beg the question against egalitarianism as well as many other moral positions. For example, Rawlsians, Nozickians, and perfectionists will each permit inefficient transfers, as long as they maximize the level of the worst-off group, result from voluntary agreements of consenting adults, and promote perfectionism, respectively; similarly, they will not permit efficient transfers that worsen the level of the worst-off group, result from coercion, or detract from perfectionism, respectively. In any event, whatever the ultimate merits of the position in question, it need not concern us here. As I stressed at this book's onset, my purpose is not to defend equality; it is to elucidate the notion by trying to determine different judgments egalitarians would make and the factors underlying and influencing those judgments. In that light, I think this section's results stand. As with Rawlsians, Nozickians, perfectionists, and others, there are some efficient transfers the egalitarian will condemn, and some inefficient transfers the egalitarian will approve.

A final point. Given the foregoing, some may raise a narrower, but far-reaching objection. Granting the general point that some efficient transfers may be objectionable and some inefficient transfers desirable, they may nonetheless draw the line at the cases I described as "perfectly efficient transfers" and "perfectly inefficient transfers." Specifically, they may insist that improving the lot of some cannot be bad *in any respect* if *no one* is thereby worsened, and similarly that worsening the

---

different *kinds* of equality. But, as noted in chapter 1, most of the book's considerations will be relevant to *whatever* kind(s) of equality one supports.

39. We have illustrated some practical implications of our results for inequality of welfare. There will be other practical implications for other kinds of inequality. But notice, implications analogous to the ones discussed may hold even for those goods that can, theoretically, be transferred one-for-one. For example, there may be practical and political considerations that dictate against permitting certain inequalities of wealth to arise, and then reducing them via even transfers from richer to poorer. Instead, it might be best to structure society's principles and institutions so there is less inequality in the first place. But principles and institutions cannot be fine-tuned. Hence, even if desirable, it is highly unlikely the effect of such changes would precisely parallel a series of even transfers. To the contrary, it is virtually certain those who would have been richer without the changes will "lose" either more or less than the others "gain." Thus, even where directly transferrable incremental goods are involved, social attempts to reduce inequality will often involve either efficient or inefficient transfers of goods.

lot of some cannot be better *in any respect* if *no one* is thereby benefited. This position has enormous appeal, and I think there are some egalitarians who would want to formulate their views to accommodate it. But while I think such a move is possible,[40] my own view is that such a position is, in the end, neither desirable nor necessary.

(My own view is that insofar as one cares about *equality* one should be willing to hold that, if everyone else remains the same, improving the lot of those who are *already* better off than *everyone else* would be bad and, correspondingly, that even if no one else gains from it, worsening the lot of those better off than everyone else would, up to a point, be good.[41] Naturally, the egalitarian could hold this and still acknowledge that in other respects, and perhaps all things considered, such moves would be good and bad, respectively. My view is supported by each of the aspects of inequality we have considered, and although they might be amended to avoid this result, I do not think it is in the spirit of egalitarianism to do so. Of course, some will insist that it is precisely because the spirit of egalitarianism has these implications that it must be rejected. This is an important claim I shall return to in chapter 9. Suffice it to say, though I think the claim has much appeal, I do not believe it ultimately succeeds in undermining egalitarianism.)

3.7 Conclusion

Let us summarize this chapter. I began by presenting the results of an informal poll comparing complex situations regarding inequality. I warned against according too much weight to the poll given the poll's nature and few respondents. Nevertheless, the poll's results were interesting and suggestive for two reasons. First, they illustrated a wide range of agreement, or lack thereof, in pretheoretical intuitions about inequality. Second, there was a striking correlation between the extent of agreement among poll respondents and the extent of agreement among chapter 2's aspects. For example, where there was virtual unanimity among poll respondents, there was also unanimity among chapter 2's aspects, and where there was almost no agreement among respondents, the aspects, too, were sharply divided.

Together these facts supported (or strongly suggested) two conclusions. First, as chapter 1 claimed and chapter 2 implies, the notion of inequality is complex rather

---

40. Basically, this might be a person-affecting or deontological version of egalitarianism of the sort briefly discussed in section 3.3. As noted then, on such a view equality will be *essentially comparative* not merely in the sense that it involves judgments about how some fare relative to others, but in the sense that our judgment about a situation's inequality will essentially depend on the alternative with which it is compared. Again, I refer the reader to my "Intransitivity," especially sections B and D, where the beginnings of this kind of view, and the motivation underlying it, are presented. As suggested earlier, the difficulties with this kind of view are enormous and its implications far-reaching. I hope to explore these and related issues in another book.

41. The qualification "up to a point" is an integral component of the egalitarian's view and not a weakening of it. For example, if A and B are the only two people, and A has 1,000 units of welfare and B 800, it would be an improvement if A lost 100, but not if A lost 800.

than simple.[42] Second, since people may be influenced by different aspects to varying degrees, together chapter 2's aspects can accommodate and explain the pretheoretical intuitions of most egalitarians across a wide range of cases.

I also suggested one reason many may have thought inequality a simple notion. In discussing inequality most have focused on certain "paradigm" cases contrasting perfect equality with inequality, or large gaps between better- and worse-off with small gaps. Unfortunately, these "paradigm" cases are very misleading in being cases about which *each* of chapter 2's aspects agree. As a result, there is widespread general agreement about such cases, which may obscure the fact that people may actually be responding to different features of the situations in assessing their inequality. Thus, many failed to see the need for exploring the underlying bases of their egalitarian judgments, naturally but mistakenly assuming inequality was a simple notion that most others assessed the same way they did (though they might care about it more or less).

I next considered how variations in group levels would affect inequality. I noted the pretheoretical intuitions of my poll respondents for cases where group levels were varied, and also suggested several firm considered judgments about such cases. These included both firm absolute judgments—for example, other things equal, raising the level of the best-off group or lowering the level of the worst-off group would clearly and unequivocally worsen inequality—and firm relative judgments, such as, regarding inequality, the worse off a group is the better it would be to raise it and the worse it would be to lower it. I argued chapter 2's aspects could accommodate and explain both the poll respondents' pretheoretical intuitions and, even more important, the firm considered egalitarian judgments.

Our discussion confirmed chapter 2's claim that aspects that agree (or disagree) regarding the Sequence might disagree (or agree) in other cases. Thus, one cannot simply reduce chapter 2's aspects to a convenient subset that will yield the same orderings of the Sequence. As claimed in chapter 2, the aspects represent elements of our thinking that may influence us in different ways depending on the situation.

Our discussion also illustrated the importance of not assessing an aspect's plausibility too quickly, for example, based on a particular example. As we saw, aspects that may seem most (or least) plausible considering the Sequence may seem least (or most) plausible considering other situations. So, as chapter 2 claimed, though for each aspect it may be possible to construct situations where the aspect's judgment seems implausible, or at least less plausible, this does not show each aspect should be rejected, revised, or accorded little weight. It shows inequality is complex, and that each aspect does not itself wholly underlie our judgments. Clearly, before finally deciding which aspects are most plausible and how much they matter vis-à-vis each other, we shall have to consider their implications for a whole range of cases. More about this in chapter 5.

---

42. While the assumption that inequality is complex can plausibly account for both the agreement and variation in people's judgments, the assumption that inequality is simple can only account for the agreement. That is, the extreme divergence in people's pretheoretical intuitions about certain cases and the ambivalence and contrary pulls many feel within themselves about certain cases are difficult to plausibly account for if inequality is a simple notion.

Another point our discussion implied is that while in most cases our theoretical considerations can accommodate and explain people's pretheoretical intuitions—and indeed usually have the appealing feature of confirming the "general sense" of the majority—they do not simply rubber stamp those intuitions.[43] Thus, even when there may be good egalitarian reasons for people's pretheoretical intuitions, in the sense of their being supported by some aspects of inequality, in many cases those intuitions will ultimately need revising once inequality's full scope and complexity is recognized.

I next considered how transfers between groups would affect inequality. We saw that together chapter 2's aspects would support the egalitarian view that for any transfer of any size or kind the transfer should go from the "highest" to "lowest" possible group. We also noted that most economists endorse the Pigou-Dalton condition, and observed that together chapter 2's aspects support PD for the cases economists were considering. But we noted PD's scope must be limited in ways having both theoretical and practical significance. Specifically, we argued that in accordance with people's pretheoretical intuitions and firm considered judgments, together chapter 2's aspects imply that a transfer's effect depends on the group levels involved, the kind of transfer in question, and the extent to which it raises or lowers the different groups.

Thus we saw that while in accordance with PD *even* transfers from worse- to better-off worsen inequality, and from better- to worse-off improve it—so long as the transfers reduce the gaps between them—it is not true that *any* transfers from worse- to better-off worsen inequality or that any from better- to worse-off improve it. For example, transfers from worse- to better-off may improve inequality if those affected are relatively poorly off and if the transfer is "sufficiently" efficient. By the same token, the same kind of efficient transfer that might be condemned were it to occur between two relatively well-off groups might be approved were it to occur between two relatively poorly off groups, and might be strongly approved were it to occur between relatively well-off and relatively poorly off groups.

In sum, once one stops focusing on the sort of transfers economists mainly considered—that is, even or one-for-one transfers—there is no simple or general rule for whether a given transfer will improve inequality. Nevertheless, it appeared our theoretical considerations can plausibly account for both the much-discussed cases of even transfers, and the less-discussed yet common cases of efficient and inefficient transfers.

In discussing transfers we noted how our reaction to complicated cases may be revealing. In some cases where inequality's aspects significantly diverge we may nevertheless feel confident about how two situations compare regarding inequality. If so, this may usefully indicate how much we actually care about certain aspects relative to others. However, sometimes we may remain unsure about how two situations compare regarding inequality, and this may be an important hint as to

---

43. Following Sidgwick, I think it would be cause for concern if our account implied that most were seriously mistaken in their egalitarian judgments most of the time. By the same token it would also be cause for concern if our account failed to provide a perspective from which to correct intuitive errors into which, for a variety of reasons, we may fall. I will return to these points.

inequality's nature. Specifically, we may determine our indecision is not due to ignorance—for example, of how the alternatives compare regarding the aspects or how much the different aspects matter—but to the fact that inequality is an incomplete notion that does not yield or permit a determinate ranking of all alternatives. As observed, we return to this point in chapter 5.

For clarity and ease of presentation, this chapter has continued to focus on simplified cases involving homogeneous groups. That is, there is inequality between, but not within groups. Let me emphasize that this feature of our diagrams did not substantively affect our central results. As I illustrate in appendix B, virtually the entire set of arguments and conclusions presented in the context of discussing variation between homogeneous groups could be straightforwardly extended, mutatis mutandis, to cases involving variations of individuals in heterogeneous groups. And this is so for cases involving different numbers of heterogeneous groups, different numbers within the groups, and different patterns of distribution within and between the groups—that is, for any situation, whatever its complexity and pattern of distribution.

Also, as noted previously, in appendix A I consider whether there may be any aspects of inequality besides those we have discussed. I examine, and reject, five suggestions. Although there are various ways one may want to revise or supplement chapter 2's aspects, I am not aware of any significantly new or different aspects of inequality that withstand philosophical scrutiny. If there are such aspects, as there may well be with such a difficult and complex notion, perhaps this book will—if only via its mistakes and the corrections they prompt—aid in their discovery.

In chapter 2 we offered intuitive and theoretical grounds for different aspects of inequality. In this chapter we have considered numerous arguments and cases that both corroborate chapter 2's central results and help guard against misinterpretations and faulty inferences based on those results. It appears that, for most cases at least, together chapter two's aspects offer a coherent, systematic, and non-ad hoc method of accommodating and explaining both the pretheoretical intuitions of most egalitarians and their firm considered judgments. Moreover, they offer a principled method and perspective from which to assess, and where appropriate to revise, egalitarian judgments. Thus, although much work remains, it appears our approach represents a promising way of elucidating the notion of inequality.

4

Averages, Individuals, or Groups: What Should an Egalitarian Focus On?

This chapter is divided into two main parts. In part 1, I consider an *Average Principle* of equality and a *Proportional Average Principle* of equality. In part 2, I closely examine the relative to the best-off person view of complaints (BOP). Both parts raise questions about the focus of egalitarian concern.

The Average and Proportional Average Principles of equality are straw men. They have little to commend them and few, if any, actual proponents. Still, I think it is worth constructing them, and then knocking them down. Considering their short-comings in detail serves several purposes. First, it precludes a certain misinterpretation of my work, which might otherwise arise. Second, it helps guard against a wrong turn in part 2 of this chapter. Third, it helps clear the ground and lay the foundation for appendix B, where I illustrate how considerations analogous to those presented in chapter three would apply to variations within heterogeneous groups. Fourth, and most important, it adds further credence to the book's central method-ological approach of understanding inequality as an essentially comparative individ-ualistic notion, rather than as an essentially distributive holistic notion.

4.1 The Average Principle of Equality

On the *Average Principle* of equality, how good a situation is regarding inequality depends on how the average levels of the different groups within that situation fare relative to one another. As background for our discussion of this principle, let me begin by commenting on a (mis)interpretation of our earlier results paralleling a common but, I believe, mistaken way of regarding inequality.

As noted in chapter 1, most implicitly assume inequality is a holistic notion. Concern about society's inequality standardly expresses itself as a concern about a factor that can only be understood and assessed from a global, or holistic, perspec-tive relating to the goodness or badness of the society *per se*, as if the society *itself* is the proper object of the egalitarian's concern. I find this view deeply wrong-headed, and this book presents an alternative way of understanding inequality. Still, I have often posed my questions in terms of how better- and worse-off groups fare regarding inequality, or of how variations in group levels, or transfers between groups, would affect inequality. And I have often stated my conclusions in similar terms. Correspondingly, it may seem at times that I, too, am advocating a holistic approach, though one focusing on *groups*, rather than society, as the proper object of the egalitarian's concern. But this is not my view.

In discussing the maximin principle I wrote that "claims to the effect that we are especially concerned about the complaints of the worst-off group are misleading, insofar as they suggest a concern on our part about the *group itself* as opposed to the *members* of that group. We do not have a special concern for some real or abstract entity 'the worst-off group'; what we have is a special concern for the worst-off members of our world, and it is *this* concern which the maximin principle expresses."[1] Similar remarks apply regarding inequality. Though it is often convenient to discuss inequality between society's different groups, the egalitarian's concern is not about the inequality between the groups *per se*, as if the groups *themselves* were the objects of concern, rather the concern is about the inequality between the *members* of those groups. Thus, ultimately, the egalitarian is concerned about how different individuals fare relative to one another. Or so I believe, anyway.

It should now be clear how I intend my arguments to be understood. But, as the preceding suggests, my view of these matters is not the only one possible. In applying Maximin, many Rawlsians focus not on the plight of the worst-off individual, or any other particular individuals, but rather on the prospects or expectations of the so-called representative member of the worst-off group.[2] Although Rawls himself is elusive about how, precisely, we are to interpret the "representative member of the worst-off group," Maximin is frequently understood to imply that the better of two situations is the one in which the average member of the worst-off group fares better. Analogously, one might claim that, contra Temkin, egalitarians should focus *not* on how particular individuals fare relative to each other, but on how the average members of different groups fare relative to each other. Thus, one might advocate a position like the Average Principle. Moreover, one might even urge that most of my arguments to this point are compatible with, and can be interpreted as supporting, such a position.

4.2 Rejecting the Average Principle

Let us turn, then, to a consideration of the Average Principle. To facilitate discussion it will be useful to introduce a new feature into our diagrams. It is illustrated in diagram 4.1. Like my other diagrams, diagram 4.1 represents a situation, or "world," with people at different levels. As before, the world can be viewed as containing better- and worse-off groups. However, in this case each group has been drawn with a sloped top, rather than a horizontal one. This represents the existence

1. See chapter 2, p. 31, especially note 10.
2. Thus, in discussing his principles of justice Rawls emphasizes that "when principles mention persons, or require that everyone gain from inequality, the reference is to representative persons holding the various social positions, or offices, or whatever, established by the basic structure .... neither principle applies to distributions of particular goods to particular individuals who may be identified by their proper names" (*A Theory of Justice* [Harvard University Press, 1971], p. 64).

DIAGRAM 4.1

of inequality within each group, corresponding to the realistic fact that as useful as it often is, in both practical and theoretical discussions, to divide society or the world neatly into different groups—for example, the upper, middle, and lower classes, or the first, second, and third worlds—it remains true that there is significant diversity within these groups. Terminologically, I shall say that a group is *homogeneous* if its members are equally well off, *heterogeneous* otherwise. Homogeneous groups are represented by figures with (completely) horizontal tops, heterogeneous groups by figures with (partially) sloped tops.

To be sure, in many respects diagrams like 4.1 remain unrealistic. For example, real societies are not neatly divided into groups of equal size, separated by gaps of equal size, with a uniform pattern of inequality within each group. Still, my diagrams are sufficient for my purposes and, as before, I think if we are careful their simplified features need not mislead us.

My criticisms of the Average Principle will focus on its implications about transfers both between and within heterogeneous groups. Consider diagram 4.2. In I there is inequality both between, and within, three equal-sized groups, A, B, and C. As drawn, people are evenly distributed such that the gaps between the better- and worse-off are the same within each group. In addition, the gaps between A and B, and B and C are the same size. In II welfare has been evenly transferred from some of the best-off to some of the worst-off. Specifically, the best-off group's bottom half has been lowered, and the worst-off group's top half raised, to the average level, that is, to the level of B's middle person. As a result the B group is twice as large in II as in I, the A and C groups are half as large.

How do I and II compare regarding inequality? Judging by appearance alone, one might be drawn to the view that II is worse than I in part because the gaps between the better- and worse-off groups are larger in II than in I. Appealing to the Average Principle, one might urge that the egalitarian's concern is (or ought to be) about how society's *groups* compare—specifically, how the *average* members of the groups fare relative to one another—and consequently, that II is worse than I. Is this plausible?

In considering this issue it will help to attach numbers to the levels of diagram 4.2. Assume that in I A ranges from levels 510 to 610, B from 350 to 450, and C

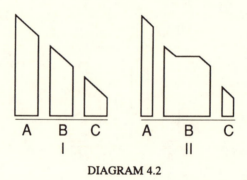

DIAGRAM 4.2

from 190 to 290.[3] In II, A ranges from 560 to 610, B from 350 to 450, and C from 190 to 240. Then in I the average levels of A, B, and C are 560, 400, and 240, respectively, in II they are 585, 400, and 215, respectively. Clearly, then, the gaps between the average members of the different groups are larger in II than in I. The question is whether this is reason to regard II's inequality as worse. I think not.

Focus, for a moment, on the A and C groups. In I, the gap between the average members of A and C is 320 units. In II, it is 370 units. But notice, in moving from I to II it is not the case that any members of C have been made worse off. Nor have any members of A been made better off. To the contrary, the only reason the gap between the average members of A and C is larger in II than in I is because the gap between some of those (originally) in A and C *has been completely removed*. Surely, this is not a reason to think II worse than I regarding inequality.

Similar remarks could be made about the gaps between A and B, and B and C. To be sure, moving from I to II the gap between those who were in A's top and bottom halves has grown larger. But, on reflection, it seems clear these larger gaps will be more than offset by the reduced gaps between those who were in the bottom of A and everyone else. Similarly, the greater gap between C's top and bottom halves will be more than offset by the reduced gaps between those who were in C's top half and everyone else.

II results from I via an even transfer of welfare from better- to worse-off. Thus, in implying that II is worse than I the Average Principle violates the most plausible version of the Pigou-Dalton condition. This is hard to accept.

The Average Principle's problem can be put more pointedly. Suppose one had two choices. Starting with a situation like I, one could either transfer welfare from some of the best- to some of the worst-off so as to bring about II or, alternatively, one could transfer welfare from the worst- to the best-off so as to make each member of the worst-off group even worse off by 20 units, while making each member of the best-off group even better off by 20 units. Clearly, the first choice would be better according to the Pigou-Dalton condition. It would also be better

---

3. There is nothing special about these numbers, other than that they serve the purposes of our discussion in a relatively clear, straightforward manner. Their important feature is they reflect the relative proportions of the gaps within and between diagram 4.2's groups.

according to *each* of chapter 2's aspects of inequality. Yet, one can easily calculate that on the Average Principle the second choice would be better than the first regarding inequality.[4] This is not merely implausible; it is absurd.[5]

To avoid the sting of this objection one might try circumscribing the Average Principle. Thus, one might claim that the Average Principle is "merely" another aspect of inequality, albeit an important one; or that it might replace some, but not all, of chapter 2's aspects. Alternatively, one might modify or interpret other aspects in light of the Average Principle. For example, one might modify aspects involving the relative to the best-off person view of complaints, so comparisons are made to the average level of the best-off group, rather than to the best-off individual. Similarly, one might urge, like certain Rawlsians, that aspects involving the maximin principle of equality focus on how the average member of the worst-off group fares relative to others.

Such views may initially seem promising. But ultimately they only prop up a position not worth preserving. Given the choice between an even transfer from the best- to the worst-off group, and one from the worst- to the best-off group, I believe the former would be *clearly and unequivocally* better regarding inequality. It is not merely that the former would be better than the latter all things considered. There is *no respect* in which the latter would be better regarding inequality.[6] If this is correct, then the Average Principle should be rejected. It is not even plausible as an aspect of inequality.

4.3 The Proportional Average Principle of Equality

One might object to the foregoing arguments by claiming that diagram 4.2 is visually misleading, and that membership in the better- and worse-off groups should be determined not by the eye but by the calculator. For example, one might urge that all situations must be evenly divided into n groups, so that each group one considers in assessing a situation contains the same proportion of the population and, moreover, for each group one considers in assessing one situation, one must consider a corresponding group representing the same proportion of the population in assessing another situation.[7] Let us call this the *Proportional Average Principle* of equality.

4. Given the figures our example assumes, on the first choice the average levels of A, B, and C would be 585, 400, and 215, respectively, while on the second they would be 580, 400, and 220, respectively. Thus the gaps between the average levels of the different groups would be larger on the first choice than the second.

5. There may, of course, be nonegalitarian respects in which the second move seems better than the first. For example, the second move may seem better regarding perfectionism. What seems absurd is the claim that the second move would be better than the first *regarding inequality.*

6. Cf. the previous note. Also, my view is that no plausible egalitarian position would *ultimately* endorse the latter over the former. As implicitly noted, I think there are *certain* considerations in virtue of which a plausible position might favor the latter over the former, but I think considerations of the very same sort will *also* favor the former over the latter and to an even greater extent.

7. One might think that as long as one retains the latter requirement one could, and perhaps should, drop the former. Though such a position seems initially plausible, I shall not discuss it separately. It faces the objections I shall be raising in this chapter, and others as well.

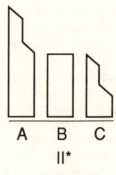

A   B   C

II*

DIAGRAM 4.3

On the Proportional Average Principle my discussion of diagram 4.2 is based on erroneous comparisons. Whereas in discussing I, I compared the average levels of three equal-sized groups, in discussing II, I compared the average levels of two groups containing one-sixth the population and one group containing two-thirds the population. This, it might be claimed, is illegitimate—to compare the two situations accurately the second should have been divided into three equal-sized groups, as represented in II* in diagram 4.3.

Given the stark contrasts within A and C, I think II* is not as natural and plausible a way of dividing the situation into three groups as is II. Indeed, given that A's worse half and C's better half are generally closer both to those in B, and to each other, than they are to the others in their "own" so-called "groups" and given the prevalent view of our own society as containing a large middle class with smaller upper and lower classes, surely most would view the described situation more as II depicts than as II* depicts. Nevertheless, advocates of the Proportional Average Principle might rightly contend that however they fare relative to others, A's worse half is still among society's best-off third and C's better half is still among society's worst-off third. Correspondingly, they might insist that for a fair and accurate comparison I must be compared with II*, not II.

The Proportional Average Principle avoids our earlier objections. Whereas the average levels of the best- and worst-off groups are higher and lower, respectively, in II than in I, they are lower and higher, respectively, in II* than in I. Thus, whereas the gaps between the average members of the different groups are larger in II than I, they are smaller in II* than in I. Correspondingly, if the composition of the better- and worse-off groups are determined as the Proportional Average Principle requires, transfers from the best- to the worst-off group will improve inequality. Similarly, on the Proportional Average Principle transfers from the worst- to the best-off group lower and raise, respectively, the averages of those groups; hence, such transfers worsen inequality. Thus, the Proportional Average Principle avoids the absurd conclusion that an even transfer from the worst-off to the best-off group might be better than an even transfer from the best-off to the worst-off group regarding inequality.

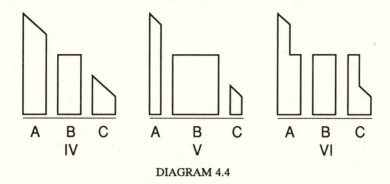

DIAGRAM 4.4

4.4 Rejecting the Proportional Average Principle

So should we reserve a place for the Proportional Average Principle in our under-standing of inequality? I think not. Consider diagram 4.4. IV is like I in diagram 4.2, except the middle group's members are equally well off. Now suppose there were an even transfer of welfare such that the best-off group's bottom half and the worst-off group's top half were moved to B's level. Surely, V would be the natural way of de-picting the result. Yet, on the Proportional Average Principle the result would—at least for accounting purposes—have to be regarded as containing equal-sized groups as in VI. This, however, seems implausible, and not merely because it seems an "un-natural" way of picturing the situation.

Consider VI. By hypothesis, A's worse half, the B group, and C's better half are all equally well off. Hence one cannot say of VI, as one could of II* in diagram 4.3, that A's worse half is among society's best-off third and that C's better half is among the worst-off third. True, only one-sixth of the population is better off than A's worse half, but this holds equally for C's better half. Similarly, while only one-sixth is worse off than C's better half, this is just as true of A's worse half. The point is that however A's worse half fares relative to others, by hypothesis, that is *exactly* how the B group and C's better half fare. Correspondingly, there is no particular reason the members of A's worse half should have been counted among the best-off group. They might just as easily, and accurately, have been counted as in the middle or worst-off groups, with some in those groups counted among the best-off group. More generally, on the Proportional Average Principle it is *completely arbitrary* in a situation like VI which of those who are equally well off are included in the best-off, middle, and worst-off groups. Thus, the Proportional Average Principle appears open to the (related) charges of treating equals unequally and of arbitrariness.

The Proportional Average Principle is also misleading. For instance, it doesn't permit the normal inference that someone in the worst-off group fares worse than most others, or even *any* others.[8] Consider, if the vast majority was equally well off,

8. There is a special case where this will be true, and unobjectionable, for any view—namely, a homogeneous situation where *everyone* is equally well-off. In such a case one might say everyone is a

and much better off than the others, the Proportional Average Principle could have to count some of those best-off among the worst-off group even though the gap between the members of the so-called worst-off group might be enormous, and even though, by hypothesis, there might be *nobody* better off than those who were arbitrarily included in the worst-off group. In the extreme case, some members of the worst-off group might have the most wretched lives possible, while others might be as well off as any who ever lived. Although in such a case the former clearly deserve to be counted in the worst-off group, it stretches the bounds of credulity to count the latter there as well.

The Proportional Average Principle seems misleading in another respect. On the Proportional Average Principle one focuses on the average levels of the better- and worse-off groups, aiming so far as possible to reduce the gaps between them. But then, dividing a society into groups A, B, and C, as in VI of diagram 4.4, naturally *suggests* a concern with how the average levels of *those* groups, A, B, and C, compare. So, if, as in VI of diagram 4.4, C's average level is lower than B's and A's, it seems as if *one* way of improving the inequality would be to raise the average level of the C group (another, perhaps less desirable, way would be to lower the average levels of the other groups). But by their very nature average views focus on groups as a whole— specifically on average levels of groups—rather than on the particular individuals and their levels within groups. Correspondingly, it is a notable feature of average views that they are generally indifferent between ways a group's average might change. Thus, on average views it won't generally matter whether a group's average is increased by raising everybody in the group a little, by raising a few a lot, by raising the group's worst-off, or by raising the group's best-off.

Together, the preceding considerations might lead one to expect that on the Proportional Average Principle one could improve VI's inequality by raising C's average, and one could do this by raising any of C's members. But, while raising any of C's worse-off would (at least up to a point) improve inequality, raising any of C's better-off would *worsen* inequality, not improve it. The reason is that as soon as any of C's better-off were raised, *even by a small amount*, they would immediately become members of the best-off group, while their place in the worst-off group would be taken by some previously included in B or A. So, in essence, the effect of raising some of C's better-off would be not to improve C's average relative to the other groups, but to change the groups' compositions so that B's and C's averages remained constant while A's increased. Thus, VI's inequality would be worsened by such a move, as none of the gaps between the better- and worse-off groups would be smaller, and some would be larger.

The foregoing suggests several related respects in which the Proportional

---

member of both the best- and worst-off groups, that is, the only group there is, and being a member of the worst-off group will not imply being worse off than anyone else. The case I am considering is a heterogeneous situation, where, as we shall see, the Proportional Average View's implications are hard to accept.

Average Principle is misleading. Normally, when one learns someone is among society's worst-off group, it is reasonable to infer that that person will fare worse than anyone in the best-off group and that someone who is no better off than that person will also be a member of the worst-off group. In addition, normally when someone is in society's worst-off group it is reasonable to infer that an egalitarian would favor improving her position, at least somewhat, and would rather benefit her than someone in the middle or best-off group. However, as case VI illustrates, on the Proportional Average Principle none of these inferences would be valid.

Notice, the main objection suggested by the preceding remarks is not that the Proportional Average Principle yields the "wrong" answers in the cases discussed. To the contrary, it is quite plausible to hold both that raising the level of some who are already as well off as all but a few might worsen inequality, and that among people equally well off it makes no difference who is raised or lowered. The main objection of the preceding remarks is that the Proportional Average Principle is misleading, perhaps even disingenuous,[9] in counting certain people as members of C, and intimating that it is actually concerned with how the average of C—*the group that includes those members*—compares with the averages of the other groups.

One wants to say that if C's better-off members were really full-fledged members of the worst-off group—in a significant, contentful, way—then raising their level should, at least to some degree, improve the worst-off group's average and thus inequality. But one notes that, ceteris paribus, the only way to raise the average of VI's worst-off group is to raise those in C's worse-off half. Hence, C's better-off seem to be members of the worst-off group in name only. They are *counted* as such, so the Proportional Average Principle can avoid the Average Principle's insuperable difficulties, but they claim no special allegiance insofar as the Proportional Average Principle is really concerned to reduce gaps between society's groups. Thus, in practice, if not in name, it is C's worse-off half whose situation matters, insofar as the Proportional Average Principle addresses the relative status of the worst-off group. This is, one wants to say, as it should be, for they really are VI's worst-off group. But then shouldn't one straightforwardly acknowledge this, and avoid the pretension that the worst-off group is C?[10]

The Proportional Average Principle faces yet another charge: being ad hoc. There is, I think, no independently plausible justification for the arbitrary and misleading unequal treatment of equals required by the Proportional Average Principle. The main motivation for looking at the situation depicted in V of diagram 4.4 as

9. I write loosely here, as I frequently do in this work. Strictly speaking, the Proportional Average View cannot *itself* be disingenuous, only its advocates can be. Here, as elsewhere when I make such remarks, I trust my meaning is plain enough.

10. Similarly, in practice there is no difference in how the Proportional Average View responds to the relative positions of the worst-off group in A, the B group, and the better-off group in C. And again, one wants to say that this is as it should be. But if it would be implausible to respond differently to the relative positions of people equally well off, why is it both appropriate and not misleading to treat them as members of different groups in calculating inequality?

better represented by VI is that one must do so if one hopes to defend some version of an Average Principle.[11] But, so motivated, such a defense is hardly inspiring. If the Average Principle's intrinsic appeal were overwhelming, or we needed an Average Principle to capture our egalitarian views, perhaps the Proportional Average Principle might seem compelling despite its shortcomings. But this is not our situation. We can dispense with both the Average Principle and the Proportional Average Principle and still do justice[12] to our egalitarian judgments.

Let me turn to a final, particularly instructive, criticism of the Proportional Average Principle, one that could equally be leveled at the Average Principle. I noted earlier that a characteristic feature of average views in general is their indifference between ways a group's average might change. Another way of putting this point is that average views ignore, and thereby obscure, the particular levels of the individuals from which the averages are derived. This feature is *especially* unappealing for a theory of inequality.

Consider again I in diagram 4.2, where there is inequality both within, and between, three groups. The Proportional Average Principle wholly ignores the inequality *within* the groups, except insofar as this affects the inequality between the groups' average levels. This implies that as long as a transfer does not change the membership of the groups—a condition that will often be so, and which I shall assume throughout this discussion—then, contrary to the Pigou-Dalton condition, the Proportional Average Principle will be completely indifferent to even transfers within groups. This is because even transfers within groups will not affect group averages; hence, it will not affect how the groups' averages compare.

The foregoing implies that the Proportional Average Principle will be wholly indifferent between an even exchange from A's best- to worst-off members, and one from A's worst- to best-off members, even if the former completely removed, and the latter significantly increased, the gaps between them. Similarly, of course, for B and C. In addition, the Proportional Average Principle would favor an even transfer from B's worst-off to C's best-off over an even transfer from C's best- to worst-off, as the former would positively effect, however slightly, how the averages of the groups compared, while the latter would have no effect. Moreover, this would be so *no matter how small* the initial gap was between B's worst-off and C's best-off, and *no matter how large* the gap was between C's best- and worst-off, and even if the transfer between B's worst-off and C's best-off would *barely reduce* the gap between them, while the transfer between C's best- and worst-off *completely removed* their gap.

The foregoing implications of the Proportional Average Principle are absurd. Why should one care about slightly reducing small inequalities between groups, but

11. One is tempted to say the motivation suggested may be the only one for the view in question, for surely there would be no inclination to put people who are equally well off into different groups—even to the extent of counting some as in the best-off group and others as in the worst-off group—except as a(n ad hoc) solution to the Average View's problems. Indeed, one person I spoke with claimed it would be "crazy" to represent the situation in question via VI rather than V, that doing so "wouldn't make any sense." This person's claims *may* be too strong, but they are not obviously so.

12. That is, as much justice as one can, given the complexities and incompleteness inherent in the topic.

not care *at all* whether large inequalities within groups are completely removed or increased?

Suppose A and B in diagram 4.2 didn't exist, so C was the only group existing in I. Would the egalitarian not care that some in C are worse off than others through no fault of their own? Surely not, especially since, for anything said so far, both C's size and the gaps between its members might be (relatively) large. But then why should the concern about C's inequality suddenly disappear when two more unequal groups, like A and B, are added to the situation?

4.5 Individuals versus Groups: A Question of Focus

I believe the problems facing the Average and Proportional Average Principles are profound and irresolvable. At their root lies not merely an unyielding focus on *averages*, but a concomitant and mistaken focus on *groups*. Measuring inequality in terms of how group averages compare suggests the egalitarian is concerned with the inequality between the groups, as if the groups *themselves* were the proper objects of egalitarian concern. This seems to me deeply mistaken. As noted earlier, I believe the core of the egalitarian's position is that it is bad (unjust or unfair) for one person to be worse off than another through no fault of her own. Ultimately, then, the egalitarian is concerned with how *individuals* in situations fare relative to one another. Correspondingly, concern about inequality between society's groups must ultimately be understood as concern about inequality between groups' *members*.

Recognizing the nature of the egalitarian's concern one sees why the egalitarian will oppose inequalities within, as well as between, groups and hence why the Average and Proportional Average Principles are unsatisfactory. After all, if it is bad for one person to be worse off than another through no fault of her own, this should be so whether or not they happen to be lumped together as members of the same group.

Note, inequalities within groups will often be less than those between groups, and to the extent this is so the former will be less objectionable than the latter. But as suggested earlier the relation in question need not hold. If p and q are, respectively, the best- and worst-off members of their group, and r is the best-off member of the next group, the inequality between p and q may well be worse than that between q and r. This is why an earlier result was qualified to state that, other things equal, *in general* the egalitarian will want transfers to go from the "highest" possible group to the "lowest" possible group. In some cases transfers from a "higher" to "lower" group may not be better than transfers within the "higher" or "lower" groups. Thus a more perspicuous statement of this conclusion would be that, other things equal, the egalitarian will want transfers to go from the best- to the worst-off individuals.[13] More generally, it is important to bear in mind that throughout this

---

13. The "other things equal" clause remains necessary as a large transfer from a to b, might be better than a small transfer from c to d, even if c and b were better off than a and d, respectively.

Our point may be put even more perspicuously, though inelegantly, as follows: for any transfer of a given size, and any four individuals A, B, C, and D, if A were better off than B, and C better off than D, then it would be better for the transfer to be *from* A rather than B, and to go *to* D rather than C.

book the terminology of "groups" is merely a useful shorthand for expressing the relevant relations between groups' *members*.

In *Reasons and Persons*, Derek Parfit rejects an Average Principle of utility by appealing to the following case.

> *Hell Three*. Most of us have lives that are much worse than nothing. The exceptions are the sadistic tyrants who make us suffer. The rest of us would kill ourselves if we could; but this is made impossible. The tyrants claim truly that, if we have children, they will make these children suffer slightly less (p.422).

Parfit writes: "On the Average Principle, we ought to have these children. This would raise the average quality of life. It is irrelevant that our children's lives would be much worse than nothing. This is an . . . absurd conclusion" (p. 422).

Utility and equality are different in important respects. The latter is comparative in a way the former is not. So the absurdity of the Average Principle of utility does not directly entail the absurdity of the Average Principle of equality. Parfit, for example, states the main objection to the Average Principle of utility is "On this principle, whether I ought to have a child . . . depends on irrelevant facts about other people's lives (p. 422)." But though it may be irrelevant from the standpoint of utility whether others' lives would be better or worse than my child's, this would not seem irrelevant regarding inequality. Still, in the end, I think both Average Principles are absurd for what may, at bottom, be the same reason. Both focus attention on *groups* in a way that ignores crucially important facts (in the one case relational in the other nonrelational) about the individuals composing those groups.

Now to part 2. In chapter 2 I argued that the relative to the best-off person view of complaints (BOP) was an intuitively plausible way of measuring individual complaints. I further argued that three aspects of inequality involving BOP might underlie and influence our egalitarian judgments. Chapter 3 confirmed the view that BOP plays a significant role—in fact, in some cases, *too* large a role—in people's pretheoretical judgments. Despite this, some think BOP is the least plausible way of measuring individual complaints. More specifically, some find the relative to the best-off person view of complaints implausible in measuring complaints by how people fare relative to the *very best-off* person. Instead, many believe that just as Rawls's Maximin Principle focuses on the worst-off group, rather than the worst-off person, so the relative to the best-off *person* view should be widened to focus on the best-off *people*, or group. In what follows I shall discuss both the motivation for, and various ways of, modifying the relative to the best-off person view of complaints. Then at the end I shall also add a brief comment about the maximin principle of equality. As we will see, part 1's results have a bearing on such issues, but other considerations are also relevant.

Like part 1, part 2 raises a question about the focus of egalitarian concern. Moreover, I believe it raises interesting points about Rawls's Maximin Principle as well as inequality. Nevertheless, the following is tangential to the book's main concerns and does not significantly affect our other conclusions. Consequently, readers who do not find BOP or maximin principles troubling may wish to skip directly to section 4.9, where I summarize part 2's main claims.

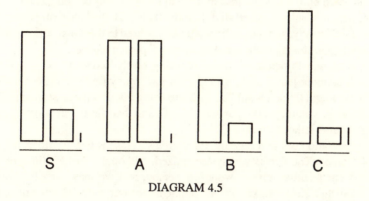

DIAGRAM 4.5

4.6 Rawls's Maximin Principle: Reasons for Focusing on the Worst-Off *Group*

Before assessing BOP, it is instructive to consider Rawls's Maximin Principle. Some believe Rawls's version of Maximin is insufficiently motivated or justified within Rawls's theoretical framework. They believe the reasoning underlying the selection of the principles of justice in Rawls's Original Position supports a Maximin Principle focusing on the plight of the worst-off *person*, rather than on the prospects or expectations of the "representative member of the worst off group" as Rawls, himself, contends.[14] Whether or not this charge can be sustained, many might claim Rawls was right to advocate the version of Maximin he did since the narrower version has implausible implications the wider one avoids.

The need for expanding Maximin's focus beyond the worst-off person is well known and easily illustrated. Consider diagram 4.5. S has one person very badly off, many others quite badly off, and many others very well off. A, B, and C are alternatives to S. In A, the worst-off person would remain unchanged, the better-off group would be slightly lowered, and everyone else would be dramatically raised. In B, the worst-off person would be slightly raised, but everyone else would be lowered, and while the others who initially fared poorly would still not be as badly off as the worst-

---

14. After telling us "it is useful as a heuristic device to think of the two principles as the maximin solution to the problem of social justice," Rawls goes on to state that it is a "fact that the two principles are those a person would choose for the design of a society in which his enemy is to assign him his place. [And] the maximin rule tells us to rank alternatives by their worst possible outcomes: we are to adopt the alternative the worst outcome of which is superior to the worst outcomes of the others" (*A Theory of Justice*, pp. 152–53). Yet if my *enemy* were assigning my place, why would he merely put me *among* the worst-off? Why wouldn't he make me the *very* worst-off? Similarly, from the standpoint of a rational self-interested person, who "in choosing between principles . . . tries as best he can to advance his interests" (*A Theory of Justice*, p. 142), wouldn't the worst possible outcome be the one in which one occupied the position of the very worst-off person from among all the alternatives being considered?

One person who explicitly questions whether Rawls's focus on groups is "*ad hoc*" and "inadequately motivated" is Robert Nozick. See *Anarchy, State, and Utopia* (Basil Books, 1974), p. 190. There are several ways Rawls might respond to such charges, but they needn't concern us here.

off person, each of them would lose more than the worst-off person gained. In C, the worst-off person would be raised slightly more than in B, the better-off people would be raised significantly, and the others would be lowered to the worst-off person's new level, each (again) losing more than the worst-off person gained.

On a Maximin Principle of justice focusing on the worst-off person, B and C would both be more just than A, with C most just. Many find this unacceptable. Although some might think it would be unjust to *bring about* A if one *started* in B or C, many believe A would be more just than B or C, and that starting in S justice dictates bringing about A rather than B or C.[15]

In consideration of the foregoing, there are two reasons to reject focusing on the worst-off person. The first is widely recognized. Although considerations of justice may focus our attention on the worst-off person, and we may even be *most* concerned about her situation, surely her plight is not our *only* (significant) concern regarding justice. To paraphrase an earlier argument of chapter 2, it is implausible that we should be deeply and genuinely concerned about benefiting the worst-off person, but not concerned at all[16] about benefiting those who fare very poorly but are (ever-so-slightly) better off than she. In bringing about B or C rather than A, members of S would be directly harming, as well as failing to *significantly* benefit, many who are themselves quite badly off—all for the sake of slightly benefiting the worst-off person. This, one might claim, would be unjust, for while failing to benefit the worst-off person might be somewhat unjust, requiring so many who are *themselves* badly off to lose *so much* (to be sacrificed?) for another's slight benefit would be even more unjust.[17]

The second reason for not only focusing on the worst-off person is important but rarely articulated. It can be illustrated as follows. Let A* and C* be large populations, say, two billion each. Let A* be perfectly equal with everyone faring very well, C* very unequal with the worst-off group faring very poorly. Finally, assume that in

15. The relevance of the starting point to our judgments may reflect two important strands of moral thinking. The first corresponds roughly to a distinction like that between the good and the right to which many nonconsequentialists adhere. The good or just situation cannot always be rightly or justly brought about. The second corresponds roughly to the asymmetry many see between harming and not helping. Although it may seem unjust to harm those already worse off than everyone else so as to benefit others, it may not seem (as) unjust not to help those already worse off than everyone else so as to benefit others.

16. Except in the case of ties. Henceforth I shall omit this qualification both in the text and notes. Though strictly speaking it is necessary for reasons given in chapter 2, the qualification plays no role, other than a distracting one, in the arguments.

17. Robert Nozick holds a much stronger position. On his view it would even be unjust to require those very well off to make small sacrifices for the sake of large gains for those much worse off. (Cf. *Anarchy, State, and Utopia*, pp. 189-97.) Many find Nozick's position implausible. In fact, many think it would not be unjust, even if it would be inefficient or bad on other grounds, to require those very well off to make large sacrifices for the sake of small gains for those much worse off. On the other hand, as my discussion suggests, where both Nozickians and many non-Nozickians might agree is that it would be unjust to require large sacrifices by some for the sake of small gains for others if those required to make such sacrifices were themselves poorly off to begin with.

Nozick, of course, would claim he has a consistent principled position, whereas his opponents do not. Although I think Nozick is wrong about this, he deserves more of a response on this issue than he is usually given. Unfortunately, I shall not provide such a response here, for to do so adequately would be difficult and carry us too far afield.

Rawlsian terms A* is *perfectly* just, and C* terribly unjust.[18] Clearly, the committed judgment of Rawlsians, and many others, would be that regarding justice A* would be much better than C*. But notice, A* and C* might be represented by A and C of diagram 4.5, except for the worst-off person. Yet, as already noted, focusing on the worst-off person, maximin would rank A and C the exact reverse of A* and C*. This seems implausible. Absent a special explanation, it does not seem the mere presence or absence of two extra people among billions could require a complete reversal in our firm assessment about the relative justness of the situations.[19]

Or consider the following. By hypothesis, A* is *perfectly* just and C* terribly unjust. It follows that on the view under criticism A would be terribly unjust, since it would be worse than both C and C*. Yet A and A*'s only difference is one extra person very poorly off. Even if we think A would be worse than A* regarding justice, it is hard to believe the mere addition of one extra person to a population of two billion could make *such* a difference as to transform a perfectly just situation into a terribly unjust one.[20] More generally, it does not seem that in a large population the mere presence or absence of a few extra people could force *radical* revision in our settled judgment about the situation's overall justness.

Basically, then, the second objection to focusing on the worst-off person is that doing so may seriously distort our judgment because the worst-off person's condition may not accurately reflect the situation's overall justness. For example, the worst-off person's condition may simply be an anomaly or fluke.

4.7 Maximin and BOP: Are They Analogous?

In light of the foregoing one can see Rawls's motivation for focusing on the expectations of the representative member of the worst-off group. Our question is whether in measuring someone's complaint regarding inequality analogous considerations

18. For Rawls a situation is *just* if "no changes in the expectations of those better off can improve the situation of those worse off," and *unjust* if "the higher expectations . . . [of the better off] are excessive . . . [such that if] these expectations were decreased, the situation of the least favored would improve" (*A Theory of Justice*, pp. 78–79).

I assume we can make some meaningful distinctions between "somewhat" and "terribly" unjust situations. For our purposes, I include among the latter category situations where the higher expectations of the better-off mean the difference between the worse-off group being very poorly off and their being very well off. (There are various ways one might expand upon and refine this rough, and incomplete, characterization, but they need not concern us here.)

19. Especially since, as described, C's worst-off person is not substantially better off than A's. Thus, the difference between comparing A* with C* and A with C is simply that A and C each contain *one* extra person who is very poorly off, though the extra person in A is slightly worse off. (See the following note for how a special explanation *could* possibly justify a reversal in judgment, but also for an [implicit] indication of why such an explanation will not usually obtain.)

20. If we learned that A's situation resulted from the (concealed) presence of a tortured slave, whose tormented struggles enabled everyone else to fare so well, we might completely revamp our judgment regarding A's justness. So I don't want to rule out the *possibility* of one person's plight significantly affecting our judgment about a situation's overall justness. But this would be an extreme, peculiar, and morally loaded example of how A and A* might be related. On most "normal" scenarios the difference one extra person would make to our assessment of a large population's overall justness would (rightly) be negligible, more or less regardless of how poor or well off that extra person might be.

militate against focusing on the best-off person and in favor of focusing on the "representative member of the best-off group." Although initially this question's answer might seem an obvious and unqualified yes, in fact it is a not so obvious and very qualified maybe.

One place the analogy may hold is with the position's starting point. Arguably, chapter 2's theoretical considerations support a "relative to the best-off person" view not, I think, a "relative to the representative member of the best-off group" view. Thus, if the latter is maintained, it needs to be on the basis of new arguments replacing or supplementing the old ones, or on the strength of the claim that some version of the relative to the best-off view is necessary to accommodate our egalitarian views, but the narrow version focusing on the best-off person has implausible implications avoided by the wider version focusing on the representative member of the best-off group.[21]

But does the narrow version need replacing by a wider one? To better answer this question, let us pursue the analogy between the relative to the best-off person view of complaints (henceforth, *BOP*) and the Maximin Principle of justice which focuses on the worst-off person (henceforth, MP). Consider diagram 4.6, which is a mirror image of diagram 4.5. For example, whereas in diagram 4.5 S had one person very poorly off, many others quite poorly off, and many others very well off, in diagram 4.6 S has one person very well off, many others quite well off, and many others very poorly off. To the extent the analogy between BOP and MP holds, our views about BOP's implications regarding diagram 4.6's inequality should parallel our views about MP's implications regarding diagram 4.5's injustice.

Discussing diagram 4.5 we claimed most would judge A better than B and C regarding justice, but MP would rank C best and A worst. Considering diagram 4.6, I think most might similarly judge A better than B and C regarding inequality, but BOP would not rank C best and A worst. Recall from chapter 2 that by itself BOP yields no rankings. Like the other ways of measuring complaints, BOP only ranks situations when combined with one of the principles of equality—the additive, weighted additive, or maximin principle.[22] Now as drawn, BOP would rank B best on all three principles. In addition, while it would probably rank A worst when combined with the additive and weighted additive principles, it would rank C worst when combined with the maximin principle.[23]

21. Advocates of such a position may look to both Rawls and Sidgwick as providing the theoretical framework for "adjusting" one's theoretical conclusions to "fit" one's pretheoretical intuitions or judgments. Rawls's discussion of "reflective equilibrium" is well known in this regard, but I take it key elements of Rawls's view are clearly anticipated by Sidgwick who basically suggests that the purpose and test of a moral theory are to organize, systematize, and explain our moral intuitions or judgments so as to (1) accommodate as many as possible—taking into account their relative strength and importance in our thinking, and (2) explain, so far as possible, why intuitively appealing judgments not countenanced by the theory have the appeal they do. See Rawls, *A Theory of Justice*, esp. pp. 20-21 and 48-51, and Sidgwick, *The Methods of Ethics*, 7th ed. (Macmillan, 1907).

22. As the contexts should make clear, throughout the ensuing discussion "the maximin principle" refers to chapter 2's maximin principle of equality while "MP" refers to a maximin principle of justice that focuses on the worst-off individual.

23. The qualification "probably" is necessary because if the weighted additive principle's weighting scheme were extreme enough, then BOP would also rank C worst on that view.

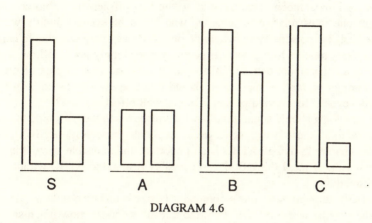

DIAGRAM 4.6

The foregoing suggests two ways BOP and MP are disanalogous. First, because BOP's rankings depend on the principle of equality it is combined with, we need not accept or reject BOP simpliciter. Although we *may* choose to accept or reject it solely in its own right, BOP's plausibility may vary depending on the principle with which it is combined. For example, I think some reasons for worrying about BOP when it is combined with the maximin principle do not apply, or matter less, given the other principles.

Second, perhaps MP's most glaring and important shortcoming is that in ranking outcomes it only focuses on the worst-off person's level, wholly ignoring everyone else. This is why, according to MP, C is better than B and B better than A in diagram 4.5. By contrast, the aspects of inequality employing BOP do not simply rank outcomes by focusing on the best-off person's level. Thus, although in diagram 4.6 A's best-off person is better off than B's who in turn is better off than C's, this by itself implies nothing about A, B, and C's inequality. Indeed, as suggested, B may be better than A and C on each aspect involving BOP, despite its best-off person being better off than C's, yet worse off than A's.

Although BOP does not take account of how everybody fares relative to everybody else, it is *not* guilty of exclusively focusing on one person's situation. BOP is a comparative view that provides a way of assessing *each* person's situation—that is, complaint—regarding inequality. Admittedly, some complaints are ignored when BOP is combined with the maximin principle, but this shortcoming, if it is one, is due as much to maximin's nature as to BOP's. Combined with both the additive and weighted additive principles, BOP yields rankings taking each person's complaint into account. Of course, whether or not BOP measures complaints in a plausible way may still be an open question. But clearly the analogy between MP and BOP breaks down precisely at one of MP's weakest points.

If we turn to the question of whether BOP measures complaints plausibly, an analogy with MP may seem apparent. One of MP's shortcomings is that it expresses tremendous concern for the worst-off person but no concern for someone ever-so-slightly better off than she. Similarly, one might argue, BOP expresses tremendous concern for how someone fares relative to the best-off person but no concern for how someone fares relative to someone who might be ever-so-slightly worse off than the best- off person. More generally, one might ask why one should care how someone fares relative to the best-off person yet seemingly not care how she fares relative to all the others better off than she. If it is bad to be worse off than one person through no fault of one's own should it not be even worse to be worse off than two—even if the second person is not as well off as the first?

The foregoing should sound familiar. It corresponds to the reasoning underlying the relative to all those better off view of complaints (henceforth, *ATBO*). But, as I argued in chapter 2, though ATBO is an important and plausible view, it is not the only such view. Thus, I think BOP can plausibly respond to ATBO without necessarily discrediting it.

On BOP, knowing someone's complaint is size x tells one nothing about how many she may be worse off than by up to x. Still, x reflects how much she would have to be raised for her to no longer be worse off than another, and hence no longer have a complaint regarding inequality. This is not an unimportant or implausible feature for a view about individual complaints to express. Moreover, it isn't that BOP cares how someone fares relative to the best-off person but not how she fares relative to anyone else; rather it is that, ceteris paribus, *whatever* our concerns about how she fares relative to everyone else, they will be fully met if she is raised to the best-off person's level.

BOP's plausibility may be clearer if we look closer at the position threatening it. On ATBO someone's complaint reflects how much she is worse off than all those better off than she. Assuming, for simplicity, this is just the total by which she is worse off than others, one can see how ATBO plausibly expresses the view that, regarding inequality, being worse off than 1 person by 1,000 units is not as bad as being worse off than 1 person by 1,000 and 10 others by 900. On ATBO one's complaint would be 1,000 in the one case and 10,000 in the other, whereas on BOP one's complaint would be 1,000 in both cases. Notice, however, on ATBO, as on BOP, knowing someone's complaint is size x tells one nothing about how many she may be worse off than by up to x. For example, a complaint of 1,000 may reflect being worse off than 1 person by 1,000, or 500 people by 2 each. Moreover, on ATBO, unlike BOP, there will be little correlation between a complaint's size and the extent to which improvements of a given amount will reduce the complaint.

Now ultimately it is not clear one really should be more concerned about someone who is 2 units worse off than 500 people than about someone who is 500 units worse off than 1 person, but even if one should, egalitarians would presumably not favor raising the former person 500 units. Regarding inequality, however great our concern for the former person's situation, it should be completely alleviated if she is raised 2 units. On the other hand, however much less our initial concern for the latter person might be (in virtue of her only being worse off than one rather than 500) some of that concern would remain even if she were raised 200—100 times more than the amount that would fully satisfy us in the first person's case! The reason for this is apparent. Once the former is raised 2 she will no longer be worse off than anyone else, whereas until the latter is raised 500 there will still be someone she is worse off than through no fault of her own.

In sum, in response to the charge that BOP expresses great concern about how someone fares relative to the best-off person, but no concern about how she fares relative to anyone else—including those ever-so-slightly worse off than the best-off person—one might claim the following: first, however great our concerns may be about how someone fares relative to those not best off, one knows those concerns will be fully satisfied if she is raised to the best-off person's level; and second, such a charge misses BOP's point, where someone's complaint reflects not so much the extent of our concern about her relative situation,[24] but the extent to which her situation would have to be improved before she no longer had a complaint. A similar defense of MP is not plausible.[25] Hence, here too, the purported analogy between MP and BOP fails.

One respect in which MP and BOP are alike is that both yield implausible judgments. However, the importance of this similarity is an open question due to (yet) another disanalogy between MP and BOP.

The maximin principle of justice was offered as the primary component in a theory of justice. That is, in most cases the better of two situations regarding social justice was simply to be the one judged as such by maximin. So if there were cases where MP's judgments were obviously unacceptable, MP clearly had to be rejected or revised. Thus, given maximin's central role in his theory, Rawls only had to consider diagrams like 4.5, and the extent of MP's deviation from our considered moral judgments, to know he needed a version of maximin other than MP.

BOP's case is markedly different. BOP has not been offered as the primary component in a theory of equality, but merely as one important element in such a theory. Specifically, we have argued inequality consists of as many as twelve aspects of which only three involve BOP. Thus, though BOP's aspects[26] yield implausible judgments in cases like diagram 4.6—as, for example, in implying B's inequality would be better than A's—this does not show those aspects should be rejected or revised. For, as observed earlier, for each of inequality's aspects we may be able to construct *some* situations where the aspect's implications would be deeply implausible. This would not show each aspect to be untenable. It might simply reflect inequality's complexity and the attendant fact that, all things considered, any given aspect's judgment may sometimes be clearly and strongly outweighed by other aspects' judgments.

Considering diagram 4.6, it is fairly easy reconciling our firm intuitive judgment that A's inequality is better than B's with the fact that BOP's aspects yield the

24. It may or may not do this depending on one's view of the matter.

25. To defend MP along similar lines one would need to show that maximizing the worst-off person's level would also improve (maximize?) the positions of everyone else poorly off; so that, in essence, alleviating our concern regarding the worst-off person would entail alleviating any other concerns we might have about others. But despite Rawls's intriguing claims about "chain connectedness" and "close knitness," it is apparent that maximizing the position of the worst-off person may do nothing to improve the positions of others badly off—indeed, it may require worsening them. (Rawls would agree. He does not even contend that chain connectedness and close knitness hold for all societies and circumstances, and he certainly would not contend they hold between each of society's *individuals*. At most, Rawls thinks that under favorable circumstances they would hold between the "representative" members of society's groups. Cf. *A Theory of Justice*, pp. 81–83.)

26. Here, as elsewhere, I use "BOP's aspects" as shorthand for "the aspects involving BOP."

opposite judgment. One need merely observe that A will probably be better than B in terms of *each* of inequality's other aspects and acknowledge that, despite their importance, BOP's aspects are not more important and (therefore) do not outweigh or play a greater role in our thinking than all the other aspects combined. Indeed, even if only one or two aspects judged A's inequality better than B's one could retain that judgment without revising BOP, depending of course on both the relative importance of the various aspects and the relative strengths of the judgments they yielded.[27]

The preceding suggests that to show BOP must be revised it is not enough to find cases where BOP's judgments[28] seem implausible all things considered. One must find a case where there is *no* respect in which BOP's judgment seems plausible. But this may be difficult to do in a non–question-begging manner. For example, in diagram 4.6 one might insist that in *no* respect is A's inequality worse than B's, hence BOP must be revised. But, of course, BOP's advocate may reject such a claim. Surely, she may aver, A's inequality is worse than B's in at least one respect. After all, the gaps between the best-off and those who are not best-off are larger in A than in B; and for each person in B worse off than another, there is someone in A worse off than another by an even greater amount.

Is there *no* respect in which A's inequality is worse than B's—so BOP needs revision—or is A worse than B in some respects, reflected by BOP, though these are outweighed by others in which A is better? This question may not have a definitive answer, but I think one way of pushing the analogy between MP and BOP plausibly supports the former position.

Consider diagram 4.7. A is *perfectly* equal, and BOP supports this judgment.[29] B's worst-off group is slightly better off than those in A, so B may be better than A regarding a maximin principle of justice. Still, let us suppose B is *terribly* unequal, and that BOP also supports this judgment. Next, suppose A and B are large populations, say, two billion each. Finally, let C be just like A, except it contains one extra person who happens to be better off than B's best-off group.

Focusing on how people compare to the best-off person, as BOP does, C's inequality would be worse than B's. Many may find this hard to accept. Regarding inequality, A is *much* better than B in every respect. Even if C's inequality is worse than A's, it may seem implausible that there is any significant respect in which in a population of two billion the mere addition of one extra person could make *such* a difference as to transform a *perfect* situation into a *terrible* one. More generally, it may seem no significant aspect of inequality should be so sensitive that the mere

27. If A is *slightly* better than B according to one aspect and B *much* better than A according to another, then, ceteris paribus, the former aspect would have to be much more important than the latter before its judgment would carry the day. On the other hand, if A is *much* better than B according to one aspect and B *slightly* better than A according to several others, then the former judgment might carry the day even if the former aspect were not more important than any, much less all, of the others.

28. Here, as elsewhere, I use "BOP's judgments" as shorthand for "the judgments yielded by the aspects involving BOP" and of course similar expressions are to be interpreted similarly. Cf. note 25.

29. Given notes 25 and 27 this note may be superfluous, but lest there be any confusion: here and elsewhere I frequently use "BOP" as shorthand for "each of the aspects involving BOP." I trust context makes plain when "BOP" is being so used and when it is not.

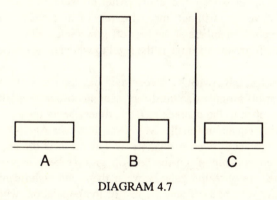

DIAGRAM 4.7

presence or absence of a few extra people in a very large population could *radically* alter its ranking.

So an objection to BOP might be raised like the second objection to MP noted earlier. One might claim that focusing on the best-off person may seriously distort our judgment because the best-off person's condition may not accurately reflect the situation's overall inequality. Perhaps the best-off person's condition is simply an anomaly or fluke.

Even in this case BOP and MP are not perfectly analogous. Rawls was concerned about social justice, about the principles and institutions governing society, whereas egalitarians may be concerned about natural justice. And it is less clear one may appropriately identify or treat someone's situation as anomalous where one's concern is natural rather than social justice. Still, suppose one ultimately decides BOP must be modified. How might one plausibly guard against the danger that focusing on comparisons to the best-off person can seriously distort a situation's inequality?

4.8 Modifying BOP: Several Suggestions

One immediate suggestion, following Rawls, would be to focus on the "representative member of the best-off group" instead of the best-off person. Unfortunately, it is not clear how to unpack the notion of the "representative member of the best-off group" other than by equating it with the average member of the best-off group. Yet replacing BOP with a "relative to the average member of the best-off group" view of complaints (henceforth, *AMBOG*) involves adopting precisely the sort of hybrid view part 1 argues against.

AMBOG's problem is that, depending on its construal, it will face similar shortcomings to those of the Average or Proportional Average Principle. Without repeating the arguments here, let us briefly recall some of these shortcomings. If AMBOG is construed along the lines of the Average Principle, so the best-off group's size can vary, then even transfers from the best-off group's worst-off members to others much worse off might worsen inequality. After all, such transfers might raise the best-off group's average, without improving *any* of its members, by lowering the (previously) worst-off members of the best-off group into a different group. And, of course, the best-off group's average is the level to which people would be compared on AMBOG.

On the other hand, if AMBOG is construed like the Proportional Average Principle, so the best-off group's size must represent a constant proportion of the population, then it is open to the charges of (sometimes) being misleading, ad hoc, and arbitrarily treating equals unequally. Moreover, however AMBOG is construed, it will be indifferent about even exchanges within the best-off group; even if, for example, an even exchange from the best-off group's best- to worst-off members would completely remove the gaps between them and significantly decrease the gaps between the very best-off and the rest of the population, while one from the best-off group's worst- to best-off members would significantly increase the gaps between the very best-off and everyone else.

AMBOG faces other problems we need not pursue. Suffice it to say, I think focusing on the "representative member of the best-off group" would be a mistake if it were understood in terms of the average member of the best-off group.

One might suggest that instead of focusing on how people fare relative to the "representative" member of the best-off group, we should focus on how people fare relative to "each member of the best-off group" (henceforth, *EMBOG*). Although a natural suggestion, I leave it for others to pursue. Ultimately I think EMBOG faces numerous shortcomings, including losing sight of perhaps the main point of BOP.

On BOP there is a significant correlation between the size of someone's complaint and how much her situation has to be improved before she no longer has a complaint. This correlation reflects much of the spirit and reasoning underlying BOP. Correspondingly, insofar as one is interested in preserving BOP's core insights one will want, so far as possible, to retain a similar[30] correlation. But on EMBOG, as with ATBO, no such correlation obtains. Someone with a relatively small initial complaint may still have much of her complaint remaining after being raised a lot, whereas someone with a relatively large complaint may only need a small improvement to eliminate her complaint.

This is not to say there aren't plausible reasons for expanding one's focus from the best-off person to the best-off group's members. There are. But I think the reasons in question would carry one a large step away from the reasoning underlying BOP toward that underlying ATBO. The question then is whether one can plausibly revise BOP without forsaking the source of its appeal. Specifically, given that the best-off person may be anomalous, can we prevent BOP from seriously distorting our egalitarian judgments other than by shifting our focus from the best-off person to (either the average member or each of the members of) the best-off group.

Let us consider two suggestions. In presenting BOP's problem, I wrote "no significant aspect of inequality should be so sensitive that the mere presence

---

30. Given the need to revise BOP, preserving the *exact* correlation may be impossible.

or absence of a few extra people in a very large population could *radically* alter its ranking." One suggestion in response to this view would be that BOP is *not* a significant aspect in the cases in question, though it *is* a significant aspect in other cases—and hence rightly plays an important role in our judgments about such cases.

Instead of revising BOP, the first suggestion limits its scope or force. Roughly, the idea is to weight BOP inversely proportional to the degree the best-off person's condition is anomalous, so the more anomalous the best-off person's situation the less weight BOP would receive. With an appropriate weighting scheme, or discount function, one need not worry about BOP seriously distorting our judgments in (relevantly) anomalous cases, as in such cases BOP would hardly affect our judgments.

The first suggestion faces implementation problems, for example, finding a non-ad hoc way of measuring degrees of anomaly, or an appropriate weighting scheme, or "drop off" rate, for BOP vis-à-vis inequality's other aspects. Still, without minimizing such problems they do not, at least theoretically, seem insurmountable. Moreover, the suggestion accords with the intuitive notion that as circumstances vary so too does the plausibility of inequality's aspects.

Unfortunately, the first suggestion faces another problem, which may be illustrated as follows. Suppose p and q are the best-off in A and B, respectively. Suppose p's and q's situations are not anomalous, so that on the first suggestion BOP's aspects rightly play a significant role in our overall judgments of A and B. Next, suppose that, giving each of inequality's aspects its due consideration and weight,[31] we would judge that, all things considered, B's inequality is worse than A's but that were it not for the significant influence of BOP's aspects on our judgment about B—which, as it were, tip the balance in A's favor—B would be better than A. Then on the first suggestion adding an extra person, r, to B who was *much* better off than everyone else might make the resulting situation's inequality (B*'s) *better* than A's. This is absurd.

Clearly the mere addition of someone *much* better off than everyone else would, if anything, only worsen a situation's inequality, not improve it. Thus, since by hypothesis B's inequality is worse than A's, all things considered, B*'s inequality would be even worse than A's, not better.

Let us spell out why the first suggestion has the counterintuitive implication noted. Suppose r is so much better off than everyone else in B* her condition is very anomalous. Then on the first suggestion BOP would hardly affect our judgment regarding B*'s inequality. Now, by hypothesis, B would have been better than A but for the significant weight attached to BOP's aspects in assessing B. This raises the possibility that B* would also be better than A if one ignored BOP's aspects in assessing B*.

To be sure, B* will be worse than B in terms of inequality's other aspects. But, unlike with BOP, in large populations the other aspects' judgments will not be significantly altered by the mere presence of one extra person who is very well off. So supposing B is a very large population, the extent to which

31. See chapter 5.

B* is worse than B in terms of aspects not involving BOP may not be enough to make B* worse than A if, as we are temporarily assuming, one ignores BOP's aspects in assessing B*. In other words, it is possible the extent to which B would be judged better than A will be greater than the extent to which B* would be judged worse than B insofar as one's judgments of B and B* were not influenced by BOP's aspects.

One can see, then, B* might be better than A if B*'s ranking were not influenced by BOP's aspects. But then on the first suggestion B*'s inequality might also be better than A's, all things considered, since, given r's situation, BOP's aspects would hardly affect our assessment of B*.

In essence, the main worry about BOP was that focusing on the best-off person could make a situation's inequality seem worse than it was. It is ironic therefore that on the first suggestion the net effect of adding someone better off than everyone else could be to improve inequality even if doing so were condemned by every aspect not involving BOP.[32] Surely, such a position is not the most plausible way to capture BOP's spirit.

The second suggestion can be put in Rawlsian terms, but it must be interpreted carefully. On the second suggestion, instead of focusing on comparisons to the best-off person, one should focus on comparisons to the "representative member of the best-off group." But this notion must not be understood as the best-off group's "average" member or, for that matter, as a hypothetical person whose characteristics are somehow "representative" of those best-off. Instead, the "representative member of the best-off group" is to be the best-off person whose position is still "representative" of the situation's inequality.[33]

Intuitively, the second suggestion will measure someone's complaint by comparing them with the best-off person, unless that person's condition is anomalous. In that case, the comparison will be made to the best-off person whose condition is not anomalous. Thus, depending on the situation and the criteria for determining when someone's condition is anomalous, the best-off group's "representative" member may be the best-off, second best-off, or fiftieth best-off. Presumably, however, for large populations at most a tiny percentage will have anomalous situations.

One can see how the second suggestion may satisfy most of what really concerns BOP's advocates, for while in theory egalitarians may want each to be no worse off than *any* others through no fault of their own, in fact they would be almost completely satisfied if each were no worse off than the representative member of the best-off group. After all, raising someone to the level in question would not only make her as well off as the vast majority in her society, it would make her as well off as *all* others whose conditions were not anomalous. Surely, as the second

32. Notice, such a move would *also* be condemned by BOP's aspects. It is because such aspects might receive less weight on the first suggestion, not because they would approve such a move, that the first suggestion has such an implausible implication.

33. For our purposes the "representative best-off person" would be more perspicuous than the "representative member of the best-off group." But given Rawls's influence I suspect many would find the former usage grating. The important point, of course, is to not let the terminology obscure the concept it expresses.

suggestion implies, such a person would have virtually no complaint.[34] Moreover, measuring complaints as it does, the second suggestion preserves BOP's significant correlation between complaint sizes and the extent to which improvements reduce complaints. Thus, someone worse off than the representative member of the best-off group by 2 will have a complaint of 2 and, even if others stand between them, 2 is all she will need to be raised to alleviate her complaint. Likewise, even if the representative member of the best-off group is the only one better off than someone, raising that person 250 will still only halve her complaint if she began worse off by 500.

The second suggestion is attractive but not entirely satisfactory. Focusing on how people compare with the representative member of the best-off group, the second suggestion *completely* ignores how people compare with any (anomalously) even better off. This implies one could dispense with the qualifiers "virtually" and "almost" in the preceding paragraph, that someone as well off as the representative member of the best-off group would have *no* complaint, and hence one should be *completely* satisfied if each were no worse off than the representative member of the best-off group. But this does not seem quite plausible. A situation where everyone is perfectly equal except for one extra person much better off may not be *significantly* worse than the perfectly equal situation that would obtain but for the extra person; still, it seems no aspect of inequality should be *completely* indifferent between the two situations.

In response to the foregoing the second suggestion might be modified. One way would be to measure individual complaints as a function of two components, the first corresponding to the gap between the individual and the representative member of the best-off group, the second to the gap between the representative member of the best-off group and the best-off person. The second component would be heavily discounted relative to the first, so complaint sizes would be almost wholly determined by how people compared with the representative member of the best-off group. Still, the second component would reflect the extent to which someone at the representative member's level would have some complaint, however slight, depending on how much she would need to be raised before she were no longer worse off than *any*.

A modified version of the second suggestion retains a significant correlation between complaint sizes and the extent to which improvements reduce complaints. Moreover, it expresses both the theoretical ideal that it is bad for someone to be worse off than any others through no fault of her own, and the practical notion that someone would have virtually no complaint if she were as well off as all whose conditions were not anomalous. Such a view neither ignores the best-off person nor allows her condition to distort our judgments seriously, for when the best-off person's condition is anomalous it will worsen inequality but not significantly. To be sure, such a view needs a way of determining when someone's condition is anomalous, along with a weighting scheme for counting the residual complaint of someone who is as well off as all whose conditions are not anomalous but not as

---

34. Someone not accepting this claim would probably not see a need for revising BOP in the first place.

well off as the best-off. But though daunting, these issues are not, in principle, insoluble and are precisely the sort needing resolution if one is to retain a view like BOP while avoiding both its shortcomings and those of other alternatives. Thus, a modified version of the second suggestion seems a promising way of capturing most of BOP's attractions.

4.9 Summary of BOP

Let us sum up our discussion of BOP. Some may think a position focusing on how people compare with the best-off person (BOP) will need modification for the same reasons as a maximin principle of justice focusing on the worst-off person (MP). But there are important disanalogies between BOP and MP. MP focuses on the position of only one person, the worst-off. BOP focuses on the comparative positions of each person relative to the best-off. On MP our concerns about how all but the worst-off fare are ignored. On BOP our concerns about how people fare relative to those not best-off will be fully met if they are raised to the best-off's level. MP was offered as the primary component in a theory of social justice. BOP was offered as one of many aspects of the notion of inequality. Given their disanalogies it is not clear BOP needs revision as MP does. Although BOP, like MP, sometimes yields implausible judgments, this may be due to inequality's complexity rather than BOP's inadequacy.

Though BOP may be defensible, we saw one might want to revise BOP to prevent distortion of our judgments when the best-off person's condition is anomalous. In considering possible revisions of BOP, we argued against shifting attention from the best-off person to either the average member or each of the members of the best-off group. We also argued against simply lessening BOP's weight in cases where the best-off person's condition was anomalous. Instead, we suggested measuring individual complaints as a function of two factors: the gap between the person and the "representative member of the best-off group" and the gap between the "representative member of the best-off group" and the best-off person—where the second factor would be heavily discounted relative to the first, and where the "representative member of the best-off group" would be the best-off person whose condition was not anomalous.

I have examined BOP closely because, given its apparent similarity to MP, I suspect many may initially regard it as the least plausible of chapter 2's elements, or perhaps the one most in need of revision. Although I have suggested one way of revising BOP, I am less attached to my particular suggestion than to the conviction that BOP's spirit and underlying reasoning represent an important element of inequality that must somehow be accounted for.

The reader will notice that my suggested revision of BOP is much more cumbersome than BOP, and that there will be no extensional difference between the two in cases where the best-off person's condition is not anomalous. Therefore, having indicated at length why and how I think BOP may be revised, I shall henceforth assume that the representative member of the best off group is also the best-off person and so, for simplicity, continue to use BOP rather than the proposed alternative. I trust my reasons for doing this are clear, and that bearing this discussion in mind the reader will not be misled by my doing so.

4.10 The Maximin Principle of Equality

Let me end part 2 by briefly commenting on the maximin principle of equality (MPE). It is unclear how best to capture the spirit and reasoning underlying MPE. For reasons presented in part 1 and briefly reviewed in discussing BOP, one cannot simply adopt Rawls's solution of focusing on the "representative member of the worst-off group" if that is interpreted as the average member of the worst-off group. Nor can one handle MPE similarly to BOP by primarily focusing on the worst-off person whose position is not anomalous. Unlike BOP, there is a close analogy between MPE and the maximin principle of justice.[35] Correspondingly, it is implausible to focus on the worst-off person whose condition is not anomalous and ignore everyone else—including those ever-so-slightly better off than she.

Like the maximin principle of justice, MPE should express a special concern for society's worst-off. Specifically, MPE should express our special concern for how the worst-off fare relative to others. There are various ways one might do this. The point to stress is that the concern maximin expresses is not merely a concern for any particular real or hypothetical person—like the worst-off person, or the worst-off person whose condition is not anomalous, or the "average" member of the worst-off group, or even the "representative" member of the worst-off group. Nor is it a concern for some real or abstract entity "the worst-off group."

Insofar as MPE focuses on the relative position of the worst-off group, it needs to focus on the relative positions of *each* of that group's members. And, of course, insofar as we are more concerned about someone's position the worse off she is, complaints must be weighted accordingly. Thus, in keeping with maximin's spirit, as well as other considerations presented in this work, one would prefer an even transfer from a member of a better-off group to a member of the worst-off group to a similar transfer within the worst-off group, but if the latter occurs MPE should approve the transfer only if it reduces the gaps between better- and worse-off.

35. The analogy is close but not perfect. As noted before, the maximin principle of justice was offered as the primary component of a theory of social justice, whereas the maximin principle of equality was merely offered as one important element of the notion of inequality. On the other hand, those pushing the analogy might contend that while the maximin principle of justice was offered as the primary component of a theory of *social* justice, it was only offered as one important element of the notion of justice (which includes the notion of social justice as but one of its components).

5

Approaches for Measuring Inequality

At the end of chapter 2, I observed that once we see what the notion of inequality involves, we may come to think it as either largely inconsistent and severely limited, or complex, multifaceted, and partially incomplete. Even if we ultimately decide that the notion of inequality is "merely" complex rather than inconsistent, as I have been assuming since chapter 2, its *practical* significance will be fairly minor unless we are generally able to compare situations regarding inequality. After all, it can be of little consequence that we regard inequality as bad, if we can't usually tell whether one situation's inequality is worse than another's. Eventually, therefore, the egalitarian would like to arrive at a measure that would enable her to accurately compare situations regarding inequality. In this chapter, I examine some measures of inequality economists have offered. In doing this, I note some significant parallels, as well as points of disagreement, between my work and theirs. I then offer my own suggestion for how one might best proceed if one wants to capture accurately a complex notion like inequality.

Four background remarks. First, though the economists' measures were offered as measures of *economic* inequality, I shall, except for Atkinson's measure, be considering them as they would apply to inequality of welfare. This does not affect my conclusions.

Second, this chapter does not offer (anything like) a comprehensive list of economists' measures of inequality. Nor is its aim to identify and critique the currently most popular measures. In fact, a fair amount of my discussion focuses on measures economists regard as passé. Still, as we will see, there is value in focusing on the measures I do; for they illuminate and support many of this book's claims and, importantly, vice versa.

Third, in this chapter and the following two I offer many criticisms of economists, but few of philosophers. Lest this be misinterpreted, let me point out that this is a case where criticism is a form of flattery. There is virtually nothing in the philosophical literature that is even relevant to the issues raised in these chapters, whereas economists have published work that is not only relevant but interesting and suggestive. Thus, my criticisms of economists' work testifies to the importance and relevance of that work to this book's concerns.

Finally, some readers unfamiliar with economic formulas may have difficulty with sections 5.1 and 5.3. Though I have tried to clearly explain the formulas presented, there is no reason to get bogged down in the mathematics. This chapter's central points should be accessible by simply skimming the formulas and reading the accompanying text. In any event, let me add that later chapters do not presuppose an understanding of the economists' measures.

5.1 The Statistical Measures

In this section, I shall consider the so-called statistical or summary measures. These include: the *range*, the *relative mean deviation*, the *variance*, the *coefficient of variation*, the *standard deviation of the logarithms*, and the *Gini coefficient*. These measures have been widely discussed in the economics literature, and there are well-known difficulties associated with each of them.[1] Still, despite their difficulties, each of these measures has, to a greater or lesser extent, been advocated as a plausible measure of inequality. In the ensuing discussion, I shall briefly examine each of these measures and suggest the source of their appeal. In doing this, important similarities will be noted between these measures and the theoretical results of chapter 2.

A preliminary comment. One criticism often made of the Gini coefficient is that it is implausible for comparing situations whose average levels differ greatly. A similar criticism has been made of the variance and, for reasons to be presented in chapter 6, I think each of the statistical measures lose plausibility when applied to such situations. In response to such criticism, advocates of the Gini coefficient have contended that even if the Gini coefficient is not acceptable for comparing all situations, it is still a useful and plausible measure for comparing situations whose average levels do not differ greatly. A similar claim might be made on behalf of the other statistical measures. Therefore, throughout the following discussion I shall assume that the statistical measures are to be employed for comparing situations that have the same number of people, the same total amount of welfare, and, hence, the same average levels of welfare. This assumption enables me to ignore μ and n in the statistical measures and, in so doing, ensures that I am comparing situations for which the statistical measures seem most plausible when I consider why they have been offered as measures of inequality. (The reason the statistical measures seem most plausible on the assumption in question will become clearer in chapters 6 and 7 where the roles of μ and n are explained and criticized. Briefly, it can be put as follows. The statistical measures contain certain features—μ and/or n—that yield controversial answers to the questions of whether, and to what extent, inequality is affected by a population's level or size. However, this is not intuitively evident except in cases where the population's level or size varies greatly. In fact, it turns out that the statistical measures' controversial features can be ignored in cases where the numbers of people and total amounts of welfare are the same, since in such cases the measures' orderings are not influenced by the features in question. Intuitively, then, certain shortcomings of the statistical measures will be most evi-

1. Among the many discussions of these measures in the economics literature, I have found A. K. Sen's to be particularly useful. In presenting these measures and the shortcomings they face, my discussion closely follows the one he provides in *On Economic Inequality* (Clarendon Press, 1973), chap. 2.

dent in cases where the levels or sizes of the populations vary; hence, the statistical measures will seem most plausible for comparing situations in which these factors are constant.)

So one way of looking at my task in this section is as follows. Statisticians have devised a large number of formulas to measure or reveal various features of a given population or curve. Of these, several have been offered by economists as plausible measures of inequality. I want to suggest what it is about the selected measures that, at least for a certain range of cases, gives them their plausibility as measures of inequality.

The Range

Let me begin my consideration of the statistical measures by looking first at the range. The range is the simplest of the statistical measures of inequality. Its formula is given by:

$$E = (\text{Max}_i \; y_i - \text{Min}_i \; y_i)/\mu$$

where $\text{Max}_i \; y_i$ and $\text{Min}_i \; y_i$ are the levels of welfare of the best- and worst-off individuals, respectively, and μ is the society's average level of welfare. Now clearly, for the sort of worlds I am presently interested in, that is, worlds where the total amount of welfare and the number of people are fixed, the average level of welfare, μ, will be constant. This means that for the purpose of ordering such worlds, the denominator of E may be ignored, as E's orderings will be identical to E*'s, where

$$E^* = (\text{Max}_i \; y_i - \text{Min}_i \; y_i)$$

According to the range, then, A's inequality will be worse than B's if and only if the gap between the best-off person and the worst-off person is larger in A than it is in B.

Serious criticisms have been leveled at the range as a measure of inequality. The most obvious is that it completely ignores the pattern of distribution between the extremes. Consider diagram 5.1.

All things considered, most would probably say that B's inequality was worse than A's, since in B one-half of the population is much worse off than the other, whereas in A the vast majority of the population is perfectly equal, though a few are fortunate to be better off, and a few are unfortunate to be worse off. The range, of course, focusing as it does on the extremes, yields the judgment that A's inequality is worse than B's. This sort of result has led many to reject the range as a plausible measure of inequality.

A second criticism of the range, closely connected with the first, is that it violates the Pigou-Dalton condition, according to which any (even) transfer from a worse-off to a better-off person worsens inequality.[2] Many have felt that any adequate measure of inequality must meet at least this minimal condition. Clearly,

---

2. See sections 3.4 and 3.6 for an extended discussion of the Pigou-Dalton condition and an explanation of the qualifying parenthetical "even."

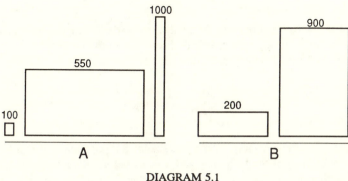

DIAGRAM 5.1

however, the range fails to do this, as it fails to reflect transfers between people who are not at the extremes.

To these criticisms, the general considerations of chapters 2 and 3 might be added. We have seen that our notion of inequality is complex and multifaceted. Correspondingly, I would argue that the range is inadequate as a measure of inequality because it does not recognize and capture the full complexity of that notion.

In light of such shortcomings one might wonder why the range was ever offered as a measure of inequality? To this question, I suggest the following answer. In chapter 2, I argued that in accordance with certain intuitions the size of someone's complaint regarding inequality would depend upon how that person fared relative to the best-off person. I also argued that in accordance with certain other intuitions—maximin intuitions—the worse of two worlds regarding inequality would be the one in which the worst-off person had the most about which to complain. Together, these intuitions combine to support the judgment that how bad a world is regarding inequality depends upon how badly the worst-off person fares relative to the best-off person. Now it is essentially *this* judgment that the range yields. I believe, therefore, that it is from these two sets of intuitions that the range derives its plausibility.

Insofar as we are caught in the grip of the intuitions underlying the relative to the best-off person view of complaints and the maximin principle of equality (see chapter 2) a measure like the range will have great plausibility. However, it must be recognized, as advocates of the range apparently did not, that the intuitions in question are not the *only* plausible intuitions underlying and influencing our egalitarian judgments. Thus, advocates of the range were mistaken in simply offering the range as a measure of inequality, rather than as a measure of one particular aspect of that notion. Similarly, however, opponents of the range were mistaken in simply focusing on its shortcomings as a measure of inequality and then dismissing it as implausible. Had they carefully considered the range's properties and the orderings it yielded, they might have seen that despite its faults it had a fair amount of intuitive appeal. This, in turn, may have led them to see that *certain* egalitarian intuitions would support a measure like the range.

The Relative Mean Deviation

In certain respects my discussion of the relative mean deviation, as well as the other statistical measures, closely resembles my discussion of the range.

The formula for the relative mean deviation is:

$$M = \sum_{i=1}^{n} |\mu - y_i| / n\mu$$

where, as applied to any society, S, n is the size of S's population, y represents, in turn, the level of each of S's members, and μ is, as before, S's average level. Once again, for worlds of the sort I am presently interested in—where n and μ will be constant—the denominator of M may be ignored. For such worlds, M's ordering will be identical to M*'s, where:

$$M^* = \sum_{i=1}^{n} |\mu - y|$$

M* sums up the absolute value of the differences between the average level and the level of each individual. In doing this, M* measures the total deviation from the average. So, according to the relative mean deviation, A's inequality will be worse than B's if and only if the total deviation from the average is larger in A than it is in B.

As with the range, the relative mean deviation has been criticized for violating the Pigou-Dalton condition, as it is insensitive to transfers within the same side of the mean. So, for example, while a transfer of 10 units of welfare from someone 1,000 units below the mean to someone 20 units below the mean would worsen inequality according to the Pigou-Dalton condition, such a transfer would have no effect according to the relative mean deviation as the total amount of deviation from the mean would remain unchanged.

Given that the relative mean deviation is insensitive to transfers *within* the same side of the mean, it directly follows that it is insensitive between transfers of any given size *to* the same side of the mean. As we saw in chapter 3, this is another feature many would find objectionable. All things considered, most egalitarians believe it would be better for an above average person to transfer n units of welfare to someone way below the average than to someone only a little below the average—that, for instance, it would be better to transfer 10 units of welfare to someone 1,000 units below the average than to someone 20 units below the average. However, according to the relative mean deviation there would be no reason to prefer the one transfer to the other, as both would reduce the total deviation from the mean by the same amount. (The reader will notice that a similar criticism could have been made against the range.)

Again, to these criticisms the considerations of chapters 2 and 3 might be added. Those considerations indicate that the relative mean deviation is inadequate as a measure of inequality because it fails to capture fully the complexity of that notion.

Like the range, the relative mean deviation has evident difficulties. So, as with the range, we may wonder why the relative mean deviation was offered as a measure of inequality. Here, too, I think our answer lies in the fact that while the relative mean deviation may not capture the *whole* of our notion of inequality, to a large extent it captures one very important *aspect* of that notion. Specifically, it reflects the combination of those intuitions underlying the relative to the average view of complaints and the additive principle of equality; for, as I pointed out in chapter 2, together those intuitions support the judgment that the worse of two worlds is the one in which the deviation from the average is greatest.

It is not surprising, then, that the relative mean deviation should have been offered as a measure of inequality. Because it appears to capture certain of our egalitarian intuitions, it will seem plausible insofar as one is caught in the grip of those intuitions. These considerations suggest that, as with the range, it would be a mistake to simply regard the relative mean deviation as a measure of inequality and dismiss it as inadequate. To do this would be to miss the source of its appeal—to fail to realize that it may capture some, though not all, of our egalitarian intuitions.

The Variance

Let us next consider the variance, whose formula is:

$$V = \sum_{i=1}^{n} (\mu - y_i)^2/n$$

For worlds of the sort we have been considering, V's ordering will be the same as V*'s, where:

$$V^* = \sum_{i=1}^{n} (\mu - y_i)^2$$

This means that for such worlds the only significant difference between the variance and the relative mean deviation is that the variance first squares the differences between the average level of welfare and the level of each individual before adding them together. (This is the only relevant difference between V* and M*.) The effect of this squaring feature is to give larger differences from the mean extra weight. For example, being 10 units worse off than the average would count for more than simply twice being 5 units worse off than the average, as the former would increase the variance by 100, whereas the latter would increase it by 25.

Because of its squaring feature the variance avoids two of the criticisms raised against the relative mean deviation. It does not violate the Pigou-Dalton condition and is not indifferent between transfers to the same side of the mean. (So, if p is worse off than q, it will always be better to raise p, n units, rather than q.) Still, the variance is not without problems as a measure of inequality. From a moral perspective, the squaring feature is an arbitrary way of reflecting the view that large deviations should be given extra weight. This renders the accuracy of the variance open to doubt, thereby lessening its plausibility. In addition, the variance is liable to the familiar general criticism that it does not fully capture and reflect inequality's complexity. (As noted earlier, the variance is often criticized as implausible when comparing situations whose average levels vary greatly. As this criticism does not apply to the kinds of situations I am presently interested in, I shall not discuss it here. However, this is an important line of criticism I shall return to in chapter 6.)

In chapter 2, I argued that the intuitions underlying the relative to the average view of complaints could combine with the intuitions underlying the weighted additive principle to influence our egalitarian judgments. Moreover, I pointed out that according to these intuitions, inequality might be measured by, first, comparing the level of each individual to the average, second, attaching weight to the figures thus arrived at so as to give more weight to large deviations, and, third, summing up the weighted figures. Now the variance measures inequality in just such a manner. I believe, therefore, that it is from the intuitions underlying the weighted additive principle and the relative to the average view of complaints that the variance derives its plausibility.

This conclusion should not be surprising given that (1) for worlds of the sort being considered the main difference between the variance and the relative mean deviation is that the variance attaches greater weight to large differences from the mean, (2) the relative mean deviation reflects the intuitions underlying the additive principle and the relative to the average view of complaints, and (3) the difference between the additive principle and the weighted additive principle is that the latter sums up complaints only after first weighting them so as to give extra weight to large complaints.

It appears, then, that like the range and the relative mean deviation, the variance reflects some, but not all, of our egalitarian intuitions. This helps to explain both its plausibility and its limitations. To the extent the intuitions underlying the weighted additive principle and the relative to the average view of complaints influence our egalitarian judgments, the variance will seem plausible. Since, however, the intuitions in question are not the only ones influencing our egalitarian judgments, the variance is best regarded as a measure of one aspect of inequality, rather than as a measure of inequality itself.[3]

The Coefficient of Variation

My discussion of the coefficient of variation will be brief, since for worlds of the sort being considered there is no significant difference between the coefficient of variation and the variance. The coefficient of variation is simply the square root of the variance divided by the mean income level. Thus its formula is:

3. Note that in explaining the variance's plausibility I say it is best to regard it as a measure of one aspect of inequality. I have not claimed it is the most plausible measure of that aspect. For example, the morally arbitrary squaring feature is no more plausible in a measure of an aspect of inequality than it is in a measure of inequality itself. More generally, as I shall stress later, I think the statistical measures are best regarded as reflecting inequality's aspects, but that even in that capacity they are inadequate and best regarded as first approximations. Better measures must still be developed to capture inequality's aspects fully and accurately.

$$C = \sqrt{V}/\mu \text{ or } C = \sqrt{\sum_{i=1}^{n}(\mu - y_i)^2/n}/\mu$$

Now for the sort of worlds under consideration C's ordering will be identical to C*'s, where

$$C^* = \sqrt{V}$$

Similarly, C*'s ordering will be identical to C**'s, where

$$C^{**} = V$$

For such worlds, then, C's ordering will be the same as V's, as in fact the relevant portion of both formulas for comparing inequality in such worlds is that corresponding to C***, where

$$C^{***} = V^* = \sum_{i=1}^{n} (\mu - y_i)^2$$

These considerations suggest that for the sort of worlds being considered the coefficient of variation will have the same strengths and weaknesses as the variance, and for just the same reasons. Like the variance, therefore, I believe the coefficient of variation is best regarded as a measure of one aspect of inequality. More specifically, I believe the coefficient of variation corresponds to those intuitions underlying the weighted additive principle and the relative to the average view of complaints.

The Standard Deviation of the Logarithm

Let us next consider the standard deviation of the logarithm. Its formula is:

$$H = \sqrt{\sum_{i=1}^{n} (\log \mu - \log y_i)^2/n}$$

For comparing worlds with the same number of people the relevant portion of H will be that corresponding to H*, where

$$H^* = \sum_{i=1}^{n} (\log \mu - \log y_i)^2$$

H* may look familiar. It bears a close resemblance to C*** and V*. The sole difference between C*** and H* is that H* weights the deviations from the average even before it squares them and adds them together. It does this by comparing the *logarithm* of each individual's level to the logarithm of the average, rather than by directly comparing each individual's *actual* level to the average. Now the logarithmic function attaches proportionately greater weight to small numbers than to large ones. As a result, H* attaches more weight to deviations below the average than to deviations above the average. It also attaches more weight to transfers occurring at the low end of the scale than to transfers occurring at the high end of the scale.

The foregoing considerations suggest the following. Like the variance and the coefficient of variation, the standard deviation of the logarithm corresponds to the relative to the average view of complaints and a weighted additive principle. However, the standard deviation of the logarithm differs from those measures in the *manner* in which it weights deviations from the mean. Whereas the variance and the coefficient of variation weight deviations above and below the mean similarly, the standard deviation of the logarithm weights deviations below the mean more than deviations above it. Still, as with the variance and the coefficient of variation, the standard deviation of the logarithm attaches extra weight to large deviations *below* the mean. So, for example, being ten units below the mean is more than twice as bad as being five units below the mean.

Various criticisms have been leveled at the standard deviation of the logarithm as a measure of inequality. Like the variance and the coefficient of variation, the standard deviation of the logarithm involves a morally arbitrary squaring feature. Similarly, the logarithmic transformation is a morally arbitrary way of capturing the view that extra importance should be attached to transfers at the low end of the scale. Additionally, it has been claimed that the standard deviation of the logarithm becomes *so* insensitive to transfers between people who are *very* well-off that it can end up violating the Pigou-Dalton condition. But perhaps the main criticism needing to be made is that it is a mistake to consider the standard deviation of the logarithm as a measure of the *whole* of our notion of inequality, as surely it does not capture the full complexity of that notion. Still, as with the other measures, it is better to try to discern the source of its plausibility than simply to dismiss it. As indicated, I believe the standard deviation of the logarithm is best regarded as giving expression to a weighted additive principle and the relative to the average view of complaints.

Before going on, let me comment on the apparent tension between the last several measures discussed. I have suggested that the variance, the coefficient of variation, and the standard deviation of the logarithm each give expression to a weighted additive principle and the relative to the average view of complaints. I have also noted that while there is nothing to choose between V and C for worlds of the kind we are now discussing, there *is* a significant difference between those measures and H in the way they weight deviations from the mean. It might seem, therefore, that H is in competition with V and C, and that we will ultimately have to choose between them and decide which sort of measure best captures the aspect in question. However, in the spirit of the rest of this book, I would suggest that before rejecting any of the measures, one should be sure they are indeed measures of the *same* aspect of inequality. In fact, it is arguable that while certain of our intuitions support a measure like V or C, others support a measure like H.

More particularly, I would suggest the following. Given the kinds of considerations underlying the relative to the average view of complaints, it may seem natural and plausible to count deviations above and below the average similarly. This is because among equally deserving people, it may seem just as bad for someone to have *more* than his fair share as for someone to have *less* than his fair share. That is, it may seem just as unfair or unjust for Fate to discriminate in *favor* of someone (to the disadvantage of others) as for Fate to discriminate *against* someone (to the advantage of others). Nevertheless, despite this position's appeal, there is also appeal to the view that deviations below the average should count for *more* than similar deviations above the average. I suspect this may be connected with an asymmetry in our thinking about the lucky and the unlucky. While we empathize with the unlucky person who suffers misfortune, and tend to feel that his burdens should be shared evenly, we tend not to begrudge the lucky person his good fortune, and tend not to feel that his benefits should be shared evenly. Such feelings intuitively support the view that deviations below the average should count for more than deviations above the average. (See the connection, noted in chapter 2, between our notion of luck and the relative to the average view of complaints.)

Despite their similarities, then, H may not simply be a more or less accurate version of C and V. Different intuitions may be underlying the different ways they weight deviations from the mean. If this is so, then it is important to identify those intuitions, and to assess their plausibility. Upon reflection, we may decide there is yet another element of inequality's complexity, and that H is best regarded as expressing that element. Alternatively, if H ultimately rests on a bias in favor of the lucky, we may decide that, despite its appeal, it should be rejected. This is because it may seem that, insofar as inequality is one's concern, such a bias is irrational and not to be accorded any weight.

A word of caution. In discussing the statistical measures we have seen how one might adopt two different views insofar as one is influenced by the relative to the average view of complaints and the weighted additive principle, one of which would be roughly captured by C and V, and one of which would be roughly captured by H. It is perhaps worth emphasizing that our discussion does not rule out the possibility that on reflection one might find other views plausible as well, or perhaps instead. Diagram 5.2 illustrates some of the views one might consider.[4] Each graph represents a possible weighting curve with the origin representing the average level, the y axis representing deviations above and below the average, and the x axis representing the amount of weight attached to deviations such that greater weight is represented by those points that are further to the right along the x axis.

A is merely for illustrative purposes. It represents the straight—that is, non-weighted—additive principle against which various weighted principles might be compared. The vertical line runs through the x axis at point one implying that deviations above and below the average will each receive their "normal" or "full"— that is, nonadjusted—weight. On this view a deviation of n above the average would count exactly as much as a deviation of n below the average, and half as much as a deviation of 2n above or below the average.

B represents the view expressed by the Variance and the Coefficient of Variation. Deviations above and below the average count equally, with extra weight being attached to greater deviations.

C represents the view expressed by the Standard Deviation of the Logarithm. Deviations below the average count more than deviations above the average, with

---

4. The following diagrams, and their interpretations, were suggested by Shelly Kagan.

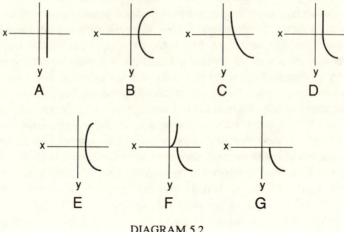

DIAGRAM 5.2

the upper half of the curve asymptotically approaching the line where deviations would only receive their "normal" or "full" (nonadjusted) weight. Notice, on this view, although large deviations above the average might actually count more in the end than small deviations about the average, the latter would be *weighted* more than the former.

D represents the view that while deviations above and below the average are both objectionable, only the latter are especially objectionable the larger they are. On this view extra weight is only attached to greater deviations below the average, with deviations above the average receiving their "normal" or "full" weight.

E represents the view that deviations above and below the average should both be weighted so that extra weight is attached to greater deviations, but that deviations below the average should count more than comparable deviations above the average.

F represents the view that extra weight should be attached to greater deviations below the average, that slight deviations above the average hardly matter at all (they approach zero weighting), and that greater deviations above the average become increasingly objectionable approaching the point where they deserve to be given their "full" or "normal" weight.

Finally, G represents the view that extra weight should be attached to greater deviations below the average, but that only deviations below the average matter—that is, we shouldn't care about deviations above the average *at all*.

I have not tried to motivate B–G, and shall not explore them further in this work (though I will confess I find E particularly appealing). I mention them because they remind us of how much work remains to be done in addressing the issues we have raised. In deciding how best to capture the positions underlying the relative to the average view of complaints and the weighted additive principle, a number of positions might be considered. These include, but are by no means limited to, C, V, and H.

One final comment regarding H. I have argued that H corresponds to a relative to the average view of complaints and a weighted additive principle. If this is so, then H's plausibility is not automatically enhanced because it captures the view that transfers between people above the average matter less than similar transfers below the average. Though very appealing, the plausibility of *this* view *may* depend on the intuitions underlying the relative to the best-off person and the relative to all those better-off views of complaints, both of which capture the view in question when combined with a weighted additive principle. The question is whether certain intuitions underlying the relative to the average view of complaints may also have this implication. Leaving this question open, let us turn to the final statistical measure to be considered.

The Gini Coefficient

At one time, the Gini coefficient was perhaps the economists' most popular measure of inequality. Probably the most common way of looking at the Gini coefficient is in terms of the Lorenz curve, which plots the percentage of a population from the least well-off to the most well-off along a horizontal axis, and the percentage of welfare that the bottom n percent of the population has along a vertical axis. Plotted on a graph like diagram 5.3, the Lorenz curve always runs from the lower left hand corner to the upper right hand corner, since 0 percent of the population always has 0 percent of the welfare, and 100 percent of the population always has 100 percent of the welfare.

In diagram 5.3, the diagonal, e, is the line of absolute equality. It would be the Lorenz curve of a situation where everyone was perfectly equal, where for all n, n percent of the population had n percent of the welfare. C, the lower and right-hand

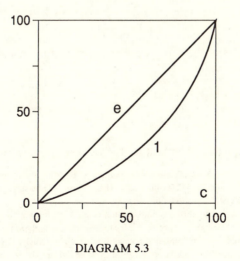

DIAGRAM 5.3

border of diagram 5.3, would be the Lorenz curve of a situation where one person (somehow) had all the welfare, since for all n < 100, the bottom n percent of the population would have 0 percent of the welfare, while, as noted already, 100 percent of the population would have 100 percent of the welfare. L would be the Lorenz curve of a fairly typical situation. Obviously, like l, the Lorenz curve for most situations will lie between e and c.

The Gini coefficient can now be defined. It is the ratio of the area between the line of absolute equality and the Lorenz curve to the triangular area underneath the line of absolute equality. Thus, the Gini coefficient of a world whose Lorenz curve is l, is given by the formula:

$$G = \frac{\text{the area between between e and 1}}{\text{the area between e and c}}$$

Obviously, the Gini coefficient can range from zero, when the Lorenz curve corresponds to e, to one, when the Lorenz curve corresponds to c. Correspondingly, for advocates of the Gini coefficient, the better of two worlds regarding inequality will be the one whose Gini coefficient is smaller; intuitively, the one whose Lorenz curve lies closer to the line of absolute equality.

Various critics have shown that the Gini coefficient faces serious shortcomings as a measure of inequality.[5] Still, the Gini coefficient has great intuitive appeal. I think, therefore, that as with the other measures it would be a mistake simply to dismiss it. Instead, one should try to determine the source of its appeal.

Despite the popularity of looking at the Gini coefficient in terms of the Lorenz curve and graphs like diagram 5.3, perhaps a more useful way of looking at it (at least for our purposes) is in terms of the relative mean difference, which is the arithmetic average of the absolute value of the differences between all pairs of incomes. It turns out that the Gini coefficient is equal to one-half of the relative mean difference. Thus, an alternative formula for the Gini coefficient is:

$$G = (1/2) \sum_{i=1}^{n} \sum_{j=1}^{n} |y_i - y_j|/n^2\mu$$

Since for worlds of the sort we are now considering, n and μ are constant, G's ordering will be the same as G*'s, where

$$G^* = (1/2) \sum_{i=1}^{n} \sum_{j=1}^{n} |y_i - y_j|$$

But G*'s ordering will be identical to that yielded by a new measure, K,[6] where K

5. See, for example, Sen's *On Economic Inequality*, A. B. Atkinson's *The Economics of Inequality* (Clarendon Press, 1975), and David Newbury's "A Theorem on the Measurement of Inequality," *Journal of Economic Theory* 2 (1970): pp 264-66.

6. The reader may be puzzled by my introduction of K, since my argument could be made without reference to it. However, though K is not *necessary* for my argument, there are various respects in which dispensing with K would make my presentation awkward or slightly misleading. Thus, in this case I have opted for a smoother, hopefully clearer presentation to an equivalent shorter, but more cryptic one.

measures inequality by adding up the absolute values of the differences between each person and all those better off than he. To see this, consider the following.

G* measures inequality by adding up the absolute values of the differences between each person and all of the members of his world (including himself), and dividing the figure thus arrived at by two. Thus,

$$G* = 1/2 \ (a + b + c)$$

where a is the sum of the absolute values of the differences between each person, and all those better off than he (so a = K), b is the sum of the absolute values of the differences between each person and all those (including himself) as well-off as he, and c is the sum of the absolute values of the differences between each person and all those worse off than he. The value of b will of course be zero, so

$$G* = 1/2(a + c)$$

Moreover, the value of a will be identical with the value of c, since for each component of a there will be an equivalent component of c. Suppose, for instance, that x who has n units of welfare, is better off than y, who has m units. Then one of a's elements will be $|m - n|$, and similarly, one of c's elements will be $|n - m|$. But obviously this will hold for any two people x and y, where x is better off than y. Therefore, since for all n and m, $|m - n|$ = $|n - m|$, a = c. So

$$G* = 1/2 \ (a + a) = 1/2 \ (2a) = a = K$$

Thus, for the sort of worlds we are now considering, the gini coefficient's ordering will be identical to K's.

K should seem familiar. In chapter 2, I argued that in accordance with certain intuitions the size of someone's complaint regarding inequality would depend upon how he fared relative to all those better off than he. I also argued that, in accordance with other intuitions, inequality could be measured by summing up individual complaints. The first intuitions supported the "relative to all those better off" view of complaints, the second, "the additive principle of equality." Together, I argued, these positions constitute a plausible aspect of inequality, one that underlies and influences our egalitarian judgments. But, of course, together these positions support a measure like K, which assesses inequality by adding up the absolute values of the differences between each person and all those better off than he.

We can now see, I think, why the Gini coefficient has the appeal it does. In accordance with certain powerful intuitions, the orderings yielded by a measure such as K will have great plausibility. But, for worlds of the sort we are now interested in, the orderings yielded by the Gini coefficient will be identical to those yielded by K. Thus, insofar as we are caught in the grip of the intuitions in question, the orderings yielded by the Gini coefficient will have great plausibility.

I might note that this way of looking at the Gini coefficient seems to be suggested by some remarks of Sen's. Speaking about income inequality, Sen writes that the following interpretation is suggested by the formula:

$$G = (1/2n^2\mu) \sum_{i=1}^{n} \sum_{j=1}^{n} |y_i - y_j|$$

"In any pair-wise comparison the man with the lower income can be thought to be suffering from some depression on finding his income to be lower. Let this depression be proportional to the difference in income. The sum total of all such depressions in all possible pair-wise comparisons takes us to the Gini coefficient."[7] Talking about welfare, rather than income, I would amend Sen's remarks as follows: in any pair-wise comparison the man with the lower level of welfare can be thought to have a "complaint" regarding inequality. This complaint may seem to be proportional to the difference between his level of welfare and that of the better-off person. How bad a world's inequality is may seem to depend upon its sum total of complaints (taking into consideration all pair-wise comparisons). It is these intuitions the Gini coefficient appears to capture.

5.2 The Statistical Measures in Perspective

I have pointed out important similarities between the statistical measures of inequality and the general theoretical considerations of chapter 2. Specifically, I have shown that, at least for certain sorts of cases, the range expresses the intuitions underlying the relative to the best-off person view of complaints and the maximin principle of equality; the relative mean deviation expresses the intuitions underlying the relative to the average view of complaints and the additive principle of equality; the Gini coefficient expresses the intuitions underlying the relative to all those better-off view of complaints and the additive principle; and the variance, the coefficient of variation, and the standard deviation of the logarithm each express intuitions underlying the relative to the average view of complaints and a weighted additive principle.

We see then that the statistical measures directly reflect four of chapter 2's twelve aspects of inequality. More generally, as diagram 5.4 illustrates, we see that between them the statistical measures reflect each of chapter 2's three ways of measuring individual complaints and each of the three principles of equality. Accordingly, on the view that each way of measuring complaints might plausibly combine with each principle of equality, one might hold that between them the statistical measures *indirectly* support nine of chapter 2's aspects. Only the aspects corresponding to gratuitousness, deviation from the median, and social inequality are not represented by (some combination of the positions underlying) the statistical measures.

The statistical measures were a major step toward elucidating the notion of inequality. Among other things, their plausibility and shortcomings led economists

7.   *On Economic Inequality*, p. 33.

		Three Ways of Measuring Individual Complaints			Three Principles of Equality		
		AVE	BOP	ATBO	MP	AP	WAP
	R :		X		X		
	M :	X				X	
Statistical	V :	X					X
measures	C :	X					X
	H :	X					X
	G :			X		X	

AVE = Relative to the Average
BOP = Relative to the Best-Off Person
ATBO = Relative to All Those Better Off
MP = Maximin Principle
AP = Additive Principle
WAP = Weighted Additive Principle

R = The Range
M = The Relative Mean Deviation
V = The Variance
C = The Coefficient of Variation
H = The Standard Deviation of the Log
G = The Gini Coefficient

DIAGRAM 5.4

to appreciate both the importance and difficulty of measuring inequality. This, in turn, led economists to understand the complexity of inequality much better than most. Still, economists did not really pursue the question of *why* the statistical measures have the plausibility they do.[8] As indicated, I think the answer to this question can be found in chapter 2.

It was, I think, unfortunate that the sources of the statistical measures' plausibility were not pursued. I think this for several related reasons. First, given the complexity and confusion surrounding the topic of inequality, there is reason to try to ascertain whether the various measures are indeed grounded on firm intuitive foundations—to be certain, for instance, that they are not *ad hoc*, and that they are truly capturing *egalitarian* intuitions, rather than other moral sentiments, which often, perhaps, accompany such intuitions.

Second, if the source of their plausibility had been pursued, it might have been recognized that the various measures are best regarded as measures not of inequality itself, but of certain *aspects* of that notion. Thus, it might have been seen that *insofar* as these measures seem plausible, it is because they reflect certain powerful intuitions that do indeed underlie our egalitarian judgments, but which are not the only ones to do so. Importantly, this might have prevented numerous wrong turns and fruitless attempts to find the better, more sophisticated, measure of inequality

8. It might be claimed that economists did pursue this question, but that they did so inadequately. My own sense of the literature is that such a charge cannot be sustained. By and large I think the economists' main shortcoming on this point is one of omission rather than commission. It isn't so much that their attempts fail, but that they fail to attempt the task in question.

that would suffice by itself and enable one to simply dispense with the "troublesome" and often conflicting statistical measures. Although, as will be noted, I think our final measure of inequality will ultimately replace the statistical measures with even more plausible measures of the different aspects, one way or another it will have to accurately accommodate the central intuitions that give the statistical measures their plausibility.

Third, if the intuitions underlying the statistical measures had been uncovered, people might have seen that inequality is even *more* complex than had been realized. So, for instance, once people recognized that the range, the gini coefficient, and the variance were supported, respectively, by the intuitions underlying the relative to the best-off person view of complaints and the maximin principle of equality, the relative to all those better off view and the additive principle, and the relative to the average view and the weighted additive principle, they might also have recognized that these intuitions might plausibly combine in other ways to influence our egalitarian judgments. Specifically, they might have recognized that each of the ways of measuring complaints could plausibly be combined with each of the principles of equality.

Fourth, only by discovering the source of their appeal is the seriousness of the conflict between the different measures likely to be appreciated. As long as one focuses on the measures themselves, it is easy to believe that they merely represent different aspects of a complicated notion that happen, on some occasions, to conflict. However, once one explores the foundations of these measures, one sees that some conflict at a very deep level with underlying intuitions that may appear to be fundamentally opposed. This is important for, as noted in chapter 2, it raises serious questions about the scope and intelligibility of the notion of inequality. (These questions, as noted previously, I shall return to in chapter 10.)

Finally, for reasons I discuss in chapters 6 and 7, I think if the sources of the statistical measures' plausibility *had* been pursued, people might have recognized that the statistical measures are best regarded as first approximations, and that even *more* accurate measures of the different aspects might be found.

One point worth emphasizing is the manner in which the argument of section 5.1 supports the general argument of chapter 2. In chapter 2, I presented various considerations showing that the notion of inequality is surprisingly complex. I argued that different intuitions influence our egalitarian judgments, and claimed that even if they are not all *equally* appealing, many really do have the intuitions in question, they have significant plausibility, and they cannot easily be dismissed. Now clearly, many economists have felt about the statistical measures the way I feel about the intuitions presented in chapter 2. In fact, it is arguable that it is precisely *because* it seemed one couldn't simply choose one statistical measure and dismiss the others that many economists first recognized inequality's complexity. The problem was not simply that competing measures were offered, but that competing *plausible* measures were offered. Thus, Meade was not atypical when, in discussing the statistical measures he wrote, "changes . . . [that] have a marked effect in reducing the degree of inequality according to one *very reasonable* measure . . . at the same time . . . have a marked effect in increasing the degree of inequality if some alternative but *equally reasonable* method of measurement is employed" (emphasis added).[9] But then, if the argument in section 5.1 is correct, and there *is* the connection between the statistical measures and the aspects of inequality I have suggested, the fact that many economists have responded to the statistical measures in the manner indicated lends further independent support to the claims of chapter 2—that we *do* have the egalitarian intuitions in question, that they *are* plausible, and that they *cannot* easily be dismissed.

5.3 Atkinson's Measure

Let me next consider Atkinson's measure, one of the most widely accepted measures of inequality.[10] On the surface, at least, Atkinson's approach seems diametrically opposed to this book's. Whereas I want to compare situations *regarding inequality*, independently of how they compare all things considered, or with respect to other moral ideals, Atkinson seems to imply that the value of inequality cannot be understood in such a manner. Let me explore the relations between our positions.

Unlike with the previous measures, it will be most useful to consider Atkinson's measure as it was originally offered, that is, as a measure of *income* inequality. I begin with a detailed presentation of Atkinson's measure, relying heavily on direct quotations from Atkinson. Though lengthy, this presentation will greatly facilitate my discussion.

Atkinson's measure, or index of inequality, is given by the following formula:

$$I = 1 - \left[\sum_{i=1}^{n} \left(\frac{Y_i}{\mu} \right)^{1-\varepsilon} f_i \right]^{\frac{1}{1-\varepsilon}}$$

where "Y_i denotes the income of those in the ith income range (n ranges altogether), f_i denotes the proportion of the population with incomes in the ith range, and . . . [μ] denotes the mean income."[11] As Atkinson observes, the above formula "may look intimidating, but the measure has a very natural interpretation as the proportion of the present total income that would be required to achieve the same level of social welfare as at present if incomes were equally distributed."[12] Let me try to clarify this "natural interpretation."

In his classic article, "On the Measurement of Inequality,"[13] Atkinson assumes that concern for inequality should be expressed in our social welfare function for ranking outcomes. Following Dalton,[14] he suggests that we consider a social wel-

9. J. E. Meade, *The Just Economy* (Allen and Unwin, 1976), p. 113.

10. I am grateful to Peter Mieszkowski and John Broome for their comments regarding the relation between my work and Atkinson's measure. In addition, my presentation of Atkinson's measure is indebted to that of Sen's in *On Economic Inequality*, pp. 38–39.

11. Atkinson, *The Economics of Inequality*, p. 48.

12. Ibid, p. 48.

13. Atkinson, *Journal of Economic Theory* 2 (1970): 244–263.

14. Hugh Dalton, "The Measurement of the Inequality of Incomes," Economic Journal 30, 1920, pp. 348–361.

fare function that "would be an additively separable and symmetric function of individual incomes."[15] On this view,

$$W = \sum_{i=1}^{n} U(y_i) = U(y_1) + U(y_2) + \ldots + U(y_n)$$

where W is the social welfare function, yi is the income of the *i*th person, and U is the individual welfare function (specifically, U gives you an individual's welfare as a function of her income). Because, by hypothesis, U is the same for all individuals,[16] if one assumes, as Atkinson does, that the function U should be increasing and concave—so that the more income one has the less additional income increases one's welfare—then it is easy to see that W will be maximized when income is equally distributed.[17] Thus, the maximum value of W will be $nU(\mu)$, since if income were distributed equally everyone would have the average level of income.

Given these assumptions Atkinson introduces the concept of "the equally distributed equivalent level of income (y_{EDE}) or the level of income per head which if equally distributed would give the same level of social welfare as the present distribution."[18] It is this concept Atkinson's measure intuitively relies on. Specifically, it can be shown that the complicated formula given for Atkinson's measure, I, is equivalent to the following one:

$$I = 1 - \left(\frac{y_{EDE}}{\mu} \right)$$

"or 1 minus the ratio of the equally distributed equivalent level of income to the mean of the actual distribution."[19] As Atkinson observes, "if I falls, then the distribution has become more equal—we would require a higher level of equally distributed income (relative to the mean) to achieve the same level of social welfare as the actual distribution. [In addition] the measure I has . . . the convenient property of lying between 0 (complete equality) and 1 (complete inequality).[20]

Now according to Atkinson, the parameter ε plays a key role in his measure. Specifically, ε "represents the weight attached by society to inequality in the distribution. It ranges from zero, which means that society is indifferent about the distri-

15. "On the Measurement of Inequality," pp. 244–245. On the standard economic model, where social welfare is understood to be a function of individual welfares, basically, the symmetry requirement means that each individual has the same individual welfare function—so that if two people have the same income they have the same welfare—and the requirement of additive separability means that "individual components of social welfare . . . [are] judged without reference to the welfare components of others, and the social welfare components corresponding to different persons are eventually added up to arrive at an aggregate value of social welfare" (Sen, *On Economic Inequality*, p. 40).

16. This is entailed by W's being a symmetric function of individual incomes. See the previous note.

17. If income were not equally distributed one could always increase W's value by transferring income from somebody above the average, say, yj to somebody below the average, say, yk. U's concavity insures that the decrease in the value of U(yj) would be smaller than the increase in the value of U(yk), and hence (given W's additive separability) that the value of W will increase.

18. "On the Measurement of Inequality," p. 250.

19. Ibid.; see also Sen's *On Economic Inequality*, p. 38.

20. "On the Measurement of Inequality," p. 250.

bution, to infinity, which means that society is only concerned with the position of the lowest income group. This latter position may be seen as corresponding to that developed by Rawls . . . where inequality is assessed in terms of the position of the least advantaged . . . . Where ε lies between these extremes depends on the importance attached to redistribution at the bottom."[21]

Atkinson offers an illuminating interpretation of ε worth citing in detail:

> Suppose there are two people, one with twice the income of the other (they are otherwise identical), and that we are considering taking 1 unit of income from the richer man and giving a proportion x to the poorer, (the remainder being lost in the process . . .). At what level of x do we cease to regard the redistribution as desirable?
>
> If . . . [one] is at all concerned about inequality, then $x = 1$ is . . . desirable. What is crucial is how far . . . to let x fall below 1 before calling for a stop . . . . The answer determines the implied value of ε from the formula $1/x = 2^{\varepsilon}$. For example, if . . . [one] stops at $x = 1/2$, this corresponds to ε = 1, but if . . . [one] is willing to go until only a quarter is transferred, then the implied ε equals 2.[22]

To the foregoing, Atkinson adds the following important note, "to calibrate ε fully we should have to consider different gaps between the rich and poor man; the [preceding] calculation . . . is only illustrative."

Once one has determined ε's value, calculating y_{EDE} and I is straightforward. Moreover, these values can be conjoined with intuitively appealing interpretations. For example, if the ratio of the equally distributed equivalent level of income to the actual distribution's average is .20, that is, if

$$\left(\sum_{i=1}^{n} \left(\frac{Y_i}{\mu} \right)^{1-e} f_i \right)^{\frac{1}{1-e}} = \left(\frac{y_{EDE}}{\mu} \right) = .20$$

then this means that the gains from redistribution to bring about equality would be equivalent to raising total income by 20 percent; or alternatively, that we could attain the same level of social welfare with only $(1 - .20 =)$ 80 percent of the present total income.

Atkinson's measure has many features that make it attractive to economists. These include the following:

1. Atkinson's measure is explicitly normative, as equality's distributional value is explicitly incorporated into the social welfare function via the value attached to ε.
2. Once we have determined ε's value we can assess whether proposals to reduce inequality or increase income are "worth it," by calculating their effect on the social welfare function (W). In particular, for most economists one outcome will be judged better than another if the value of its equally

21. Atkinson, *The Economics of Inequality*, p. 48.
22. Ibid, p. 49.

distributed equivalent income (y_{EDE}) is higher. This implication of Atkinson's measure has great practical appeal.

3. Atkinson's measure has the "virtue" of being neutral as between strikingly disparate distributional objectives. Thus, as noted previously, someone could accept his formal conditions for measuring inequality—that is, for measuring how bad situations are regarding "inequality"—who in fact attaches *no* weight to distributional considerations, and hence who assigns ε the value zero. By the same token, someone who is only concerned with the worst-off's level could accept Atkinson's measure, and assign ε the value infinity.

4. Atkinson's measure is neutral between those who think inequality is intrinsically bad and those who think it is only extrinsically bad. For example, strict utilitarians could assign a value to ε corresponding exactly to the extent to which there is diminishing marginal utility of income, in which case the value of I would reflect *only* the extent to which inequality was *inefficient*. Alternatively, ε's value could incorporate a distributional concern about inequality *itself* beyond the extent to which inequality is inefficient (for the standard utilitarian and economic reasons).

5. For all values of ε less than infinity, Atkinson's measure is compatible with the economic "requirement" of pareto optimality. That is, pareto improvements[23] will always increase the value of the social welfare function W, even if they worsen the situation's inequality.

6. For all values of ε between zero and infinity, Atkinson's measure reflects many of the egalitarian judgments noted previously in this work. For example, it captures the Pigou-Dalton condition in its most plausible form.[24] In addition, it implies that, other things equal, increases in the best-off or decreases in the worst-off will worsen inequality, and that for any transfer of any size or kind it will be best if the transfer goes from the "highest" possible person to the "lowest" possible person.[25]

Given the foregoing, it is not surprising that Atkinson's measure has been widely accepted. But it will also not be surprising that I have many worries about it. My main worry is that Atkinson's measure offers too many too much. While it provides common ground, or a common approach, for a wide variety of distributional concerns, I think it does this in a way that—at least in certain respects—eviscerates its plausibility as a measure of inequality. More cautiously, compatible as it is with utilitarian, Rawlsian, and antiegalitarian views, I believe Atkinson's measure obscures what is *distinctive* about the egalitarian's concern. Equality, I have urged, is an essentially *comparative* notion. Egalitarians believe it is bad (unfair or unjust) for some to be worse off than others through no fault of their own. It is this belief which a measure of inequality should reflect, and although Atkinson's measure is

23. Any increases in the income or welfare of some, which do not decrease the income or welfare of another.

24. Roughly, any (even) transfers from worse- to better-off will worsen inequality, while those from better- to worse-off will improve inequality (at least up to the point where the gaps between better- and worse-off are removed). See sections 3.4–3.6.

25. Again, see sections 3.4–3.6.

compatible with this belief,[26] it is not wedded to it. Thus, as suggested earlier, Atkinson's measure is also compatible with other nonegalitarian and even anti-egalitarian positions.[27]

I worry, then, about the third and fourth "advantages" noted previously. I also worry about the first and second. As the reader knows, I fully agree with Atkinson that one's measure of inequality should be normative, and not merely descriptive. That is why from the outset my concern has been with one situation's inequality being *worse* than another, rather than with one situation's having *more* inequality. But normative concerns can enter into our deliberations about inequality at two levels. First, there may be "purely internal" egalitarian reasons for caring about some inequalities more than others. Second, there may be "external" nonegalitarian reasons for caring about some inequalities more than others, because, for example, trade-offs are necessary between our egalitarian and other moral concerns. I agree with Atkinson that eventually we must address the latter concerns to arrive at a social welfare function reflecting our all-things-considered judgments. But I think we must probably get clear about the former concerns before we can get clear about the latter, not vice versa (see section 5.7).

Similarly, I worry about the simplifying assumption that we merely need to determine the trade-off between income and inequality to determine our social welfare function. Concern about income is but one part of our larger concern about utility, and our concerns about utility and equality are only two of many moral concerns we might have. What about freedom, perfectionism, proportional justice, maximin, and so on? One could care about each of these factors in addition to caring about utility and equality. Does this mean Atkinson's measure needs modification to reflect the relevant trade-offs between all such factors before we could compare situations regarding inequality? If so, Atkinson's measure would look very different than it does now. In addition, it would probably lose much of its appeal and point. Our measure of inequality would have turned into a rather odd way of revealing what factors matter to us and how much they matter relative to each other. It would be good to know such things, but I doubt they must be reflected in our measure of inequality.

I also have a worry about the fifth "advantage." I realize most economists think it conceptually true that if one outcome is pareto superior to another then it must be better all things considered. But for reasons noted in chapter 9 I am not convinced of this. In particular, it is arguable—though controversial— that egalitarians should maintain that in *some* cases pareto improvements worsen a situation all things considered. Consider, for example, the effect of raising one person a certain amount in an otherwise perfectly equal world. It is by no means clear—to me anyway—that the gains in utility and perfection accruing to that one person must *necessarily* outweigh the egalitarian complaints of those left behind. There might be ten billion left behind. Even if each of their complaints would be relatively small, together they might outweigh the gains

26. See subsequent discussion.

27. Many of these assertions have been previously articulated and/or defended, and many will receive further support in subsequent chapters.

of the one person benefited.[28] In sum, I think it is at least an open question whether the egalitarian objection to certain pareto improvements might be sufficiently strong as to condemn those improvements all things considered. Thus, I find it a shortcoming of Atkinson's approach that it appears to link inequality with social welfare in a way that rules this out.

Other objections to Atkinson's measure are possible. As noted already, Atkinson assumes the social welfare function (W) would be an additively separable and symmetric function of individual incomes. Sen raises doubts about the assumption of additive separability,[29] and I have doubts about the symmetry assumption. Suppose A and B both have the same incomes, but A is healthy and B severely handicapped. Why should we believe a given increase in income would improve A's and B's welfare the same amount? For that matter, why believe the individual welfare function U will not only be the same for everybody but be increasing and concave. This assumption assures that income transfers from the richer to poorer will improve inequality on Atkinson's measure. But under certain circumstances additional income might well increase A's welfare by *more* than it would increase B's, even if A were richer than B.[30] Finally, considering the distributive value of a $50 transfer from someone with $100,000 to someone with $10,000 we may judge that ε's value should be 3, whereas considering such a transfer from someone with $50,000 to someone with $30,000 we may judge that ε's value should be .5. Must one or both of these judgments be wrong? On Atkinson's measure we must ultimately determine a single value for ε, which would then be used in weighting each person's individual contribution to social welfare. Yet it may seem that different values for ε would be appropriate in different circumstances.

I think, then, that Atkinson's measure faces numerous problems. Nevertheless, it is widely accepted, and this isn't simply because it provides common ground for a variety of distributional concerns. Rather, Atkinson's measure seems plausible *as a measure of inequality* precisely because, as noted already, for all values of ε between zero and infinity, Atkinson's measure reflects many of the egalitarian's judgments. Let me next briefly suggest why this is so.

In essence, Atkinson's assumptions reflect the following views. First, that the best situation will be the one where income is equally distributed. Second, that deviations from the average worsen inequality. Third, that the total cost to social welfare arising from inequality will be an additive function of the "cost" in terms of individual welfare resulting from the inequality. That is, if we added up the gains in individual utility for each person below the average that would result if the total income in their world was equally distributed, we would know how much the inequality had adversely affected the situation. And finally, that greater deviations

28. At least on many of inequality's aspects. Whether or not one thinks this is so might well depend on the details of the case imagined. One example where I think a pareto improvement would be worse, all things considered, is suggested by Tim Scanlon in "Nozick on Rights, Liberty, and Property," *Philosophy and Public Affairs* 6 (1976): 3–25. The example I have in mind is cited in note 41 of chapter 9, and though it would have to be suitably modified to fit my current purposes, I think this could be done.

29. See Sen, *On Economic Inequality*, pp. 39–41.

30. For example, if A were healthy and rich, and B *severely* handicapped and poor, A might be a more efficient "utility machine" than B, so that A would get more utility from additional income than B.

from the average matter more than lesser deviations,[31] so that the worse off some-one is the better (worse) it will be for income to be transferred to (from) him.

The preceding should sound familiar. If we think of each person worse off than the average as having an egalitarian complaint proportional to how much utility they would have gained had income been distributed equally—or alternatively, as having a complaint inversely proportional to the ratio between how much utility they have in the actual distribution to how much they would have if income were distributed equally—then we can see that basically Atkinson's measure reflects those intuitions underlying a relative to the average view of complaints with a weighted additive principle of equality.

Despite its shortcomings, then, it is no accident Atkinson's measure seems plausible even to those who genuinely value equality. This is because for values of ε between zero and infinity Atkinson's measure reflects the basic intuitions that lend plausibility to the variance (V), the coefficient of variation (C), and the standard deviation of the logarithm (H). Moreover, by asking us to explicitly incorporate our distributional concerns into the parameter ε, Atkinson's measure avoids the morally arbitrary squaring feature common to V, C, and H in attaching greater weight to larger deviations below the average. In addition, Atkinson's measure avoids the morally arbitrary square root feature common to C and H, and for values of ε less than infinity it avoids H's problem of becoming so insensitive to transfers at very high levels that it runs afoul of the Pigou-Dalton condition.[32]

In sum, despite the worries expressed, there is much to be said for Atkinson's measure. But as I have tried to indicate, Atkinson's measure is not plausible because of the way it inextricably links inequality to income, utility, and social welfare; rather, it is plausible despite the way it does this. Thus, I think Atkinson's measure does not pose a threat to this book's approach. To the contrary, I think this book helps illuminate both the shortcomings of Atkinson's measure and the source of its appeal.

In conclusion, I think Atkinson's measure, like the statistical measures, is best regarded not as a measure of the whole of inequality but as a measure of one important aspect of inequality. I also think that given the worries expressed here, it is probably best regarded as a useful but flawed method for capturing that aspect.

5.4 The Intersection Approach

In his book *On Economic Inequality*, A. K. Sen introduces an approach for measuring inequality, which I shall refer to as the *intersection approach*. In this section, I shall argue that the intersection approach has serious shortcomings in virtue of which it is not the most plausible method of capturing and reflecting a complex notion like inequality.

In fairness to Sen, let me emphasize at the outset that most of the criticisms of this section are not directed at the intersection approach as Sen himself understood

31. With the extent to which this is so being reflected in our value for ε.
32. Even in its most plausible form.

and advocated it. For the most part Sen's claims on behalf of the intersection approach are both modest and plausible. He merely suggests than an intersection approach may be a fairly useful measure of inequality, one that "opens up a new set of possibilities," that perhaps more adequately corresponds to our notion of inequality than the standard measures of inequality, and that, most important, "helps to sort out the relatively less controversial rankings from those that are more doubtful (p. 74)."[33]

Sen never suggests that an intersection approach will be fully adequate in the sense of being the most complete measure of inequality at which we might arrive. Still, there are two reasons for detailing the problems facing an intersection approach. First, doing so is a useful prophylactic against the temptations of those who would be less careful than Sen, and who might otherwise claim more on behalf of the intersection approach than Sen himself did. Second, and more important, as we shall see in the next section the shortcomings of the intersection approach help illustrate a more promising way of proceeding in order to accurately capture a complex notion like inequality.

Let us begin our discussion of the intersection approach with a bit of background. At the beginning of *On Economic Inequality*, Sen writes the following:

> We may not be able to decide whether one distribution x is more or less unequal than another, but we may be able to compare some other pairs perfectly well. The notion of inequality has many aspects, and a coincidence of them may permit a clear ranking, but when these different aspects conflict an incomplete ranking may emerge. There are reasons to believe that our idea of inequality as a ranking relation may indeed be inherently incomplete. If so, to find a measure of inequality that involves a complete ordering may produce artificial problems, because a measure can hardly be more precise than the concept it represents (pp. 5–6).

Later, after showing that each of the standard measures of inequality faces problems, and noting that each yields a complete ordering, Sen continues:

> Arbitrariness is bound to slip into the process of stretching a partial ranking into a complete ordering. It is arguable that each of these measures leads to some rather absurd results precisely because each of them aims at giving a complete-ordering representation to a concept that is essentially one of partial ranking (pp. 47–48).

So, Sen believes, as we do, that the notion of inequality is complex, multifaceted, and partially incomplete, and that none of the standard measures of inequality will alone suffice to capture that notion. It is in this context that he offers his proposal for how we might arrive at a useful measure of inequality. Sen's suggestion is that we take an intersection relation, Q, of a selected subset of the various measures of inequality that have been (or presumably might be) offered. He claims that "in eschewing exclusive reliance on any one measure and on the complete ordering generated by it, Q restrains the arbitrariness of such measures" (p. 74). On

---

33. Throughout this section page references are to Sen's *On Economic Inequality* unless noted otherwise.

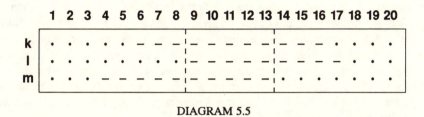

DIAGRAM 5.5

Sen's proposal, Q will yield the judgment that A's inequality is better than B's if and only if A is better than B according to each of the selected measures (and similarly for the relations "worse than," "equivalent to," "at least as good as," and "at least as bad as").

Intuitively, Sen's reasoning might be put as follows. A number of measures of inequality have been offered, each of which has some plausibility and yet each of which, by itself, is inadequate. If, therefore, we are interested in comparing the inequality of two situations, A and B, we would do well to look at more than one of the standard measures. In particular, we might do well to select carefully several of those measures and see what each says about A and B. If each of the measures is in agreement about how A and B compare, then we may confidently conclude that that is how A and B do compare. If, on the other hand, the measures yield opposing judgments, then the intersection approach would yield no judgment regarding A and B.[34]

My first criticism of the intersection approach may be made with the aid of diagram 5.5, where k, l, and m represent possible measures one might employ in arriving at an intersection relation. The marks next to them indicate how each measure corresponds to our intuitions about twenty cross-world comparisons. Each comparison is between two worlds, A_n and B_n. A dash (–) indicates we are certain the measure has yielded a correct judgment about how A_n compares to B_n. A dot (.) indicates this is not the case—either we are certain the measure has yielded an incorrect judgment, or we are not certain whether the judgment is correct or incorrect.

For instance, suppose that in judging between what we may refer to as the two

34. In such a case one might merely note that the intersection approach is silent on the issue of how A and B compare. Alternatively, one might conclude that due to the complex and incomplete nature of inequality, A and B are noncomparable regarding inequality. These two responses would correspond to weaker and stronger versions of the intersection approach. Sen's own view, expressed in correspondence, is the former—more plausible—version, that in such a case the intersection approach is just silent regarding how A and B compare.

Notice, to conclude that A and B are noncomparable regarding inequality would only be to conclude that one cannot say either that one is better than the other or that both are equivalent. That is, it would be to conclude that the notion of inequality does not permit us to make either of those judgments. It would not be to conclude that A and B are noncomparable along the dimension in question, as if one or the other was not the proper kind of object or situation about which judgments of inequality could be made. To the contrary, on the view in question one could make the judgment that neither was better than the other regarding inequality.

11-type worlds, A_{11} and B_{11}, we are certain the inequality is worse in A_{11} than in B_{11}, then the dashes in column 11 of diagram 5.5 imply that according to all three measures A_{11} is worse than B_{11}. Similarly, according to diagram 5.5, k and l both yield the correct judgment about 14-, 15-, and 16-type worlds, while m does not. For the 1-3- and 18-20-type worlds the diagram does not reveal whether the various measures agree with one another. Depending on the cases, the measures may all agree but we may be certain they are wrong, or they may disagree but we may be uncertain about which, if any, is correct.[35]

We are now in a position to see that an intersection relation employing measures k, l, and m will not accurately capture and reflect our notion of inequality. According to diagram 5.5, k, l, and m conflict in their judgments regarding the 4-8- and 14-17-type worlds. This means that an intersection relation employing those measures will yield no judgment about how A_n and B_n compare in those cases. Clearly, however, a fully adequate measure of inequality should yield a judgment in such cases. After all, by hypothesis, not only are we certain in each of those cases that A_n and B_n are comparable regarding inequality, but we are certain how they compare. Specifically, we are certain that l's judgments are correct for the 4-8-type worlds and that k's judgments are correct for the 14-17-type worlds.

The preceding considerations suggest a general and deep problem facing the intersection approach. The problem, whose roots will be explained in greater detail shortly, is that often an intersection approach will fail to yield an ordering when an ordering should be yielded, and this may be so even in cases where it is quite clear what the correct ordering is. Surely, however, a measure that accurately captures and expresses our notion of inequality ought to at least yield those orderings of which we are certain. More generally, just as Sen is correct that a fully adequate measure should not be *more* complete than the notion it expresses, yielding orderings where orderings shouldn't be yielded, so it shouldn't be *less* complete, failing to yield orderings where they should be yielded.

In defense of the intersection approach it might be suggested that one must distinguish between measures that are *strongly misdirecting* and ones that are *mildly misleading*, where a measure, m, will be strongly misdirecting if for at least one comparison between two situations we are certain that m yields the wrong judgment, and mildly misleading if for every instance where we are certain how two situations compare m yields the correct judgment. (The reason for regarding m as mildly misleading is that presumably it will yield judgments in some cases about which we are initially uncertain, and where, after employing the intersection relation Q, we will feel that no judgment can be made.) It might then be claimed that only measures that are mildly misleading may be used in arriving at Q.

Now I readily grant that if one may only employ mildly misleading measures in arriving at Q, the particular criticism just presented will collapse. Q will no longer fail to yield orderings in cases about which we are clear. However, I am most

---

35. Notice that we may be certain some of the measures are wrong and still be uncertain about whether a conflicting measure is correct. Such a situation could obtain, for example, if we were certain that A_n was not better than B_n, but were uncertain as to whether A_n was worse than, equivalent to, or perhaps noncomparable with B_n. (See the previous note for the sense of noncomparability in question.)

skeptical about the likelihood of our arriving at several intuitively acceptable non-
ad hoc measures that are only mildly misleading and not strongly misdirecting. In
fact, I believe that if we could find even one such measure we would gladly embrace it as our measure of inequality until someone greatly surprised us by revealing
another measure that genuinely differed from the first and yet handled all the cases
we were sure about equally well. I might add, here, that Sen himself seems to
presume that Q will be derived from some of the standard measures of inequality,
each of which, there is good reason to believe, is strongly misdirecting and not
merely mildly misleading.[36] In short, if the intersection approach is to be regarded
as a serious and realistic one it cannot be stipulated that only mildly misleading
measures are to be employed in arriving at Q. Hence, there is good reason to think
the intersection approach will have the previously noted shortcoming.

It might be claimed that the foregoing objection misses the whole *point* of the
intersection approach, that we cannot be "certain" or "sure" of *any* of our egalitarian
judgments in advance of, or unless they are yielded by, the intersection relation Q.[37]
I believe this claim is deeply mistaken and begs the question against the most
fundamental objection to the intersection approach. To see this, it may help to offer
a more concrete illustration of why an intersection approach is not the best way of
capturing a complex, multifaceted notion.

Consider the relatively trivial notion of basketball ability, shared by (among
others) the players, coaches, and fans of basketball. Like inequality, the notion of
basketball ability is a complex notion. A number of aspects or factors are relevant
to our judgment of whether one person is a better basketball player than another.[38]
Among these are the ability to score points, to get rebounds, to play defense, to
handle the ball, and to lead the team. For the sake of discussion, let us suppose that
the five suggested aspects constitute the notion of basketball ability, and that we are
able to arrive at an accurate measure of each of these aspects. It is easy to see that
the intersection relation Q derived from these measures would not adequately capture and reflect the notion of basketball ability.

Suppose there are two basketball players, D and F. D is the greatest scorer,
rebounder, defender, and team leader in the game's history. F is well below average
in all these respects. F is a better ball handler than D, but just barely (F diligently
practiced ball handling since early childhood, but his natural talent is so minimal,
and D's is so vast...). *Without question*, D would be a better basketball player than
F. In fact, D's basketball ability is *vastly* superior to F's. Yet an intersection approach applied to the measures of the aspects of basketball ability would fail to

36. Many of the reasons for believing the standard measures of inequality are strongly misdirecting
have already been noted, and were previously noted by Sen and others. Other important reasons for
believing the standard measures are strongly misdirecting will be given in chapters 6 and 7.

37. This claim was suggested to me by both Amartya Sen and John Broome. I am not sure if they
were actually endorsing it, or merely calling it to my attention as a possible response that might be given.

38. For the purposes of this discussion I am assuming a direct correlation between one person's being
a better player than another and that person having greater basketball ability. This does not affect the
substance of my remarks and greatly simplifies my presentation. I am aware that it is often said that
certain players are better than their abilities would suggest and others are worse than their abilities
permit.

yield the judgment that D is better than F. Clearly, then, such an approach would not suffice as a measure of basketball ability.

It is perhaps worth noting that one needn't resort to wild examples to illustrate the point in question. For instance, at the professional level we are frequently able to judge which of two players has more ability, yet it is rare for one professional to be at least as good as another in *all* of the respects relevant to determining our overall judgments. Similarly, among professionals almost every center is a better rebounder than almost every guard and almost every guard is a better ball handler than almost every center, yet in many, and perhaps most, cases we have little difficulty in judging whether a given center has more basketball ability than a given guard. Suffice it to say, such judgments cannot be accounted for on an intersection approach based on the aspects of basketball ability.

The problem with intersections is they don't allow trade-offs. They don't allow trade-offs that take account of the *number* of different measures supporting conflicting judgments, or of the relative *significance* of the different measures supporting conflicting judgments, or of the *degree* to which the different measures support conflicting judgments. So, for example, on an intersection approach, if the measures from which the intersection is derived yield opposing judgments regarding A and B, there is no room for contending that A might be better than B because it is better in four of five important aspects, or because the aspects in which A is better are more significant than those in which B is better, or even, as we have seen, because A is *much* better than B in terms of four aspects and only *slightly* worse in terms of a fifth.

It is no doubt true that sometimes when different facets of a multifaceted notion point in different directions a ranking cannot be expected to emerge. But it by no means follows that *whenever* different facets of a multifaceted notion point in different directions a meaningful ranking cannot emerge. Fortunately, this is as true for the notion of inequality as it is for the notion of basketball ability, for as we have seen inequality is an incredibly complex and multifaceted notion whose facets will diverge in many, and perhaps most, cases.[39]

39. In presenting the intersection approach Sen readily acknowledged that the orderings yielded by the intersection relation Q "might be rather severely incomplete and precisely how incomplete would depend on the extent to which the various . . . measures [from which Q is derived] conflict" (p. 72). The results of chapters 2 and 3 confirm Sen's fears on this score, assuming, as I believe Sen did, that Q was to be derived from the measures of inequality's different aspects.

There are ways of avoiding severe incompleteness in the orderings yielded by the intersection relation Q if one is "careful" in one's selection of measures from which Q is to be derived. For example, instead of including measures of each of the different aspects of a multifaceted notion—as we implicitly did in our basketball examples—one might "conveniently" omit measures of those more "troublesome" aspects that frequently conflict with other aspects of the notion in the judgments they yield. Or, instead of directly focusing on measures of a multifaceted notion's aspects, one might focus on several relatively plausible measures that have been (or presumably might be) offered as measures of the *whole* of the notion.

In such cases the orderings yielded by Q may not be "severely" incomplete, but Q will still face the central problems noted earlier. As long as one of the measures from which Q is derived is strongly misdirecting, there will be orderings Q fails to yield about which we are certain. Moreover, whatever the nature of the measures from which Q is derived, Q will not allow trade-offs of the sort we noted.

There are other, deep, problems with the suggestions in question. Let me mention one for each.

There are purposes for which an intersection approach is well suited. For instance, one could possibly determine the greatest all-around basketball players by appropriately employing an intersection approach. In addition, as we implicitly supposed throughout chapter 3, one might feel confident that any ordering yielded by a carefully selected intersection relation would be uncontroversial.[40] For the reasons noted, however, an intersection approach is not the most plausible way of attempting to capture fully a complex and multifaceted notion.

5.5 A Better Alternative

Let me next offer a suggestion for how best to proceed if one is interested in arriving at a measure that (as) accurately (as possible) captures and reflects a complex and multifaceted notion. To do this, it will be helpful to consider again the

---

Clearly, a measure that simply ignores one or more "troublesome" aspects of a multifaceted notion has no claim to being an accurate measure of the whole of that notion. At best, such a measure might reflect a truncated version of the notion in question, and might yield orderings that "generally" correspond with those of the original notion. Similarly, measures of the whole of a complex notion might be "relatively plausible" as long as the orderings they yielded corresponded "more or less" accurately with those that would be yielded by "most" of the different aspects of the notion "most" of the time. Correspondingly, there is no particular reason to believe that an intersection of such measures (or for that matter any other combination of such measures we might arrive at in a non-*ad hoc* way) would even reflect, let alone accurately capture, each of the complex notion's different aspects giving each its due weight in relation to the others.

40. There are various positions one might take regarding what we may conclude when employing a carefully constructed intersection relation Q. Let us distinguish four: (1) any judgment yielded by Q will be uncontroversial; (2) any judgment that Q fails to yield will be controversial; (3) any judgment yielded by Q will be less controversial than any judgment not yielded by Q; and (4) judgments yielded by Q will "tend" to be less controversial than judgments not yielded by Q.

As noted earlier, Sen's official line is simply to suggest that Q "helps to sort out the relatively less controversial rankings from those that are more doubtful" (p. 74). This cautious remark commits Sen to no more than position 4. However, unofficially, I think (based on conversation) that Sen is inclined to endorse, and even defend, both positions 2 and 3.

There are, I think, several perspectives from which positions 2 and 3 may initially seem plausible. Ultimately, however, my own view is that while 1 may be defensible, 2 and 3 are not. My reasons for rejecting 2 and 3 can be gleaned from our earlier example of the basketball players D and F. There is *no* question in my mind that D, who is the greatest scorer, rebounder, defender, and team leader in the game's history, is a better player than F, who is well below average in all those respects, even though F is a slightly better ball handler than D. To be sure, the extent to which D is better than F would be even greater if D were a better ball handler than F, but the fact that this is not so is not enough to render the judgment that D is a better player than F controversial. Indeed, I contend there would not be a single knowledgeable and unbiased player, coach, or fan of basketball who would be uncertain as to whether D was better than F. Hence, I reject 2.

Similarly, suppose there were a player, E, who was *slightly* better than F in terms of each of the aspects of basketball ability. I grant that the judgment that E would be a better player than F would be uncontroversial, but I reject the claim that it would be less controversial than the judgment that D would be a better player than F. Asked which was the better player among D, E, and F, I contend that knowledgeable and unbiased players, coaches, and fans would be unanimous in selecting D, and that, if anything, there would be less hesitation in choosing between D and F than in choosing between E and F. In addition, I think much more would be required to shake our confidence that D is better than F, than to shake our confidence that E is better than F. Hence, I also reject position 3.

notion of basketball ability, a notion that is more trivial, less widespread, and less controversial than the notion of inequality. The notion of basketball ability is analogous to that of inequality in certain respects, and disanalogous in others.[41] However, for my present purposes, I am mainly interested in the fact that both notions are complex and multifaceted.

Suppose we wanted to arrive at an accurate measure of basketball ability, that is, at a method or procedure for comparing any two people in terms of their basketball ability. How might we best go about doing this? As trivial and obvious as this might seem, I would suggest we should start by getting as clear as possible about what the various facets are constituting the multifaceted notion of basketball ability. Having done this, we should then combine these facets into a single measure in such a way as to accord each its proper weight. In this way, we might arrive at a measure that (as) accurately (as possible) captures and reflects the notion we want. (Note, as we will see in sections 5.6 and 5.7, giving each aspect its "proper" weight may or may not involve giving each aspect a constant weight.)

The idea here might be fleshed out as follows. If we were interested in arriving at a measure of basketball ability, we might begin by asking ourselves the following question: when we judge one player to be better than another, what aspects are relevant to the judgment we make? As suggested in the previous section, our answer to this question will presumably include such factors as the ability to score points, to get rebounds, to play defense, to handle the ball, and to lead the team. Once we were clear on what aspects are involved in our notion, we might then seek to arrive at a measure of each aspect. Each measure would tell us how skilled players were with respect to the aspect in question, and would give us a way of comparing players along that dimension. For instance, we might think we could accurately measure a player's scoring ability by how many points he averaged per game. If so, then someone who averaged eighteen points would have more scoring ability than someone who averaged twelve. Our ultimate aim, of course, would be to arrive at a measure of these measures accurately corresponding to the notion of basketball ability. Essentially, this would involve determining the relative importance of each of the aspects of basketball ability, and then combining the measures of the different aspects accordingly. For instance, if we determined that rebounding ability was twice as important as scoring ability, then in our final measure of the notion of basketball ability someone's rebounding ability, as determined by the appropriate measure for that aspect, would count twice as much as someone's scoring ability, as determined by the appropriate measure for *that* aspect.

The intuitive idea here is quite simple. If we are seriously interested in comparing two people in terms of their basketball ability, then we should compare them in terms of *each* aspect relevant to that ability, and count each aspect in accordance with how important it is to a person's ability to play basketball. If we do this, then we should arrive at the correct judgment given our multifaceted notion of basketball ability.

Now in the case of basketball ability, we *might* be able to come up with a precise and wholly satisfactory measure for each of the aspects composing that

---

41. In the following section I shall return to the significance, or lack thereof, of the disanalogies between basketball ability and inequality.

notion. Similarly, we *might* be able to come up with a precise and wholly satisfactory weighting of each of the various measures. (For instance, we might decide that each steal is worth so many rebounds, that each rebound is worth so many points, that each point is worth so many assists, and so forth.) If both these conditions held, then presumably we might arrive at a measure of basketball ability yielding a total ordering of all basketball players. Much more likely, however, we might be fairly confident about our methods for measuring certain aspects, such as rebounding[42] or scoring, but less confident about our methods for measuring other aspects—e.g. the ability to handle the ball or to lead the team. In addition, we may have no firm rule for counting each aspect exactly so much and no more in comparison to the others. Thus, for instance, while we may be confident that scoring twenty points is more important than getting three rebounds, we may be unclear whether scoring fifteen points is more important than getting eight rebounds.

The importance of such uncertainty is that, if we are truly faithful to the spirit of the procedure we have presented, our ultimate measure of the notion of basketball ability will undoubtedly be complex, messy, and incomplete. Still, as Sen rightly reminds us, "a measure can hardly be more precise than the concept it represents" (pp. 5-6). Neither our uncertainty in these matters nor a measure accurately mirroring these uncertainties will necessarily reflect a failure to understand or capture accurately the notion of basketball ability; rather, they might be the appropriate and inevitable[43] result of a complex, multifaceted, and incomplete notion.

The point to stress is whether our notion of basketball playing ability is complete or incomplete, if we want to capture that notion accurately we must accurately reflect each of the aspects composing that notion. It is highly unlikely that any method will just *happen* to do this. Rather, to arrive at the sort of method we want we must do some careful thinking. First, we must get clear on what the various aspects *are* constituting the notion of basketball ability. Then, we must arrive at a method accurately reflecting *each* of these aspects. I have suggested this would probably involve a two-step process. Step one would involve arriving at a measure for each of the aspects. This would enable us to compare each player in terms of each aspect. Step two would involve determining the relative importance of the various aspects comprising the notion of basketball ability and combining the values yielded by the measures arrived at in step one accordingly.

Naturally, in both steps our decisions will be guided, though not wholly determined, by our pretheoretical intuitions about who the better basketball players are.[44]

---

42. "Rebounding" is used here in place of "the ability to rebound." For brevity's sake, analogous substitutions are also sometimes used for basketball ability's other aspects.

43. So long as our thinking is guided by the notion itself.

44. More specifically, in both steps, though probably the second more than the first, we would go through the sort of process John Rawls describes in order to insure that our decisions reflect the "considered" judgments we might make in a state of "reflective equilibrium." (See *A Theory of Justice* [Harvard University Press, 1971], pp. 46-50. Also, see Norman Daniels's "Wide Reflective Equilibrium," *Journal of Philosophy* 5 [1979]: 256-82.) Thus, for instance, our initial judgments about how much to count each aspect will be influenced and altered by our pretheoretical notions about who the better players are, while our judgments about who the better players are will in turn be influenced and altered by our developed views about how much to count each aspect.

Central to the approach I have been advocating is that it will involve precisely the sort of trade-offs precluded by the intersection approach.[45] Thus, before rendering a final judgment as to how two alternatives compare, such an approach will take into account the number and relative significance of the aspects supporting possible judgments as well as the degree to which the different aspects support those judgments.

Incidentally, I believe comparisons between basketball players are often made in roughly the way discussed, as a typical assessment of two players might run something like this: "True, x scores more than y, but rebounding is as important as scoring, and y gets more rebounds than x." "Yes, but each blocked shot is worth about three points, and while x has about three blocks a game, y rarely blocks shots." "Still, one must not underestimate the way y sparks his team, x on the other hand . . ."

If the discussion is a fairly informed and dispassionate one—so the perceptions of the participants are not too distorted by partisan bias—eventually the two players will be compared in terms of each of the aspects of basketball ability. The relative importance of these aspects will be roughly and intuitively calculated, and an overall judgment will be made as to the relative abilities of the two players. Anyway, whether or not something like this actually *does* occur—I think it does—it seems such a process *should* occur both when our concern is with comparing basketball ability, and when our concern is with comparing inequality. More generally, I think such an approach is a reasonable way of attempting to capture and reflect our complex and multifaceted notions.

5.6 Objections and Replies

Some believe I have ignored certain obvious or characteristic disanalogies between basketball ability and inequality in ways rendering the preceding discussion suspect. Let me consider several such objections.

First, one might object that the analogy between basketball ability and inequality is strained because it is clear from the start that basketball ability is a complex of other abilities and that the question is one of weighting, whereas it is much less clear that this is so regarding inequality. I grant the disanalogy in question but fail to see its force. I have not employed the basketball analogy in (question-begging) support of my view that inequality is complex. I have offered arguments throughout this book in support of inequality's complexity, and asked the best way of proceeding in order to capture—that is, measure as accurately as possible—a complex notion. Once it is granted that a notion *is* complex, I think the best way of trying to measure that notion *will* involve a weighting of its aspects along the lines of the basketball example. So for my purposes the analogy is apt, as the relevant question is *whether* basketball ability and inequality are both complex, not the transparency or timing of our recognizing their complexity.

Second, one might object to my analogy because one thinks basketball ability is

45. See the previous section.

an additively separable[46] notion whereas inequality is not. That is, one might think that how good someone is regarding basketball ability is a simple (though weighted) *additive* function of how good that person is regarding each of the separate aspects of basketball ability, where our judgment about how good someone is regarding each aspect is independent of our judgment about how good that person is regarding the other aspects, but that how good a situation is regarding inequality is *not* a simple (though weighted) additive function of how good that situation is regarding inequality's aspects, where our judgment about how good a situation is regarding each aspect is independent of our judgment about how good that situation is regarding the other aspects.

This objection raises several interesting and important issues, but as with the preceding objection I do not see how it undermines my suggested approach for arriving at a measure of inequality. I confess that in my discussion I proceeded as if basketball ability were additively separable in the manner in question. But I only did this for reasons of clarity and simplicity and nothing about my suggested approach hinges on this.

Consider the following view. Though rebounding is an important aspect of basketball ability, and other things equal one would always prefer a better rebounder to a worse rebounder, how much someone's ability to rebound ultimately matters depends on his whole package of basketball skills. For example, great rebounding ability matters more in someone whose other characteristics make him well suited to play center, such as size, lack of speed, and a good inside shot, than in someone whose other characteristics make him well suited to play guard, such as lack of bulk, ballhandling, and a good outside shot. Similar remarks might be made about the other aspects of basketball ability. On this view, how good a basketball player someone is, all things considered, will depend on how good he is regarding the different aspects of basketball ability *and the complex non-additive relation between those aspects.*

In fact, I accept this view. Hence, I do not believe basketball ability is additively separable. But having said that, I would suggest that my basic account of how we might best go about arriving at an accurate measure of basketball ability will be unchanged. It is still the case that we must first get clear on what the various aspects *are* constituting the notion of basketball ability. Then, we must combine these aspects into a measure in such a way as to accord each its proper weight, where this would probably involve a two-step process. Step one would involve arriving at a measure for each aspect that would enable us to compare each player in terms of that aspect. Step two would involve determining the relative importance of the various aspects of basketball ability *in combination with each other* and then weighting and combining the values yielded by step one's measures accordingly.

I do not wish to minimize the difficulties one would confront in trying to construct an accurate measure of basketball ability if that notion is nonadditively separable, any more than I wanted to minimize the difficulties in constructing such a measure on the alternative assumption. My point is simply that my suggestion for

---

46. The notion of additive separability was introduced in section 5.3. See note 15, and the surrounding text.

how best to proceed if one wants to arrive at a measure of a complex notion does not depend on whether the notion with which one is concerned is additively separable. Correspondingly, the claimed disanalogy between basketball ability and inequality regarding additive separability—which may or may not obtain—does not affect my position.

Importantly, then, my claims about seeking a measure that will accord each of inequality's aspects its "proper" or "due" weight should *not* be construed as implying that each of inequality's aspects must be accorded a *constant* weight. Perhaps certain aspects will be more or less significant in combination with others—for example, if a situation is already very good in terms of aspect A, it may matter less that it (also) be good in terms of aspect B. Or perhaps promoting A will initially be more important than promoting B, but once a situation is "sufficiently" good regarding A further incremental gains will matter less and it will then be more important to promote B than A. In other words, whether additive or not, nothing in my claims precludes the trade-off function between aspects from being as complicated as necessary.

Third, one might object to the analogy between basketball ability and inequality by arguing that they are entirely different kinds of notions embedded within entirely different contexts. For instance, one might contend that basketball is a specific game with precise rules and well-defined aims in virtue of which one could expect basketball ability's aspects and their relative importance to be identifiable—say, in terms of their instrumental efficacy toward achieving the aims of basketball. The case is otherwise, one might contend, regarding morality in general and inequality in particular. There is no specific code or practice of morality or inequality with precise rules and well defined aims in virtue of which one could expect inequality's aspects and their relative importance to be identifiable. Correspondingly, although my suggested approach may seem perfectly plausible for arriving at a meaningful measure of basketball ability, there is no reason to expect my approach to meet with success in arriving at a meaningful measure of inequality.

This objection is significant, and some variation of it might be forwarded by two important, though very different, traditions in moral philosophy. Subjectivists deny the objectivity of value. Hence, they would deny the existence of any truths or facts about the world that could guide our reasoning about inequality's aspects in such a way as to result in an (objectively) meaningful measure of inequality. Aristotelians, on the other hand, are objectivists about ethics, but they deny that the subject matter of ethics permits precision. On an Aristotelian view the good is what the good man does. The good is recognized by the person of practical wisdom and is a matter of perception or judgment; it is decidedly *not* something that can be codified in an accurate system of rules or measures we might then consult in the course of moral deliberation.[47] (Presumably the subject matter of basketball might be far more precise and permit the sort of meaningful measure unavailable for ethics.)

This is not the place for me to respond to the deep worries of subjectivists or Aristotelians. Instead let me observe that their worries are not merely about my

47. See Aristotle's *Nicomachean Ethics*, for example, book 1, chapters 3 and 7, and book 2, chapters 2, 6, and 9.

particular approach, they are worries about *any* approach for trying to arrive at a meaningful measure of inequality.

My conclusion at the end of the preceding section was modest. All I claimed is that my suggested approach is "a reasonable way of attempting to capture and reflect our complex and multifaceted notions." This conclusion stands despite subjectivist and Aristotelian worries. After all, I did not claim my approach would necessarily *succeed*; rather, I offered it as "a suggestion for how best to proceed if one is interested in arriving at a measure which (as) accurately (as possible) captures and reflects a complex and multifaceted notion." Though here as elsewhere in philosophy there are no guarantees, I believe it is a suggestion worth considering.

If the subjectivists or Aristotelians are right, perhaps a meaningful measure of inequality is not to be had. Still, there are many respects in which it would be useful to have such a measure. Hence, unless we are already convinced they *are* right— and I take it many are not—there is reason to pursue my suggested approach.

In sum, although there are disanalogies between basketball ability and inequality, they do not impugn my earlier claims.

5.7 Methodology, Additive Separability, and the Hermeneutic Tradition

The preceding remarks about additive separability have some bearing on my methodology. In addition, I suspect they may have some bearing on the nature of the conflict between the analytic and hermeneutic traditions. Let me conclude this chapter by commenting on the former and speculating (no doubt foolishly!) about the latter.

As noted in the Introduction, some people are suspicious of my attempt to understand the notion of inequality independently of other ideals and the particular contexts with which it is normally associated. Although I suspect most who share this view are simply not egalitarians, at least not in my sense of the word, some might object to my methodology on general hermeneutic grounds. They will insist that trying to understand inequality, or any other ideal, out of the particular historical context in which it is embedded is to lose sight of the point of the philosophical enterprise, as any concept elucidated in such a manner will be unconnected with the real world and hence be lacking in significant grounding or relevance. "What" they might ask "does the inequality of my abstract sterile diagrams have to do with inequality as it is experienced in the world and as it influences the course of human events?" On this view my methodology commits the analytic philosopher's classic mistake of seeking to understand the whole by analyzing its parts, while failing to recognize that the parts themselves cannot be understood independently of the whole.

It is not my intention, here, to defend analytic philosophy or to compare the relative strengths and weaknesses of the analytic and hermeneutic traditions. But I do want to suggest that my methodology is compatible with certain important insights of both traditions. I believe there are many cases where one cannot *fully* understand the parts independently of the whole. On the other hand, as the hermeneutic tradition itself insists, neither can one fully understand the whole independently of the parts. This, of course, is the famous—or infamous— hermeneutic circle. And it raises the troubling question, "if to know the whole one must know the part, and to know the part one must know the whole, how is knowledge of anything possible?" How are we to enter (or exit?) the circle to establish a starting place or perspective (not to say foundation) from which to develop our understanding of both part and whole?

Not surprisingly, here my sympathies lie with the analytic approach. It is not as if the whole is composed of something *other* than its parts. Hence, if we want to understand the whole, it makes perfect sense to *begin* by trying to identify and understand its parts. And in doing this it does not seem unreasonable to *start* by carefully considering each part separately. But, as the hermeneutic tradition suggests, we must recognize that any understanding of the nature and significance of the different parts that we reach in this manner will only be tentative with respect to our ultimate goal, which is to understand the whole by understanding each part *and its nature and role in relation to the others.*

My view here parallels my earlier discussion regarding the best way of proceeding if one has a complex notion that is nonadditively separable. Suppose we wanted to know whether one situation was better than another all things considered, and we couldn't tell just by "looking" at them. (Alas, our judgment failed us and those we might [otherwise] have thought possessed practical wisdom were unable to help.) We might throw up our hands in despair, or perhaps decide that there couldn't "really" be any significant difference between them. Alternatively, we might proceed first by trying to get clear on what aspects *are* relevant to our all-things-considered judgments, and then by trying to combine these aspects into a measure in such a way as to accord each its due weight. As before, I think this might involve a two-step process. Step one would involve arriving at a measure for each aspect that would enable us to compare each outcome in terms of that aspect. Step two would involve determining the relative importance of the various aspects *in combination with each other* and then weighting and combining the values yielded by step one's measures accordingly—where, of course, this recognizes that according each aspect its "due weight" *may* require a complex, nonadditive, function involving variable weights.

Naturally, I favor the last approach, and see this book and its methodology as important for carrying out step one. As before, I grant that the described process may not succeed. Perhaps in seeking a method or measure—even a rough and incomplete one—for comparing situations all things considered, one is seeking yet another philosopher's stone. Still even if such an effort ultimately falls short of its aim, I believe the attempt to identify and clarify our different moral ideals reveals much about our moral concepts and the role they play in our moral thinking. I have found this to be so regarding Mill's contributions to our understanding of utility, Rawls's contributions to our understanding of justice, and my own modest contributions to our understanding of equality.

The foregoing suggests one way of interpreting a central insight of the hermeneutic tradition. Perhaps the insight that the part cannot be understood independently of the whole reflects the similar insight of the Gestalt tradition that the whole may be greater or less than the *sum* of its parts where the basic point is *not* that the whole is somehow composed of something *other* than its parts—it obviously isn't!—but rather that parts often combine in *nonadditive* ways in constituting the wholes of which they are parts. Thus, to note a nonphilosophical case, giving someone a more beautiful nose may or may not result in his having a more beautiful face, depending on the nature of the relation between a person's features and the beauty of his face. (Perhaps the more beautiful nose will be too big, or too small, for the size of the person's eyes or mouth.) Similarly, to note a moral case, increasing a situation's utility may or may not improve it—even a little—depending on the nature of the relation between utility and other ideals. So, for example, on a Kantian view of proportional justice the moral value of increased utility will depend on whether the beneficiary of the increased utility deserves her good fortune. (Recall Kant's dictum that "the sight of a being who is not graced by any touch of a pure and good will but who yet enjoys an uninterrupted prosperity can never delight a rational and impartial spectator. Thus a good will seems to constitute the indispensable condition of being even worthy of happiness.")[48]

Understood as an insight about additive separability, I think the hermeneutic claim that the part cannot be understood independently of the whole is interesting, important, and too often neglected. I have discussed additivity elsewhere[49] and shall not explore it here; but briefly, I think many positions in philosophy—especially analytic philosophy—implicitly assume additive separability where it is unclear such assumptions are defensible. Correspondingly, I think the hermeneutic tradition offers valuable criticism insofar as it calls such assumptions into question. On the other hand, I also think it is no accident additive assumptions are so pervasive. While such assumptions raise many worries, and are no doubt unwarranted in *some* cases, there are many cases where it is far from clear how we might think about morality or rationality in the absence of such assumptions.

In any event, for the reasons given here and in the preceding section I think accepting the nonadditive separability of our moral ideals does *not* undermine my methodological approach. To be sure, we may learn further insights about the nature and role of inequality when we later consider its relation to other ideals. Accordingly, we should regard the results of our present inquiry as preliminary. Still, the process of understanding must begin somewhere, and what better place to start than to try to identify and clarify as carefully as possible the different parts that compose the whole and whose relation to each other we ultimately seek to understand? This book begins the task for the ideal of equality.

48. Grounding for the Metaphysics of Morals, first section, first paragraph (James W. Ellington's translation).

49. Larry S. Temkin, "Additivity Problems," in *Encyclopedia of Ethics*, ed. by Lawrence Becker and Charlotte Becker (Garland Publishing, 1992) pp. 15-18. For a rich discussion of additivity, see Shelly Kagan's "The Additive Fallacy," *Ethics 99* (1988): 5-31.

I conclude that my methodology is compatible with the hermeneutic insight that one cannot fully understand the part independently of the whole, at least on one plausible interpretation of that insight. More particularly, I conclude that my methodology is not objectionable as long as we do not naively assume that morally ranking outcomes will be a simple (perhaps weighted) additive function of separate values and ideals.

6

Inequality's Sensitivity to Affluence or Well-Being

(1) Is our notion of inequality sensitive to society's overall level of affluence or well-being?

Alternative version of the same question:

(1a) Does inequality matter more in a poor society than in a rich one?

In this chapter I shall offer an answer to (1) and (1a) and consider how best to capture that answer in a measure of inequality. As we shall see, this is one area where much of the economics literature needs revising.

A brief comment before proceeding. Although (1) and (1a) are (largely) adequate for our purposes, I think there are better ways of formulating the question in which I am interested. Better than (1) would be:

(2) Is our notion of inequality sensitive to the levels of affluence or well-being of the individuals between whom inequality obtains?

Better than (1a) would be:

(2a) Does inequality matter more when people are badly-off then when they are well-off?

Questions (2) and (2a) are more in keeping with this book's approach. However, because most economists have thought about this issue in terms of (1) and (1a), I begin the discussion in their terms. This will help us to avoid begging certain questions in our formulation of the issue, and to see why the economists' measures of inequality have certain features. Eventually the discussion will illustrate how (1) and (1a) can be misleading, and thus why (2) and (2a) are preferable.

6.1 The Correct View

Does inequality matter more in a poor society than a rich one? The literature on this question has been divided and confusing. Despite this, I think that for a large class

157

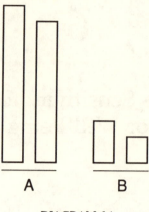

DIAGRAM 6.1

of cases, including most usually considered, this is one of the few significant questions about inequality for which there is a clear, straightforward answer. Later, I will try to explain the source of at least some of the literature's confusion. First, let me discuss what the correct answer should be.

Consider diagram 6.1. As drawn, the absolute size of the gaps between the better- and worse-off are the same in A and B. Despite this, I think most would rightly judge B's inequality worse than A's. In B, the worse-off have relatively little compared with the better-off. In A, on the other hand, not only are the worse-off better off (than those in B), but they fare much better relative to the better-off.

Of course, there is a straightforward sense in which it *could* be maintained that A has just as *much* inequality as B. For example, if A and B's worse-off groups have n people, and the gap in each world is c, it *might* be claimed that in both worlds the total amount of inequality is n(c). Still, that A and B have the same amount of inequality in *this* sense does not entail that A's inequality is as bad as B's; and indeed, as already indicated, I think it is not.

To indicate further some of the reasons for thinking B's inequality worse than A's, it will be useful to assign numbers to A's and B's group levels. Suppose that in A the better- and worse-off are at levels 11,000 and 10,000, respectively, whereas in B they are at levels 2,000 and 1,000.[1] Then the difference between A's inequality and B's can be looked at as follows. In A the worse-off half has 47.6 percent of the welfare, in B it only has 33.3 percent. Moreover, in A the worse-off group's members fare 90.9 percent as well as the better-off group's members, whereas in B they only fare 50 percent as well.

---

1. Naturally, one doesn't have to be able to determine how much welfare individuals actually have in order to make certain judgments about how they would compare if they had certain amounts. I point this out in order to remind the reader that while in this example and others I often proceed *as if* we are able to determine welfare levels and, correspondingly, zero levels precisely, the point of my examples does not depend on our being able to do this.

Another way of looking at this situation is to consider the size of the gap between what the worse-off have and what it seems they "should" have, relative to how well-off they actually are. For example, although on the relative to the best-off person view of complaints it will seem for both A and B that the worse-off have 1,000 less units than they "should," in B those 1,000 units represent a 100 percent increase (that the worse-off were denied by Fate), while in A they only represent a 10 percent increase.

Finally, one can see how the relative position of the worse-off group will be more sensitive to changes in B than in A. For example, in B increasing the worse-off by 200 would involve a 10 percent increase in how well they fare relative to the better-off (from 50 percent as well off to 60 percent as well off); whereas in A increasing the worse-off by 200 would involve only a 1.8 percent increase in how well they fare relative to the better-off (from 90.9 percent as well-off to 92.7 percent as well off). Similarly, in B the size of the gap between the better- and worse-off will have gone from representing a 100 percent increase in the worse-off's level to a 66.6 percent increase in their level—a rather significant change of 33.3 percent. In A, on the other hand, the size of the gap between the better- and worse-off will have gone from representing a 10 percent increase in the worse-off's level to a 7.8 percent increase—a much less significant change of only 2.2 percent.

This point is generalizable. On each of the ways of looking at A's and B's inequality an increase of n units will have a greater impact on B's inequality than on A's. Moreover, the same point goes for decreases, and applies whether it is the worse-off who change or the better-off. (Naturally, the greater impact will be for the better if the worse-off increase or the better-off decrease, and for the worse if the the worse-off decrease or the better-off increase). Analogous remarks could be made concerning how the worse-off fare relative to the average.[2]

Employing chapter 2's terminology, B's worse-off have more to complain about than A's. They have been more unlucky, treated less kindly by Fate. Moreover, this is so not merely with respect to their absolute levels, *but with respect to how they fare relative to the others in their world*. After all, in A the worse-off fare 90.9 percent as well off as the best-off person, 95.2 percent as well off as the average person, possess 47.6 percent of the total welfare, and so on. In B, on the other hand, the worse-off fare only 50 percent as well off as the best-off person, only 66.6 percent as well off as the average person, possess only 33.3 percent of the total welfare, and so on. Not surprisingly, then, I think we will, and should, regard B's inequality as worse (more unfair and unjust) than A's.

The foregoing considerations suggest the following. In measuring how bad a situation's inequality is one cannot simply focus on the absolute size of the gaps between better- and worse-off. One must also take account of the extent to which those gaps represent a significant difference in how well the worse-off fare relative

2. For example, in A, the worse-off group's members fare 95.2 percent as well as their world's average member, whereas in B, they fare only 66.6 percent as well. Similarly, if, in accordance with the relative to the average view, it seems A and B's worse-off have 500 units less than they "should," that may seem more significant in B, where those 500 units represent 50 percent of the worse-off's welfare, than in A where they represent only 5 percent of the worse-off's welfare.

to others. So, for example, a gap of 5,000 between the better- and worse-off may be very offensive if the worse-off *only have* 5,000, less offensive if they have 20,000, and hardly offensive at all if they have 1,000,000. More generally, how bad a gap of n units is depends upon how well off the people are between whom the gap obtains. Thus, in this sense, a clear answer can be given to (1) and (1a). "Yes." Our notion of inequality *is* sensitive to society's overall level; inequality matters *more* in a poor society than in a rich one.

An important proviso. As note one indicates, my example in this section assumes a precise zero level. It also involves each person being well above zero. I am well aware my arguments would need revision to accommodate the lack of a precise zero level, as well as cases involving people near or below the zero level. But I shall not offer the necessary revisions here, as my point in this section is merely to persuade the reader of my conclusion, and I trust for that purpose my simplified example and arguments are compelling—at least in the Millian sense of being "sufficient to determine the intellect."[3] Similarly, I grant that my "clear" answer is less clear in cases where everyone in the poor society is *far* below the zero level, or where even those in the "rich" society are below the zero level. Unfortunately, such cases raise a host of complicated questions that, though philosophically interesting, I cannot address here. Still, my discussion holds for most cases with which people have been (or might be) concerned. For points related to these claims, as well as my general conclusion, see sections 6.2, 6.4, and 6.6.

6.2 Objections and Responses

Some reject the preceding conclusion. Their argument runs roughly as follows. In a society of plenty promoting equality may be desirable, but in one of scarcity it is neither desirable nor acceptable. Suppose, for example, two people are stranded on an island whose resources can only support one. If outside help will not arrive in time to save both, it would be morally worse (as well as irrational?) to promote equality by dividing the island's resources. That is, given the choice between A and B in diagram 6.2 one ought to choose A, since an unequal situation where one survives is morally preferable to an equal situation where both die. Thus, the argument concludes, inequality matters less in a poor society than a rich one. (Note, this argument does *not* depend on the claim that lives below the subsistence level are

---

3. Some readers may think the whole idea of zero levels is mistaken. Maybe they think every possible life *must* be worth living, or that it makes no sense to think a life might either be, or not be, worth living since we can't compare life to nonexistence. Or maybe they think that zero levels are merely social constructs, with different societies having different views about when life ceases to be worth living and there being no further fact about whether a life is, or is not, worth living. I shall not try to argue against such positions. Suffice it to say, I find them deeply implausible. I recognize that there is probably no precise zero level, and that even the range within which life ceases to be worth living is open to rational dispute. Nevertheless, I believe it is both meaningful and true to hold that while some lives would be worth living, others would not. In any event, even readers who part company with me here may find it illuminating to grant me my claim for the sake of argument. I suspect they may find that analogous arguments to those I present might be constructed using premises they accept.

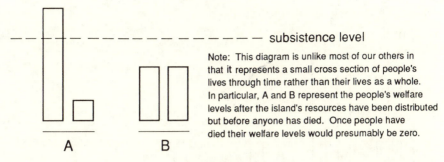

subsistence level

Note: This diagram is unlike most of our others in that it represents a small cross section of people's lives through time rather than their lives as a whole. In particular, A and B represent the people's welfare levels after the island's resources have been distributed but before anyone has died. Once people have died their welfare levels would presumably be zero.

DIAGRAM 6.2

not worth living, merely that they are not *sustainable*. Thus proponents of such an argument can grant that the lives of those in B are worth living, and hence would be worth preserving *if one could*, but they think that despite this B's equality is worse than A's inequality since it results in two dying instead of one.)

Arguments like the foregoing are popular. This is unfortunate. Such arguments fail because they fall into the trap—warned about in chapters 1 and 2—of confusing two separate questions: When is one situation worse than another regarding inequality? and When is one situation worse than another *all things considered*? Such arguments do *not* establish that inequality matters less in a poor society than a rich one. They merely remind us that inequality is not all that matters.[4]

Undoubtedly, A is better than B all things considered. But this does not mean that A's inequality is better than B's—it is not. Nor does it mean A's inequality doesn't matter. Surely, the egalitarian would say, A's worse-off person has a significant complaint regarding inequality. He is much worse off than the other person through no fault of his own and this is unfair and unjust. Moreover, the difference between the quality of their lives is most significant. It is a difference measured in terms of the necessities of life—a difference, quite literally, between who lives and dies. To suggest such inequality doesn't matter is ludicrous. A's inequality is *very* bad and it matters a great deal.[5] Still, as bad as A's inequality is, if the cost of removing it were a situation where none survived, even the egalitarian could admit the moral unacceptability of such a cost.

The foregoing is, I think, uncontroversial and can be straightforwardly applied to the argument in question. Consider diagram 6.3. No doubt we would rather transform A* into B* than A into B. However, this does not show A*'s inequality is worse than A's, any more than our preference for A over B shows B's inequality is worse than A's. Clearly, regarding inequality A's worse-off person will have more to

4. Note, my claim here is that such arguments fail to establish that inequality matters less in a poor society than a rich one. As I will note, such arguments *may* support the oft-heard claim that only a rich society can "afford the luxury of equality." But that is a very different claim. One which is compatible with the view that inequality matters more in a poor society than a rich one.

5. The nonegalitarian would, of course, deny these claims. In making them I am wearing the egalitarian's hat. As throughout this book, my concern is to explicate the egalitarian's position, not to defend it.

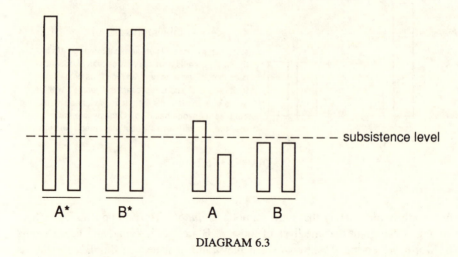

DIAGRAM 6.3

complain about than B's.[6] Similarly, for all the reasons presented in 6.1, A's worse-off person will have more to complain about than A*'s. Obviously then (since A, A*, and B are two-person worlds), just as A is worse than B *regarding inequality*, so it is worse than A*.

The argument I have been criticizing may support the oft-heard claim that only a rich society can "afford the luxury" of equality. However, even if this is so, it is only because inequality is not all that matters and, in particular, because the moral costs of removing inequality may be higher in poor societies than in rich ones. The argument does not impugn our earlier result: inequality matters more in a poor society than in a rich one.

There are a number of arguments similar to the one just considered to which the same points should be made. Let me discuss but one other. Some economists and philosophers contend that until society becomes fairly advanced inequality is desirable because it is more conducive to civilization's development. This contention generally involves two claims: first, for a variety of familiar reasons (concerning incentives, risk taking, capital accumulation, and so on), a poor society is more likely to become rich if some are exceptionally well-off than if all are equal; and second, the benefits gained from the development engendered by inequality are sufficient to outweigh the costs of that inequality.

Now for my present purposes, I shall not debate the plausibility of these two

6. Strictly speaking, of course, there is no *worse*-off person in B, as all are equally well-off. I trust, however, there is no serious danger of confusion here. Throughout this work I will sometimes speak of the worse- or better-off person where people are equally well off or of the worst- or best-off person where strictly speaking there is no such person as a whole group of people is worst- or best-off. In these, and similar cases, I trust my meaning is plain. For the sake of my arguments, the "worse-" or "better-off" person in a case where all are equally well off may be any member of the situation; similarly, where appropriate, the "worst-" or "best-off" person in a situation may be thought to be any member of the worst- or best-off group. Such claims could be put in terms of a "representative" member of the situation or groups in question, but for our purposes this is unnecessary and possibly misleading.

claims. Instead, I want to emphasize that *even if* correct they do not impugn our earlier result. Those who have thought otherwise have failed to distinguish between the question of when one situation is worse than another regarding inequality and the question of when one situation is worse than another all things considered. The claims in question *may* support the judgments that, all things considered, it is better for a poor society to be unequal than equal,[7] and that only a rich society can "afford the luxury" of equality. But they do not support the judgments that even with respect to *inequality* it is better for a poor society to be unequal than equal, or that inequality matters less in a poor society than in a rich one.

I have considered two typical arguments that have led some economists and philosophers to deny that inequality matters more in a poor society than a rich one. Such arguments rest on a confusion of the two distinct questions already noted. Once one is careful to avoid this confusion, it becomes evident that section 6.1's considerations are compelling.

6.3 Four Approaches for Capturing the Correct View

We have seen that in measuring inequality one cannot merely focus on the absolute size of the gaps between the better- and worse-off. One must also consider the relative position of the worse-off vis-à-vis others. More specifically, we have determined that:

S: inequality matters more in a poor society than in a rich one.[8]

In this section I shall present four approaches for capturing S—so designated because it reflects our notion of inequality's *sensitivity* to a society's overall level. Briefly, my reasons for considering these approaches are as follows. The first approach is incorporated into many economists' measures, and (hence) is (implicitly) adopted by most economists. The second approach has glaring shortcomings that help illuminate similar, but less glaring, shortcomings in the first approach. The third approach has significant initial appeal, and is perhaps the most natural approach to which one might turn once the first approach's weaknesses are appreciated. The fourth approach is perhaps the least natural, and to my knowledge no one else has advocated it. Nevertheless, it is ultimately the most promising.

Ultimately, then, my discussion of the first three approaches will serve two purposes: first, to undermine particular positions people hold or otherwise might incline toward and, second, to highlight both desirable and undesirable features of which an approach to capturing S should take account. But that is the work of later sections. My task here is merely to describe the four approaches, each of which can

7. Even this is questionable, as one must bear in mind the differences between process and static judgments. From the fact that A *together with its successors* would be better than B *together with its successors*, it doesn't follow that A is better than B.

8. But cf. the proviso at the end of section 6.1 where we grant that S may need to be qualified, or its scope limited. Henceforth I shall drop this reminder.

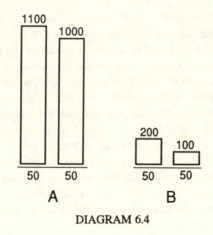

DIAGRAM 6.4

be combined with chapter 2's aspects. For simplicity, I shall illustrate the basic idea of these approaches in terms of the additive principle of equality (AP) and the relative to the best-off person view of complaints (BOP). The application of these approaches to other egalitarian views is analogous and will not be pursued here.

Recall that on AP and BOP inequality is measured by first determining the size of the gap between each person and the best-off person, and then adding together the numbers arrived at—where the larger the sum, the worse the inequality (see chapter 2). Now as chapter 2 argues, this way of measuring inequality has much to recommend it. However, focusing as it does on the absolute size of the gaps between the worse- and the best-off it needs supplementing if it is to capture S. This, of course, is where the four approaches come in.

The first approach is simple and straightforward. On this approach one (first) measures inequality as suggested previously, but (then) divides the resulting sum by the number representing society's average level. As we shall see, one way of interpreting this approach—but not the only one—is to view it as involving two steps; the first step determining the "absolute" amount or degree of inequality obtaining, and the second determining how bad it is for a society at that overall (average) level to have that "absolute" amount of inequality.

Consider diagram 6.4. Clearly, if one simply compares A's and B's inequality by measuring the size of the gap between each person and the best-off person, and then adding these numbers together, A will be just as bad as B, as what might be called the "inequality index" of A—henceforth, I(A)—would equal the "inequality index" of B, or I(B). That is, $I(A) = (1,100-1,000)50 = I(B) = (200-100)50 = 5,000$. However, on the first approach B would be worse than A, since B's average level (150) is significantly lower than A's (1,050), while the "absolute" amount of inequality is the same (5,000). More particularly, on the first approach $I(B) = (200-100)50/150 = 33.33 > I(A) = (1,100-1,000)50/1,050 = 4.76$. One can see, therefore, how the first approach yields the desired result regarding A and B and how it reflects inequality's sensitivity to society's (average) level. How much the "absolute" amount of a society's inequality matters depends upon how well off (the average member of) that society is. The better off a society is the less a given "absolute" amount of inequality matters.

Whereas the first approach may (but need not) be viewed as attempting to capture inequality's sensitivity *after* summing up complaints—by "relativizing" the sum to society's average level[9]—the other three approaches are most naturally interpreted as attempting to capture inequality's sensitivity *before* summing up complaints, that is, at the stage where one is determining the size of individual complaints. The second approach does this by measuring the size of the gap between the best-off person and the person whose complaint is being measured, and then dividing by the best-off person's level.

One can see the effect this would have on our judgment regarding A and B. Instead of A's and B's worse-off members having the same size complaints—given that $(1,100-1,000) = (200-100)$—A's would have smaller complaints than B's, since $(1,100-1,000)/1,100 = 1/11 < (200-100)/200 = 1/2$. So, on the second approach each of A's worse-off would have a complaint of $1/11$, and $I(A) = (1/11)50 = 4.5$, whereas each of B's worse-off would have a complaint of $1/2$, and $I(B) = (1/2)50 = 25$. As with the first approach, therefore, the second yields the desirable result that B's inequality is worse than A's. More generally, the second approach reflects S by relativizing individual complaints to the best-off person's level. Intuitively, the idea is that to be n units worse off than the best-off person matters less (regarding inequality) if the best-off person is well off than if he is not well off.

The third approach is similar to the second. It determines someone's complaint by measuring the gap between the best-off person and her, and then dividing by her level. On the third approach, then, each of A's worse-off would have a complaint of $(1,100-1,000)/1,000 = .1$ and $I(A) = (.1)50 = 5$. Similarly, each of B's worse-off would have a complaint of $(200-100)/100 = 1$ and $I(B) = (1)50 = 50$. So, like the others, this approach captures the view that B's inequality is worse than A's, and reflects the general fact that inequality matters more in a poor society than in a rich one. It does this by relativizing each complaint to the level of the person who has the complaint. Intuitively, the idea of this approach is that to be n units worse off than the best-off person matters less (regarding inequality) when one is well off than when one is not well off.[10]

Like the third approach, the fourth attempts to capture S by relativizing each individual complaint to the level of the person who has the complaint. However, on the fourth approach one measures the gaps between the worse-off and the best-off person, and then "discounts" the numbers arrived at by a certain percentage, depending upon how well off the people are whose complaints are being measured. Intuitively, the idea of the fourth approach is the same as that of the third, but the fourth tries to capture this idea by weighting people's complaints in such a way that the better off they are the less each unit of difference between them and the best-off

---

9. Some readers have been unclear about this. The point is simply that *one* way of looking at the first approach is that after summing up complaints it takes the average, with the idea being that it takes the average of the summed complaints in order to reflect inequality's sensitivity.

10. Although there are similarities between them, as we shall see there are interesting and significant differences between the second and third approaches.

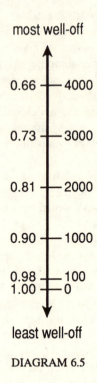

most well-off

least well-off

DIAGRAM 6.5

person counts. In practice, this might involve using a scale of the sort shown in diagram 6.5.

The numbers on the scale's right side represent welfare levels. The numbers on the left represent how much to count each unit that someone *at* that level is worse off than the best-off person. For example, on this scale someone 10 units worse off than the best-off person would have a complaint of 10 if he was at level 0 (a complaint of 1 for each unit he was worse off), and a complaint of 9.8 if he was at level 100 (a complaint of .98 for each unit he was worse off). More generally, someone n units worse off than the best-off person would have a complaint of n(1) if he were at level 0, n(.98) if at level 100, n(.9) if at level 1,000, n(.81) if at 2,000, and so on. Using this scale, then, each of A's worse-off would have a complaint of $(1,100-1,000).90 = 90$, while each of B's worse-off would have a complaint of $(200-100).98 = 98$. This would yield the desired result regarding A and B, as I(A) $= 90(50) = 4,500$, while I(B) $= 98(50) = 4,900$.

Let me emphasize that the above scale is merely illustrative. Constructing the actual scale would require a careful and thorough determination of the extent to which someone n units worse off than the best-off person has less to complain about if he is well off than if he is poorly off. *Eventually*, this project needs pursuing (and ultimately one would want such a scale for those below, as well as above, the zero level), but for my present purposes it is sufficient to note that, like the others, the fourth approach captures the view that B's inequality is worse than A's, and reflects

S. As indicated, it does this by relativizing each person's complaint to her level via a conversion scale as shown.

This completes my presentation of the four approaches. Between them they represent three logical ways that one might attempt to relativize the size of someone's complaint. The first approach relativizes someone's complaint as a function of both her level and others' levels; the second approach relativizes someone's complaint as a function of others' levels; and the third and fourth approaches relativize someone's complaint as a function of her level. I have claimed that each of the four approaches may be combined with chapter 2's aspects, and shown how each, in its own way, reflects S. In the next section, I shall consider some problems facing the first three approaches. These problems suggest that while for many cases each approach may suffice, it will be something like the fourth that most adequately reflects the way inequality is sensitive to a society's level.

Note. In the ensuing discussion I shall continue to illustrate my claims in terms of AP and BOP. However, similar problems arise on other aspects of inequality.

6.4 Problems with the First Three Approaches

In this section I shall detail some problems facing the first three approaches. If it seems I continue doing this long after establishing their implausibility—and I do!— this is because I am not just interested in undermining the first three approaches. I am also interested in highlighting features of which an approach to S should take account.

I start with a problem facing the second approach. Consider three worlds, C, D, and E, each having two groups of fifty people such that the worse-off are at level 100, while the better-off are at levels 1,000, 10,000, and 100,000, in C, D, and E, respectively. Clearly, D's worse-off, who are 9,900 units worse off than their better-off, have much more to complain about than C's, who are 900 units worse off than their better-off, while E's worse-off, who are 99,900 units worse off than their better-off, have by far the most to complain about. Correspondingly, D's inequality is significantly worse than C's, and E's is significantly worse than D's.

Diagram 6.6 helps graphically illustrate the extent of the differences between C, D, and E. The height of C's and D's columns have been drawn roughly to scale. Due to space limitations, the column representing E's better-off is shown disappearing into a cloud. Drawn to scale, it would extend ten times the length of D's tall column, or roughly four times the length of this page. Considering diagram 6.6, and imagining the full height of E's tall column, our earlier conclusions seem obvious, and even understated. D's worse-off do indeed appear to have *much* more to complain about than C's, and E's *much much* more to complain about. Correspondingly, D's inequality seems *much* worse than C's, and E's *much much* worse.

How much worse is "*much*" worse? How much worse is "*much much*" worse?

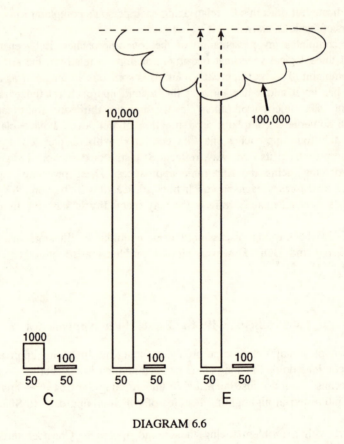

DIAGRAM 6.6

My own feeling is that D's worse-off would have at least five to ten times as much to complain about as C's.[11] They are, after all, no better off than C's worse-off, and they are ten times *worse* off relative to their best-off. Similarly, I believe E's worse-off have at least five to ten times as much to complain about as D's (and thus twenty-five to a hundred times as much to complain about as C's worse-off). Now if pressed I would probably argue for the higher figures. But for my present purposes it will suffice to note that at the *very least* D's worse-off will have a complaint one and a half times (50 percent) larger than C's, and similarly E's worse-off will have a complaint at least one and a half times [50 percent]) larger than D's (and thus more than two times (100 percent) larger than C's worse-off). Correspondingly, at the *very least* D's inequality will be one and half times as bad as C's, and E's at least one and a half times a bad as D's (and thus more than twice as bad as C's).[12]

11. More specifically, this would be my feeling insofar as I was caught in the grip of the relative to the best-off person view of complaints, which is the case presently being considered.

12. This follows directly on the view presently under consideration, where inequality is measured by adding up individual complaints, and where individual complaints are measured by comparing each individual to the best-off person.

Reflecting on diagram 6.6, it is obvious that these figures, chosen arbitrarily, are ridiculously low. As low as they are, however, they are high enough to illustrate a serious shortcoming of the second approach. To see this, one need only apply the second approach to C, D, and E, and note that on that approach: C's worse-off would have a complaint of $(1,000-100)/1,000 = .9$, D's a complaint of $(10,000-100)/10,000 = .99$, and E's a complaint of $(100,000-100)/100,000 = .999$; moreover, $I(C) = 45$, $I(D) = 49.5$, and $I(E) = 49.95$. According to the second approach, then, both in terms of how much the worse-off have to complain about, and how bad their inequality is, the differences between C and D, D and E, and E and C would be on the order of 10 percent, 1 percent, and 11 percent, respectively.[13] But, as just noted, at the *very least* the differences between these worlds should be 50 percent, 50 percent, and 100 percent, respectively. Thus, the second approach falls far short of reflecting the extent of the differences between C, D, and E.

The source of the second approach's problem is easy to spot. It lies in the way that it measures individual complaints. Because it divides the size of the gap between the best-off person and the person with a complaint by the best-off person's level, improvements in the best-off person's level increase both the numerator *and* denominator of the ratio measuring complaint size. Naturally, while one's complaint will tend to increase insofar as it does the former, it will tend to decrease insofar as it does the latter.

Thus, the second approach contains two opposing elements in the way it measures complaints whose net effect, as seen, is to soften drastically and implausibly the extent to which increases in the best-off person's level exacerbate individual complaints. Now obviously, it is the dividing of the size of the gap by the best-off person's level that is responsible for the implausible results noted. I would next like to show that this feature is implausible in its own right, and not merely in virtue of its unintuitive implications.

Consider the following dialogue between Tom, an advocate of the second approach, and John. The conversation concerns a world that has been transformed from a D- to an E-type world. For simplicity though, imagine it is a two-person world, composed of Bill and Bob, Bob being the worse-off.

J: Poor Bob. He's so unlucky. It was bad enough when he was worse off than Bill through no fault of his own by 9,900. Now he is worse off by 99,900. I thought he had a large complaint before, but compared with his complaint *now* that seems trivial. The inequality *was* bad, now it's *outrageous*.

T: Calm down John. While it's true the gap between Bob and Bill is now much larger, you seem to be forgetting or ignoring the fact that Bill is now *much* better off. Before, Bill only had 10,000 units of welfare, now he has 100,000. Bearing this in mind, surely you can see that while Bob has a *bit* more to complain about than previously, he doesn't have too much more to

---

13. These figures are arrived at by subtracting the size of complaint or index of inequality of the poor world, from the size of complaint or index of inequality of the rich world, and dividing that number by the size of complaint or index of inequality of the poor world.

complain about (before he had a complaint of .99, now it is slightly larger, .999).

J: You can't *possibly* be serious! *Of course* I'm not forgetting that Bill is now much better off. It is *that very fact* that makes Bob's situation so much worse regarding inequality. You think Bill's being better off somehow mitigates the effect of the much larger gap between Bob and Bill. That's absurd! In the absence of an accompanying improvement in Bob's welfare, there is *no way* that an increase in *Bill's* welfare could contribute—even partially or indirectly—to a lessening of Bob's complaint. To the contrary, Bill's vast improvement greatly and unequivocally increases Bob's complaint.

I side with John. It isn't, as the second approach seems to imply, as if the adverse effects of Bill's improvement always outweigh (though only slightly) its positive effects. Rather, there *are* no positive effects from Bill's improvement regarding inequality, for there is no respect in which Bob fares better relative to Bill in an E-type world than in a D-type world. The point here can be summed up as follows. The second approach measures inequality as if *even regarding inequality* there is a positive or partially redeeming feature of the best-off person becoming even better off (even in the absence of related gains to the worse-off). Since this isn't so, the second approach seems unacceptable.

Before going on, let me note that the third and fourth approaches do not face the problem noted here. To be sure, those approaches' advocates would agree that it is worse to be n units worse off than the best-off person when the best-off person is badly off than when he is well-off. But they would contend that the second approach's advocate goes wrong in (implicitly) connecting the smaller complaint in the one case with the best-off person's being better off—as if *his* being better off were the feature responsible for the smaller complaint, rather than the *worse-off* person's being better off (and thus, for the sort of reasons indicated in 6.1 having less complaint). Since they don't make that mistake and, more particularly, since each in their own way relativizes complaints to the level of the person with the complaint rather than that of the best-off person, the third and fourth approaches can accommodate both our judgments about C, D, and E, and the related judgment that as Bill's position significantly improves, Bob's complaint greatly and unequivocally increases.

A corollary of these considerations is that the third and fourth approaches are also better suited than the second to handle cases where the best-off don't improve and the worse-off do. Consider diagram 6.7.

All three approaches capture the view that q's complaint will be greater in A than B. However, the way they do this is strikingly different. On the second approach, the sole factor responsible for this is the larger gap between p and q in A than in B. On the third and fourth approaches that is only one of two relevant factors—the other being the fact that q is worse off in A than B.[14] But surely, those

_____

14. These remarks follow directly from the way in which the three approaches measure individual complaints.

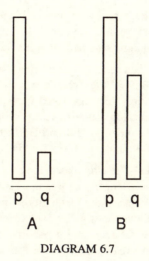

DIAGRAM 6.7

considerations that gave rise to the different approaches in the first place—that is, those underlying S—would support the view that A's larger gap is *further* worsened by q's being worse off in A than B (since absolute gap size is not all that matters, and since, for instance, in A each unit by which q is worse off than p represents a more significant improvement relative to what he has than in B).

The specific conclusion yielded by our considerations is that the third and fourth approaches are more plausible than the second for cases like A and B as well as C, D, and E. But a stronger conclusion is suggested. On examination, the second approach is not a plausible way of capturing inequality's sensitivity to a society's (overall) level.

Let us next focus on the first—economists'—approach, which, though differing markedly from the second, suffers from a similar shortcoming. Consider again C, D, and E. On the first approach, inequality is measured by summing up the differences between the best-off person and each worse-off person, and then dividing the number reached by the average level. So, on this approach I(C) = (900)(50)/550 = 82, I(D) = (9,900)(50)/5050 = 98, and I(E) = (99,900)(50)/50,050 = 100. On the first approach, then, the differences between C and D, D and E, and C and E regarding inequality are on the order of 20 percent, 2 percent, and 22 percent, respectively. Now in each case, these figures represent a twofold improvement over those yielded by the second approach. However, given our earlier conclusion that at the *very least* the differences between these worlds should be on the order of 50 percent, 50 percent, and 100 percent, respectively, clearly the first approach, like the second, falls well short of reflecting the extent of the differences between C, D, and E.

The problem here can be highlighted with a revised version of Tom and John's dialogue (with Tom now advocating the first approach). Again, the dialogue concerns Bill and Bob's two-person world, which has been transformed from a D- to an E-type world.

J: Alas. Though I didn't really expect Bill and Bob's gap to get much smaller, even in my most pessimistic moments, I never expected it to grow so tremendously. The inequality *was* bad, now it's *outrageous*.

T: Calm down, John. You seem to be ignoring the fact that the average level is now *much* higher. Before, the average was only 5,050, now it's 50,050. Bearing this in mind, surely you must see that despite the much larger gap the inequality hasn't become too much worse. [In fact, it's less than 2 percent worse, as the inequality index in Bill and Bob's two-person world has only increased from 1.96 ((9,900)(1)/5050) to 1.996 ((99,900)(1)/50,050).]

J: You can't be serious! The *only* reason the average is so much higher now is because *Bill* is much better off. But it is precisely that very fact (that Bill *is* much better off) which makes the inequality so much worse. On your view, Bill's being better off supposedly has two opposing effects. Insofar as it increases the gap between better- and worse-off, it tends to increase inequality, while insofar as it increases the average it tends to decrease inequality. I fail to see how Bill's being better off has the second effect. Surely, as Bill's position vastly improves the situation's inequality greatly and unequivocally worsens.

Again, I side with John. Because any increase in the best-off person's level increases the average, the first approach, like the second, measures inequality as if *even regarding inequality* there is a positive or partially redeeming feature of the best-off person becoming even better off (even in the absence of related gains to the worse-off). Since this seems wrong, I think the first approach, like the second, is unacceptable.

Note, I am *not* arguing that the first approach is just as implausible as the second. Although on both approaches increases in inequality are sometimes softened to an implausible extent, the second's softening effect is more extreme than the first's. Moreover, whereas in most realistic cases the second's softening effect would stand out as clearly unacceptable, for many cases, the first's would barely be noticeable (since increases in the best-off person's level may only negligibly affect the average of a large population). Nevertheless, it remains true that the first approach measures inequality as if, even regarding *inequality*, there would be *something* beneficial (however slight) about the best-off becoming even better off. This makes the first approach theoretically unsatisfying, even for those cases where its judgments seem plausible.

Some might attempt to defend the first approach by appealing to the *way* in which it measures inequality. As noted earlier, they might argue that the first approach measures inequality in what may be viewed as a two-step process. Step one sums up the gaps between the best-off person and those worse-off, and can be viewed as determining the "absolute" amount of inequality obtaining. Step two divides the resulting number by society's average and (hence) can be viewed as determining how bad it is for a society at that level to have that "absolute" amount of inequality. It may seem, therefore, that this approach—unlike the others?—gives us exactly what we want in a measure of inequality, a way of determining how bad a society's inequality is.

I have several worries about this line of reasoning. First, a formula does not carry its interpretation on its sleeve,[15] and as we shall see the first approach can be given a rather different reading. Second, I worry about any interpretation that focuses our attention on "society's inequality." Focusing on "society" and relativizing inequality to society's average is, for a variety of reasons, both natural and intuitive. Nevertheless, doing so is mistaken or misleading in at least two respects. First, it suggests that it makes sense to speak of a society as being at a given level of welfare. But it doesn't. *Societies* aren't at levels of welfare—people *in* societies are.[16] Second, it misconstrues the proper objects of our concern. Inequality's "badness" doesn't consist of *society* being in such a position, it consists of society's *members* being in such a position. *Individuals* are the "victims" of inequality, not the artificial or abstract entity "society."

It may seem I have taken this construal of the first approach too literally. For instance, instead of viewing the second step as determining "how bad it is for a society at that level to have that 'absolute' amount of inequality," perhaps it should be viewed as determining "how bad it is for a group of individuals with that average level of welfare to be worse off than the best-off person by the amount they (taken collectively) are." Admittedly, such a move (however inelegant) would allow one to sidestep the first of the two charges just cited. It might even allow one to temporarily forestall the second. In the end, however, such a move does nothing to blunt the basic point of the charges. The question is, What does *society's average* have to do with it? How is the mere fact that one world has a higher *average* than another *itself* supposed to make it the case that the gaps between the better- and worse-off matter less in the one than the other?

It is a commonplace to observe that although the average American family has 2.2 children, nowhere is such a family to be found. It is also a commonplace for reformers to be unimpressed with statistics purporting to show how today's average American is much better off than his earlier counterpart. The reformer wants to know *who it is* that is supposedly so much better off. Is it all Americans, or only the rich, or the white, or the young, or the males? It is easy to see why the reformer insists on an answer to such questions, for even where abstract statistics are useful bellwethers of pervasive trends, there will always be those whom the trend has left—or perhaps even pushed—behind.

These remarks are so obvious as to be almost trivial. Still, there is a lesson to be learned from them, which the first approach ignores. That the average person is relatively healthy or has a relatively high income does nothing to lessen the plight of the severely handicapped or the extremely impoverished. Similarly, that the

---

15. As Shelly Kagan nicely put it in correspondence.

16. Of course societies do have average levels of welfare, but they are not themselves at those levels. Society's average level describes a relation obtaining between the total amount of welfare society's members possess and society's total number of people. It is a useful, though crude, guide for judging how well society's members fare. It does not represent how well some ontologically significant entity "society" fares. Similarly, insofar as it makes sense to say that one society is better off than another, this is just an abbreviated way of saying something about how the society's *members* fare relative to each other.

I shall say more about this issue in chapters 9 and 10.

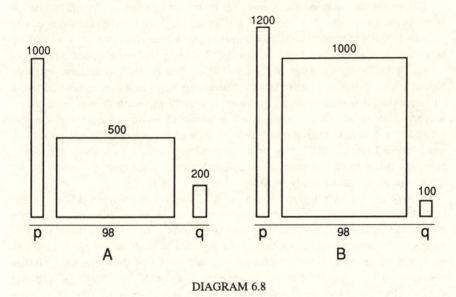

DIAGRAM 6.8

average person is relatively well-off does nothing to lessen the extent to which it is bad for someone not well-off to be worse off than the others in his world. Thus, as we saw, that the average is much higher in an E- than a D-type world, does nothing to lessen either the extent to which the worse-off would have more to complain about in E than in D, or the extent to which E's inequality is much worse than D's.

My point may be illustrated in a slightly different manner. Although, as noted, the first approach *may* be viewed as attempting to capture inequality's sensitivity *after* adding up individual complaints, it may also be viewed differently. Specifically, the way it measures inequality is logically equivalent to the following one: first, determine each person's complaint by dividing the size of the gap between him and the best-off person by the average, and then sum up the individual complaints. After all, since $(a + b + c)/k = a/k + b/k + c/k$, the effect of dividing the "absolute" amount of inequality by the average is to count each unit by which someone is worse off than the best-off person as having a significance inversely proportional to the average.

Looking at the first approach in this way, the shortcoming I have been discussing is easily demonstrated. Consider diagram 6.8. In A, the gap between p and q is 800. Since A's average is 502, q will have a complaint of 800/502 = 1.6 on the method of measuring inequality that is equivalent to the first approach. In B, the gap between p and q is 1,100 units, yet, since B's average is 993, q will have *less* to complain about than he had in A—as 1,100/999 = 1.1. This suggests that on the first approach the gap between p and q is less significant in B than in A. But this is absurd. In B, p is *better* off than he was in A and q is *worse* off. Surely *these* features must serve to *increase* the significance of p and q's gap. Just as surely, the fact that in B the others better off than q are even *better* off than they were in A couldn't possibly *lessen* the significance of p and q's gap. On the relative to the best-off person view of complaints, their improved position would be irrelevant to the size of q's complaint; on the other ways of viewing complaints their position would not be irrelevant, but would serve to *increase* q's complaint; on *no* plausible view could their improved position serve to *decrease* q's complaint. This is because there is no respect in which q fares better relative to others in B than in A.

In sum, the first approach is implausible because it measures inequality as if people had complaints inversely proportional to the average. Of course, because normally there is a positive correlation between one society having a higher average than another and most of its people being better off, in most cases the first approach's comparative judgments may be quite plausible. Still, it is important to recognize that even when the first approach gets the "right" answer, it does so for the wrong reasons. For instance, in diagram 6.8, the first approach yields the result that on BOP B's inequality is better than A's. This result may seem plausible, but if it does, it will be because the increased significance of the gap between p and q seems to be *offset* by the decreased significance of the gaps between everyone else and p. Thus, even if B *is* ultimately better than A, because everyone *else* fares better, it remains true that regarding inequality q fares worse in B than A. This is a feature of the situation of which a fully adequate measure of inequality should recognize and take account. And it is a serious shortcoming of the first approach that it fails to do this.

It should now be clear why I earlier expressed a preference for question (2), Is inequality sensitive to the levels of affluence or well-being of the individuals between whom inequality obtains? over question (1), Is our notion of inequality sensitive to society's overall level of affluence or well-being? And similarly, for question (2a), Does inequality matter more when people are badly off than when they are well-off? over question (1a), Does inequality matter more in a poor society than in a rich one? Although for most purposes either set of formulations will suffice, (1) and (1a) may tend to make an approach like the first seem especially appropriate. Moreover, once that mistake is made, it may (long) go undetected given the general correlation between one society having a higher average than another and most of its members being better off. Yet, as I have argued, adopting an approach like the first *would* be a mistake. Ultimately, our concern about inequality is not a concern about how *societies* fare relative to one another, but a concern about how *individuals* fare relative to one another. And in the end, this is why (2) and (2a) are preferable to (1) and (1a), and why relativizing the size of someone's complaint to his level is acceptable, but relativizing it to the *average* is not.

Let me turn now to a problem facing each of the first three approaches. I shall illustrate how it applies to the third approach, and indicate in note 19 how it applies to the first and second. Consider diagram 6.9 and suppose, for the sake of the ensuing discussion, that the level of a normal life will be around 100, that someone at level one will barely be above the level at which life ceases to be worth living (the zero level), and that differences of less than two

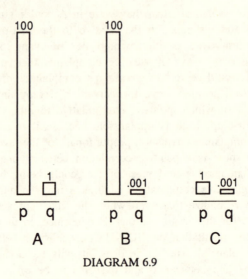

DIAGRAM 6.9

units are basically insignificant so, for example, there would be very little to choose between a life at level n and a life at level n + 2.[17]

In A, q is at level 1, and p at 100. In B, q is at .001 and p at 100. In C, q is at .001 and p at 1. By hypothesis, in C the difference between p and q is basically

17. Here, as throughout much of this work, the particular numbers and scale I use are arbitrary. If the reader finds my combination of claims implausible—that is, if the reader finds it hard to reconcile the view that differences of less than two are insignificant with the view that a life at level one is barely worth living while one at level 100 is normal—then the reader can alter the views and the ensuing discussion accordingly, for example, assume a normal person's level will be 1,000, or perhaps 10,000, and then, if one wants, alter p's level in A and B of diagram 6.9. For any plausible scale where positive numbers represent lives worth living, zero represents the level at which life ceases to be worth living, negative numbers represent lives worth not living, and the better off someone is the larger the number representing her welfare level; this book's arguments could be made, mutatis mutandis, employing that scale.

Having said that, let me emphasize that on the scale I am using in this example the numbers 1 and .001 are assumed to be meaningful and accurate, and the differences between those levels are insignificant. Some people have objected to my diagram and the ensuing argument by claiming that my drawing fails to accurately reflect the difference between 1 and .001, given that the former is *1,000* times larger than the latter. This objection is mistaken. Though 1 *is* 1,000 times larger than .001, by hypothesis, the (real) difference between people at those levels is insignificant. Indeed, if anything my diagram *exaggerates* the difference between the two levels—on an accurate portrayal, the two levels would be visually indistinguishable. (Consider the difference between someone whose net worth was 1 cent and someone whose net worth was zero. Other things equal, surely a loan officer would treat them identically, even though the former's net worth is infinitely larger than the latter's! Analogously, it is perfectly plausible to assume, as I do in this example that, substantively, the gap between someone at level 1 and someone at level .001 is insignificant or negligible, even though 1 is 1,000 times larger than .001.)

Finally, let me acknowledge the obvious fact that in this and other examples I am assuming a level of precision that probably doesn't exist and that we certainly could never achieve. That is, for the sort of scale I assume, one couldn't distinguish between levels 1 and .001, let alone determine that two people were both (exactly!) at level .001. But this fact doesn't affect the logic of my argument, and assuming this level of precision is useful, as it enables me to easily illustrate the problem in which I am interested.

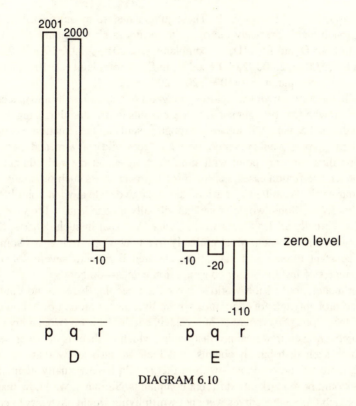

DIAGRAM 6.10

insignificant. In fact, we are imagining that in our example the difference between them is negligible—both in absolute terms and relative to their difference in the other cases. Likewise in our example the difference between q's level in A and B is negligible—both in absolute terms and relative to the differences between p and q in those cases. Given these assumptions the following conclusions seem clear. First, B's inequality will be worse than A's, but only by a very small amount (correspondingly, q's complaint will be larger in B than A, but only slightly), and, second, both A's and B's inequality will be much worse than C's (correspondingly, q's complaint will be much larger in A and B than in C).

But recall, the third approach measures inequality by summing up individual complaints where individual complaints are measured by dividing the size of the gap between the best-off person and someone worse off by the worse-off person's level. Hence, on the third approach q's complaint would be $(100-1)/1 = 99$ in A, $(100-.001)/.001 = 99,999$ in B, and $(1-.001)/.001 = 999$ in C. Correspondingly, B's inequality would supposedly be 1,000 times worse than A's, and even C's inequality would be 10 times worse than A's. Such results are clearly unacceptable.

Next, consider diagram 6.10. In D, p and q are virtually equal. P is at level 2,001, and q at 2,000. R is at level −10. Though alive, the quality of his life is so poor it is represented as being below the zero level—the level at which life ceases to be worth living.

Obviously, regarding inequality, r would have a greater complaint than q in D, and similarly, for that matter, in E. These judgments are incontrovertible. Yet, the third approach yields precisely the opposite results as r's complaint would be *less* than q's in both D and E: in D, r's complaint = (2,001 − −10)/−10 = −201.1 < q's complaint = (2,001 − 2,000)/2,000 = .0005; in E, r's complaint = (−10 − −110)/−110 = −10/11 < q's complaint = (−10 − −20)/−20 = −1/2.

As with the results it yields regarding diagram 6.9, these results are unacceptable. Derek Parfit, who first brought some of these points to my attention, suggested a description that rather nicely, if somewhat roughly, sums up the situation. He observed that the third approach would never do because it "goes wild near zero, and crazy below."

Having illustrated my point with simple examples, let me add it is not only in simple or science-fiction cases that the third approach faces such problems. It faces them in our world. Admittedly, it is a matter of large debate at what point life ceases to be worth living. Some would argue that virtually no one leads a life worth living, others that virtually all lead lives worth living. As usual in such debates, the truth lies somewhere in between. Most probably live lives worth living, but some—victims of constant disease and starvation, children born with severe spina bifida, certain inmates of institutions or concentration camps—do not.

Unfortunately, out of the world's five billion people, there are no doubt thousands, and probably tens of thousands whose lives hover around or below the zero level. Of these, one person may be at level ten, another at level two, another at level five. Moreover, even if we cannot distinguish which of them is at which level, we know some such distribution obtains. But then we also know that on the third approach many of these people—who in fact should have virtually identical complaints—would have markedly different complaints. Similarly, we know that on the third approach those whose lives were not worth living would have *less* to complain about regarding inequality than the world's second best-off person. Indeed, this understates the situation.[18] On the third approach those whose lives were not worth living would have *nothing* to complain about as the negative weightings should turn their complaints into approbation. Regarding inequality, they should be grateful for their good fortune! This, of course, is absurd.

In contrast to the third approach, the first two would not face these problems regarding our world (now). Nevertheless, as noted previously, there are situations where they too would face such problems.[19]

18. As Shelly Kagan noted in bringing the following point to my attention.
19. Consider the diagram below:

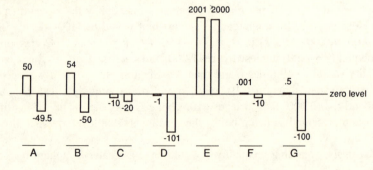

Before proceeding let me briefly note and comment on one response to the foregoing discussion.[20] One might urge that our welfare scale only assign positive numbers greater than one to people's welfare levels, even those whose lives are not worth living. Clearly, such a scale would enable the first three approaches to at least sidestep—if not exactly directly answer—the charge that they "go wild near zero and crazy below."

In support of this view it might be claimed that no one knows where the zero level is much less how to interpret negative levels. I have some sympathy with this claim, but even so the view in question seems implausible and ad hoc. Specifically, it is one thing to acknowledge the difficulty of ascertaining the zero level, or interpreting negative levels, it is another to claim that our welfare scale should only assign positive numbers greater than one. What is the motivation for this position *other* than to avoid the problems discussed earlier? If someone's life is not worth living, why should it be assigned a positive value?

Perhaps we are to understand our scale of welfare on analogy with the Kelvin scale for temperature, as the Kelvin scale, unlike the Centigrade and Fahrenheit scales, has no negative numbers. Even so, on the Kelvin scale absolute zero is a meaningful temperature one can at least theoretically, if not practically, reach. Is there a priori reason to believe there cannot be an absolute zero level for welfare one might at least theoretically, if not practically, reach? Put differently, if we grant someone could possibly be at level two, can we rule out the possibility of someone worse off being at level one, and someone even worse off at level one-half? If not, then it seems the preceding response should be revised, and the first three approaches would still be open to the *theoretical* objection that they would go wild (very) near zero, even if they might successfully evade the charge of "going crazy below."

In sum, this response requires a non–ad hoc basis for giving our welfare scale a floor of one. I fail to see what that basis would be. Moreover, even if this response enabled the first three approaches to avoid the "wild and crazy" implications noted previously, they would still disproportionally, and hence implausibly, measure different complaints. For example, consider a two-person world where the better-off person is at level 100,000. On the third approach raising the worse-off person from level 10 to level 20 would lower her complaint by more than half. Surely this is implausible, even if it is less obviously objectionable than the results noted earlier.

Clearly, B's inequality is (ever so) slightly worse than A's, and D's inequality is worse than C's and E's. However, on the first approach A's inequality—$(50 - -49.5)/.25 = 398$—would be nearly eight times worse than B's—$(54 - -50)/2 = 52$; and D's inequality—$(-1 - -101)/-50.5 = -1.98$—would be better than C's—$(-10 - -20)/-15 = -.66$—and E's—$(2,001 - 2,000)/2,000.5 = .0005$. The second approach would also yield the result that D's inequality—$(-1 - -101)/-1 = -100$—would be better than C's—$(-10 - -20)/-10 = -1$—and E's—$(2,001 - 2,000)/2,001 = .0005$—as well as the equally implausible result that G's inequality—$(.5 - -100)/.5 = 201$—would be better than F's—$(.001 - -10)/.001 = 10,001$. Thus the first and second approaches are theoretically unsatisfying since, as the foregoing illustrates, they face theoretical problems analogous to those faced by the third approach.

Unfortunately, we live in a world where these theoretical problems could become practical. It seems likely this would be the case, for a while anyway, in the event of a nuclear holocaust—if we assume, of course, that some survived.

20. Some version of this response has been suggested to me (though not necessarily endorsed) by several people, including John Broome, Tyler Cowan, and Thomas Scanlon.

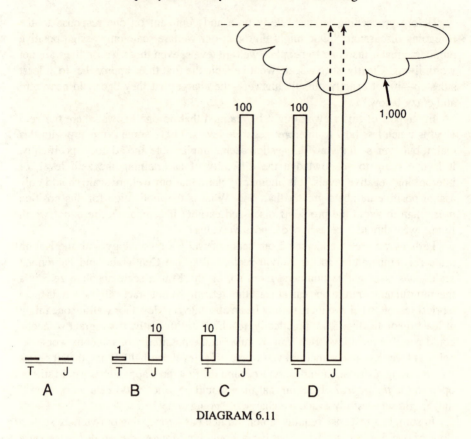

DIAGRAM 6.11

Let me turn now to the final problem I want to discuss. This problem also faces each of the first three approaches. It may be illustrated with the aid of the following story. John and Tim are equally deserving people who start out with lives barely worth living. As it happens, John is ever-so-slightly better off than Tim, he has .001 units of welfare to Tim's .0001 units;[21] however, for obvious reasons this goes unnoticed. Slowly but steadily their positions improve, but at different rates. In particular, for each (portion of a) unit Tim's life improves, John's improves by ten times that amount. As time passes, the following situations obtain: when Tim is at level 1, John is at 10; when Tim is at 10, John is at 100; when Tim is at 100, John is at 1,000. These situations are represented as B through D, respectively, in diagram 6.11.

B's and C's columns have been drawn roughly to scale regarding each other. John's column in D would, if drawn to scale, be seven times taller than the

21. Here, again, I am assuming both a scale according to which the difference between .001 and .0001 would be insignificant and a level of precision that is not ascertainable. While the level of precision I assume facilitates my presentation, my point does not depend upon our being able to achieve such precision.

height shown, and D would stand to C as C stands to B. For obvious reasons, the correct scale for A, representing the initial situation, has been left to the reader's imagination.

Now I claim that regarding inequality D is worse than C, C worse than B, and B worse than A. Most will grant this is obvious after examining these worlds directly, and reflecting upon how badly Tim fares relative to John in each. However, one may also conclude this by reflecting on the manner in which Tim and John's world is transformed from A to D. As the story was told, it is as if Fate is steadily apportioning welfare according to an unwavering rule: ten for John, one for Tim. Now given that John and Tim are equally deserving, in the absence of later developments that "even things up," even one allocation in accordance with such a rule will seem somewhat unfair and unjust. Surely, however, if one allocation in accordance with such a rule is bad, two such allocations would be worse, three would be worse still, and so on. Extended, such reasoning supports the judgment that A through D are getting worse regarding inequality.

As usual, I am not making any claim about how A through D compare, all things considered. Nor, for that matter, am I making any claim about how *much* worse the inequality is getting.[22] For now I am simply making the limited and I think indisputable claim that the worlds are getting worse regarding inequality. Why, one may wonder, have I belabored such an obvious claim? Because the first three approaches are indifferent between A through D! (This will be evident shortly, and is easily proved with a few simple calculations.)

Look again at diagram 6.11, and make a sincere effort to imagine A and D drawn to scale. Now carefully consider how Tim and John compare in those worlds. Even taking into consideration, as one should, Tim's improved position, it's obvious D's inequality, where there is *much* to choose between Tim and John, is worse than A's, where there is virtually nothing (.0009) to choose between them. Correspondingly, it's clear the first three approaches won't suffice, since according to them A's inequality is as bad as D's.

The preceding example illustrates a general problem with the first three approaches. The problem is that these approaches are "mean-independent" as some economists use that term. That is, they measure inequality independently of the mean level *in the sense that* proportional increases in people's levels do not affect inequality. So if, as with A through D, one world is a scaled-up version of another—as if everyone's level has been multiplied by a fixed amount—the two worlds will be equivalent regarding inequality.

It is easy to see why the three approaches have this feature. If everyone's level is multiplied by a fixed amount, k, then the size of the gaps between the better- and worse-off will be k times larger. But, of course, the average level, the level of the best-off person, and the level of each person with a complaint will also be k times

---

22. This is important. I am not committing myself to the view that the "badness" associated with the rule's repeated applications can be captured by an additively separable function. It may or may not be the case that two applications of the rule are (exactly) twice as bad as one, that three applications are three times as bad, and so on. My claim is simply that if it really is unfair, and hence bad, for Tim and John to be treated in accordance with the rule in question once, it will be worse for them to be so treated twice, worse still for them to be so treated three times, and so on.

larger. So, for each of the three approaches the result of multiplying everyone's level by k will be that *both* the numerator and denominator of the formula measuring inequality will be k times larger. Naturally, the k-fold increases in the numerator and denominator will cancel each other out. Thus, the net effect of multiplying everybody's level by k will, on the first three approaches, be zero.[23]

In sum, the first three approaches measure inequality in a way that is indifferent to proportional increases in everyone's levels. But, as many economists have noted, there is no reason to think our measure of inequality should have this feature and, as our discussion of A through D shows, there is good reason to think it should not.

One point deserves emphasis. Notwithstanding their many problems, it remains true, as noted earlier, that the first three approaches reflect the view that inequality matters more at low levels than high ones. Hence, where mean-independent measures go wrong is *not* in their answer to the general question, Does inequality matter more at low levels than high levels? but in their answer to the more particular question, How *much* more does inequality matter at low levels than high levels? Examples like A through D illustrate that mean-independent measures give *too much* weight to inequality at low levels. Thus, as we have seen, on a mean-independent measure, a gap of .0009 between the better- and worse-off when the worse-off are at level .0001 will be as bad as a gap of 90,000 when the worse-off are at 10,000. This is clearly implausible. A gap of .0009 at level .0001 is worse than a similar size gap at level 10,000, and it may even be worse than a gap of 9 or 90 or 900 at level 10,000 (though the latter seems very unlikely). But it is surely *not* worse than a gap of *90,000* at level 10,000.

In sum. Though inequality matters more at low levels than high levels, it does not matter as *much* more as mean-independent measures imply. Put differently, although gaps between the better- and worse-off matter less at high levels than low levels, the rate at which gaps decrease in significance is not (nearly) as high as mean-independent measures imply.

6.5 Atkinson versus Sen

I have emphasized the preceding point partly because it is one about which many have been confused. As we shall see in section 6.8, most of the statistical measures of inequality employ the first approach for capturing inequality's sensitivity. Corre-

---

23. This result may be demonstrated as follows. Let $w1$ be a world with a certain amount of inequality, and $w2$ a scaled-up version of $w1$, say, where each person is k times better off than his counterpart in $w1$. On the first approach, a world w's inequality would be measured by the following formula: $I(w) = (bw - yiw)/\mu$ where bw represents the level of w's best off person, μ represents w's average level, and y_iw represents, in turn, the level of each individual in w. On the first approach, then, $I(w1) = (bw1 - yiw1)/\mu1$, and $I(w2) = (kbw1 - kyiw1)/k\mu1 = (k/k)(bw1 - yiw1)/\mu1 = (bw1 - yiw1)/\mu1 = I(w1)$. Similarly, on the second approach, $I(w1) = (bw1 - yiw1)/bw1$, but then again, given that everyone in $w2$ is k times better off than his counterpart in $w1$, $I(w2)=(kbw1 - kyiw1)/kbw1 = (k/k)(bw1 - yiw1)/bw1 = (bw1 - yiw1)/bw1 = I(w1)$. As for the third approach, on that approach $I(w1) = (bw1 - yiw1)/yiw1$. But then again it will be the case that $I(w2)=(kbw1 - kyiw1)/kyiw1 = (k/k)(bw1 - yiw1)/yiw1 = (bw1 - yiw1)/yiw1 = I(w1)$.

spondingly, most of the statistical measures are mean-independent, and this is a feature economists have recognized and rightly criticized as implausible. But consider the remarks of two of the most prominent writers on economic inequality. After noting that most of the statistical measures are mean-independent, A. B. Atkinson suggests that "it might reasonably be argued that as the general level of income rises we are more concerned about inequality—that I (our inequality index) should rise with proportional additions to income."[24] While after noting that most of the statistical measures "have the property of being invariant if everyone's income is raised in the same proportion," A. K. Sen asks, "Is this a property we want? Can it be asserted that our judgment of the extent of inequality will not vary according to whether the people involved are generally poor or generally rich?"[25] And later, in partial answer to his question, Sen writes, "One can argue that for low income levels the inequality measures should take much sharper note of the *relative* variation . . . . On the other hand, I have heard it argued that inequality is a 'luxury' that only a rich economy can 'afford,' and while I cannot pretend to understand fully this point of view, I am impressed by the number of people who seem prepared to advocate such a position. Though the considerations run in opposite directions, that in itself is no justification for making the inequality measure *independent* of the level of mean income" (Sen's emphasis).[26]

Setting aside Sen's attempt to be fair-minded, these passages suggest the following. Atkinson and Sen agree our inequality index I should not be invariant to proportional increases; but whereas Atkinson seems to think I should increase in such cases and that inequality matters more at high levels than low ones, Sen seems to think I should decrease in such cases because inequality matters less at high levels than low ones.[27]

Our earlier discussion suggests that Atkinson and Sen are both partly right and partly wrong. It also suggests that insofar as they go wrong, it may be because they mistakenly assume that the issue of whether I should increase with proportional increases is ultimately the same as the issue of whether inequality matters more at low levels than high levels. Given that assumption, Atkinson, who correctly recognizes that proportional increases worsen inequality is driven to the implausible contention that inequality matters more at high levels than low ones; while Sen, who strongly and rightly feels that inequality matters less at high levels is thereby driven to the equally implausible contention that proportional increases lessen inequality (as if, in diagram 6.11, A's inequality could be worse than D's).

We see, then, that Atkinson and Sen were both half right in the positions that *led* them to question mean-independent measures. However, we also see that in the end

24. A. B. Atkinson, "On the Measurement of Inequality," *Journal of Economic Theory* 2 (1970): 251.

25. A. K. Sen, *On Economic Inequality* (Clarendon Press, 1973): 36.

26. Ibid., pp. 70–71.

27. Some readers of Sen view him as genuinely neutral on the question of whether inequality matters less at high levels than low ones, and I readily grant that what Sen actually *says* carries the appearance of neutrality. Obviously, I believe that in fact Sen's sentiments run along the line suggested, but whether or not this is so doesn't really matter for my central point. The issue isn't really about what two particular people—Atkinson and Sen—actually think, but about two opposing ways of viewing the inequality index I.

they were unsatisfied with mean-independent measures for the wrong reason. They felt mean-independent measures were inappropriately *neutral* as to whether inequality matters more at low levels than high levels.[28] But, as we have seen, mean-independent measures not only give *greater* weight, they in fact give *too much* weight to inequality at low levels.

It is interesting to speculate as to why economists like Atkinson and Sen may have been guilty of the oversight I've suggested. In part, I suspect it was due to misleading terminology, together with a failure to appreciate the source of the statistical measures' plausibility. Had economists discerned the intuitions underlying the statistical measures, they might have noticed not only that the statistical measures' numerators correspond to ways of measuring gaps between better- and worse-off, but also—as I noted before and shall return to—that most of those measures incorporate the first approach for capturing inequality's sensitivity by including the average in the denominator. Correspondingly, they may have seen there is a perfectly straightforward sense in which those statistical measures *are* mean-dependent in a way that is relevant to whether inequality matters more at low levels than high levels. This is the sense in which the gaps between better- and worse-off are relativized to the average.[29]

The point is, I suspect economists implicitly recognized mean-independence as being relevant to sensitivity, without being clear about the *kind* of mean-independence that is relevant. Thus, when they discovered most statistical measures were invariant to proportional increases, given the unfortunate terminological coincidence that formulas with that property were regarded as mean-independent, they naturally concluded that those measures were *neutral* as to whether inequality matters more at low levels than high ones. They did not realize that while the statistical measures *are* mean-independent in the one sense, the sense of being invariant to proportional increases, they are *not* mean-independent in the other sense, the sense of being neutral as to whether inequality matters more at low levels than high ones; and it is the latter sense, not the former, that is (indirectly) relevant to the issue of sensitivity.

Ironically, once the mistake was made, it was probably their relatively sophisticated view of inequality that prevented economists from discovering it. Thus, for instance, recognizing inequality's great complexity, Sen naturally supposed the dispute in question stemmed from that complexity, rather than from an error by his opponents (and, being fair-minded, he thought this despite not "understanding fully" their position's appeal). Whereas if, like most philosophers, he was unaware

---

28. Neutral in the sense that they gave neither more nor less weight to inequality at low levels relative to high levels, not in the sense that they were compatible with either position.

29. Actually, as we saw, how bad the gaps between the better- and worse-off are is ultimately dependent on *their* levels, and not the *average* level. Still, as we also observed, given the correlation between those factors, there will tend to be a correlation between the "badness" of the gaps looked at as a whole, and the average level. Hence, one can see how one might come to think inequality's "badness" was dependent on the average and, moreover, how measuring inequality that way would tend to yield close approximations to the correct results. Correspondingly, one can see it wouldn't be too far off the mark to maintain that society's average level is indirectly relevant to how bad its inequality is.

of inequality's complexity, he might have sought the source of his opponents' error and, in so doing, discovered that the dispute had its roots in a shared mistake.

Earlier, I pointed out that many have thought inequality matters more at high levels than low levels because of a confusion of two separate questions: When is one situation worse than another, all things considered? and When is one situation worse than another regarding inequality? The preceding discussion illustrates that that is not the only confusion which might lead to such a view. As we have seen, one may be led to such a view if one recognizes that the inequality index I should increase with proportional increases, and confuses that with the issue of whether inequality matters more at low levels or high ones.

Thus, we see further why the issue of sensitivity has been disputed. We also see there is good reason why Sen could not "understand fully" the view that inequality matters more at high levels than low levels; for the basis of that view lies not, as he had surmised, in inequality's complexity, but rather in certain common, yet none-theless mistaken, confusions.

6.6 Advantages of the Fourth Approach

In light of the preceding sections, the fourth approach seems especially promising. For, as reflection reveals, not only does the fourth approach reflect the fact that inequality matters more at low levels than high levels, it avoids each of the problems cited previously. Thus, it captures inequality's sensitivity in a way that:

1. focuses on the levels of the *individuals* between whom inequality obtains rather than on the average of society;
2. reflects the view that an increase in the best-off person's level unequivocally worsens inequality;
3. reflects the view that an increase in someone's level should lessen his complaint relative to those better off, not only because the gaps between them are smaller, but also because those gaps should count for less (even if only *slightly* less) given his improved position;
4. readily allows it to handle cases where people are near or below the zero level; and
5. enables it (via a "properly constructed" scale) to avoid giving inequality too much weight at low levels, so that, in particular, proportional increases worsen inequality.

As we have seen, the fourth approach is preferable to the first regarding (1) and (2), to the second regarding (2) and (3), and to each of the first three approaches regarding (4) and (5).[30]

Our discussion has revealed a number of features the fourth approach's scale must possess. For example, in addition to implying that a gap of n matters more at low levels than high levels, it must imply that a gap of n at level x counts less than

30. I leave it to the skeptical reader to verify these claims (assuming, of course, the details of such an approach could eventually be worked out). Just a little reflection should suffice in this regard.

most well-off

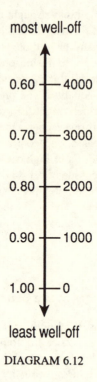

least well-off

DIAGRAM 6.12

a gap of k(n) at level k(x)—that is, the inequality index should increase with proportional increases. Another feature of the scale is that it should be nonlinear.[31] That is, as welfare levels increase the significance of a gap of a given size should not decrease at a constant rate. Consider for example diagram 6.12. Diagram 6.12 exemplifies a linear scale. A gap of n units is discounted at the constant rate of .1 for every 1,000 units of welfare. On this scale a gap of n units would count for *zero* if someone were at level 10,000, and would receive a negative weight—that is, count positively!—if someone were above level 10,000.

This point is generalizable. If our scale is linear—so that as welfare levels increase the significance of a gap's size decreases at a constant rate—then at some point the weighting will equal zero, so that "complaints" at that level will not count at all. Worse yet, beyond that point the weighting will become negative. This means that "complaints" will now be positively valenced so that inequality at very high levels will count as a good thing! This result is clearly unacceptable.

Similarly, as welfare levels increase the significance of a gap's size should not decrease at an *increasing* rate. Otherwise there would again be some point at which gaps would receive zero weight and beyond which they would receive negative weight. Thus, I conclude that the fourth approach's scale should be such that, as welfare levels increase, the significance of a gap's size should decrease at a *de-*

31. This point, and the following two paragraphs, are indebted to Shelly Kagan.

creasing rate so that gaps always receive *some* weight, even if—at *very* high levels—the weight is negligible. (I here ignore the possibility of discontinuous curves, which hold little attraction for me. But I acknowledge that one might resist these claims if one allows discontinuity in one's weighting function; for example, if one holds, as some do, that one can reach a certain [very high] level at, and beyond, which inequality doesn't matter *at all*.)

I have noted several features that our scale must possess if we pursue the fourth approach and argued that the fourth approach has many advantages over the first three. But it must be admitted that I have not constructed anything like an adequate scale, that doing so will undoubtedly be a difficult and complex task, and that until an adequate scale is constructed the fourth approach will be no more than a suggestion, inapplicable in practice. It may appear therefore that I have overlooked the first three approaches' *positive* features, that unlike the fourth approach they are simple, easy to apply, and complete. However, I have not overlooked these features; rather, I question their relevance and plausibility.

Consider the following "simple" question. How much less significant is a gap of n at level 1,000 than at level 500? Is it 1 percent, 10 percent, 25 percent, or what? The answer to this question is by no means obvious. For that matter, it is by no means obvious that there is a precise answer to be given. Perhaps the best answer one could give is, say, that it is "somewhere in the neighborhood" of 10 percent less significant. I don't know, yet, how to answer such a question. But the very fact that this is so—that I could only hope to answer such a question after much hard work and careful deliberation—makes me skeptical of approaches that are simple, easy to apply, and complete (in either sense).

I think, then, it is no criticism of the fourth approach that it is not simple or easy to apply. To the contrary, here, as in most cases involving complex notions, it seems likely that the cost of simplicity and easy applicability will be theoretical implausibility and unintuitive results (as, for instance, attend the first three approaches). As far as being incomplete—in the sense of programmatic—it is no shortcoming of the fourth approach as an *approach* to capturing sensitivity that it is not yet fully fleshed out. That work remains before an adequate scale can be constructed is not itself reason to doubt that such a scale can be constructed. Also, that such a scale may turn out to be imprecise is not itself reason to think it will thereby be inaccurate. To the contrary, such imprecision may be necessary for accuracy—as what one wants, so far as possible, is an approach that is neither more nor less precise than the sensitivity to be captured. All in all, then, given its appeal and the ease with which it could handle the other approaches' difficulties, I believe the fourth approach is a (the most?) promising way of capturing inequality's sensitivity to the levels of those between whom inequality obtains.

6.7 Sensitivity and the Weighted Additive Principle

What is the relation between the additive and weighted additive principles given the kind of sensitivity I have been discussing? I have claimed the fourth approach is compatible with each of chapter 2's aspects. However, it *may* seem that the effect

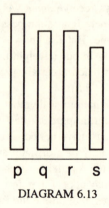

DIAGRAM 6.13

of applying the fourth approach to a position like the relative to the best-off person view of complaints (BOP) and the additive principle of equality (AP) is in essence to forsake the additive principle for a weighted additive principle (WAP). Consider, for example, diagram 6.13.

If one combined the fourth approach with AP and BOP, on the resulting view, V, s's complaint would count for more than simply twice that of q's or r's. Correspondingly, given the choice between raising q and r one unit each, or s two units, according to V we should do the latter. But of course these are exactly the results one would get if one adopted BOP and WAP. Hence, one might wonder whether AP really is, as chapter 2 suggests, a genuine alternative to WAP.

I think it is. To see this, one need only bear in mind that although there are certain similarities in their application, the intuitions underlying the notion that inequality matters more at low levels than high levels differ from those underlying WAP. Thus, the issue between advocates of the additive and weighted additive principles concerns not the adequacy of the former intuitions, about which both should readily agree, but the adequacy of the latter ones—that is, whether a special concern for a world's worst-off members warrants attaching extra weight to their complaints, even though their being worse off than others is already reflected in the size of the gap between them and the best-off person, and the extent to which we count that gap given the level at which they are. The difference between the two positions can be highlighted with the aid of diagram 6.14.

According to V, s's complaint would be the same in A and B. According to W, on the other hand, which is like V except that it involves a weighted additive principle rather than just an additive principle, s would have a larger complaint in A than B, since W attaches extra weight to the complaints of a world's worst-off members, and since s is A's very worst off member but one of B's best-off members. Thus, although V and W would agree that for both cases s's complaint would be more than twice that of q's or r's, they would disagree about whether the "break-even" point between increases in q's or r's welfare and increases in s's welfare would be the same. According to V, it would take the same size increase in q's welfare in both A and B to offset a lesser increase in s's welfare, whereas according

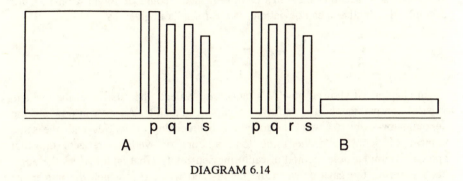

p q r s   p q r s

A   B

DIAGRAM 6.14

to W, it would take a greater increase in q's welfare in A than in B to offset a lesser increase in s's welfare.

Thus, despite having certain features in common, AP and WAP remain as distinct ways of measuring complaints, even when combined with the fourth approach. This is what I wanted to show. Of course, advocates of the additive and weighted additive principles will each argue that it is their principle that, when combined with the fourth approach, accords each person's complaint its correct weight. I shall not rehash the various arguments for their positions. My own view of the matter remains essentially unchanged from chapter 2.[32] Each is plausible. Neither can simply be dismissed.

6.8 Sensitivity and the Statistical Measures

We have noted that one fairly natural way of reflecting the notion that inequality matters more at low levels than high levels would be to divide the number representing the gaps between the better- and worse-off by the number representing society's average level. However, we saw that such a method—corresponding to the first approach discussed—is *not* the best way of reflecting inequality's sensitivity. More specifically, we saw that the first approach faces numerous shortcomings, and offered another approach that avoids the shortcomings while focusing more directly on the fact that our notion of inequality is sensitive not merely to *society's* level, but to the levels of the individuals between whom inequality obtains (and, even more particularly, to the levels of those with complaints).

Given this, one can partly see why, in chapter 5, I suggested that the statistical measures—which, I argued, are best regarded not as measures of the whole of inequality but of various aspects of it—are good only as first approximations, and

32. It is not completely unchanged. When combined with the fourth approach I find the additive principle slightly more plausible relative to the weighted additive principle than I did before. However, I do not find substantial differences in the way I view them.

that even more accurate measures of those aspects could be found. Consider, for example, the relative mean deviation, whose formula is given by:

$$M = \sum_{i=1}^{n} |\mu - y_i|/n\mu$$

In chapter 5 I showed how M's numerator reflects the relative to the average view of complaints and the additive principle of equality. As we can now see the denominator—which I was able to ignore by focusing on worlds with the same number of people and the same total amount of welfare—reflects the first approach's implausible method of capturing sensitivity. That is, it divides the number measuring the gaps between the better- and worse-off (which the numerator yields), by μ, society's average level. (It also divides the numerator by n, society's population size. This feature of M, and most other statistical measures, is discussed in chapter 7.) Thus, if this chapter's argument is correct, the relative mean deviation will not be the most accurate measure of the aspect involving the relative to the average view of complaints and the additive principle. A more accurate measure would employ a different way of capturing inequality's sensitivity to the levels of those between whom inequality obtains.

A similar point could be made about the range, the coefficient of variation, and the Gini coefficient, each of which divides the number measuring the gaps between the better- and worse-off by society's average. One can see, then, part of the reason why, in chapter 5, I noted that focusing on worlds with the same size population and the same total amount of welfare would enable me to ignore certain controversial features of the statistical measures.[33] More particularly, one can see one way the statistical measures should be altered to capture best the different aspects they reflect. They should be supplemented so as to reflect accurately the extent to which inequality matters more at low levels than at high levels, and this should involve relativizing the gaps between the better- and worse-off not to society's average level, but to the individual levels of those with complaints.

A final comment. It is not only the statistical measures that reflect inequality's sensitivity in the manner discussed. Atkinson's measure does too, and so do many of the other measures economists have offered. Moreover, some measures, such as the variance, take no account of the view that inequality matters more at low levels than high ones. Suffice it to say, I think any plausible measure of inequality will eventually have to be modified, or constructed, along the lines this chapter suggests.

---

33. The other part of the reason will become clear in chapter 7.

7

Variations in Population Size

The issue of whether inequality is affected by a society's size has received little attention—in part, because debates regarding the "ideal" size of populations have focused on broadly utilitarian concerns and, in part, because the issue is one about which most have (implicitly) agreed. Nevertheless, the issue is complicated and will be resolved, if at all, only with careful deliberation.

Note, as throughout this book, the following discussion assumes an impersonal teleological view of inequality. But in this chapter, perhaps more than any other, this assumption is not innocuous. Though I think many of the ensuing arguments support an impersonal teleological view, it might be argued that they merely beg the question against deontological or person-affecting views, and that many of this chapter's arguments and conclusions would have to be revised on such views. Unfortunately, as implied earlier, an examination of this issue lies beyond this chapter's scope, as it broaches deep topics that could only be adequately explored in another book. Thus, this chapter only begins the task of considering how variations in population size affect inequality. Even so, I think it raises important questions, questions whose significance extends far beyond the topic of inequality, and which up to now have been virtually ignored.

7.1 The Standard View

In considering how, if at all, size variations affect inequality, it will be useful to address a position that I shall call the *Standard View*, introduced here with the aid of diagram 7.1.

As drawn, A's and B's better- and worse-off groups are at the same levels but B's groups are twice as large as A's. Regarding *inequality* many would judge A and B equivalent. As they might put it, since the *pattern* of inequality is identical in A and B, there is nothing to choose between them—the "mere" fact that B is larger than A is irrelevant to how they compare regarding inequality.

The judgment that A and B are equivalent expresses the Standard View, according to which:

> *P*: Proportional variations in the number of better- and worse-off do not affect inequality.

191

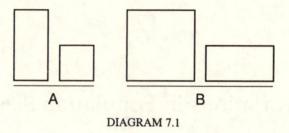

A   B

DIAGRAM 7.1

On the Standard View size is not *itself* relevant to inequality. Variations in size will only matter insofar as they affect the *pattern* of inequality, for example, by altering the better- and worse-off's levels or the ratios between them.

Each of the economists' statistical measures imply P. Moreover, while the statistical measures have been criticized for being invariant if the better- and worse-off's *levels* vary proportionally, they have not, to my knowledge, been criticized for being invariant if the better- and worse-off's *numbers* vary proportionally. Given the economists' scrutiny of the statistical measures, this suggests the latter property, unlike the former, is widely accepted. I think, then, the Standard View is appropriately named.[1] In fact, I think many, and perhaps most, would accept P without argument.

P has great plausibility and widespread appeal. But it is neither obvious nor uncontroversial. To the contrary, P stands in need of argument rarely, if ever, offered. This is not yet to say P must be rejected. Rather, it is a serious question under what circumstances, or to what extent, it should be accepted, rejected, or modified.

1. John Broome has suggested this discussion may be misleading. He doesn't think there really is a *standard* view among economists, as he thinks most economists have simply not *thought* about the issue. In part I agree with him. I think most economists, like most others, have not really considered the issues this chapter addresses. Still, in part I think this is because the Standard View is *implicitly* accepted as natural, obvious, or uncontroversial. If the Standard View appeared objectionable or controversial, then surely economists *would* have recognized that it was implied by the statistical measures, and those measures would have been criticized accordingly. The fact that this didn't occur suggests, to me anyway, that my moniker is not too misleading. (Perhaps I am giving economists more credit than Broome thinks they deserve.)

Also, some economists have explicitly addressed the question of variable population, and those I know of accept the standard view. For example, in *On Economic Inequality* (Clarendon Press, 1973), A. K. Sen adopts what he calls the *Symmetry Axiom for Population* (*SAP*), which he describes as "a relatively unobjectionable assumption" and "an undemanding axiom" (p. 59). Yet, as Sen makes explicit, SAP allows the Lorenze curve (or Gini coefficient) to be applied to populations of variable size in a way that directly entails the Standard View. Thus, as I read Sen, he is endorsing both SAP and the Standard View.

Let me add that while I think few have previously thought about the issue, those philosophers and economists with whom I have discussed it strongly endorse the Standard View—at least initially. So, as indicated, I think the Standard View is appropriately named even if its acceptance is largely implicit (perhaps even dispositional?) rather than explicit.

Finally, having said all that let me point out that here, as elsewhere, little hinges on my terminology. Even if the Standard View is *not* "standard" in the sense of being widely—even if only implicitly—accepted, I think the issues raised in this chapter have important and far-reaching implications.

There are, I believe, strong considerations that can be adduced on *both* sides of the question. In the following sections I shall present some of these considerations, without pursuing all of their many implications and complications. Though my discussion must be incomplete, I hope it is sufficient to convince the reader of the issue's importance and complexity.

7.2 Considerations Supporting the Standard View

I begin by considering reasons for accepting P, with its implication that A and B are equivalent. (Note, throughout this chapter all references to A and B refer to diagram 7.1). Though the reader may already be convinced of P's truth, I ask that the reader bear with me in this section and the next, as they are important for both setting up, and balancing against, sections 7.4–7.7.

In chapter 2, we argued that one aspect of inequality is concerned with *social* rather than natural inequalities, where the judgment that one society is better or worse than another regarding inequality will be a judgment about the principles and institutions of those societies responsible for (social) inequality. It is easy to see how such an aspect might support P's plausibility.

Consider the following example. Suppose representatives of the worse-off met with the U.S. administration to complain about America's inequality. It seems likely they would not be consoled—indeed, would be completely unmoved—by assurances that the sizes of the better- and worse-off groups were changing, and at the same rate. The reason for this is clear. Presumably, the worse-off's representatives want the government to *do* something about America's inequality. They want to see changes in the inheritance and tax laws, the judicial process, the educational and vocational systems, and so on. In other words, in meeting with the administration their concern is with the principles and institutions governing American society. But then, it is easy to see why they won't be consoled by the assurances in question; such assurances do not address *their* concern.

One can see, then, how a concern for social equality might support the judgment that A and B are equivalent on the implicit assumption that A and B differ solely in size—that is, that they are alike in all other relevant respects, including their principles and institutions. More generally, I think the preceding helps explain P's widespread appeal. Many economists and others who have endorsed P have been mainly concerned with social justice. Their interest has been in determining whether a society seeking equality should pattern its principles and institutions after those of Britain, Russia, America, or some other model altogether. Given their concerns, there is good reason to accept P.

Two comments regarding the foregoing. First, the assumption that A and B are alike except in size is necessary if one wants to conclude—based on a concern about social inequality—that they are equivalent regarding inequality. For example, it might be the case that A's principles and institutions are much better (or worse) than B's, but that A's and B's gaps between the better- and worse-off are the same due to other, *natural*, circumstances. In such a case, a concern for social equality would support P, but not the judgment that A and B are equivalent.

Second, I believe the concern about social inequality is a legitimate and important egalitarian concern. Hence, I think there *are* significant reasons for accepting P.
However, this does not settle the issue of how size variations affect inequality. After
all, the concern for social equality is not the *only* significant aspect of the
egalitarian's concern and, as we shall see later, other considerations suggest rather
different conclusions.

A second aspect of inequality supporting P is the one judging inequality in terms
of "gratuitousness." Recall, on this aspect a situation's inequality will be gratuitous,
and hence bad, insofar as the "costs" of a redistribution of (the sources of) welfare
would be relatively small, and the "gains" relatively large. Thus, as we saw, on this
aspect a situation where just a few are well off while the vast majority are badly off
would be much less objectionable than one where just a few are badly off while the
vast majority are well off, since in the former situation, unlike the latter, a redistribution of (the sources of) welfare would (presumably) involve a tremendous loss in
the quality of life for some, with virtually no gain for those thus "benefited." Such
a position supports P, since if the pattern of inequality is identical in two societies,
so that (we suppose) their only difference is that one is proportionally bigger than
the other, then the relative "costs" and "gains" of a redistribution of (the sources of)
welfare to the better- and worse-off should be the same in the two societies. Correspondingly, their inequality will seem equally gratuitous, and hence equally objectionable.

Two other aspects of inequality supporting at least P's spirit, and hence its
intuitive plausibility, are the maximin principle of equality combined with the relative to the average view of complaints (MP & AVE) and the maximin principle of
equality combined with the relative to the best-off person view of complaints (MP
& BOP). Recall, on MP & AVE and MP & BOP how two societies compare
regarding inequality will depend on how much those societies' worst-off members
have to "complain" about regarding inequality, where this will depend on how they
fare relative to the average and best-off persons in their societies. Basically, then,
on these positions one society's inequality will be worse than another's if the gaps
between the average or best-off person and the worst-off are larger in the one
society than the other. Because the size of the gaps between the average or best-off
person and the worst-off would not be affected by proportional variation in a
society's population, such positions intuitively support P.

Note, the preceding discussion ignores maximin's "tie breaking" clause according to which if the worst-off groups had the same size complaint in two situations,
that situation would be best whose worst-off group was smallest. Clearly, if
maximin's tie-breaking clause applies, proportional increases will worsen inequality
on the views in question. However, it is a very complicated and controversial
question whether such a clause should apply in cases where different people would
be in the worst-off groups because there are different numbers in existence—a
question I cannot pursue here.[2] In any event such worries need not detain us, since

2. I, in fact, think a principle like maximin is controversial whenever one is comparing outcomes with
different people in the worst-off groups. Rawls and Parfit might disagree. In particular, they might hold
that a principle like maximin isn't controversial when comparing situations where different people are

even if maximin's "tie-breaking" clause applies, the aspects in question would still support a position very close to P. Though strictly speaking proportional increases in the number of better- and worse-off would worsen inequality, the extent to which they do so would only make a difference in the case of ties. Correspondingly, proportional increases would not "significantly" affect a situation's inequality.

There is another way of thinking that may support P. It may be illustrated with the following nonegalitarian example. Suppose there were four societies, F, G, H, and I, such that those in F were susceptible to chickenpox, those in G and H were susceptible to diabetes, and those in I were susceptible to AIDS. There is a straightforward sense in which one might judge that *regarding illnesses* G and H were equivalent to each other, worse than F, and better than I. Such judgments might be simply, and strictly, judgments about the *kinds* of illnesses obtaining in the societies. Correspondingly, they would be independent of the societies' sizes or, for that matter, of the prevalence of the respective diseases within each society. That is, such judgments would be independent of both the absolute numbers and the percentages of those afflicted with the diseases.

Analogously, suppose there were four societies, F, G, H, and I, whose only inequalities were due to birth defects. Specifically, suppose that the only inequalities were between those born with a limp and those born without one, in F's case; between those born born blind and those born sighted, in G and H's cases; and between those born with spina bifada and those born without it, in I's case. As before, there is a straightforward sense in which someone who cared about natural inequality might judge that *regarding inequality* G and H were equivalent to each other, worse than F, and better than I.[3] Such judgments might be simply, and strictly, judgments about the *kinds* of inequality obtaining. They would be independent of the societies' sizes, or even the prevalence of the inequality within each society. That is, they would be independent of both the absolute numbers and the percentages of the societies who were worse off relative to the better-off. Clearly, then, such judgments would support P, on the assumption that "mere" proportional variations in the number of better- and worse-off would not affect the *kind* of inequalities obtaining—at least not in the sense described here.

There is still another way of thinking that may support P. To illustrate it, consider again our nonegalitarian example involving G and H whose members were susceptible to diabetes. Although, as we have seen, there is *one* sense in which one might judge that *regarding illnesses* G and H were equivalent to each other, there is *another* sense in which one might judge that regarding illnesses G was worse than H if, for example, most of G's population was afflicted by illness, while few in H's

---

involved, as long as the worst-off groups are the same size. Still, both Rawls and Parfit recognize difficulties in applying such a principle when different people are in the worst-off groups because there are different numbers in existence. Some of the complexities raised by these issues are broached in my "Intransitivity and the Mere Addition Paradox" (*Philosophy and Public Affairs* 16 [1987]: 138-87), and I hope to pursue them further on another occasion.

3. Strictly for the purposes of this argument I am assuming that the inequality between those born with spina bifida and those born without it is worse than that between those born blind and those born sighted, which in turn is worse than that between those born with a limp and those born without one. Insofar as this assumption is incorrect, my example could be revised accordingly.

population were. More particularly, there is a straightfoward sense in which, from a health standpoint, one might judge G more dangerous or worse than H if, say, 80 percent of G's population were seriously ill, while only 20 percent of H's were, and this is so even if in *absolute* terms there might be more people seriously ill in H than in G due to H's being a larger society.

The preceding suggests a sense in which our judgment about how two societies compare regarding illnesses (or, alternatively, in terms of their citizens' health) may depend on the societies' *patterns* of illnesses in terms of both the *kind* and *prevalence* of their illnesses—that is, on the *relative* rather than absolute numbers of those afflicted by illness. Similar reasoning suggests there may be a sense in which our judgment about how two societies compare regarding inequality may depend on the societies' *patterns* of inequality in terms of both the kinds of inequalities obtaining (in the sense indicated) and the extent to which the inequalities are pervasive (that is, the relative numbers of "victims" of inequality in each society). Thus, in our earlier example where G and H both involve inequality between the deaf and those who hear, there is a sense in which we would not regard G and H as equivalent regarding inequality if, say, 80 percent of G were deaf, while only 20 percent of H were, and where we *would* regard them as equivalent if the same percentage were deaf in the two societies. Moreover, this is so whatever might be the case regarding the *absolute* numbers who were deaf. So, even if *more* people were worse off than others through no fault of their own in H than G—because H was larger—there is a sense in which we might regard H's inequality as equivalent or even preferable to G's depending on the *relative* number of deaf in the two societies.

The view I have been discussing has different implications than the previous one in cases where size variations are not proportional—specifically, in cases where a society's *kinds* of inequality remain constant, but the *numbers* of better- and worse-off change disproportionately so that the relative numbers of better- and worse-off vary. However, as should be clear, it has the same implications as the previous one in cases where size variations are proportional. Hence, this view also supports P.

I have noted six positions that support P, or at least the judgment that proportional variations do not significantly affect inequality. The first position concerns only social inequality. The others may concern both social and natural inequality. I have not claimed each position is equally plausible. But I think each represents an intelligible way of judging inequality that cannot simply be dismissed. Moreover, however exhausting, my discussion is not necessarily exhaustive. Other positions may also support P. In sum, it is not surprising P has been widely accepted. It is intuitively appealing and is supported by a number of intelligible and plausible positions.

7.3 A General Argument for the Standard View

We have noted how four of chapter 2's aspects directly support P. From this the reader may correctly infer that chapter 2's (eight) other aspects do not support P (see section 7.4). Although proponents of P may initially find this surprising, they may not find it disturbing. Instead, they may insist that even if some aspects of inequality do not *themselves* directly entail P, they should be supplemented, if necessary, to reflect P. In support of their position, they may offer a general argument supporting P, one pushing an analogy between a society's (overall) level and its size. More particularly, they may contend that just as one must take account of the levels of those between whom inequality obtains, so one must take account of the size of the society in which inequality obtains. Their argument might run as follows.

As we have seen, although in one sense there may be just as *much* inequality in a world where n people are at level 1,000 and m are at level 2,000, as in one where n are at level 1,000,000 and m are at 1,001,000, the inequality is less offensive in the latter world than the former, since in the latter the worse-off fare better relative to the others in their world. Likewise, although in one sense there may be just as *much* inequality in a world where n people are 1,000 units worse off than m people, as in one where n thousand people are 1 unit worse off than m people, the inequality is less offensive in the latter than the former, since in the latter the worse-off fare better relative to the others in their world.

More generally, just as C will be better than D regarding inequality if the inequality measured as a function of the gaps between the better- and worse-off is the same in C and D, but C's *levels* are higher than D's, so C will be better than D if the inequality measured as a function of both the gaps and levels is the same in C and D, but there are *more* people in C than D. In both cases this is because the egalitarian is not simply concerned with how *much* inequality a world has; he is concerned with how *bad* it is. More specifically, he is concerned with how the worse-off fare relative to the better-off.

The heart of this reasoning might be put as follows. Egalitarianism is not like utilitarianism. Utilitarianism, as is often pointed out, is an additive principle. Moreover, if the core of utilitarianism is that more of the good is better than less of the good, then it seems utilitarianism is *essentially* an additive principle. It is concerned not with who has what, but rather with *how much* there is. Conversely, egalitarianism, it might be claimed, is concerned not with how much there is, but with who has what. That is, it might be claimed that the fundamental concern of egalitarians is with the good's distribution, not its maximization. Thus, it might seem that egalitarianism is *essentially* a distributive principle, not an additive one. But then, even when "the good" being considered is equality itself, or more particularly, how much people have to complain about regarding inequality, it might seem egalitarians should be concerned not merely with the sum total of complaints, but with their distribution.

On this view, then, a measure of inequality focusing on the sum of individual complaints cannot, by itself, be a useful or plausible one—even if those complaints have been weighted to take account of the levels of those with complaints. This is because, by itself, such a measure reveals nothing about the distribution of complaints and, on this view, that is the egalitarian's central concern.[4]

_____

4. Someone might worry that on different views about individual complaints facts about distribution *already* enter into our measurement of complaints, so that taking further account of the distribution of complaints is both unnecessary and unwarranted. Specifically, one might hold that the view in question

Note that although the above reasoning parallels earlier remarks supporting the maximin principle of equality, it might be applied to each of chapter 2's aspects. What it suggests is that just as the ways of measuring inequality must be supplemented to capture the notion that a given amount of inequality will be less offensive if it is spread out among people well off rather than among people poorly off, some need to be further supplemented to capture the notion that a given amount of inequality will be less offensive if it is spread out among a large number of people rather than a small number. Thus, for example, we do not want to dismiss those aspects of inequality employing an additive principle for, as our earlier results show, they can reflect significant features of inequality's pattern. Nevertheless, we want to be sure that when one of those aspects implies that C is worse than D, it is because C's pattern of inequality really is worse than D's, and not simply because C has a lot more people with complaints.

One can see how advocates of this reasoning would apply it to A and B of diagram 7.1. They could admit that the sum total of individual complaints is larger in B than A. Nevertheless, they would claim that A's pattern of inequality is identical to B's. More particularly, they would emphasize that B's *distribution* of complaints is not worse than A's. In sum, they would contend that, relative to the others in their world, B's worse-off do not fare worse than A's. Hence, they would maintain A's inequality is just as bad as B's.

Before going on, let me present one way of supplementing chapter 2's aspects to reflect such reasoning. First, note that the aspects only need supplementing where populations of different size are involved. If two worlds have populations of the same size, there is no problem.[5] Second, note that the advocates of such reasoning accept P, the view that proportional variations in the number of better- and worse-off do not affect inequality. Given these facts, the following way of comparing two worlds of different sizes suggests itself. First, carry out the thought process of "transforming" one of the worlds into a world with a population the same size as the other world's population, but with the same proportion of better- and worse-off that it presently has. Then, compare the inequality of the "transformed" world with that of the other world, using chapter 2's approaches.

For example, suppose we want to compare C and D, where D is larger than C. We might do this by comparing C* with D, where C* is the same

---

involves an illegitimate double counting of our distributional concerns. I take it this is precisely what advocates of the view in question would deny. They would assert, for reasons suggested in the text, that distributional concerns must enter our egalitarian deliberations both at the level of measuring individual complaints and at the level of assessing the collective effect of those complaints. Of course, whether we should be satisfied with their assertion is another matter. See my subsequent comments.

5. In such cases the orderings yielded by the aspects will seem perfectly plausible—at least, insofar as we are caught in the grip of the intuitions underlying those aspects, and assuming they have already been supplemented to reflect the fact that inequality matters more at low levels than high levels. (Throughout the discussion that follows, I assume the aspects should and will be supplemented to capture the sensitivity of the notion of inequality to the levels of those between whom the inequality obtains. However, for ease and clarity of expression I ignore this in my presentation.)

size as D but has a pattern of inequality identical to C's.[6] Given the first point just noted, there will be no problem comparing C* with D; and given the second, this will tell us how C compares with D, since C and C* will be equivalent regarding inequality.

I mention this particular method of taking population size into account for two reasons. First, it is pretty clear how such a method would reflect the reasoning in question and would imply that A is equivalent to B. Second, it is equivalent to a method many economists' measures employ, according to which the various additive approaches are supplemented by simply dividing the number arrived at by the number of people in society. Interestingly, it might plausibly be claimed that the result of this process is a number representing society's average level of complaint. I shall return to this later, but for now the key points to note are (1) as indicated (and as a bit of mathematics reveals) the orderings yielded by the economists' process are identical to those yielded by the method outlined previously; and (2) such a method represents a way of taking into account the number of people between whom inequality obtains.

I have considered the view that each aspect of inequality must be supplemented so as to reflect P by taking account of society's numbers as well as its levels. I have tried to present the intuitions and arguments underlying that view as powerfully as possible, since many economists subscribe to it, and since I suspect many philosophers would as well if they thought about the issue. Nevertheless, despite its appeal, I believe the view should be rejected. My reasons for this follow.[7]

6. So, if C has m people and D n people, then if there were k people at a given level in C, there would be (n/m)k people at that level in C*.

7. Shelly Kagan has suggested that instead of giving a single general argument for the Standard View I have blurred two distinct arguments. Specifically, he thinks the parallel argument between levels and size should be presented, and responded to separately, from the pattern, or distribution argument. On Kagan's view, the parallel argument should be fundamentally understood as supporting a *discount* rate for inequality relative to both population levels and size. So, just as inequality matters less at high levels than low levels, it matters less when populations are large rather than small.

I think this is mistaken. More accurately, I don't find the parallel between levels and size plausible if it is understood in the manner suggested. Roughly, I think the *reason* a discount rate seems plausible for levels is that, for all the reasons given in chapter 6, the worse-off seem to fare *better* relative to others if the gaps between the better and worse remain the same but the population's welfare increases. But there are not parallel reasons to think a discount rate will be plausible for size. That is, the kinds of considerations presented in chapter six will not imply that the worse off will fare better relative to others if the gaps between the better and worse remain the same but the population's size increases. Thus, I think if a parallel is to be drawn between the two cases it should be understood in terms of the way in which level and size variations affect the pattern of inequality or distribution of complaints, rather than the way in which both support discount rates for inequality. (And, of course, my point here is merely to present a general argument which I think *might* be offered in support of the Standard View; I am not endorsing that argument.)

Note, as we shall see, I think there *may* be reasons to adopt a kind of discounting rate for inequality as population size increases. And perhaps this—which has important implications for the views we are discussing—is really all Kagan intends to suggest. But these reasons are distinct from the reasons for supporting a discounting rate as levels increase, and hence are not supported by drawing a parallel between levels and size. Thus, while one might draw a parallel between levels and size *after* showing that—for very different reasons—a discount rate is appropriate for both; one cannot show that a discount rate is appropriate for both by appealing to a parallel between levels and size.

7.4 Considerations Opposing the Standard View

In this section I shall offer several arguments for rejecting the standard view. Let me begin by responding to the general argument of section 7.3.

I claim we should not supplement each of inequality's aspects so as to reflect P. In claiming this I am, among other things, denying that egalitarianism is essentially distributive in the manner suggested. I readily grant that egalitarians are concerned with distributions and not merely totals—with who has what, rather than with *how much* there is. Nevertheless, I believe the egalitarian's concern is not so much essentially distributive as it is essentially comparative. The egalitarian has no intrinsic concern with how much people have; her concern is with how much people have *relative to others*. One way of putting this[8] is that the egalitarian is concerned not so much with the distribution of goods but with the satisfaction of moral claims—specifically, with the satisfaction of certain moral claims based on how people fare relative to others.

The foregoing point is, I think, important. While egalitarians *are* concerned with how the good is distributed, that is not their ultimate concern. Their ultimate concern is that some have less while others have more. To say this is basically to reiterate my earlier claim that the ultimate intuition underlying egalitarianism is that it is bad (unfair or unjust) for some to be worse off than others through no fault of their own. Now as we have seen this intuition is not easy to interpret. Its content is complex and it manifests itself in various ways. Nevertheless, I think it is this intuition that lies at the heart of the egalitarian's position and underlies her concern about distributions. This intuition also underlies my objection to section 7.3's reasoning.

Consider again diagram 7.1. According to section 7.3 each of inequality's aspects should be supplemented to imply that B is not worse than A. This, however, seems implausible. True, as section 7.2 shows, insofar as we are caught in the grip of the intuitions underlying certain aspects of inequality, B may not seem significantly worse than A.[9] Still, insofar as we are caught in the grip of the intuitions underlying the other aspects, why *shouldn't* we regard B's inequality as worse than A's?

Consider. As noted in chapter 2, the additive principle reflects the view that if it really is bad for one person to be worse off than another through no fault of his own, it should be even worse for two people to be in such a position. Similarly, the relative to all those better off view of complaints reflects the view that if it is bad to be worse off than one person through no fault of your own, it should be even worse to be worse off than two. But then, in accordance with these views, B's inequality *is* worse than A's, and I fail to see why these views should be ignored, revised, or supplemented so as to avoid this result. After all, not only are B's

---

8. Suggested to me by Thomas Scanlon.

9. This would be so, for instance, on either the relative to the best-off person, or the relative to the average view of complaints. Notice, however, it would not be so on the relative to all those better off view of complaints.

worse-off at the same level as A's, and not only are the gaps between the better- and worse-off just as great in B as in A, but in B there are *twice* as many in the position of being worse off than others through no fault of their own, and there are *twice* as many that they are worse off than.

One can see how the reasoning underlying an additive principle and a relative to all those better off view of complaints (AP & ATBO) would combine to oppose P. On such a position proportional increases in a society's population would worsen inequality, as it would result in there being *more* people with *larger* complaints regarding inequality. Analogously, I think the reasoning underlying many of inequality's other aspects will also oppose P. Specifically, let me add—without repeating the many relevant claims and arguments of chapter 2—that I think P is opposed by the reasoning underlying AP & AVE, AP & BOP, WAP & AVE, WAP & BOP, WAP & ATBO, MP & ATBO, and Deviation.

The point to stress, here, is that even if one grants that in a certain sense the kind of inequality is no worse in B than in A, and even if one grants (the more controversial claim) that in a certain sense the pattern or distribution of complaints is no worse in B than in A, it is crucial to bear in mind *why* the egalitarian cares about kinds of inequality, or patterns and distributions, in the first place. If, as suggested, it is because she regards it as bad for some to be worse off than others through no fault of their own, then there is good reason to regard B as worse than A. After all, to paraphrase the basic insight of the utilitarians, more of the bad is worse than less of the bad, and in many respects there is, in the end, more of what the egalitarian regards as bad in B than in A.

Let me note another way of putting the objection to P. In chapter 6, I considered the example of Tim and John, two equally deserving people whose positions improved as if Fate were steadily apportioning welfare according to an unwavering rule: 1 for Tim, 10 for John. So, when Tim was at level 1, John was at level 10; when Tim was at level 100, John was at level 1,000, and when Tim was at level 1,000, John was at level 10,000. I claimed that as time passed the situation was worsening regarding inequality. In support of that claim, I argued that if Tim and John really were equally deserving, then, in the absence of later developments that "evened things up," even one allocation of welfare in accordance with a rule like "1 for Tim, 10 for John" would be somewhat unfair; but that surely, if one such allocation was bad, two would be worse, three would be worse still, and so on. But notice, analogous reasoning suggests that B is worse than A and, more generally, that proportional increases in population size worsen inequality.

Suppose there are a million people in each group of A, two million in each group of B, and that the better- and worse-off are at levels 2,000 and 1,000, respectively. Suppose, also, that each of the better-off are named "John," each of the worse-off "Tim." Then, in each world, it is as if Fate has apportioned welfare in accordance with an unwavering rule like: (R) if there are two equally deserving people named "John" and "Tim" give 2,000 units to John, and 1,000 units to Tim. But now, if the people really are equally deserving, it would be bad for Fate to allocate welfare in accordance with R even once, worse for R to be used twice, and still worse for it to be employed three or more times. In other words, since it really is bad for welfare to be apportioned in accordance with R, the more times R is followed, the worse it is (unless later uses rectify earlier ones). Moreover, this is so whether or not R is repeatedly applied to the same individuals, or to different individuals.[10] But if this is right, then it would seem that B is worse than A, since in B it is as if R has been applied two million times, while in A it is as if R has been applied one million times.

Again, the point here can ultimately be couched in terms of the basic intuition underlying egalitarianism. I claim that the inequality between Tim_1 and $John_1$ will offend the egalitarian because she regards it as bad for one person to be worse off than another through no fault of her own. But then if it really is bad for Tim_1 to be worse off than $John_1$, it should, for the same reason, be bad for Tim_2 to be worse off than $John_2$, and thus, it should be even worse if, *in addition* to Tim_1 being worse off than $John_1$, Tim_2 is worse off than $John_2$. Extended, this reasoning leads straightforwardly to the judgments that B is worse than A and that proportional size increases worsen inequality.

One way of putting our point is as follows. In general, numbers count. This is true in most spheres of life, and morality is no exception to it. Moreover, it is not only true for utilitarians, but for most who employ moral ideals in the assessment of outcomes. Other things equal, more pains are worse than less pains, more infringements of liberty are worse than less infringements of liberty, more injustices or inequalities are worse than less injustices or inequalities. Even deontologists can accept such claims (though they deny that what we ought, morally, to *do*, is always to maximize the good or minimize wrong doing).

Not everyone accepts the view that numbers count in the moral realm.[11] But most do. And I think they are right in doing so (even though I also think there are good reasons to believe numbers probably do not count in the *simple* additive way most have implicitly assumed.)[12]

10. I am not claiming that both kinds of repeated applications would be *equally* bad, just that both would be bad. It is an open, and interesting, question which application, if either, would be worse taking all the relevant factors into consideration. Similarly, let me repeat the important disclaimer of chapter 6's note 22. I am *not* committing myself to the view that the "badness" associated with R's repeated applications can be captured by an additively separable function. It may or may not be the case that two applications of R are (exactly) twice as bad as one, that three applications are three times as bad, and so on. My claim is simply that it is unfair, and hence bad, for welfare to be allocated in accordance with R once, worse for R to be used twice, worse still for R to be used three times, and so on. Thus, I am not simply committing what Shelly Kagan has called the additive fallacy (see note 11 in this chapter). I am aware that there are nonadditive functions where two applications of R might not be twice as bad as one, and also nonadditive functions where two applications might be *better* than one. But I do not find the second nonadditive function *plausible* for the case in question.

In sum, I think my argument is plausible and *persuasive*, but not necessarily compelling. Still, though I acknowledge that an argument (involving externalities) *might* undermine my position, I do not see such an argument on the horizon, and doubt such an argument would ultimately succeed.

11. John Taurek explicitly denies that numbers should count in his rich and widely discussed article, "Should the Numbers Count?" *Philosophy and Public Affairs* 6 (1977): 293-316. Other authors who raise serious questions about whether numbers count in all cases include Bernard Williams and G.E.M. Anscombe. See the concluding comments of "2. The structure of consequentialism," in William's "A Critique of Utilitarianism," in *Utilitarianism: For and Against*, ed. J. J. C. Smart and Bernard Williams (Cambridge University Press, 1973) esp. pp. 92-93, and also Anscombe's "Modern Moral Philosophy," *Philosophy* 33 (1958): 1-19.

12. Shelly Kagan challenges a number of widely held assumptions about additivity in a fascinating article "The Additive Fallacy," *Ethics* 99 (1988): 5-31. Other reasons to worry about simple additivity

Consider again our earlier example of two societies G and H both of whose members were susceptible to diabetes. We saw that there is a sense in which we might judge G and H equivalent regarding illness regardless of their respective sizes or even the prevalence of diabetes within each society. Such a judgment would strictly be about the *kinds* of illness in the societies—and, by analogy, we saw that a similar kind of judgment might be made regarding inequality. We also saw that there was *another* sense in which we might judge that regarding illness G was worse than H, if, for example, most of G's population was afflicted by illness, while few in H's population were. Such a judgment would be a judgment about both the *kind* of illness in the societies, and the (relative) prevalence of the illness—and again, by analogy, we saw that a similar kind of judgment might be made regarding inequality. But there is clearly yet *another* sense, and a crucially important one, in which we would judge the situation regarding illness to be worse in H than in G if there were *more* people with diabetes in H than in G. Such a judgment would reflect the view that, from one perspective at least, it would be better if all illness were eradicated in H than in G. Here, too, I think a similar kind of judgment might be made regarding inequality.

Suppose, for example, that G were the size of Haiti, and H the size of China. If 80 percent of G suffered from diabetes and 10 percent of H, then as we have seen there is a sense in which we might judge G and H equivalent, and another sense in which we might judge G worse than H. Still, as suggested previously, there is a third sense in which we would judge H worse than G. After all, while in G four million would be ill, in H a *hundred* million would be ill. Given the choice between the eradication of all diabetes in G and the eradication of all diabetes in H, few would think we ought to flip a coin. Most would say that here, as elsewhere, numbers count, that other things equal it is better to eradicate more illness rather than less.

On reflection, I think similar considerations apply in the case of equality. If 80 percent of G and 10 percent of H were worse off than the better-off by a certain amount, then as we have seen there is a sense in which we might judge G and H equivalent regarding inequality, and another sense in which we might judge G worse than H. Still, I think there is a third sense in which we should judge H worse than G. After all, while in G four million would be worse off than one million, in H over a *hundred* million would be worse off than over *nine hundred* million. Given the choice between the (magical?) eradication of all inequality in G or H, we ought not, I think, to flip a coin. Here, as elsewhere, numbers count.

---

are contained, implicitly, in my "Intransitivity" and in section 7.9. It is perhaps worth emphasizing that some reasons people are drawn to the view that numbers don't count, or that additivity should be rejected, are in fact compatible with an additive model for moral ideals but not with a *simple* additive model. There may be good reason to retain the view that two pains or deaths are worse than one, that three are worse than two, and so on, and yet to reject the view that two pains or deaths are necessarily *twice* as bad as one, that three are three times as bad, and so on. Thus, for example, while I think strictly speaking utilitarians and others are right to insist that massacring seven million and one is worse than massacring seven million, I suspect that Anscombe and Williams may be correct in thinking that the objective difference between those cases may not be nearly as great as the objective difference between murdering two people and murdering one, and may, in fact, be (virtually?) insignificant. I raise these issues only to leave them aside. Though deep and important, they are not central to our current concerns.

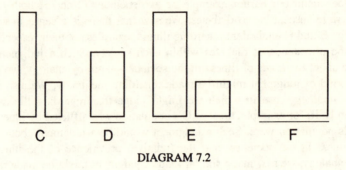

DIAGRAM 7.2

Some will insist that equality is not bad in the same way illness is. More generally, they will insist that equality and utility are different *kinds* of moral ideals and that the two ideals can, and should, be treated differently. On this view, the fact that numbers count regarding utility is completely irrelevant to—that is, suggests *nothing* about—whether numbers count regarding equality. I sympathize with this view, which is why I have mainly tried to motivate my claims by appealing to elements *internal* to egalitarianism—for example, by showing how my claims reflect both the basic intuition underlying egalitarianism and particular aspects of inequality. Still, ultimately I am not sure our moral ideals are isolated from each other in the way suggested. Depending on how moral ideals combine to yield all-things-considered judgments, at least some may need to share certain formal or structural features if we are to avoid unacceptable implications.

Consider diagram 7.2. As drawn, C represents an unequal society, D a perfectly equal society with less total utility. E and F are just like C and D, respectively, except they are twice as large. Looking at C and D, many would judge that D is better than C all things considered. They would judge the (slight) loss of utility in moving from C to D regrettable, but outweighed by the (substantial) gain in equality. Similarly, looking at E and F, many would judge that F is better than E all things considered. Again, they would judge the loss of utility in moving from E to F regrettable, but outweighed by the gain in equality. More important, few if any would approve a redistribution between the better- and worse-off in C so as to bring about D, yet oppose a redistribution between the better- and worse-off in E so as to bring about F. That is, most would agree that *if* moving from C to D were desirable, moving from E to F would *also* be desirable.

The foregoing claims may seem obvious and uninteresting, but they have important implications. Depending on how one thinks moral ideals combine to yield all-things-considered judgments, they imply that if numbers count for utility, they must also count for equality. Consider. Suppose one thinks that the move from C to D is only a *slight* improvement all things considered, because the gain in equality is just *barely* enough to outweigh the attendant loss in utility.[13] Then it looks as if

---

13. If this doesn't seem plausible for A and B as drawn, imagine them redrawn (along with C and D) such that it *does* seem plausible. That is, imagine the level of those in B lowered (or raised?) further, so

F would be *worse* than E if numbers count for utility but not for equality. After all, E and F are twice as large as C and D. This means that the loss in utility in moving from E to F will be *twice* as great as the loss in utility in moving from C to D, and hence, on the view in question, that the move from E to F will be much worse than the move from C to D regarding utility. Yet if numbers don't count for equality or, more specifically, if we accept P—the view that proportional increases do not affect inequality—then the gain in equality in moving from F to E will be *exactly* the same as the gain in equality in moving from D to C. But then it looks as if the gain in equality in moving from F to E *won't* be sufficient to outweigh the attendant loss in utility, since, by hypothesis, the gain in question is *barely* enough to outweigh a loss in utility that is only *half* as large. In sum, if moving from E to F is significantly worse than moving from C to D regarding utility, and no better regarding equality, then it is easy to see that, all things considered, moving from E to F could be undesirable even if moving from C to D were desirable.[14] But this, of course, is contrary to the "obvious and uninteresting" view noted earlier.

The preceding considerations suggest that perhaps different moral ideals can not be fully and adequately characterized in isolation from each other. Specifically, a plausible and coherent account of the role moral ideals play in relation to each other and our all-things-considered judgments may require at least some ideals to share certain formal or structural features in common.[15] Thus, as we have seen, if we want to hold on to the view that numbers count regarding utility, we may also have to be prepared to hold that numbers count regarding equality.

---

that in moving from A to B the loss in utility would be *barely* outweighed by the gain in equality. I presume, of course, that someone who genuinely cares about both equality and utility will want to permit *some* losses regarding either of the ideals for "sufficient" gains regarding the other.

14. This argument was developed by Derek Parfit and me, during a series of discussions about this topic. It is powerful, but not conclusive. David Aman and John Broome have pointed out that one could avoid the argument's apparent implications by adopting a multiplicative function for moral ideals rather than an additive one. For example, instead of adding together numbers representing how good situations are regarding utility and equality in order to arrive at one's all-things-considered judgment, one might multiply the relevant numbers. Such a function would enable one to maintain that while moving from E to F is significantly worse than moving from C to D regarding utility, and *no* better regarding equality, the move from E to F will be desirable if the move from C to D is. Though such a move accommodates what many people would (at least initially) want to say about the particular situations in question, I am not sure that it can be independently motivated or ultimately defended. Prima facie, at least, it strikes me as odd, implausible, and (hence) ad hoc to contend that how good a situation is, all things considered, will depend on, among other things, how good it is regarding utility *times* how good it is regarding equality. (Can one think of any *other* moral ideals that might be related in a *multiplicative* manner?) Still, I think the suggestion is worth pursuing since there are serious difficulties with the more natural and intuitively appealing additive approach. (Cf. notes 9 and 11. I take it Kagan might be quite sympathetic to Aman and Broome's suggestion. I am less so, since the difficulties I see with the additive approach, though significant, do *not* undermine the argument I have presented.)

15. John Broome develops and exploits this theme—that a coherent account of the role moral ideals play in our all-things-considered judgments may require them to share certain formal or structural features—in his book *Weighing Goods* (Basil Blackwell, 1991). Broome's arguments and conclusions are rather different from mine, and I am not always sure what to make of them. But I find his claims fascinating, and even where I am skeptical of his results, I am sympathetic with his attempt to draw substantive conclusions about the relations between, and natures of, moral notions previously regarded as (logically or conceptually) disparate.

The foregoing result may be surprising. But on reflection it is not, I think, perplexing or disturbing. To the contrary, I find the result plausible and welcome both on general theoretical and intuitive grounds, and in virtue of the further support it offers the particular conclusions for which I have been arguing. Suffice it to say, I accept the view that if moving from C to D were desirable, so too would be moving from E to F. I also accept the view that in an important sense the latter move would be worse than the former regarding utility. This leads me to believe there is an important sense in which the latter move would be better than the former regarding inequality. But, of course, this implies that E is worse than C regarding inequality, which in turn implies that there is reason to reject P and the judgment that A and B are equivalent regarding inequality.

To sum up. I believe there are strong reasons to reject the Standard View. I have claimed P is in tension with the most fundamental intuition of egalitarianism, and opposed by the underlying reasoning of most of equality's aspects. I have also claimed P conflicts with the basic fact that numbers (usually) count; specifically, that it is plausible to believe that numbers count not only for morality in general, but for equality in particular. Finally, I have argued that a coherent and plausible account of moral ideals may require us to hold that numbers count for equality—and hence that P must be rejected—if we want to hold, as many do, that numbers count for utility.

I conclude there are (at least) eight aspects of inequality opposing P, and that those aspects should not be supplemented to reflect P.

Before going on, let me address a concern many may hold about this section's views.[16] As indicated, I think most accept the view that numbers count in the moral realm. Given the choice between saving one life and five, they believe that other things equal we should save the five. But many who accept "the basic fact" that numbers count in *this* sense would deny that it is better if more people exist with lives worth living. Numbers do not count in *that* way, they think. For example, they may accept Jan Narveson's view that "morality has to do with how we treat whatever people there are . . . . We are in favor of making people happy, but neutral about making happy people."[17] On such a view, one improves an outcome regarding utility if one increases the total (or average) level of utility for the people who exist in that outcome, but not if one simply adds more people with lives worth living to that outcome. Correspondingly, one may think that proportional variations in population size do not affect an outcome's desirability regarding utility and argue that, just as this is so for utility, it should also be so for equality. In sum, one may grant that there is an important sense in which numbers count, without believing it is better if more people are living. Hence, one may think the "basic fact" that numbers count is not incompatible with P.

There are various ways to flesh out such a view. For simplicity, I shall assume

16. Some readers may recognize Parfit's *Mere Addition Paradox* as my initial point of departure for the following reflections. See part 4 of *Reasons and Persons* (Oxford University Press, 1984), esp. chap. 19.

17. Jan Narveson, "Moral Problems of Population," *Monist* 57 (1973): 73 and 80. See also Narveson's pioneering work, "Utilitarianism and New Generations," *Mind* 76 (1967): 62-72, for further discussion of his view.

the view entails three principles: (R) When comparing outcomes with the same number of people, the best outcome regarding utility will be the one with the greatest total utility (note, for same number of cases, this principle will be extensionally equivalent to an average principle or to Parfit's principle of beneficence, Q^{18}); (S) The mere existence of extra people with lives worth living does not improve an outcome regarding utility, though it doesn't worsen it either;[19] and (T) Proportional increases in a population's size do not affect an outcome's value regarding utility.

The preceding is an extremely important view, with significant implications for our discussion. But it raises a host of complicated and far-reaching problems I cannot fully pursue here. Let me mention, without elaborating on, three of these.

First, I think it is hard to consistently maintain that increasing utility is good if it results from improving the lot of already existing people, yet neutral if it results from the mere addition of extra people. Consider our earlier claim that other things equal it is better to eradicate more illness rather than less. This view implies that, other things equal, in any given world it would be better to cure 200,000 cases of diabetes than 100,000 cases. But if we accept this, should we deny that curing 200,000 diabetics in a world of 2 billion would be better, regarding utility, than curing 100,000 diabetics in a world of 1 billion? Even if the costs were higher to accomplish the former than the latter, mightn't they be justified regarding utility? I find this hard to deny. But then, for similar reasons, in considering diagram 7.2 I find it hard to deny that moving from E to F will be worse than moving C to D regarding utility.[20] But this position is hard to reconcile with T, the view that proportional increases in population do not affect an outcome's value regarding utility. After all, on T, C's utility should be equivalent to E's, and D's should be equivalent to F's. Yet if C's utility is equivalent to E's, and moving from E to F is worse than moving from C to D, how could D's utility be equivalent to F's?

Second, while it may seem plausible to contend that the addition of extra lives worth living does not improve an outcome's utility, it is much less plausible to contend that the addition of extra wretched lives does not worsen an outcome's utility. That is, there may be an important asymmetry in our intuitions about lives above and below the zero level for welfare. Yet on reflection this asymmetry may be indefensible. If additional lives below the zero level can adversely affect an

18. See section 125 of *Reasons and Persons*.

19. Gregory Kavka suggests the existence of extra lives worth living may worsen a situation if their lives are *restricted* in the sense of being "significantly deficient in one or more of the major respects that generally make human lives valuable and worth living" ('The Paradox of Future Individuals," *Philosophy and Public Affairs* 11 [1982]: 105). I am not sure I agree, but to avoid unnecessary complications let us assume throughout the ensuing discussion that extra lives worth living are not restricted in Kavka's sense. The existence of such lives, which Parfit says are above the *Bad Level*, will not worsen an outcome regarding utility, though on the view under discussion they will not improve it either (see section 147 of *Reasons and Persons*).

20. Recall that there is a loss in total utility on each of the moves in question, and that for each unit of net loss in the latter move there will be two units of net loss in the former. One position that would challenge the significance of these claims—an average principle of utility—is discussed, and argued against, later.

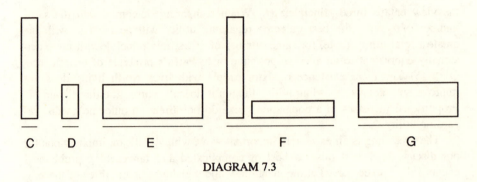

DIAGRAM 7.3

outcome's utility—as I think they can—why can't additional lives above the zero level improve an outcome's utility?[21]

Finally, and most importantly, consider diagram 7.3. As drawn, C and D are the same size as each other, so too are E, F, and G. In addition, F is assumed to include the C group as well as an extra group with lives well worth living. It follows that on the view under consideration C will be better than D regarding utility (from R), and E will be equivalent to D and G (from T and R, respectively). In addition, G will be better than F[22] (from R) and F will not be worse than C (from S). But note, if D, E, and G are equivalent, and C is better than D, then C should be better than than G. Yet if G is better than F, which is not worse than C, G should not be worse than C. But it cannot be true both that C is better than G and that G is not worse than C. Hence it appears that the view under consideration is internally inconsistent.

There are various ways of responding to the foregoing. But without under-estimating the appeal, ingenuity, or importance of the available responses, let me add that I know of no way of preserving Narveson's view that we value "making people happy, but [are] neutral about making happy people" without either limiting the scope of our principle of utility, so that it applies in some cases but not others, or adopting a principle of utility that is *essentially comparative*—not in the sense that I have argued equality is essentially comparative, but in the sense noted in section 3.3, that how good or bad a situation is regarding utility would depend on the alternatives to which it was compared, and not solely on the intrinsic, or internal, features of that situation.[23] But then, either way, the view in question will threaten the transitivity of our all-things-considered judgments, for reasons sketched in section 3.4 (see especially note

21. See my subsequent discussion for further considerations relevant to this point. See also Parfit's *Reasons and Persons*, chap. 18, where the asymmetry in question is discussed in some detail. Finally, let me add, without argument, that I believe the asymmetry in question may be incompatible with the transitivity of our all-things-considered judgments. I shall not pursue this here, because as we shall see next, I think the view under discussion threatens the transitivity of our all-things-considered judgments regardless of whether we accept the asymmetry in question.

22. As drawn, G's total (and average) utility is greater than F's.

23. This, in fact, is what accounts for the inconsistent judgments regarding diagram 7.3's alternatives.

15) and argued at length elsewhere.[24] But, of course, many believe that our all things considered judgments *must* be transitive or that denying this would undermine one of the deepest tenets of practical reasoning. Thus, accepting the view in question will not be easy.[25]

In sum, it may seem that while there is an important sense in which numbers count, it is not better, even regarding utility, if more people are alive.[26] But despite this position's appeal and significance, it faces many complex and difficult questions. Therefore, without pretending to have settled the issues raised by this position, I leave it aside in the remainder of this chapter.[27]

7.5 Rejecting Average Solutions and the Economists' Approach

In the preceding section I argued that there are strong reasons to reject the Standard View, P, that proportional size variations will not affect inequality. I suspect many readers were surprised at my arguments and results, and that some will continue to resist the conclusion that there is reason to reject P. Perhaps the most common and natural way of resisting my conclusion is to adopt *average* views regarding both utility and equality. In chapter 4 I argued against two kinds of average principles of equality. In this section I discuss, and reject, yet another kind of average view. In fact, I believe my remarks cast doubt on the legitimacy of average views in general.

Roughly, on an average view of utility one society will be better than another regarding utility if the average level of utility is higher in the one society than the other. Similarly, on an average view of equality one society will be better than another regarding equality if the average level of equality is higher in the one society than the other—or, as I prefer to put it, if the average level of "complaint" that people have regarding inequality is smaller in the one society than the other.

Many find an average view of utility independently plausible and appealing. Many also find an average view of equality independently plausible and appealing. For example, many economists measure a society's inequality by adding up the gaps between the better and worse off (in one way or another) and then dividing the number arrived at by the society's size. In essence, such an approach can be seen as measuring the average level of inequality (or the average level of "complaint" regarding inequality). Surely, the prevalence of such approaches is no accident. Such measures are formulated to yield judgments about average levels of inequality because many economists (and others)

24. See my "Intransitivity." In this article I explicitly address Narveson's view and variations of it, and argue that they have the features and implications described in the text.

25. Again, see my "Intransitivity" for further discussion of these matters.

26. This is the simplest statement of the basic view I have been discussing. Variations of the view are possible but these need not concern us here.

27. I remind the reader of my introductory remark, that this chapter "broaches deep topics that could only be adequately explored in another book . . . [and hence] only begins the task of considering how variations in population size affect inequality."

find it plausible to believe that one society will be better than another regarding inequality if the average level of inequality is smaller in the one than the other.[28]

Clearly an average view of equality will support P for many of inequality's aspects. In fact, an average view would support P for each of inequality's aspects except the one concerning social justice—which supports P by itself—and those involving the relative to all those better off view of complaints and either the additive or weighted additive principle. For example, proportional size variations would not affect the average level of complaint on any of the aspects involving the relative to the best-off person or the relative to the average view of complaints. Similarly, both the average degree of gratuitousness and the average deviation from a state of absolute equality will be unaffected by proportional size variations. Thus, for most aspects, one could maintain P by adopting an average view of equality. Correspondingly, for most aspects, an average view of equality will combine with an average view of utility to support the intuitively plausible judgment about diagram 7.2 that *if* moving from C to D were desirable, moving from E to F would also be desirable. After all, the fact that E and F are twice the size as C and D will not affect how they compare in terms of average utility or, for most aspects, average inequality. Correspondingly, the moves from E to F and C to D will involve the same size losses and gains in terms of average utility and, for most aspects, average inequality. (Henceforth, I will drop the qualifier "for most aspects." Unless noted otherwise, this section's discussion concerns those aspects for which an average view would support P.)

Although average views have a fair amount of initial appeal, *at most* they offer further reasons for accepting P. They do not, I think, undermine the significant considerations for opposing that view. In any event, I think the average views should be rejected. Let me explain why.

My first objection is to the average view of equality—specifically, to measuring inequality by dividing the total amount of a society's inequality by its size. To illustrate my objection it will be helpful to consider an example that closely parallels the one in chapter 6 where Bill started off better than Bob, and then became still better off. Just as that example cast doubt on the first and second approaches for capturing the fact that inequality matters more at low levels than high levels, for similar reasons, this example casts further doubt on the reasoning of section 7.3. More specifically, it raises serious questions about the economists' method of supplementing the different aspects where, for the aspects employing the additive principle, the numbers obtained by using that principle are divided by the population size.

Suppose we came across a world, W, where some are worse off than others. Suppose our initial observations reveal W to be sharply divided into two groups, but

---

28. There is some logical tension between the claim made here and my earlier observation that many economists may have been primarily concerned about social inequality. However, the tension is reduced if one adds the implicit psychological assumption that the average level of inequality in a society is, at least in most cases, reliably correlated with the kinds of principles and institutions in a society responsible for inequality.

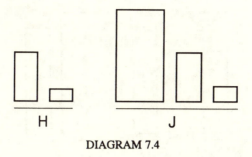

DIAGRAM 7.4

that later we discover a third group, larger and even better off than the rest, living a short distance away. So, considering diagram 7.4, our first picture of W resembles H, our revised picture resembles J. How would the realization that W resembles J and not H alter our view of W's inequality?

I claim the presence of the third group worsens W's inequality in a straightforward and unequivocal manner. It is not as if, regarding inequality, the negative features of the third group outweigh the positive ones. Rather, just as there would be no positive effects from Bill's improvement in chapter 6's example (see section 6.4), so there would be no positive effects from the presence of the third group on W's inequality.

What positive effects could there be? Presumably, we find W's inequality objectionable even before we discover the presence of the third group. And presumably this is because we regard it as bad for the one group to be worse off than the other through no fault of its own. But then, how could the discovery of a third group *better off* than the other two in any way mitigate W's inequality? Surely, the presence of an even better off group could only serve to aggravate those features of W to which we objected in the first place.

After all, the worse-off in J fare just as badly relative to the group we had thought was best-off as they did prior to our discovering the third group. It just turns out that in *addition* to being worse off than *that* group, there are others they are even worse off than. Clearly, this can in no way make J's inequality less offensive than H's. But neither can the fact that it turns out the group we had thought was best-off is not best-off after all. All this could do is make the inequality seem even worse, since they too turn out to be worse off than others through no fault of their own. The only other candidate for a feature in J not present in H that might mitigate J's inequality is the status of the third group itself. However, I fail to see how the fact that there is a group who is better off than anyone else, and hence who has nothing to complain about regarding inequality, could in any way lessen the complaints of those less fortunate than they, or otherwise alleviate their world's inequality. This seems no more plausible than the contention that the seriousness of the larger gap between Bob and Bill that results from the improvement in Bill's position can be partially offset by the fact that Bill is now much better off than he was before. To the contrary it is precisely because Bill is much better off that Bob fares worse than he did before, and hence that the inequality is worse. Similarly, it is precisely

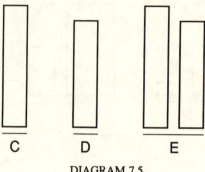

DIAGRAM 7.5

because the third group is better off than the other two, that the two previously known groups fare even worse relative to the other members of their world than had been realized, and hence that W's inequality is worse than we first thought—that is, prior to our discovery that W resembled J, not H.

The upshot of all this is that the economists' method of dividing the total amount of a society's inequality by the society's size is inappropriate and implausible. Such a method would fail to properly reflect the unequivocal manner in which the presence of the third group worsens W's inequality, since the presence of that group would increase both the numerator and denominator of the formula expressing that method. Thus, the problem with such a method isn't so much that it sometimes yields the wrong answer (though I think it does when combined with certain plausible aspects of inequality), but that even when it yields the right answer it measures inequality as if, even regarding inequality, there is a positive or partially redeeming feature of one group being better off than all the others.

Average views also face other, more well known, shortcomings. Consider, for example, diagram 7.5. Let D represent a world where everyone is better off than today's best-off, C a world where everyone is even better off, though not by a lot, and E a universe containing both C and D. Parfit has argued that all things considered, E is not worse than C.[29] I think he is right. However, even if he is not, this much seems clear: it would be most implausible to contend that the fact that E has a lower average level of utility than C provides one with a reason to maintain that E is worse than C. E *does* have a lower average level of utility. But this is so in virtue of the fact that E includes D *as well as* C, and it is very difficult to see how the *mere addition* of a group of people, all of whom have lives that are exceedingly rich, and who in no way lessen the quality of lives of C's people, could *worsen* the situation solely in virtue of their presence lowering the *average* level of utility.[30]

29. See Parfit's discussion of The Mere Addition Paradox (esp. pp. 158–59) in "Future Generations: Further Problems," *Philosophy and Public Affairs* 11 (1982): 113–72; also see *Reasons and Persons*, chap. 19.

30. Thus far, the argument is taken straight from Parfit. As will become apparent, I try to follow Parfit's clear and forceful presentation when I advocate analogous positions in the ensuing discussion.

I am not denying that there may be plausible (even if not conclusive) reasons for ranking E worse than C. Perhaps the fact that E's worse-off fare worse than C's would be such a reason, or the fact that E is unequal while C is not. Surely, however, the mere fact that E's average utility is lower than C's is not itself such a reason.

Let me be clear about the implications of the foregoing for the conflict between average utilitarianism (henceforth, *AvU*) and total utilitarianism (henceforth, *TU*). In claiming that E's lower average utility is not itself reason to prefer C to E, I am not claiming that AvU is implausible *as a moral theory* (though I think it is), or even that it is less plausible than TU. However, I am implying that AvU lacks TU's intrinsic appeal. Let me explain further.

Earlier, I suggested that the ultimate bedrock intuition underlying utilitarianism is that more of the good is better than less of the good. This is an extremely powerful intuition and one that supports TU when combined with the view—what I call the "pure" utilitarian view—that utility is all that matters. Thus, it is no coincidence that the greatest and strongest advocates of utilitarianism—Bentham, Mill, and Sidgwick—were total utilitarians. Those men were "pure" utilitarians. They believed that in the end only utility matters—that all other ideals, such as liberty, justice, and equality, have value only because, and to the extent, they promote utility. But clearly, if the bedrock intuition of utilitarianism is that more of the good is better than less of the good, then *insofar* as one is a *utilitarian*, that is, insofar as one is concerned strictly (purely) with utility, one will be, as each was, a total utilitarian.

Average utilitarians might of course try to deny this. They might claim that AvU has just as much intrinsic appeal as TU. However, I fail to see the kind of powerful intuitions underlying AvU that clearly underlie TU. Thus, even in those cases where TU seems most implausible—because, unlike the pure utilitarian, one rejects the view that only utility matters—one can always feel the pull of TU, the force of the claims that utility matters (even if it is not *all* that matters) and that more of the good is better than less of the good. The same cannot be said for AvU. In those cases where AvU seems most implausible—as, for instance, when it implies that a world where a few are exceedingly well-off would be better than a world where many are just as well-off and others are almost, though not quite, as well-off—it seems completely devoid of intrinsic appeal. So the problem with AvU is not just that in such cases it yields an implausible judgment as to which world is better; rather, there is simply no force to the average utilitarian claim as to why the one world is supposedly better. Yes, it has a higher average level of utility. So what?

I think, then, that *insofar* as one is a *utilitarian* one should be a total utilitarian. However, as indicated already, this does not entail that TU is more plausible than AvU, all things considered. Because utility is not all that matters, it could be that AvU's judgments correspond to our all-things-considered judgments more adequately than TU's. Whether or not this is so (and in fact I doubt that it is), I think AvU is best regarded not as a principle reflecting our utilitarian intuitions but rather as a compromise of sorts between those intuitions and others. Not surprisingly, I think it is not the best such compromise at which we could arrive. Following the argument in chapter 5, I think the best such compromise won't be found by looking

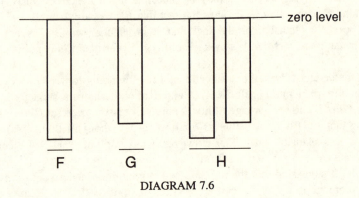

DIAGRAM 7.6

for a simple straightforward method, which just happens to correspond to our considered judgments. Instead, I believe we must first get clear about the ideals we value, next come up with a measure for each ideal, and then decide how much to weight them. Only then would we be in a position to come up with a (no doubt complex and partially incomplete) measure that plausibly combined each of our ideals according them each their due weight.

In sum, I believe that insofar as one is a utilitarian E will be better than C in diagram 7.5. Moreover, I think this becomes evident as soon as one focuses on what it is the utilitarian cares about—that is, as soon as one gets clear on the basic intuition underlying utilitarianism.[31]

Similar remarks can be made regarding negative utilitarianism, or for that matter positive utilitarianism in its treatment of disutility. Negative utilitarianism holds both that disutility is bad and that disutility is all that matters. Of course most believe negative utilitarianism is wrong regarding the latter claim. But that is not my present concern. My present concern is to point out that insofar as one cares about disutility one should care about total and not average disutility.

Consider diagram 7.6. Let G represent a world where there is tremendous disutility. In fact, imagine that each person in G is worse off than any person who has ever lived, well below the level at which life ceases to be worth living. Let F be a world where everyone is even worse off—though not by a lot—and H the universe containing both F and G. Surely, insofar as one is concerned about disutility, one would want to say that G represents a terrible situation, and F an even worse one. But then it seems clear one would also want to say that H is worse than F, since in H there is far more of what one regards as bad than in F.[32]

31. Note I say "evident." I do not say "self-evident" or "uncontroversial." I have not forgotten that there are other appealing ways of regarding utility besides those of total or average utilitarianism. For example, on the view discussed at the end of section 7.4 E won't be better than C, but neither will it be worse. (But see section 7.4 and the following paragraphs for reasons to worry about this view.) Also, let me add that I think total utilitarianism must itself be modified along lines suggested in section 7.9.

32. This example closely parallels Derek Parfit's example of Hell Three in *Reasons and Persons*, p. 422. It was written several years before the publication of Parfit's book, but Parfit and I have had many

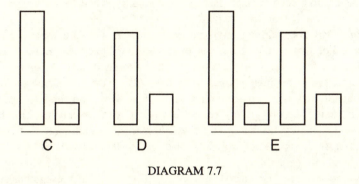

DIAGRAM 7.7

Of course, an average (negative) utilitarian might try to resist this conclusion. She might contend that one should be concerned with the average amount of disutility, and that, as such, H would be better than F. This however seems implausible. Why should the fact that H has a lower *average* level of disutility than F make H more palatable to someone concerned about disutility, when the only reason it *has* that lower average is because it contains the G group *as well* as the F group? How could the mere addition of such a group *really* improve the situation in the eyes of one who thought that disutility was bad? Suffice it to say, I think it could not.

Notice, these remarks may have even more force than the preceding ones, and they not only tell against average views, but against views like those discussed at the end of section 7.4. This is because for situations where people are very badly off, it is hard to deny that the addition of extra people with lives that are much worse than nothing would make the outcome worse. Moreover, I might add, for reasons alluded to in section 7.4, I think this is a strong argument for accepting the comparable claim that the addition of extra lives worth living makes an outcome better.

It should now be even clearer why measures of inequality focusing on average inequality should be rejected. Consider diagram 7.7. Let D represent a world where the gap between the better- and worse-off is very large, C a world where the gap between the better- and worse-off is even larger, and E the universe containing both. Two things should be clear. First, on certain aspects of inequality, for example, the additive principle and the relative to the best-off person view of complaints, E's average level of inequality will be lower than C's. Second, that fact alone is not *itself* reason to think E is better than C regarding inequality. Suppose, for instance, that D's inequality is worse than the most extreme inequality on earth today. Since the egalitarian regards inequality as bad, naturally she would regard D's situation as very bad. But then, the question can forcefully be asked: how could the *mere fact* that on certain aspects E has a lower *average* level of inequality than C make E

discussions about these topics, and I am afraid I no longer remember whether I developed this example independently of Parfit or in collaboration with him, or whether here, as so often elsewhere, I am simply indebted to him for bringing this point to my attention.

more palatable to someone concerned about inequality, when the only reason it *has* that lower average is that it contains D *as well as* C?

Again, I am not claiming anything about how E and C compare, all things considered. For that matter, I am not even claiming that there is no reason for the *egalitarian* to prefer E to C. What I am claiming is that (1) given the fact that the egalitarian regards inequality as bad, (2) given the corresponding fact that the egalitarian will regard both C and D as very bad, and (3) given the further fact that E involves the *mere addition* of D to C, surely it is implausible to contend that the egalitarian would find E's inequality preferable to C's insofar as, and *simply in virtue of the fact* that, on certain aspects it has a lower *average* level of inequality.

Here as elsewhere one must begin by focusing on what the egalitarian cares about if one wants to determine how E and C compare regarding inequality. Once one does this one will see, I think, that while in accordance with certain egalitarian intuitions E will be better than C, in accordance with others (in fact most) E will be worse. So, for instance, E will be worse according to the intuitions underlying the additive principle and the relative to the best-off person view of complaints. This is because those intuitions reflect the egalitarian's concern for how *each* person compares with the best-off person. More particularly, they reflect the views that (1) it is bad for one person to be worse off than another through no fault of her own, (2) the size of someone's complaints depends on how she fares relative to the best-off person (the level at which she would no longer be worse off than another), and (3) it is worse if in addition to *one* being worse off than another through no fault of her own there are others who are *also* in such a position.

Now I am not going to repeat here chapter 2's arguments or the supporting arguments of chapters 3, 5, and 6, where I tried to establish that the additive principle and the relative to the best-off person view of complaints reflect genuine egalitarian concerns. What I want to stress is that *insofar* as the egalitarian *is* concerned with those views, he will regard E as worse than C *notwithstanding* the (irrelevant) fact that on those views E's *average* level of complaint is lower than C's. Analogous remarks could be made about inequality's other aspects and their relation to average views.

Ultimately, then, an average view is no more plausible for egalitarianism than for utilitarianism. One cannot defend P by invoking an average view of inequality and combining it with an average view of utility for cases like those depicted in diagram 7.2.

7.6 The Shrinking World

I have argued that while in certain respects proportional increases do not affect inequality, in other respects proportional increases worsen inequality. Together these considerations suggest that, all things considered, proportional increases will worsen inequality. Defenders of P may continue to resist this conclusion. They may object that if proportional increases worsen inequality, then proportional decreases should improve it. Thus the egalitarian should favor a *Shrinking World*. More particularly, for any pattern of inequality, the *best* world will be the one with the *smallest* number of people in the better- and worse-off groups consistent with that pattern. This, it may be contended, is absurd.[33]

How should the egalitarian respond to the above objection? I think there are various ways an egalitarian might try to deny this claim—that if proportional increases worsen inequality, then for any pattern of inequality, the *best* world will be the one with the *smallest* better- and worse-off groups.[34] But in the end I don't think the egalitarian *needs* to deny that claim. Why can't she accept it, but deny that such a view is absurd?

Consider again A and B in diagram 7.1. Surely it *would* be absurd to claim that a two-person world with the same pattern of inequality as A and B—let us call it the *Shrunken World*—would be better than A or B *all things considered*. But if inequality really *is* objectionable, if it really *is* bad (unfair or unjust) for some to be worse off than others through no fault of their own, then why shouldn't we say that the Shrunken World is better than A or B *regarding inequality*? After all, in the Shrunken World there is only *one* person worse off than another through no fault of his own, whereas in A and B there are *many* such people.

Put simply, I am unpersuaded that this objection seriously challenges this chapter's arguments. It reminds one of the antiegalitarian argument that egalitarians should favor a world with only *one* person in it, or even a world with *nobody* in it, to any world with *some* inequality—no matter how slight the inequality, how large the world, or how rich the lives of those in it. Such an objection is crushing against "pure" egalitarianism—the view that equality is the *only* ideal that matters. But nobody is a "pure" egalitarian, and such an objection leaves any other version of egalitarianism unscathed. Why shouldn't the egalitarian insist that the former worlds are better than the latter one *regarding inequality*, but admit that they are worse *all things considered*? Far from being absurd, such a view seems obviously right.

The Shrinking World objection is not silly, and it *may* lead us to attach less weight to inequality when population sizes are small, along the lines suggested at the end of chapter 5. But ultimately I think the Shrinking World objection leaves this chapter's arguments unfazed. Like some arguments discussed in chapter 6, I think it derives (most of) its force from a conflation of two separate questions: When is one situation worse than another all things considered? and When is one situation worse than another regarding inequality?

33. I am grateful to Peter Mieskowski for bringing the foregoing objection to my attention during an ongoing seminar on rationality and equality sponsored by the Rice Center for the Study of Institutions and Values.

34. Perhaps the easiest and most natural way of doing this would involve rejecting an impartial teleological view of inequality in favor of a deontological or person-affecting view. On the latter views I think one could argue that the cases of proportional addition and proportional substraction are disanalogous—that is, that while an Expanding World worsens inequality, a Shrinking World doesn't improve it. I mention this possibility but will not pursue it. Unfortunately, as indicated previously, in this work I must restrict myself to considering how size variations affect inequality on an impartial teleological view.

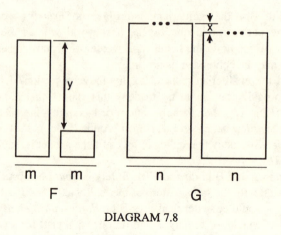

DIAGRAM 7.8

7.7 The Repellant Conclusion

There is another argument that might be offered in support of P. Unlike the preceding one, it is a powerful argument not easily dismissed. In order to present it, let me first introduce

> *The Repellant Conclusion*: For any world F, let F's population be as large (though finite) as one likes, and let the gaps between F's better- and worse-off be as extreme as one likes, there will be some unequal world, G, whose population is "sufficiently" large such that no matter how small G's gaps between the better- and worse-off might be G's inequality will be worse than F's (even if everyone in G is better off than everyone in F).

Diagram 7.8 helps illustrate the Repellant Conclusion, according to which no matter how large y and m are (as long as they are finite) or how small x is (as long as it is nonzero), there will be some number n (much larger than m), such that G's inequality will be worse than F's.

The Repellant Conclusion is similar to Parfit's Repugnant Conclusion[35] except that it addresses egalitarian rather than (broadly) utilitarian concerns. Moreover, like the Repugnant Conclusion the Repellant Conclusion is suitably named, as most would find it strongly counterintuitive (to put it mildly!).

I contend that most people would readily reject the Repellant Conclusion (*RC*). But if this is right, then RC appears to challenge the plausibility of my arguments against P. Specifically, one might argue that accepting P enables one to avoid RC, while rejecting P threatens to support RC.

Consider. If F and G were the same size in diagram 7.8 (so m = n), F's inequality would clearly be worse than G's—as could be easily shown. But then if P is

35. Parfit's Repugnant Conclusion is presented in *Reasons and Persons*, chap. 17, and discussed here in section 7.9.

true—so proportional size variations do not affect inequality—increasing n will not affect G's inequality. Hence, if one accepts P, one can reject RC, as no matter how large n becomes G's inequality will be worse than F's, and to an unchanging degree. On the other hand, suppose one rejects P, holding instead that proportional size increases worsen inequality. Then no matter how much F's inequality might be worse than G's if they were the same size, since doubling G's size would worsen its inequality, and redoubling it would worsen it further, it appears that if only G's size were doubled *enough* times *eventually* G's inequality would be worse than F's just as RC maintains.

As indicated, I think the preceding argument is powerful. After all, it is not merely nonegalitarians who would reject RC, and the claim that G's inequality might be worse than F's. Surely—at least initially—most egalitarians would too. Thus the foregoing argument considerably raises the costs of attacking P. In fact, I am sure some will think it raises them prohibitively. Whether this is so will be considered next. But this much already seems clear. To be successful, any attack on P must ultimately be accompanied by reasons to revise our intuitive reaction to the Repellant Conclusion or by an account of how one might plausibly reject both P and RC.

7.8 Reconsidering the Repellant Conclusion: One Response

I have argued that inequality's aspects should not be supplemented so as to reflect P. But as we have just seen, opposing P raises the specter of the Repellant Conclusion (RC). Does this mean I think we should embrace RC? Is it really plausible to conclude that G's inequality may be worse than F's in diagram 7.8? *Must* we conclude this if we oppose P? In this section and the next I present two responses to these questions. The first basically embraces RC, while offering an *explanation* of why it seems so counterintuitive. The second offers a way of rejecting RC while still opposing P. Neither response is wholly satisfactory. But they are, I think, worthy of consideration.

The first response might be put as follows. If someone maintains that F is worse than G in diagram 7.8, it seems fair to ask *why* he thinks that. If, for example, his response is to point out how much worse off the worst-off are in F than in G, one might grant the point but deny that it provides sufficient reason to reject RC. It is true that in accordance with both the relative to the average and the relative to the best-off person views of complaints, F's worst-off fare worse than G's. Correspondingly, when combined with the maximin principle of equality they rank F worse than G. Still, the views in question represent but two of inequality's aspects, and while they express legitimate concerns of the egalitarian they are not his only legitimate concerns.

Admittedly, the controversialism of the judgment that G is worse than F may be evidence that we attach special importance to the concerns opposing that judgment, and hence that special weight must be accorded to the aspects expressing those concerns. Alternatively, it may simply indicate that the comparison between F and G elicits and heightens our intuitions underlying those aspects, rendering those aspects salient[36] so that—since we are then caught in the grip of those aspects—we judge F worse than G. Either way, however, one could argue that insofar as we are influenced by inequality's other aspects we could, and should, accept RC.

This line might be pursued further. I argued that, in accordance with certain egalitarian intuitions we will be concerned not merely with the sum total of complaints, but with the distribution of complaints. More specifically, I argued that in accordance with our special concern for the worst-off, both the maximin principle and the weighted additive principle will seem especially appealing. Accordingly, it might be urged, insofar as the egalitarian is especially concerned with the distribution of complaints, that fact should be reflected in the manner and extent to which he fleshes out and gives weight to those two principles; it is *not* the case that those, or any other principles, should be *further* supplemented to express that concern.

In other words, one might argue that, insofar as one is especially concerned with the worst-off's complaints, one should attach extra weight to those measures involving the maximin principle. Similarly, insofar as one is concerned with the distribution of complaints, but doesn't want to focus solely on the worst-off's complaints, one should attach extra weight to those measures involving the weighted additive principle. However, once one has done that, there is no more to be done. That, by itself, attaches all the weight to distributional considerations that should be attached. Hence, any attempt to adjust the additive and weighted additive principles to further take into account the size of the better- and worse-off groups is, on this view, mistaken.

The claim here might be illustrated as follows. Suppose, for a moment, that G's population in diagram 7.8 was the same size as F's, so that n = m. It would then be the case that each of chapter 2's aspects would rank F worse than G. Now imagine that G's population begins to grow. Notice that if y is very large and x is very small, n would have to become much larger before *any* of inequality's aspects ranked G worse than F—this is especially so given that the quality of lives of the worse-off is much lower in F than in G (since we have already agreed that inequality matters more at low levels than at high levels, and that the aspects should be supplemented to reflect this). Thus, even if one attaches equal weight to each aspect, n will have to be vastly larger than m before the majority of aspects rank G worse than F. And, if one attaches extra weight to those aspects involving the maximin and weighted additive principles, n will have to be still larger before the aspects yield the overall judgment that G is worse than F. Nevertheless, one might contend, at that point, when n is *so* much larger than m—that is, when G is so *immensely* huge relative to F—we should simply admit that G's inequality is worse than F's.

We could, of course, avoid this conclusion by supplementing the aspects as discussed in section 7.3, by attaching lexical priority to aspects entailing P, or by simply contending that *together* the various factors ranking F worse than G will surely outweigh the various factors opposing that ranking. But, it might be urged, the first two options are untenable, and the third is ultimately unlikely. Having

---

36. Cf. section 3.2's brief discussion of salience regarding the way a salient factor may disproportionately influence our judgments. Clearly that discussion is relevant to the position being considered here.

already taken into consideration the vast differences in the gaps between the better- and worse-off, the fact that F's worse-off fare worse than G's, and the fact that we may want to attach extra weight to those aspects involving the maximin and weighted additive principles,[37] we should just be prepared to acknowledge that there may be *so* much more inequality in G than in F, that even taking all the distributional factors into consideration, G's inequality is worse than F's.

Further reflection on this point may help explain why judging G worse than F is, initially, so counterintuitive. Although appeals to intuitions have an important role to play in moral philosophy, many are wary of wildly implausible cases, and of attempts to "disprove" a given theory by showing that it yields counterintuitive responses to such cases. What such cases often illustrate, many contend, is not the failure of the theory in question, but rather a failure of imagination on our part or, more particularly, the fact that our commonsense intuitions have not been developed to handle such cases.[38]

The relevance of this to our present discussion is that most people are used to comparing populations of approximately the same size, or populations that perhaps differ by a factor of 10 or maybe 100. But surely, if y is *very* large, and x is *very* small, *each* of inequality's aspects would rank F worse than G for such populations. In other words, for the kinds of comparisons people usually make or think about, if one population was patterned like F, and another like G, *all* of inequality's aspects would judge the F-like one worse. But then, we might naturally come to think that *whenever* one population has a distribution like F while another has one like G, the former's inequality will be worse than the latter's. Still, however natural, this view may be false. For, as suggested, it may be that if only the latter's population were *enough* larger than the former's, its inequality would be worse.

In sum, we may be so accustomed to comparing situations where a distribution like F's would be worse than one like G's that we cannot make the conceptual adjustment necessary to fully internalize what a situation would be like where this was not so. That is, our ordinary intuitions may fail us in the case where G is so *immensely* huge relative to F. Hence, this may account for our intuitive—yet nonetheless mistaken?—judgment that G's inequality *must* be better than F's.

7.9 Reconsidering the Repellant Conclusion in Light of the Repugnant Conclusion: A Second Response

I am sympathetic to the preceding response. Still, it is difficult to swallow that G's inequality may be worse than F's all things considered, and unsatisfying to think that only a "failure of imagination" or maladjusted intuitions prevent me from seeing this. So in this section let me present a second response that, though compatible with the first, affords a way of rejecting RC.

37. If in fact this seems desirable after further reflection (and I am not at all certain it would).

38. See Richard Hare's "Ethical Theory and Utilitarianism," in *Contemporary British Philosophers*, ed. by H. D. Lewis (Allen and Unwin Press, 1976): 113-31.

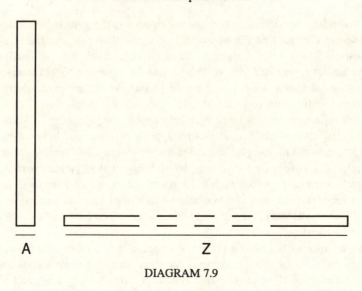

DIAGRAM 7.9

It will be useful—and independently interesting—to present the second response via a discussion of Derek Parfit's

> *The Repugnant Conclusion*: For any possible population of at least ten billion people, all with a very high quality of life, there must be some much larger imaginable population whose existence, if other things are equal, would be better, even though its members have lives that are barely worth living."

Consider diagram 7.9. According to the Repugnant Conclusion if only there are *enough* people in Z, Z will be better than A, and this is so no matter how large A is, and even if those in A are *very* well off while those in Z have lives that are barely worth living. As Parfit writes, "this conclusion [is] very hard to accept."[39]

Reflecting on the Repugnant Conclusion most of us are reminded that we are not strict utilitarians. Although utility matters a lot, it is not all that matters. But we also learn a further, deeper lesson. We learn that by itself mere increases in the quantity of utility are not sufficient (or so we think) to outweigh significant losses regarding other ideals we value. This is why Z is worse than A. Though better regarding utility, it is not better regarding equality, and it is much worse regarding other ideals, like perfectionism and maximin.

The importance of the further lesson cannot be exaggerated. It suggests that there may be an upper limit regarding how good a situation can be regarding utility. And if this is so for utility, it is probably also so for the other ideals and, hence, there may also be an upper limit regarding how good a situation can be, all things considered.

Consider an analogy from sports. In a gymnastics meet, the best all-around gym-

39. *Reasons and Persons*, p. 388.

nast is decided by adding together each person's score in each event. For women, there are four events, each with a maximum score of 10, for a maximum total score of 40. Although theoretically one can approach, and even attain, a perfect performance, one can never exceed the maximum score. So, to be the best all around gymnast, it isn't enough to near, or even attain, perfection in the floor exercises. One must also be good on the balance beam, the vault, and the uneven parallel bars.

On reflection, it seems something like this may also hold for our all-things-considered judgments. Perhaps in comparing situations all things considered, we must compare them in terms of each ideal, where there is a maximum score they can get for each ideal, determined by how much the ideals matter vis-à-vis each other. Suppose, for example, that in assessing outcomes the ideals of perfectionism (P),[40] utility (U), equality (E), and maximin (M) were equally important and all we cared about. Then we might assign numbers to situations such that the highest score a situation could get for each ideal would be, say, 100 and the "perfect" situation would score 400. Similarly, to note a more complicated example, if we thought P was one and a half times as important as U, and twice as important as E and M, then we might assign numbers to situations such that the highest score a situation could get would be, say, 150 for P, 100 for U, and 75 each for E and M.

Now a perfect situation regarding U would have infinite utility. So no finite world will be perfect. Correspondingly, while adding people with lives worth living will always improve a situation's utility, there is an upper limit on how much improvement is possible. Hence a world may approach the maximum score for utility, but it can never reach that level or go beyond it. Thus, mere increases in utility alone will not, in general, outweigh significant losses in other respects.

To illustrate this position, let us make the simplifying assumption that each ideal matters equally, and let us (arbitrarily) assign scores to A and Z of up to 100 for P, E, M, and U. A is perfect regarding E, and (by hypothesis) very good for P, M, and U. So let us suppose that $E = 100$, $P = 80$, $M = 80$, and $U = 80$. A would then have an all-things-considered score of 340. Z is perfect regarding E and, we may suppose, nearly perfect[41] regarding U, but it is much

---

40. As with our other ideals, it is not a simple matter to characterize perfectionism. For our purposes, let me loosely describe perfectionism as an ideal that ranks outcomes according to the extent to which they realize that which is "best" or "highest" in human (or global?) achievement. On different views the best outcome might be the one with the "greatest" achievements in social, political, moral, cultural, intellectual, or individual development. In what follows I shall assume that such achievements are directly correlated with how well off the best-off are. That is, for the purposes of discussion I assume—and it is *only* a simplifying assumption—that improvements in the best-off group's level are directly correlated with improvements regarding perfectionism. (I realize that perfectionists need not be elitists, but there may be cases where their views overlap and my assumption is not only useful but plausible.)

41. As Parfit originally presents the Repugnant Conclusion there is no reason to suppose Z is "nearly perfect" regarding U, only that it is better than A. So, if $U = 80$ for A, we know $U > 80$ for Z; for example, it might be that $U = 81$ for Z. But on the position we are now discussing, there will be some population size such that if Z were that size it would not merely be better than A, it would be nearly perfect regarding U. Although we could just as easily make our point using the "weaker" assumption that Z is (merely) better than A regarding U, the assumption that Z is "nearly perfect" strengthens the force of our example and better illustrates the position under discussion.

worse regarding P and M. For Z, then, let us suppose E = 100 and U = 99, but P = 20 and M = 20. Z would then have an all-things-considered score of 239—a full 100 points lower than A's on a scale of only 400! One can see, then, how such a model can account for the genuine repugnancy of the Repugnant Conclusion. Of course, the extent of the repugnancy will depend on how A and Z in fact compare for P, M, and U—or any other relevant ideals—as well as how much those ideals matter to our all-things-considered judgments.

There is a logical limit to how much one can reduce a situation's inequality, but no logical limit to how much utility obtains. Because of this, it is natural to suppose there is a limit to how much one can improve a situation regarding equality, but none regarding utility. Nevertheless, this supposition seems mistaken. However much more we may care about one ideal relative to another, they play similar roles in our all-things-considered judgments. Thus, most believe that, other things equal, transforming a situation into one perfect, or nearly perfect, regarding E, U, or P, would not be better *all things considered* if it involved significant losses regarding P and U, P and M, or E and M, respectively.

The gymnastics model can be contrasted with a more familiar model concerning utility, one involving four basic assumptions.

1. Utility is intrinsically valuable, even if it is not the only thing that is.
2. Insofar as one cares about utility, one should care about total utility.
3. How good a situation is regarding utility is a simple additive function of how much utility sentient beings have in that situation.
4. How good a situation is all things considered is an additive function of how good it is regarding each ideal, so insofar as a situation gets better regarding utility it will, to that extent, be getting better all things considered.

Assumptions 1–4 have great appeal. In fact, I suspect they represent perhaps the most natural and prevalent way of thinking about utility and its connection to our all-things-considered judgments. Nevertheless, together 1–4 support the Repugnant Conclusion. After all, given 1–3 extra lives, if worth living, will make an outcome better regarding utility. But then, if adding an extra person improves a situation *at all*—even in only one respect, and even if, because the person's life is barely worth living, it is just a tiny bit—assumptions 3 and 4 imply that if only there are *enough* people in Z, it would be better than A. That is, if only Z is large enough its all-things-considered score will be higher than A's, as its score for utility will be sufficiently higher than A's to outweigh the extent to which it has lower scores for other ideals like perfectionism and maximin.

In terms of assumptions 1–4, the gymnastics model can capture 2. It can also capture 4. But it denies 3—how good a situation is regarding utility is a simple additive function of how much utility sentient beings have in that situation. Thus, while it grants that doubling the *amount* of utility in a situation improves it regarding utility, it denies that it necessarily does this by a factor of two. Correspondingly, it denies 1—utility is intrinsically valuable—*in the sense* that each unit of utility has intrinsic value of a constant amount that increases a situation's objective value in direct proportion to that amount. On the other hand, the model *is* compatible with utility being intrinsically valuable *in the sense* that it can regard utility as a significant factor in all-things-considered judgments beyond the extent it promotes other ideals.

Faced with the paradoxes involving future generations, and hoping to avoid the Repugnant Conclusion, Derek Parfit has contended that there may be *no* respect in which the "mere addition" of extra people to an already large and well-off population improves the situation.[42] But many find this implausible. They think that, if nothing else, the addition of extra people with lives worth living must always improve utility. The gymnastics model captures this belief, while avoiding the unpalatable conclusion that sheer increases in a situation's *amount* of utility must always significantly improve it, either regarding utility or all things considered.[43] To be sure, from the subjective perspective each extra life worth living will be as important to its possessor as every other. But from the objective perspective, though each extra life will matter *some*, after a point they will matter less and less.

In light of the preceding, let us reconsider the Repellant Conclusion. Specifically, let us note that a second response to the Repellant Conclusion would be to adopt a gymnastics model for inequality and its underlying aspects. Such a response could avoid the Repellant Conclusion, as the same considerations relevant to the Repugnant Conclusion might apply, mutatis mutandis, to the Repellant Conclusion.

Clearly, there is an upper limit to how good a situation can be regarding inequality—namely where there is *no* inequality—and (hence) also an upper limit to how good a situation can be regarding each of inequality's aspects. Suppose, on the gymnastics model, there were also a lower limit on how bad a situation could be regarding inequality, and (hence) also a lower limit to how bad a situation could be regarding each of inequality's aspects. Then considering diagram 7.8 there would be good reason to regard G's inequality as worse than F's.

If, as we have assumed, m and y are very large in diagram 7.8, then F's score will already be approaching *very near* the lower limit for *each* of inequality's aspects. Correspondingly, even if G's inequality is worse than F's in terms of many of inequality's aspects, on the gymnastics model G's inequality will only be *slightly* worse—that is, only a bit closer to the lower limit—in terms of those aspects. On the other hand, as we have seen, G's inequality will be *much* better than F's in terms of at least four aspects. Specifically, while F's score will approach the lower limit for each of inequality's aspects, G's will approach the upper limit for at least four aspects. In sum, on the gymnastics model there will be good reason to reject the Repellant Conclusion, as the slight respects in which G is worse than F will surely be heavily outweighed by the much larger, though fewer, respects in which G is better than F. Thus, *all things considered* F's inequality will be worse than G's.

Let me conclude this section with several comments. First, as implied earlier, the gymnastics model provides a way of rejecting P, as well as the Repellant Con-

---

42. See part 4 of *Reasons and Persons*.

43. On the gymnastics model the addition of extra lives worth living might worsen a situation all things considered if, for example, it only slightly improved the situation's utility while significantly worsening its inequality. This has important but controversial implications for Parfit's Mere Addition Paradox, the Absurd Conclusion, and How Only France Survives, but I cannot pursue these matters here. See part 4 of *Reasons and Persons*, and my critique of part 4 in Jonathan Dancy's forthcoming volume *Reading Parfit* (Basil Blackwell).

clusion. Thus, the gymnastics model is compatible with the primary results of section 7.4, namely, that there are powerful reasons to hold that B's inequality is worse than A's in diagram 7.1 and, more generally, that proportional size increases worsen inequality. By the same token the gymnastics model suggests that in essence inequality's aspects should be supplemented in such a way that doubling a population's size will worsen its inequality but *not* by twofold (or more). So, for example, while B's inequality will be worse than A's, it will not be twice as bad.

Second, once one recognizes that proportional size increases do not worsen inequality proportionally, for example, that B's inequality will be less than twice as bad as A's, this raises the possibility of clearly and *unequivocally* rejecting the Repellant Conclusion. That is, in diagram 7.8 it may be not only that F's inequality is worse than G's *all things considered*—as our previous discussion illustrates—but that in fact F is worse than G in terms of *each* of inequality's aspects, as most intuitively assume.

Suppose, for example, that proportional size increases worsened inequality at a decreasing rate. More specifically, suppose that for each aspect of inequality if a situation's inequality had a disvalue of v with a population size p, it's disvalue would be 1.5v with a population of 2p, 1.75v with a population of 4p, 1.875v with a population of 8p, and so on. Then for each aspect proportional size increases would worsen inequality at a rate approaching a limit of 2v. So, for each aspect proportional increases alone could worsen a situation's inequality by up to, but not more than, twice as bad as it originally was. But then, consider again F and G in diagram 7.8, and suppose F and G were originally the same size (so, m = n). Clearly, as noted earlier, if y were very large and x very small, F's inequality might be *much* worse than—that is, far more than twice as bad as—G's in terms of each of inequality's aspects. But then, on the previous assumptions, F's inequality would remain worse than G's for each aspect, notwithstanding any proportional increases in G's population—that is, no matter how large n might become.

Let me emphasize that the preceding merely illustrates one way a gymnastics model might enable one to avoid the Repellant Conclusion for *each* of inequality's aspects, as well as all things considered. It is an open question what the details of such an approach would actually look like and hence whether such an approach would ultimately be plausible for each of inequality's aspects.

Third, the preceding discussion dovetails with the argument of section 7.4 where I suggested that "a plausible and coherent account of the role moral ideals play in relation to each other and our all-things-considered judgments may require at least some ideals to share certain formal or structural features in common." In section 7.4 I argued that if we want to hold that numbers count regarding utility, we may also have (and want) to hold that numbers count regarding equality. Similarly, if we accept that there is an upper limit to how good a situation can be regarding inequality, we may have (and want) to accept that there is an upper limit to how good a situation can be regarding utility. Moreover, if we adopt something like a gymnastics model for utility to avoid the Repugnant Conclusion, we may want (and have) to adopt something like a gymnastics model for equality to avoid the Repellant Conclusion. My hunch is that these various positions ultimately stand or fall together. But I have not tried to prove this.

Finally, let me acknowledge that a gymnastics model for moral ideals raises many vexing issues I cannot pursue. For example, while it may seem plausible to think there is an upper limit to how good a situation can be regarding utility or equality, it seems much less plausible to think there can be a lower limit to how bad a situation can be regarding utility or equality—as if, after a point, it doesn't really matter (much) any more whether extra people are excruciatingly tortured, or the gaps between the haves and have nots increase still further. (This may correlate with our phenomenological response to such situations, but on reflection our considered moral judgments resist the deadening effect that prolonged exposure to grave evils may have on our intuitive sensibilities.) Yet it is not clear one can have upper limits without lower limits, at least without facing serious problems of coherence and consistency.[44] Similarly, if one adopts a gymnastics model, and combines it with what I have elsewhere[45] called the *Intrinsic Aspect* view of assessing outcomes, one may have to accept the "absurd" conclusion of Parfit's How Only France Survives, according to which it might be *better* if everyone but the best-off died, even if all those who died had lives *well* worth living, and even if the lives of the best-off were worsened as a result. On the other hand if, to avoid such implications, one combines the gymnastics model with what I have called the *Essentially Comparative* view of assessing outcomes, then the threat of intransitivity looms for our all-things-considered judgments.[46]

I mention the foregoing because I do not want to minimize the difficulties facing a gymnastics model for moral ideals. Still, the gymnastics model is hardly alone in facing grave difficulties of this sort and, reflecting on the Repugnant Conclusion, it seems clear that what is perhaps the most natural and prevalent way of thinking about utility and its relation to our all-things-considered judgments—as represented by assumptions 1–4—must be rejected. Whether we should ultimately accept the gymnastics model, a variation of it—for example, one that rejects the additive assumption in 4 as well as 3—or pursue an entirely new alternative to 1–4 I must leave open for now. For the purposes of this section the main point of introducing the gymnastics model is to show that there are approaches one might pursue that would enable one to reject both P and the Repellant Conclusion.

7.10 Summary and Assessment

This concludes most of what I want to say about the issue of whether size affects inequality. Because this is an issue about which I think most have been mistaken, or at least misled, my discussion has been rather long. It may be summed up as follows.

Many have felt there is a clear answer to the issue of whether size variations

---

44. This is perhaps the main claim of Parfit's fascinating chapter 18 in *Reasons and Persons*. The claim is one that Parfit and I have jointly discussed and developed over the years.

45. In my "Intransitivity."

46. See my "Intransitivity" for a preliminary discussion of these issues. I hope to pursue them at greater length on another occasion. For Parfit's example of How Only France Survives, see *Reasons and Persons*, section 143.

affect inequality. They have accepted the Standard View, P, that proportional variations in size would not affect inequality, and hence have felt inequality's aspects
should, where necessary, be supplemented accordingly. They have also felt that
where two worlds have the same amount of inequality—measured as a function of
the gaps and levels of the better- and worse-off—that world would be worse which
had fewer people. More generally, they have felt that one world will be worse than
another regarding inequality, if it has a higher average level of complaint. Now such
views have a fair amount of initial appeal. Especially if one thinks, as most have,
that our notion of inequality is essentially distributive. Nevertheless, such views are
untenable, at least as they stand.

To be sure, there are plausible and important reasons supporting P. And insofar
as we are especially concerned about certain kinds of social or distributional judgments, those reasons may ultimately carry extra weight in our final judgments of
inequality. Still, focusing on the basic intuitions underlying egalitarianism, the importance of numbers for morality—including equality—and the interconnected relations of moral ideals, one sees there are also powerful and important reasons
opposing P. Moreover, reflection reveals that how bad a situation is regarding inequality has nothing to do with its *average* level of inequality; hence, the
economists' approach to size variations must be rejected (see section 7.11). In sum,
although some aspects of inequality support P, most do not, and the latter should not
be supplemented to do so.

One apparent cost of opposing P is the Repellant Conclusion. We have seen how
one might respond to such a cost in one of two ways. One might accept the cost,
but deny that it is too high. Specifically, one might offer an explanation for why RC
is counterintuitive but in fact acceptable. Alternatively, one might deny that RC is
the cost of opposing P, by advocating a new way of thinking about moral ideals and
their underlying aspects, which enables one to reject both P and RC. Such an
approach faces serious problems, but ultimately I think there are strong reasons to
pursue it regardless of one's views about P and RC.

In this chapter I have mainly focused on the question of how proportional size
variations affect inequality. This is because the most interesting and difficult issues
concerning size variations surround that question. Once one decides whether
inequality's aspects should be supplemented to reflect P (or avoid RC), it is a
relatively straightforward matter to determine, at least in principle, how size variations that are not proportional would affect inequality. Still, though "relatively
straightforward" it is worth emphasizing that actual size variations will almost
never be proportional, and that in such cases most of inequality's aspects have
different implications about the manner and extent to which size variations affect
inequality.

For example, on the assumption that inequality's aspects should not be supplemented to support P or avoid RC, chapter 2's twelve aspects will yield nine distinct
answers to the question of how, if at all, size variations affect inequality. Specifically, in accordance with the different aspects, size variations will have (1) no effect,
(2) a relatively insignificant effect, (3) a relatively significant and direct effect
(increases worsening inequality, decreases lessening it), or (4) a relatively significant and inverse effect (increases lessening inequality, decreases worsening it),

depending on whether the variation affects those who are best-off, worst-off, at the average level, at the median level, or at some other level. For an elaboration and defense of these claims, see appendix C.

Ultimately, then, I think the issue of how size variations affect inequality mirrors the complexity of inequality itself. Correspondingly, it is an issue that will only fully be resolved when (and if) we have determined how much to count each of inequality's aspects. In any event, whether this chapter's specific claims ultimately prove correct, I hope I have convinced the reader that the Standard View of this issue can no longer be assumed without argument, and probably needs to be revised or replaced. Indeed, to be bolder, I believe this chapter's arguments are compelling against the view that each of inequality's aspects should be supplemented so that proportional size variations do not affect inequality. If, despite these arguments, the reader remains unconvinced, that might be evidence that the notion of inequality is even *more* complicated than I have claimed. Perhaps, it could be argued, while in accordance with certain powerful intuitions (those my arguments appeal to) the aspects should not be supplemented in the manner suggested, in accordance with others (those my opponents would presumably appeal to) they should.

I have explored the question of how, if at all, size variations affect inequality not merely because it raises important theoretical issues, but also because any answer to it will have significant practical implications regarding intergenerational inequality and obligations toward other generations. It will be relevant to whether we should strive for increases or decreases in the *size* of the better- or worse-off groups of future generations, as well as their levels. Moreover, this will be relevant both for our assessment of the inequality within the future generations themselves, and for our assessment of the inequality between the future generations and other generations. I trust this point is evident, and that its importance for the egalitarian needs no elaboration or defense.

Finally, let me conclude this section by commenting on the status of two positions introduced earlier. In section 7.2 I argued that in addition to four aspects of inequality supporting P, there were two *other* positions, or ways of thinking, supporting P. Specifically, I suggested there were senses in which we might judge two situations equivalent regarding inequality if either the *kinds* or *patterns* of inequality were the same in the two situations. Since I think these ways of thinking may plausibly underlie and influence people's egalitarian judgments—for example, the judgment that A and B are equivalent in diagram 7.1—this naturally raises the question as to whether the positions noted represent two new aspects of inequality.

There is, I think, no definitive answer to this, but for the purposes of this work perhaps the best, or least misleading, answer is no. I have mainly focused on articulating inequality's aspects insofar as they are relevant to answering when one situation is better or worse than another regarding inequality. Strictly speaking, I think the positions in question do not address that question; rather they address different questions, counterfactual questions, about certain ways in which it *would* be better or worse for a society to be regarding inequality. Put differently, even if the positions are best regarded as new aspects of inequality, I think they do not, in fact, yield the sort of judgments with which I am concerned.

Consider again the illness analogy. The judgment that a society susceptible to

AIDS is "worse regarding illness" than one susceptible to diabetes is not, finally, a judgment about which *situation* is worse regarding illness; it is, rather, a judgment about which *illness* is worse. Such a judgment supports the counterfactual conclusion that *if* the two societies had the same number of ill, the one with diabetes would be better off than the one with AIDS. Similarly, it tells us that we, and the afflicted in our society, would be better off *if* we suffered from diabetes rather than AIDS. But such a judgment does not tell us which society's illness it would be better to eradicate—if, for example, ten were afflicted by AIDS, and a million by diabetes—as it would, I think, if it were really a judgment about which of the *situations* were worse. True, one might think saving ten from AIDS would be better than curing a million of diabetes, but this would be for maximin, humanitarian, or some other such reasons and not for independent reasons associated with the kind of judgment under discussion.

Similar remarks may be made about the second position noted previously. Alternative situations are frequently judged in terms of their patterns, and there is little question that such judgments are plausible and legitimate, and often reflect the relative poignancy or alarm with which we might view the situations. Still, I suspect such judgments are best understood counterfactually, not as strict judgments of the situations themselves. For example, the judgment that a society where 80 percent suffer from diabetes is "worse regarding illness" than one where 20 percent suffer from diabetes tells us that, other things equal, the average person is healthier in the latter society than the former. But this does not tell us in which society eradicating diabetes would be better—the former may only have ten victims, and the latter a million. Instead, such a judgment tells us that *if* the two societies were equal size the latter would be worse than the former, and that our society would be worse if its pattern were more like the latter than the former.

Analogous claims could be made about egalitarian judgments based on the kinds or patterns of inequality in the situations being judged. Though plausible and intelligible, ultimately I think such judgments are best understood counterfactually. Rather than telling us how the two situations *themselves* compare, they tell us how they *would* compare if they were equal size or, more practically, which kind or pattern of inequality it would be better for our society to emulate.

If the preceding is correct, then the positions I have been discussing may help *explain* the Standard View's appeal without actually *supporting* that view, and the claims of section 7.2 should be emended accordingly. If the preceding is not correct, then we should probably make room for two more aspects in our understanding of inequality. Here, as elsewhere, there is room for discussion and dispute.

7.11 Population Increases and the Statistical Measures

Let me conclude this chapter with some brief comments paralleling those of section 6.8. Having argued that inequality's aspects should not be supplemented to reflect P and, more particularly, that one ought not to divide the number representing the gaps between society's better- and worse-off by the number representing society's size, one can see further why, in chapter 5, I claimed the statistical measures are best regarded as first approximations and that focusing on worlds with the same size populations would enable me to ignore certain controversial features of the statistical measures.

Consider again the relative mean deviation, with its formula of:

$$M = \sum_{i=1}^{n} |\mu - y_i|/n\mu$$

In chapter 5, we saw that M's numerator reflects the relative to the average view of complaints and the additive principle of equality. In chapter 6, we saw that by dividing the number measuring the gaps between the better- and worse-off (which the numerator yields), by μ—society's average level—the denominator incorporates an implausible method of capturing the view that inequality matters more at low levels than high levels. By the same token, we can now see that by dividing the numerator by n—the number of people in the society—the denominator relativizes the gaps between the better- and worse-off to the population's size. This, we have argued, is a mistake. Thus, if this chapter's argument is correct, a more accurate measure of the aspect reflecting the relative to the average view of complaints and the additive principle would not have the offending feature.

A similar problem faces the variance, the coefficient of variation, and the standard deviation of the logarithm, each of which divides the number measuring the gaps between the better- and worse-off by the size of the population. Indeed, as we have noted, most of the economists' measures incorporate the feature in question, as most economists have (implicitly) adopted the view that proportional size variations do not affect inequality. Clearly, for most aspects I think the offending feature should be removed. Inequality should not be measured by dividing the gaps between the better- and worse-off by the size of the population.

If inequality's aspects should be supplemented to account for size variations they should be supplemented to avoid RC, not to support P. Hence, if anything, they should be supplemented along the lines implied by section 7.9.

8

Between Whom, or What, Does Inequality Obtain?

In this chapter I want to consider an issue raised by Dennis McKerlie in a fascinating article called "Equality and Time."[1] Roughly, the issue is whether the proper unit of egalitarian concern should be people's lives, taken as a whole, or selected portions of their lives. As we will see, this is yet another area where I think there is a generally accepted, unexamined view, which on reflection is fraught with difficulties. Unfortunately, it is also yet another area where I must content myself with illuminating some problems rather than solving them.

Three preliminary comments. First, some philosophers have recognized that the proper "units" with which a distributive principle should be concerned may depend on our views about personal identity.[2] I accept this position. But my claim here is different. My claim is that determining the proper unit of egalitarian concern is a complex matter *independently* of questions about personal identity. Thus, the ensuing discussion makes the simplifying assumption—strictly for argument's sake—that the concept of personal identity is simple and unproblematic; in particular, that there is a single person whose identity is clear and unchanging from birth until death.

Second, my discussion of this issue is heavily indebted to McKerlie. Although I have worries about many of McKerlie's particular examples, arguments, and conclusions—and have revised or replaced them accordingly—I am largely sympathetic to the spirit of his article, and see this chapter as preserving and supporting his important, and seldom recognized, insights.[3]

Finally, let me add that while my concern here is with egalitarianism, analogous considerations have implications for other ideals too—for example, Rawls's maximin principle of justice.

---

1. *Ethics* 99 (1989): 475–91.

2. For example, see Thomas Nagel's "The Justification of Equality," *Critica* 10 (1978): 3–31. Reprinted as "Equality" in Nagel's *Mortal Questions* (Cambridge University Press, 1979), pp. 106–27. See also Derek Parfit's *Reasons and Persons* (Oxford University Press, 1984) chap. 5, and Parfit's "Comments," *Ethics* 96 (1986): 832–72.

3. Readers of McKerlie's article will recognize great overlap between our work on this topic. Though most of the overlap is due to his influence on me, some of it is due to my influence on him, through my role as an anonymous reviewer for *Ethics*.

8.1 Three Views about the Proper Unit of Egalitarian Concern

In chapter 2, I pointed out that it is easy and natural to focus on two individuals and consider how they fare regarding inequality. But this raises an obvious question. In comparing two individuals regarding inequality, what should we focus on? Or, as I shall put it in this chapter, what is the proper unit of egalitarian concern?

Dennis McKerlie claims, rightly I think, that most people implicitly assume that insofar as one is an egalitarian, one should be what he calls a *complete lives* egalitarian. As its name suggests, on a complete lives view the proper units of egalitarian concern are the complete lives of individuals. Thus, on a complete lives view, an egalitarian should be concerned about A's being worse off than B to the extent, and only to the extent, that A's life, taken as a *complete whole*, is worse than B's, taken as a *complete whole*.

McKerlie points out, correctly, that despite its being widely assumed, complete lives egalitarianism is only one of a number of views an egalitarian might adopt regarding the proper units of egalitarian concern. Other views include what McKerlie calls *simultaneous segments* egalitarianism and *corresponding segments* egalitarianism. Roughly, a simultaneous segments egalitarian would divide history into a series of temporal stages, say, twenty years each, and measure inequality in terms of the inequalities obtaining between people's lives within the same temporal stages; a corresponding segments egalitarian would divide each person's life into a series of stages, for example, childhood, early adulthood, middle age, and old age, and measure inequality in terms of the inequalities between the comparable stages of people's lives.

These views may be illustrated with the aid of diagram 8.1. T1-T5 are temporal segments of twenty years each. A and B are two people, each of whom live eighty years, and whose lives are divided into four twenty-year segments. The numbers next to A and B represent how well off they fare during the different segments of their lives, as well as during the temporal segments T1-T5. Since A lives from T1 through T4, there is no number next to A under T5.[4] Similarly, since B—born twenty years later than A—lives from T2 through T5, there is no number next to B under T1. Obviously, our diagram implicitly makes a large number of simplifying assumptions—for example, that we can assign a number corresponding to the quality, or welfare, in each segment of someone's life. Strictly for the purposes of discussion, we shall also assume a simple additive model for measuring quality of life, according to which the overall quality, or welfare, of someone's life is a direct additive function of the

---

4. One might think one should put a zero rather than nothing where nonexistence is involved. Doing so would not affect our subsequent discussion regarding whole lives egalitarianism or corresponding segments egalitarianism, but would make a difference regarding simultaneous segments egalitarianism. However, I think that putting a zero where nonexistence is involved would strongly conflict with the spirit of simultaneous segments egalitarianism and yield highly implausible implications. Hence, I shall not pursue this line. Obviously, if one feels that despite problems there *should* be a zero rather than nothing where nonexistence is involved, one will also feel my discussion needs to be revised accordingly.

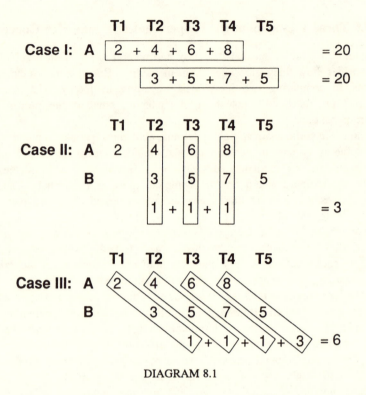

DIAGRAM 8.1

welfare of her life's segments.[5] Though unrealistic and implausible, our simplifying assumptions enable us to illuminate the views under discussion in a clear, simple, and straightforward way. The points I shall be making could be made using more realistic assumptions. But to do so would require a much longer and convoluted discussion.

If we suppose that a score of two represents a very poor quality of life, and a score of eight a very high quality of life, diagram 8.1 indicates that A's quality of life was very poor during the first segment of her life, very high during the last

5. For example, if, like A, the "scores" of the segments of someone's life are 2, 4, 6, and 8, the "score" corresponding to the overall quality of her life will be 20, and the overall quality of her life will be equivalent to that of someone whose four segments received, respectively, scores of 5, 5, 5, and 5, or, for that matter, 8, 6, 4, and 2. Now, in fact, I think the simple additive model is seriously deficient. I think the sequence 2, 4, 6, 8 is much preferable to the sequence 8, 6, 4, 2, even if the *total* amount of welfare in the two lives is identical. But in this chapter I want to leave aside the objections one might raise to the additive model for assessing the overall quality of someone's life. To be sure, doing this runs a certain risk, since some of the intuitions and judgments to be discussed may be influenced by one's views regarding the limitations of the additive model. Still, assuming a simple additive model greatly facilitates our discussion, and if we are careful we should be able to prevent our simplifying assumption from leading us astray. More particularly, it should be apparent how the conclusions we shall be arguing for could be reached even if we adopted a more complex and realistic view regarding how best to judge the overall quality of a life. (Cf. chapters 5 and 7 for further comments about additivity.)

segment of her life, and that each segment of her life was better than the previous one. Diagram 8.1 also indicates that no segment of B's life is either as poor or as good, respectively, as the first and last segments of A's life; that, taken as a whole, the overall quality of A's and B's lives are equivalent;[6] that B is worse off than A during each temporal segment they are contemporaries (T2–T4); and that during the first three segments of her life B is better off than A was during the first three corresponding segments of her life, though B is worse off during the fourth segment of her life than A was during the corresponding segment of her life. Most important, for our present purposes, diagram 8.1 illustrates the three approaches discussed previously for measuring the inequality between A and B. Specifically, cases I, II, and III illustrate how one might compare A and B regarding inequality on, respectively, complete lives, simultaneous segments, and corresponding segments egalitarianism. On complete lives egalitarianism there would be no objectionable inequality between A and B, since their lives are equivalent in terms of overall quality. On both simultaneous and corresponding segments egalitarianism there would be objectionable inequality between A and B, corresponding, respectively, to the extent of the differences in quality between the simultaneous and the corresponding segments of A's and B's lives.

8.2 Problems with Complete Lives Egalitarianism

I believe that each of the three views regarding the proper unit of egalitarian concern may seem plausible in some cases, and implausible in others. In this section, I present considerations intended to cast doubt on the adequacy of the standard view, complete lives egalitarianism. In the following section, I cast doubt on the adequacy of alternative views, and in the process suggest that complete lives egalitarianism cannot simply be dismissed.

I begin with an example involving a conversation between the Devil and God. It pertains to God's treatment of two of His servants, Job1 and Job2.

D: I see You have finally seen the dark.

G: What are you talking about?

D: I am talking about Your treatment of Job1 and Job2, whom I have been watching, with amazement, for forty years now. So far as I can tell, Job1 and Job2 are equally devoted to You, equally moral, equally skilled, equally hardworking, in short, equally deserving in every relevant way imaginable.

G   (somewhat impatiently): They *are* equally deserving! So what?

D: So, Job1's life has been filled with all the blessings life can bestow. His herds and crops flourish. He and his family are healthy and wealthy. He has

6. Recall that for the sake of this chapter I am assuming a simple additive view, where the overall quality of someone's life will be a straightforward additive function of the quality of the different segments of that person's life. So, for both A and B the "score" representing the overall quality of their lives will be 20. (See the previous note.)

the love and respect of all who know him. In addition, his plans are realized, his desires fulfilled, and he has complete inner peace. Job2, on the other hand, has led a wretched life. His health is miserable, his countenance disfigured. He has lost his loved ones. He is a penniless beggar who sleeps fitfully in the streets, and whose efforts and desires are constantly frustrated.

G: I know the condition of my faithful servants Job1 and Job2. Exactly what is it about their condition that you find so disturbing?

D: Nothing. That's the point! I have obviously misunderstood and underestimated You. I thought that You would have treated both like You've treated Job1. And, simpleton that I am, I would have treated both like Job2. But what You have done is truly ingenious. You have created a situation dripping with injustice. To treat two equally deserving people so *grossly* unequally . . . it really is *exquisitely devilish*.

G: Bah! You once again display your limited powers. If you had my prescience you would know that the situation is not "dripping with injustice," because the "gross" inequality you are seeing is a mere temporary phenomenon, a misleading appearance which arises because you are only looking at one part of the picture. If, like Me, you saw the whole picture, you would realize that the situations of Job1 and Job2 will be reversed during the second half of their lives, so that in fact the overall quality of their lives, taken as a whole, will be *completely equal*.

D: (grinning broadly, knowing he's won): Bravo! You really *are* the Master. I couldn't have given a better answer myself.

God's treatment of Job1 and Job2 exemplifies what McKerlie called "changing places egalitarianism." Like McKerlie (and the Devil!), I reject the implication of whole lives egalitarianism that there can be no egalitarian objection to a situation involving differential treatments of equally deserving individuals—no matter how significant, sustained, widespread, systematic, and even perverse, those differential treatments are—as long as the roles of the equally deserving individuals are interchanged so that each receives an equivalent share of the treatments meted out.

In addition to whatever other objections one might have to God's treatment of Job1 and Job2, I find the (first) forty years of inequality between Job1 and Job2 objectionable. I think it is unfair or unjust for Job2 to be so much worse off than Job1 through no fault of his own, and my objection to the unequal situation does not disappear—though it is, to some extent, altered[7]—when I learn that Job1 will subsequently be worse off than Job2 to an equivalent degree. The fact that over the second half of their lives Job1 will be much worse off than Job2 through no fault of his own is not *irrelevant* to my assessment of the inequality obtaining between them during the first half of their lives, but neither does the latter inequality simply cancel out, or remove the objectionable character of the former inequality. I think *both* periods of inequality are objectionable, whether considered separately or together. In sum, even looking at the whole picture, I think God's treatment of Job1

7. The importance of this qualification will become clearer shortly.

and Job2 could be criticized on egalitarian grounds, and I think it is a shortcoming of the whole lives view that it is unable to accommodate this.[8]

Some people object to examples involving God. There are many reasons for this we need not consider here. The important point to note is that analogous examples of "changing places egalitarianism" could be given that would be wholly social in character and origin. On my view, a caste system involving systematic and substantial biases towards, and differential treatment of, the members of different castes might be objectionable on egalitarian grounds *even if* the demographic composition of the castes periodically changed so that each person was a member of each caste and the *overall* quality of each life was equivalent.[9]

For the sake of later discussion, let us illustrate the point we have been making with diagram 8.2. (Recall that on the scale employed in my diagrams two represents

8. Derek Parfit has pointed out that this example, and the following one involving a caste system, are impure. He worries that perhaps our reactions to these examples stem not from their inequality, but from the fact that they involve the gratuitous or unnecessary mistreatment of certain people during certain parts of their lives. I accept the point that my examples are impure, but I still believe they illustrate my central claim. It is true, of course, that it seems wholly unnecessary for God to treat Job1 or Job2 poorly during any portion of their lives. He could treat them both splendidly for their whole lives. But if the sole basis of our reaction to my example is that we object to the gratuitous mistreatment of people during parts of their lives, then we should be equally offended if, for the first half of their lives, God treated both Job1 and Job2 as he originally treated Job2, and then afterward he treated both as he originally treated Job1. But while the total extent to which Job1 and Job2 are gratuitously mistreated may be the same in the two cases—in each they are mistreated for half their lives—I find my original example much more offensive. This is because in my original example I am not merely offended that Job1 and Job2 are gratuitously mistreated for half their lives; I am particularly offended that for half their lives Job2 fares miserably *while Job1 fares splendidly*, whereas for the other half Job1 fares miserably while Job2 fares splendidly.

Similarly, on Parfit's suggested view it should be much worse, and in *no* respect better, if God treated both Job1 and Job2 for their whole lives as he originally treated Job2. But while it would have clearly been worse in some respects for God to gratuitously mistreat Job1 and Job2 for their whole lives, it is one thing for God to treat them both badly, quite another for God to treat Job2 badly *while he treats Job1 well*, and then later to treat Job1 badly while he treats Job2 well. Clearly, the latter situation "drips with injustice" in a way the former does not. (I do not deny that the former situation drips with injustice; perhaps it violates our concern for proportional justice—that there should be a proportion between living well and faring well. But the example could be changed to alleviate this concern. And in any event, my point is simply that the latter situation drips with injustice *in a way* the former does not, namely regarding our egalitarian concern that it is bad for some to be worse off than others through no fault of their own.)

In sum, I stand by my earlier claim, that "in addition to whatever other objections one might have to God's treatment of Job1 and Job2, I find the (first) forty years of inequality between Job1 and Job2 objectionable."

Finally, if one continues to find these examples objectionable one might consider similar cases of inequality with solely natural causes. Let A be *much* worse off than B through no fault of his own. Supposing such inequality would bother us if it persisted for their whole lives, would our egalitarian concern *totally* disappear if we learned that natural causes were at play that would reverse their situations for the second half of their lives? Mine would not.

9. This point is reminiscent of one made by John Schaar in "Equality of Opportunity and Beyond," in *Nomos IX: Equality*, ed. by R. Pennock and J. Chapman (Atherton Press, 1967), pp. 228–49. Schaar argued that complete equality of opportunity might succeed in altering the demographic composition of society's groups—so, for example, more blacks and women might be doctors, and more white males be garbage collectors—yet do little or nothing to alter the basic social and economic inequalities between those groups that many find objectionable. Schaar's position is discussed further in chapter 10.

	T1	T2	T3	T4	
Case IV: A	8 +	8 +	2 +	2	= 20
B	2 +	2 +	8 +	8	= 20

	T1	T2	T3	T4	
Case V: A	5 +	5 +	5 +	5	= 20
B	5 +	5 +	5 +	5	= 20

DIAGRAM 8.2

a very poor quality of life and eight a very high quality of life.) On the complete lives view it doesn't matter that in case IV, B, through no fault of his own, is significantly worse off than A for half of his life. Nor does it matter that A, through no fault of his own, is significantly worse off than B for half of *his* life. All that matters, on the complete lives view, is that taken as a complete whole the *overall* quality of the two halves of A's and B's lives is the same. Thus on complete lives egalitarianism there is no reason to prefer the situation depicted in case V to that depicted in case IV, and this is so even though A and B are *perfectly* equal throughout the course of their lives in case V, and *significantly* unequal throughout the course of their lives in case IV. This is a conclusion many may find hard to accept.

As it should be clear, both a simultaneous segments view and a corresponding segments view would yield the judgment that case IV is worse than case V regarding inequality. By measuring the inequality between A and B as a function of the inequality between their simultaneous and corresponding segments, the two views will be extensionally equivalent for cases like IV and V.[10] By measuring inequality along the lines suggested by diagram 8.1, each view would yield a perfect score of zero for case V's inequality and a (very high) score of twenty-four for case IV's inequality.

8.3 Support for Complete Lives Egalitarianism: Problems with Alternative Views

Should the whole lives view be rejected entirely, and replaced by some combination of the simultaneous and corresponding segments views? I think not. Both of the other views have implausible implications of their own. Indeed, in some cases the judgments yielded by both the simultaneous and corresponding segments views seem less plausible than the judgment yielded by the whole lives view. Consider diagram 8.3.

---

10. This follows from our earlier assumptions about what is to count as simultaneous and corresponding segments in our examples.

	T1		T2		T3		T4		
Case IV: A	8	+	8	+	2	+	2		= 20
B	2	+	2	+	8	+	8		= 20
	6	+	6	+	6	+	6		= 24

	T1		T2		T3		T4		
Case VI: A	8	+	8	+	8	+	8		= 32
B	2	+	2	+	2	+	2		= 8
	6	+	6	+	6	+	6		= 24

DIAGRAM 8.3

According to both the simultaneous and corresponding segments views, case IV's inequality will be as bad as case VI's. According to the whole lives view, case VI's inequality will be worse than case IV's. Even if one believes that case IV's inequality is objectionable, it is hard to believe it is *just* as objectionable as case VI's. However bad it may be for one person to be much worse off than another for half of his life, and much better off than the other for the other half, it seems it would be much worse for the one person to be worse off than the other for his entire life.

Consider the following. Suppose an egalitarian were forced to choose between two severe caste systems whose only difference was that in the first system each person would occupy but one caste for his entire life, whereas in the second each person would occupy each caste over the course of his life. As objectionable as both caste systems may be, it seems clear that most egalitarians would prefer the second to the first. A caste system that distributes undeserved benefits and burdens so that some live like kings while others live like paupers will be objectionable to an egalitarian. But it will be more objectionable if the same people always receive the benefits and others always receive the burdens, than if all share, in turn, both the benefits and the burdens.[11]

11. Once again, because this example involves caste systems one might worry that our objections to these cases are that they involve the gratuitous or unnecessary mistreatment of certain people during portions of their lives. But presumably this will be so for both caste systems. So the question is why gratuitous mistreatment of people will strike us as more objectionable if embedded in a system where the same people are always burdened while others are always benefited, than if embedded in a system where each person, in turn, shares both burdens and benefits. Again, although I do not deny that various factors may influence our judgment about such cases, it seems clear that one reason we regard the first situation as worse than the second is that we find it much worse regarding inequality. That is, *qua* egalitarian, I have no difficulty judging the first situation worse. Thus, while this example may be "impure," I still think it amply illustrates my point. (See note 8.)

On both simultaneous and corresponding segments views, how two people have fared relative to each other in the past will be *completely* irrelevant to whether it would be better for the one to be better or worse off than the other in the future. This seems implausible, and to the extent it does the whole lives view may seem attractive. But note, it is not exactly clear how an egalitarian *should* count past inequalities between contemporaries.

Suppose that for the first half of their lives A and B have been, respectively, the beneficiary and the victim of a severe caste system such that, on the scale we have been employing, A has been at level eight and B at level two. Other things equal, should an egalitarian favor retaining the severe caste system but reversing A's and B's places within it, so that for the second half of their lives A would be at level two and B at level eight? This is what a whole lives view would seem to imply, since the result would be that over the course of their entire lives the overall quality of A's and B's lives would be equal. Or should the egalitarian favor removing the caste system entirely, so that for the second half of their lives both A and B were at level five? This is what the simultaneous and corresponding segments views would seem to imply, since it would minimize the overall extent to which there was any inequality between the relevant segments of A's and B's lives. Such a position has an intuitively attractive purity. If an inegalitarian system is truly objectionable, shouldn't an egalitarian clearly and unequivocally oppose and seek to dismantle it, rather than favor its perpetuation with different victims?

But of course purity is not always a virtue in the complex world of morality. And it has long been recognized that an egalitarian may have to permit, and even require, certain inequalities (say, present, short term, or income inequalities) to reduce or remove other more objectionable inequalities (say, future, long-term, or welfare inequalities). Perhaps the egalitarian should support a system that would favor B over A during the second half of their lives, but not as strongly as the original caste system favored A over B. Maybe B should be raised to level six or seven, and A reduced to level four or three. Such a position might appear to be a plausible compromise between the others, favoring the amelioration of inegalitarian systems without simply ignoring how people have fared relative to each other in the past.

As with many other questions raised in this book, we see that different answers are possible to the question of how an egalitarian should count past inequalities between contemporaries. Different answers may seem plausible depending on one's views regarding the proper unit of egalitarian concern; and of course, conversely, one's views regarding the proper unit of egalitarian concern may in turn be influenced by the plausibility of the answers they yield to the question at issue.

8.4 A Fruitful Test Case

We have considered several examples where simultaneous and corresponding segments egalitarianism would be extensionally equivalent. But they are different views that will yield different judgments about many cases. Thus, even if one grants that there are cases where the judgment yielded by the whole lives view should be rejected in favor of the judgment yielded by the simultaneous and corresponding

	T1	T2	T3	T4
Case IV: A	8	8	2	2
B	2	2	8	8

	T1	T2	T3	T4	T5	T6
Case VII: A	8	8	2	2		
B			2	2	8	8

DIAGRAM 8.4

segments views, one needs to determine whether one is being influenced by one or both of the latter views (or of course some other view entirely). Toward this end, one will want to consider examples like that of diagram 8.4. Case IV is familiar from diagrams 8.2 and 8.3. In discussing those diagrams, we saw that the simultaneous and corresponding segments views would agree with each other, and oppose the whole lives view, in judging case IV's inequality to be objectionable. Case VII is just like case IV, except that B has been born forty years later. Does this make no difference, some difference, or all the difference regarding whether there is objectionable inequality between A and B?

Cases IV and VII would be judged equivalent on the whole lives view. Both would be perfect regarding inequality. Cases IV and VII would also be judged equivalent on the corresponding segments view. Both would be equally objectionable. Cases IV and VII would be judged differently on the simultaneous segments view. Whereas case IV's inequality would be objectionable, case VII would be perfect regarding inequality. This suggests the following. If one thinks that cases IV and VII are both objectionable regarding inequality, and *equally* so, one probably accepts the corresponding segments view and completely rejects the simultaneous segments view. If one thinks that cases IV and VII are both objectionable regarding inequality, but that case IV's inequality is worse, one is probably influenced by both the corresponding and the simultaneous segments views. If one thinks case IV is objectionable regarding inequality, but case VII is not, one probably accepts the simultaneous segments view and completely rejects the corresponding segments view.

Note, depending on their clarity and certainty, one's judgments about examples like diagram 8.4 might be even more revealing. More particularly, they might indicate any one of a number of specific positions. For example, if one thinks cases IV and VII are clearly and unequivocally perfect regarding inequality, one probably accepts the whole lives view and completely rejects the other two views. If one thinks cases IV and VII are clearly and unequivocally objectionable regarding inequality, one probably accepts the corresponding segments view and completely rejects the other two views. If one thinks case IV is clearly and unequivocally objectionable regarding inequality, but case VII is clearly and unequivocally perfect regarding inequality, one probably accepts the simultaneous segments view and completely rejects the other two views. If one thinks there is *no* difference between cases IV and VII regarding inequality, but is ambivalent about them—in the sense that one feels some pull toward both the judgment that their inequalities are perfect and the judgment that they are objectionable—one probably attaches some weight to both the complete lives view and the corresponding segments view, but no weight to the simultaneous segments view. If one thinks case IV is clearly and unequivocally objectionable regarding inequality, but is ambivalent about case VII, one probably attaches some weight to both the simultaneous and corresponding segments views, but no weight to the complete lives view. If one thinks case VII is clearly and unequivocally perfect regarding inequality, but is ambivalent about case IV, one probably attaches some weight to both the complete lives view and the simultaneous segments view, but no weight to the corresponding segments view. Finally, if one thinks that cases IV and VII are not equivalent regarding inequality, and that neither is clearly and unequivocally perfect nor clearly and unequivocally objectionable, this may be because one is influenced by all three of the different views regarding the proper unit of egalitarian concern.

8.5 Summary and Implications

I have discussed three views regarding the proper unit of egalitarian concern. These views are independent of each other, in the sense that each of their judgments may be in agreement or disagreement depending on the particular case in question. Variations of the three views are possible, as their spirit might be interpreted or their details developed in ways other than those suggested. Entirely different views may also be possible.

The point of my discussion has not been to provide a definitive and exhaustive account of the proper unit of egalitarian concern. Nor has it been to establish that the standard, complete lives, view is less plausible than a simultaneous or corresponding segments view, much less that a complete lives view should be rejected in favor of one or both of the other views. Rather, it has been to suggest that there is no simple, clear, or obvious account to be given. Several views may seem plausible, each of which faces numerous complexities and problems, including many not even touched upon here. So, for example, it is not clear on the simultaneous or corresponding segments views what grounds are to be employed for arriving at "appropriate" segments for comparison. Selecting certain segments will yield wildly implausible implications, while selecting other segments may seem arbitrary and ad hoc. Also, as McKerlie notes, egalitarians will need to consider the problem of quality versus quantity for lives or segments of unequal duration.

Let me next make two observations regarding the practical significance of our results. First, on a simultaneous segments view inequality only matters between contemporaries, that is, between the simultaneous segments of overlapping generations. Correspondingly, on such a view inequality will matter within, but not between, past, present, or future (nonoverlapping) generations. Thus, for example, to the extent a simultaneous segments view seems plausible, vast consumption of the world's resources would be objectionable if, other things equal, it has an adverse effect on inequality within the present generation or within some other generations, but it would *not* be objectionable if its effect would "merely" be to leave the present generation much bettter off than either past or future ones.

Second, different views about the proper unit of egalitarian concern may have direct implications for the moral desirability of transfers between overlapping generations, for example between the young and old. Consider the following. Do we think the elderly are better off than the young? Even if they are *financially* better off, is this enough to offset losses in hearing, eyesight, memory, health, and loved ones? If not, then insofar as a position like simultaneous segments egalitarianism is plausible, someone who cares about equality of welfare will favor transfers from the young to the old. On the other hand, even if we think today's elderly are significantly worse off than today's young, that fact, by itself, will tell us nothing about the moral desirability of transfers between the young and old on either the whole lives view or the corresponding segments view. To the contrary, both views might support transfers from the elderly to the young, *even on the assumption* that the former are (currently) much worse off than the latter. Clearly, on the whole lives view the relevant question regarding the moral desirability of transfers between the young and old will not be how the two groups compare *now*, but how they compare over the course of their lives. Similarly, on the corresponding segments view the relevant question will not be how today's elderly compare with today's young, but rather, to put it roughly, how today's elderly compare with tomorrow's elderly and how today's young compare with yesterday's young.

One can see then how an egalitarian view about the desirability of exchanges between the young and old will depend on both the proper unit of egalitarian concern, and empirical facts about how the young and old compare with respect to that concern. If more than one view is plausible regarding the proper unit of egalitarian concern, then several egalitarian reasons may be relevant to the desirability of exchanges between the young and old. And these reasons may or may not support the same conclusion.

I think this chapter's considerations also have other interesting implications. For example, they are clearly relevant to the sort of questions introduced, and set aside, in chapter 1, concerning inequality's scope and the proper nature or structure of an egalitarian theory. They are also relevant to the deep and important topics of transitivity and temporal neutrality. Unfortunately, I cannot pursue these issues here.

Finally, let me observe that until this chapter I have implicitly assumed a whole lives view for the purposes of discussion. Nevertheless, I think most of my questions and claims would apply, mutatis mutandis, to simultaneous or corresponding segments views. For example, on a simultaneous segments view, should one determine the size of someone's complaint during a given segment of her life by comparing the quality of her life during that segment to that of the best-off person, the average person, or all those who are better off, during that segment? Similarly, in assessing how bad a temporal segment's inequality is, should one adopt a maximin principle, an additive principle, or a weighted additive principle, of equality? The importance of these questions, and the considerations relevant to deciding them, do not seem to be substantially affected by the proper unit of egalitarian concern.

9

A Criticism of Egalitarianism Rejected

The task of this book has been to *understand* our notion of inequality. I have tried to determine what the egalitarian cares about, and what factors are relevant to assessing situations regarding inequality. I have not argued one *should* be an egalitarian. Nor, till now, have I tried to defend egalitarianism against the claims of nonegalitarians. However in this chapter I want to address a position that, perhaps more than any other, underlies the reasoning of most nonegalitarians. It may also underlie the reasoning some are attracted to deontological or person-affecting versions of egalitarianism. As we shall see, I believe the position has enormous appeal, and influences thinking about many topics besides inequality. I also think the position can be effectively challenged in ways that cast doubt on many positions and have significant implications for our understanding of the good.

9.1 Extended Humanitarianism: An Implausible Version of Egalitarianism

Some people have suggested an approach to understanding our notion of inequality that is markedly different from this book's. According to this approach the egalitarian wants each person to fare as well as he possibly can, but he is especially concerned with the worse-off.[1] On this view the egalitarian will tend to favor redistribution between the better- and worse-off, even if a loss in utility accompanied such redistribution. Naturally, how much loss in utility to the better-off would be compensated by lesser gains to the worse-off would depend upon how much greater weight, or priority, was attached to our concern for the worse-off. In any event, on this view the worse off someone was the greater priority they would receive in our moral deliberations. This is only a rough statement of the view in question but it is sufficient for my purposes. The key point to note is while on this view the egalitarian has a special concern for the worse-off, his ultimate goal is for each to fare as well as possible.

Since humanitarians are people who want to improve the lot of the worse-off

---

1. This approach was suggested in conversation by Susanna Goodin. It was also suggested by Thomas Nagel who refers to "a very strong egalitarian principle ... [which] is constructed by adding to the general value of improvement a condition of priority to the worst off" (from *Mortal Questions* [Cambridge University Press, 1979], p. 110).

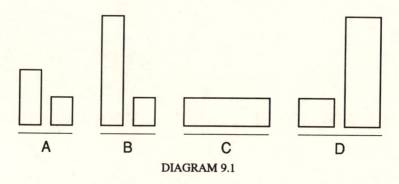

DIAGRAM 9.1

(their principle concern being to relieve suffering), I shall call such a view "extended humanitarianism." Derek Parfit has recently called such a view *The Priority View*, expressing the fact that the view's focus is on giving priority to the worse-off.[2]

As a version of egalitarianism, the problems with extended humanitarianism are many. It completely fails to reflect, and is unable to account for, most of the egalitarian views noted in chapter 2—for example, those yielding the judgments that the Sequence is getting better and better, that it first gets worse then better, and that the worlds are all equivalent regarding inequality. This is because on extended humanitarianism the Sequence would clearly and unequivocally worsen as the better-off group decreased and the worse-off group increased.

In addition, extended humanitarianism is unable to account for the fact, noted in chapter 3, that most people would agree that lowering the best-off group to the level of those next best-off would clearly and unequivocally improve a situation's inequality. Nor could this view account for the conclusion—argued for in chapter 6—that proportional increases in a population's levels would worsen inequality not improve it.

Similarly, extended humanitarianism cannot plausibly account for why the egalitarian feels guilt or shame about how he fares relative to others (see chapter 10). Thus, although on this view the egalitarian would have reason to regret that the worse-off fare badly, and that neither he nor society is doing enough about their lot, his only regret about how *he* fares should be that he is not even *better off*, not that he fares well, while others fare worse.

Finally, consider the diagram 9.1. On extended humanitarianism there would be no reason for the egalitarian to prefer A to B. In fact, there wouldn't even be reason to prefer C to D.

The problem with this view is clear. *It is not concerned with equality.* Equality describes a relation obtaining between people that is *essentially comparative.* People are more or less equal *relative to one another.* Extended humanitarianism is concerned with how people fare, but *not* with how they fare relative to each other.

2. In his unpublished manuscript "On Giving Priority to the Worse-off" (1989). As noted in chapter 1, I think Parfit's terminology may be more perspicuous than mine. But having employed my terminology for many years prior to Parfit's, I shall stick with it.

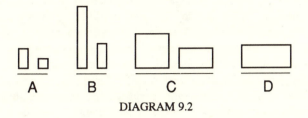

DIAGRAM 9.2

Extended humanitarianism resembles utilitarianism in the following respect. Just as equality will often be endorsed by utilitarianism as a means to promoting its end, so too equality will often be endorsed by extended humanitarianism as a means to promoting its end. However, on neither view is value attached to equality *per se*.[3] Extended humanitarianism is no more deserving of the name egalitarianism than utilitarianism is.

9.2 Extended Humanitarianism versus Egalitarianism

As a plausible analysis of what the egalitarian really cares about, extended humanitarianism is a nonstarter. Nevertheless, I think I understand its motivation. People are drawn to extended humanitarianism not as a position expressing what the egalitarian *does* care about, but rather as a position expressing what the egalitarian *should* care about. More accurately, it may seem the reflective egalitarian is forced to extended humanitarianism—that is, that it is the closest thing to an egalitarian position one can plausibly adopt. Thus the gist of this view is *not* that extended humanitarianism is a plausible version of egalitarianism, but rather that one should be an extended humanitarian *instead* of an egalitarian.

Many people are attracted to such a position. Often they are influenced by considerations of the following sort. Consider diagram 9.2. Suppose we could transform A into B. Many find it hard to believe there could be *any* reason not to do this. In B, *everybody* is better off than they were in A. In fact, B's worse-off have even better lives than A's better-off. True, there is greater inequality in B than A. But so what? Doesn't that just show we shouldn't attach weight to inequality *per se*? After all, one might wonder, how *could* B's inequality be bad, *when there is no one for whom it is worse*?

Or consider C and D, and imagine that C is a world where half are blind, D a world where all are. One *could* always transform C into D by putting out the eyes of the sighted. However, many find the view that this would improve the situation in even one respect *more* than incomprehensible; they find it abominable. That D is more equal than C gives one *no reason at all*, they think, to transform C into D; and

---

3. These remarks parallel a point of Thomas Scanlon's in "Nozick on Rights, Liberty, and Property," *Philosophy and Public Affairs* 6 (1976): 3–25. Scanlon notes that to "a humanitarian, equalization is merely a means to the improvement of the lot of those currently worst off" (p. 8).

only a hardened misanthrope, or someone motivated by the basest form of envy, could think otherwise. After all, they ask, how *could* D's greater equality make it better in *any* respect, if there is *no one* for whom it *is* better?

Such considerations have tremendous force, and I believe they underlie the thinking of most nonegalitarians (indeed, when lecturing on inequality I have almost invariably encountered some version of the foregoing). Correspondingly, one can see how such considerations might drive someone who cares about the worse-off, and who favors redistribution where it (sufficiently) benefits the worse-off, from egalitarianism toward a position like extended humanitarianism. Alternatively, such considerations might drive one toward person-affecting or deontological versions of egalitarianism; versions according to which inequality is only bad when there is someone for whom it is bad,[4] or according to which inequality can only be removed in certain morally acceptable ways (with putting out people's eyes not being among them!).

9.3 The Slogan

I believe that extended humanitarianism is a plausible position in its own right. Hence I believe there is reason to be an extended humanitarian *in addition* to an egalitarian. I also believe the preceding considerations are *extremely* plausible. But they are not, in the end, compelling. They do not force the egalitarian to abandon his view in favor of extended humanitarianism, or to adopt a person-affecting or deontological version of egalitarianism. If one decides to adopt such positions, it should be for reasons other than those presented.

At the heart of the preceding considerations is a position I shall refer to as

> *The Slogan*: One situation *cannot* be worse (or better) than another if there is *no one* for whom it *is* worse (or better).

It is the Slogan that gives the preceding considerations their powerful rhetorical force. But the Slogan can, and should, be challenged. In the remainder of this chapter I shall mount such a challenge. In doing this it will be useful, and illuminating, to present, interpret, and criticize the Slogan in its own terms. In particular, I want to assess the Slogan and its implications in a much wider context than simply its role in challenging (certain versions of) egalitarianism. This will allow us to see the Slogan's shortcomings more clearly, and enable us to evade the charge of attacking the Slogan (or begging the question against it) simply in order to preserve egalitarianism. Of course, in this book my primary interest in the Slogan concerns its implications for egalitarianism, and I shall return to these at this chapter's end.

---

4. In my article, "Intransitivity and the Mere Addition Paradox," *Philosophy and Public Affairs* 16 (1987): 138–87, I argued that a person-affecting version of egalitarianism, and in fact person-affecting principles in general, threaten the transitivity of our all-things-considered judgments. Correspondingly, someone deeply wedded to transitivity may regard such views as incoherent. For example, Derek Parfit informs me (in correspondence) that he now thinks it is incoherent to claim that inequality is only bad when it is bad for someone because he assumes the transitivity of our all-things-considered judgments.

But as we will see, I think the Slogan has far-reaching implications that should be questioned whatever one's views about egalitarianism.

Let me turn now to a direct consideration of the Slogan itself.

Like certain other slogans—for example, each person is deserving of equal consideration and respect—the Slogan enjoys widespread acceptance. As we will see, it underlies many arguments in philosophy and economics, and those appealing to it span the range of theoretical positions, including deontological, consequentialist, and rights-based views. In addition, as with some more famous slogans, most believe that the Slogan expresses a deep and important truth. So, like a powerful modern-day Occam's razor, often the Slogan is wielded to carve out, shape, or whittle down the domain of moral value.

Unfortunately, the Slogan is almost always invoked both implicitly and rhetorically. Perhaps it has been thought to be an ultimate moral principle—that which provides the justification for *other* claims, but which cannot, and need not, *itself* be justified. More likely the Slogan has been thought so obvious as to not even require explicit acknowledgment, let alone explication or defense. "After all" one might rhetorically ask, "how *could* one situation be worse than another if there is *no one* for whom it *is* worse?"

In the following sections I shall present considerations relevant to assessing the Slogan and the arguments invoking it. My central claims are three. First, *widespread agreement about the Slogan is more apparent than real*. The Slogan is ambiguous, subject to many interpretations with different implications. Hence, uncritical acceptance of the Slogan covers up the fact that no single position is being invoked or agreed upon. Second, *substantive interpretations of the Slogan are neither obvious nor uncontroversial*. Thus, rhetorical appeals to the Slogan are unwarranted in support of significant moral positions. Third, even if there are some plausible interpretations of the Slogan, *the Slogan does not support most of the particular positions it has been thought to support*.

In sum, I shall argue that the Slogan and the arguments invoking it are at best misleading and at worst mistaken. Minimally, then, the Slogan requires explication and defense heretofore lacking. In addition, most positions appealing to it must either be rejected or supported on other grounds.

9.4 Cases Where the Slogan Is Implicitly Involved

Let me begin by indicating some of the cases besides those involving inequality where the Slogan seems to be implicitly involved.

(1) A situation is *pareto optimal* if no one's lot could be improved without worsening the lot of someone else. Economists think nonpareto optimal situations are inefficient. Many, in fact, think that whenever we could improve the lot of some, without worsening the lot of anyone else, it would be irrational, and wrong, not to do so. This position presupposes the Slogan. After all, if a nonpareto optimal situation *could* be better than a (more) pareto optimal one, though there was no one for whom it was better, it need not be either irrational or wrong to fail to transform the former into the latter.

(2) The Slogan also explains why some find Rawls's difference principle (*DP*) more plausible than egalitarianism, and others find it too egalitarian to be plausible. When DP allows vast gains for the better-off to promote tiny gains for the worse-off, it is often defended by invoking the Slogan. Likewise, DP is criticized via the Slogan for failing to permit gains to the better-off that are not accompanied by gains to the worse-off.[5]

(3) Although the point of Nozick's Wilt Chamberlain example is that liberty upsets patterns, much of its force seems derived from the Slogan. Thus, Nozick writes:

> Each of these persons *chose* to give twenty-five cents of their money to Chamberlain. They could have spent it on going to the movies, or candy bars .... Can anyone else complain on grounds of justice? ... After someone transfers something to Wilt Chamberlain, third parties still have their legitimate shares; their shares have not changed.[6]

Again, the implication seems to be that if no one is worsened by the exchange, it cannot be bad.

Note, I am not claiming that the Slogan actually supports Nozick's example. Nor am I claiming that Nozick was relying on, or intending to appeal to, the Slogan in presenting his example. My claim is simply that much of its *force* is derived from the Slogan. Since the inequality between Chamberlain and those who paid to see him play results from voluntary agreements between consenting adults, it is at least arguable that the inequality between Chamberlain and his fans is not objectionable, as his fans are not worse off than Chamberlain *through no fault of their own*. Furthermore, it is natural to assume that the inequality between Chamberlain and his fans is not worse for either, since if both sides weren't benefited by it they wouldn't voluntarily agree to it.[7] Correspondingly, Nozick asks us to focus on the inequality between Chamberlain and those "third parties" who did not pay to see him play. Since presumably third parties are worse off than Chamberlain through no fault of their own, Nozick stresses the fact that third parties "*still* have their legitimate shares; *their* shares have not changed." But in stressing this fact the way he does, I think Nozick—whether wittingly or not—naturally leads many of his readers to assume implicitly that, since their shares have not changed, third parties are not worse off as a result of the exchanges between Chamberlain and his fans. Thus, I think Nozick's example invites us to suppose that there is no one for

---

5. Actually, Rawls's *lexical* version of the difference principle allows some gains of the sort in question, but at various places in the text Rawls seems to rule out any inequalities that do not "maximize, or at least contribute to, the long-term expectations of the least fortunate group in society" (*A Theory of Justice* [Harvard University Press, 1971], p. 151; see also pp. 64–65, 78–79, 83, and 150). My point here is not about Rawls's considered view regarding the permissibility of gains to the better-off that are not accompanied by gains to the worse-off, but to illustrate another example where the Slogan has been appealed to—namely, to criticize the suggestion that gains to the better-off might only be permissible if they also benefit the worse off.

6. Robert Nozick, *Anarchy, State, and Utopia* (Basic Books, 1974), p. 161.

7. This assumption may, of course, be mistaken, but many economists and others would accept it and, as we will see, this is not irrelevant to the appeal of Nozick's example.

whom the voluntary exchanges are worse in virtue of which we should condemn those exchanges, and hence his example draws force from the Slogan's appeal.

Consider how our view about Nozick's example might change if we added a few details. Suppose we found out that with his increased wealth Chamberlain drove up the price of housing, food, and medical care such that third parties, though they "*still* have their legitimate shares," are no longer in a position to provide for their children adequately. That is, suppose, in fact, that as a result of Chamberlain's wealth and market forces third parties (including elderly and children!) are now much worse off than they were before. Presumably, Nozick would still contend that the voluntary exchanges between Chamberlain and his fans were morally permissible and that no one else could "complain on grounds of justice."[8] But I suspect many would no longer share his firm convictions. Certainly, it would no longer seem so "obvious" or "uncontroversial" that there was nothing wrong with many people *choosing* "to give twenty-five cents of their money to Chamberlain."

In sum, many find Nozick's Wilt Chamberlain example powerful and appealing. But I think much of its power and appeal is derived from the Slogan. Take away the implicit assumption that there is no one for whom the voluntary exchanges are worse, and Nozick's example is far less compelling.

Similar remarks apply to several of the cases noted subsequently. I am not claiming that the authors mentioned were actually relying on, or intentionally appealing to, the Slogan in advocating their positions. Nor am I claiming that the Slogan actually applies to the cases mentioned (see, for example, note 12). My claim is that it is easy to assume implicitly—perhaps wrongly—that the Slogan is relevant to the positions in question, and this helps account for their force and appeal.

(4) Locke's theory of acquisition holds that people have a property right to any unowned thing they mix their labor with "at least where there is enough and as good left in common for others."[9] Nozick writes of this position that "the crucial point is whether appropriation of an unowned object worsens the situation of others."[10] It seems the implication is that as long as there is no one for whom acquiring the property is worse, it cannot be bad.

Similarly, Nozick follows Locke when he writes, "A medical researcher who synthesizes a new substance (out of easily obtainable materials) that effectively treats a new disease and who refuses to sell except on his own terms *does not worsen the situation of others* by depriving them of whatever he has appropriated" (emphasis added).[11] Here, Nozick's remarks seem to implicitly evoke the Slogan in support of his position that the researcher does nothing wrong if he keeps his product off the market.[12]

---

8. This is why I do not contend that Nozick actually relies on the Slogan in making his claim. He would make his claim independently of the Slogan's applying to his example. But, as will be suggested, others are less likely to find his example convincing if they don't think the Slogan supports it.

9. See Locke's *Second Treatise on Civil Government*, sections 26–33, (the passage in quotes comes from section 26).

10. *Anarchy, State, and Utopia*, p. 175.

11. Ibid., p. 181.

12. Interestingly, among those rejecting Nozick's conclusion most insist that it is precisely because

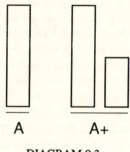

DIAGRAM 9.3

(5) Consider diagram 9.3. In discussing such a diagram, Derek Parfit wrote:

> Let us compare A with A+. The only difference is that A+ contains an extra group, who have lives worth living, and who affect no one else . . . it seems [hard] . . . to believe that A+ is *worse* than A. This implies that it would have been better if the extra group had never existed. If their lives are worth living, and they affect no one else, why is it bad that these people are alive?[13]

Here, too, the Slogan seems to support Parfit's position, for the question is, How could A+ be worse than A when there is no one for whom it is worse?[14, 15]

the medical researcher does worsen the situation of those he deprives of his medicine that he acts wrongly in keeping his product off the market. This is, I suspect, further indirect support for my claim regarding the Slogan's widespread appeal as it suggests (though does not entail) that most who reject Nozick's conclusion do so not because they reject the Slogan but rather because they think it doesn't apply to Nozick's example.

13. Derek Parfit, "Future Generations: Further Problems," *Philosophy and Public Affairs* 11 (1982): 158–59.

14. I vividly recall the first time I heard the Mere Addition Paradox, from which this example is taken. I was auditing a graduate seminar Parfit was teaching at Princeton when he drew pictures of A and A+ on the board and asked us how they compared. Several students suggested that A+ was worse than A, since it involved inequality. Parfit immediately offered the following response. How could A+ be worse than A, when it involves the *mere addition* of an extra group of people all of whom have lives worth living and who affect no one else; everyone in A exists in A+ *and is just as well off*—it is just that *in addition* there is the extra group of people whose lives are well worth living; thus, by hypothesis, A+ *isn't* worse for those in the A group, who are just as well off in A+ as A, and it *isn't* worse for those in the extra group, since their lives are worth living and *they* wouldn't exist in A, so how could A+ be worse than A, when there is *no one* for whom it is worse? I recall that at the time I, and most of my colleagues, found this response crushing. I now think this is because we were caught in the Slogan's grip.

Interestingly, Parfit himself claims he was not appealing to the Slogan when he asked us how A+ could be worse than A if there was *no one* for whom it was worse, and when he wrote of A+'s extra group "If their lives are worth living, and they affect no one else, why is it bad that these people are alive?" And there is textual evidence to support his claim. After all, in "Future Generations" Parfit introduced the Future Individuals Paradox (later called the "Non-Identity Problem" in *Reasons and Persons* [Oxford University Press, 1984]), which challenges the Slogan (see section 9.5). In addition, Parfit explicitly wrote the following: "There is one feature of A+ which seems morally regrettable. It is true here, as it is not in A that some people are worse off than others through no fault of theirs. There is natural inequality, or what some would call natural injustice. But if this inequality is not perceived, and involves no social injustice, it seems hard to believe that this feature is so bad as to make A+ worse than A" (pp. 158–59).

Thus it appears that in "Future Generations" Parfit thought A+ is worse than A regarding inequality, but not all things considered; yet according to the Slogan there would be no respect in which A+ might be worse than A (see section 9.6). Still, whatever Parfit's own view of his example, I am convinced that many who accepted Parfit's claims about how A and A+ compare were being influenced by the Slogan. (I know I was originally, as were many others I have discussed this issue with through the years.)

15. Interestingly, and importantly, in part 4 of *Reasons and Persons* Parfit adopts the strong position that A+'s inequality isn't bad *at all*. Parfit accepted this position when I confronted him with the following considerations. Already in "Future Generations" Parfit "denied that extra lives . . . have intrinsic moral value" (p. 158). Thus, Parfit believed that the lives of A+'s extra people have no intrinsic value. This implied that there is no positive respect in which A+ is better than A, a position he accepted. But then, if A+'s inequality is bad *at all*, it seems one should reject the claim that A+ is not worse than A, since there would be one respect in which A+ was *worse* than A, and *no* respect in which it was *better*. In other words, if one believes, as I am tempted to, that extra people's lives have intrinsic value, then one can maintain, as Parfit did in "Future Generations," that while A+'s inequality is bad, it's not so bad as to make A+ worse than A. If, on the other hand, one believes, as Parfit does, that extra lives have no intrinsic moral value, then it looks as if one must give up the claim that there is something bad about A+'s inequality or reject the view that A+ is not worse than A. As indicated, faced with these considerations—which he once accepted, but now rejects—Parfit endorsed the view that A+'s inequality doesn't matter in *Reasons and Persons*.

Parfit was not usually a non-egalitarian. In most cases he wanted to attach some weight to inequality. However, in *Reasons and Persons* he argued that the case of an expanding population is different. He claimed that there is nothing objectionable about inequality if it is brought about by the mere addition of extra people all of whom have lives worth living.

Parfit's claim was significant (see my "Intransitivity"). But let me note that it is hard to see a relevant difference between his case and others the egalitarian finds objectionable. Consider the following diagram:

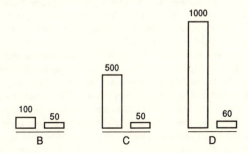

However they compare all things considered, most people would agree that C and D's inequality is worse than B's. The egalitarian might express this by saying that the worse-off have more to complain about in C and D, than in B. This doesn't mean the worse-off would actually complain more (they might not), nor does it mean the worse-off fare worse in C and D, than in B (they don't). It merely expresses the fact that the egalitarian regards individuals as the proper objects of moral concern, and that what he is concerned about is *not* how people fare, but how they fare *relative to others*. The point is, the egalitarian regards it as bad (unjust and unfair) for some to be worse off than others through no fault of their own. Because of this, he would find C and D more objectionable than B, *even though there is no one for whom they are worse*. For the same reason, I think the egalitarian would find A+ more objectionable than A even though there, too, there is no one for whom it is worse. In sum, I think once one gets clear about the egalitarian's concerns, one sees that the same reasons that lead people to the conclusion that C's inequality is bad, and worse than B's, lead to the conclusion that A+'s inequality is bad, and worse than A's.

(6) In "Rights, Goals, and Fairness" Thomas Scanlon observes "rights . . . need to be justified somehow, and how other than by appeal to the human interests their recognition promotes and protects? This seems to be the uncontrovertible insight of the classical utilitarians."[16] Many extend Scanlon's view to argue against the intrinsic value of respecting rights. Thus, it is contended that since the whole point of a system of rights is (must be?) to promote and protect human (or sentient) interests, there is not reason to respect (apparent) rights in those (rare) cases where doing so fails to promote or protect anyone's interests. Analogously, many claim there is nothing intrinsically bad about violating (apparent) rights when this benefits some and harms no one. These claims derive much of their force from the Slogan, according to which a situation where rights are respected (or violated) *cannot* be better (or worse) than one where they are not, if there is *no one* for whom it *is* better (or worse).

(7) Finally, we may note that standard objections to rule-utilitarianism, virtue-based, and deontological theories often parallel those noted against equality and rights-based theories. That is, they involve constructing cases where no one benefits and some are harmed, or where some benefit and no one is harmed, if only one does or doesn't (a) follow the rule, (b) act virtuously, or (c) do one's duty.[17] Once more, much of the force of these objections seems to rest on the Slogan's appeal.

I have dealt with this point in detail for two reasons: first, because it implicitly contains some of the considerations that lead me to favor an impartial teleological version of egalitarianism over person-affecting or deontological versions; and, second, because it has important implications for certain of chapter 7's results. For instance, if Parfit's position in *Reasons and Persons* could be defended—that while inequality is generally bad, A+'s inequality is not—that would raise doubts about my claim that inequality's aspects should not be supplemented to reflect the view that proportional size increases do not affect inequality. The considerations offered in discussing that issue, together with those sketched previously, lead me to think my earlier results stand.

Two further comments. First, readers of "Intransitivity" may recognize that I am here implicitly defending what I call an *Intrinsic Aspect* view of inequality, according to which how good a situation is regarding inequality depends solely on internal or intrinsic features of that situation. In "Intransitivity" I point out that Parfit's Mere Addition Paradox turned in part on what I called an *essentially comparative* view of inequality (see section 3.3), and I claimed that such a view has great appeal. It does, but in fact I have always favored an Intrinsic Aspect view of inequality for the reasons suggested already. Second, let me observe that Parfit no longer accepts the essentially comparative view of inequality defended in *Reasons and Persons*. Parfit now believes such a view has unacceptable implications (see "Intransitivity" for a discussion of these implications).

16. Reprinted in *Public and Private Morality*, ed. by Stuart Hampshire (Cambridge University Press, 1978), p. 93.

17. One might think that the Slogan couldn't be used against deontological theories, since deontological theories make claims about what we ought to *do*, and deny that these claims presuppose any views about the relevant goodness of outcomes. But I think this is not quite right. Deontologists insist that duty is not the same as promoting the best possible outcome, but most deontologists would admit that acting wrongly is bad, and that *other things equal* an outcome where one has acted wrongly will be worse than an outcome where one has acted rightly. Thus if someone can construct a case where breaking one's promise or lying will be worse for *no one*, they can use the Slogan to conclude that in such a case there is *no* respect in which the outcome would be worse if one broke one's promise or lied. Hence, on the assumption noted earlier, breaking one's promise or lying must not be wrong in such a case. Thus the Slogan might be invoked to undermine the claim that breaking one's promise or lying is intrinsically wrong, that is, that there is always something wrong about such actions independently of their consequences. I have heard such arguments invoked against deontologists. In response, deontologists

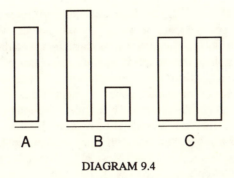

DIAGRAM 9.4

These are merely some of the many positions implicitly involving the Slogan. The list is by no means exhaustive. As we shall see, one should be wary of any appeals to the Slogan. Hence, one must seek other justifications for the positions one finds plausible.

9.5 The Non-Identity Problem

In "Future Generations: Further Problems," Derek Parfit presents the *Non-Identity Problem*, an ingenious argument which challenges the Slogan. A variation of it is shown in diagram 9.4.

Let A represent a generation contemplating two policies. On the *live for today* policy, they have children immediately, and deplete the natural resources for current uses. B would result; *they* would be better off, but their children would fare less well. On the *take care of tomorrow* policy, they postpone having children a few years, and conserve their resources. C would result; *they* would fare slightly less well than they do now, but the children they have would fare as well as they.

Most believe the "take care of tomorrow" policy should be adopted. But this is incompatible with the Slogan given two plausible assumptions: (*P*) the children born in B would be *different people* than the children born in C (being conceived several years later they would come from different sperm and ova, be raised by older and wiser parents, and so on), and (*Q*) one cannot harm or act against the interests of someone who will never exist and, more particularly, one does not harm someone by failing to conceive her (so, by refraining from sex for a month, a woman does not harm any of the millions of people who might have existed if she

must either deny that right or wrong actions themselves contribute to the goodness or badness of outcomes, insist that in such cases there really *must* be someone for whom the promise breaking or lying will be worse (perhaps the moral agent doing the action), or reject the Slogan. Note, on the last alternative deontologists claim it is not only wrong if I lie, it is bad—it makes the outcome in one respect worse—and they claim this is true even if there is *no one* for whom my lie is worse. It is a testimony to the Slogan's appeal that many find this position nonsensical.

had had sex and conceived).[18] Given these assumptions,[19] there is *no one* for whom the "live for today" policy would be worse: not the parents, who fare better in B than in either A or C; not the children in B, because *they* wouldn't exist if the "take care of tomorrow" policy was adopted; and not the children in C, because they don't exist and never will exist if the "live for today" policy is adopted. On the other hand, if the "take care of tomorrow" policy is adopted there *will* be someone for whom it is worse, namely the parents. Thus, unless we alter our judgment about which policy is better, the Slogan needs to be revised, if not rejected.

I have discussed Parfit's argument with many nonphilosophers as well as philosophers. Almost all find it perplexing. Most, at least initially, try to undermine it. Some question assumption P (often on [weak] theological grounds), others assumption Q. Some simply insist something *must* be wrong with the argument, though they know not what!

Among those accepting Parfit's argument, few believe the Slogan should be rejected outright. They point out, rightly, that the most Parfit *establishes* is that there is a limited and fairly peculiar range of cases in which the Slogan does not apply. These are cases where future generations are involved and, more particularly, cases where one's choices determine *who* comes to be. In most cases of moral concern these conditions do not obtain and for such cases, it is contended, the Slogan remains plausible.

These reactions are not atypical. They point to both the strength and widespread appeal of the Slogan, as well as the need to supplement Parfit's argument if, as I believe, appeals to the Slogan should be resisted.

9.6 Interpreting the Slogan

The Slogan is ambiguous. For example, it might be used as shorthand for any of the following claims.

1. One situation *cannot* be worse (or better) than another *in any respect* if there is *no one* for whom it *is* worse (or better) *in any respect.*
2. One situation *cannot* be worse (or better) than another *in any respect* if there is *no one* for whom it *is* worse (or better) *all things considered.*
3. One situation *cannot* be worse (or better) than another *all things considered* if there is *no one* for whom it *is* worse (or better) *in any respect.*

18. An average ejaculation contains between 120 and 750 million sperm cells. If one thinks of all of the partners a woman might have sex with during the time each month when she is fertile, and if one thinks that each sperm would combine with her ovum to create a unique individual, the number of possible people she might conceive each month is astronomical. It is surely implausible to think that she acts against each of their interests if she refrains from sex. Moreover, although it might be true that if she had had sex with Tom she might have conceived a particular individual, Tom Jr., it seems implausible to contend that she acted against Tom Jr.'s interest when she had sex with her husband Barry, and conceived Barry Jr. instead.

19. I shall not defend these assumptions. They are defended ably by Parfit. See "Future Generations," esp. pp. 113-19.

4. One situation *cannot* be worse (or better) than another *all things considered* if there is *no one* for whom it *is* worse (or better) *all things considered*.

In this chapter my concern is with the Slogan understood as shorthand for 1. Claim 2 is not plausible, and 3 and 4 are much weaker and less interesting than 1. More important, claims 3 and 4 would not license many conclusions for which the Slogan has been invoked.[20]

The nonegalitarian who insists that there is *no reason at all* to put out the eyes of the sighted uses the Slogan to support the view that equality has *no* intrinsic value. At best, 1 could support such a conclusion. Claims 3 and 4 could not. In fact, 3 and 4 are compatible with equality being the most important ideal. They merely rule out the conclusions that equality is all that matters and that equality matters more than everything else combined. Such conclusions are not very interesting and one need hardly invoke the Slogan to support them.

Similarly, few would deny that keepings one's promise, or respecting rights, or acting virtuously is not always the best thing to do all things considered. More interesting are the claims that there is *no* reason to keep one's promise, or respect rights, or act virtuously, in cases where there is no one for whom it is better. I believe opponents of deontological, rights-based, and virtue theories often invoke the Slogan to support the latter, stronger claims. Again, at best 1 could support such claims, 3 and 4 could not.

Finally, I think Nozick's Wilt Chamberlain example is intended to illustrate not merely that voluntary transactions that leave no one worse off are acceptable *all things considered*, but that there is *nothing* wrong with them—that is, *no* reason to prevent them. Here, too, the Slogan could only support such a view interpreted as 1.

Another reason for focusing on 1 is that 3 and 4 derive much of their plausibility and rhetorical appeal from 1. After all, if one situation *could* be worse than another in some respect, even if there was no one for whom it was worse in even one respect (and hence all things considered), then why couldn't it be worse all things considered? Presumably the one situation *would* be worse than the other, all things considered, if there was no respect in which it was better, or if the respect(s) in which it was better were not sufficient to outweigh the respect(s) in which it was worse. Surely there is no a priori reason to rule out such possibilities if 1 is false.

Together, the preceding makes plain the Slogan's full force. It isn't merely that one situation *is* never worse than another if there is no one for whom it is worse—as if this might be true in some respects, but not "all things considered." Rather, it is that one situation *cannot* be worse than another if there is no one for whom it is

---

20. Some readers may wonder why I bother to distinguish between 1–4 and defend my understanding of the Slogan as shorthand for 1. Jonathan Dancy, for example, suggested in correspondence that I might do away with this section as it "merely lists interpretations of the Slogan which have tempted nobody." I wish Dancy were right, but experience has taught me he is not. This section was only added to the chapter after earlier drafts elicited numerous comments and questions about the best way of interpreting the Slogan. Indeed, in the face of my arguments a number of people claimed the Slogan *should* be interpreted as 3 or 4 rather than 1. Obviously, for the reasons given in the text, I think they are mistaken. Still, I think this section will help avoid unnecessary errors or confusion.

worse—as if there is *no* respect in which this might be so and, hence, no *question* that in some cases the positive features might outweigh the negative ones. It is this strong position, expressed by 1, that underlies and explains people's confident rhetorical uses of the Slogan.

In what follows, then, I shall understand the Slogan as shorthand for 1, unless otherwise noted. Doing so will be sufficient to establish my central claims. In fact, I believe the considerations adduced also provide reason to be skeptical of 3 and 4; though this is not to deny that in *most* cases A will not be worse (or better) than B all things considered, if there is no one for whom it is worse (or better).

The Slogan is most naturally interpreted as making a claim about what is relevant to a situation's being good. This means that 1 is itself subject to interpretation, as the content and implications of the Slogan will depend on one's theory, or theories, of the good. Thus, appearances to the contrary, people endorsing the Slogan are in fact endorsing very different positions if they hold different theories of the good. This will become clearer, along with its importance, as the chapter progresses.

To assess properly the Slogan and the arguments invoking it, it is necessary to consider whether any plausible theories of the good support them. In the next sections I shall focus on three candidates: the *Mental State Theory*, the *Subjective Desire Fulfillment Theory*, and the *Objective List Theory*. Though other alternatives are possible, I believe that my arguments could be applied to plausible alternatives and, hence, that the theories considered are sufficient for my central claims.

Two remarks before turning to section 9.7. First, one benefit from assessing the Slogan is that it forces us to get clearer about theories of the good, and to make important distinctions easily neglected. As we shall see, one may usefully distinguish between theories about *self-interest*, which tell us what is good or bad *for* someone, and theories about *outcomes*, which tell us what makes an outcome good or bad. Unfortunately, perhaps partly due to the Slogan's appeal, the differences between these theories are often blurred or overlooked. I believe that some theories put forward as "theories of the good" are most plausible as theories about self-interest, whereas others are most plausible as theories about outcomes. Correspondingly, some theories that are easily dismissed as "full theories of the good" may yet deserve attention when "properly" interpreted. In addition, the most plausible "full theory of the good" may be different from, but include elements of, each such theory.

Second, although sufficient for my present purposes, sections 9.7–9.9 raise more questions than they answer, and at that they raise but a small portion of the unresolved questions regarding theories of the good. Unfortunately, this crucially important area has been sorely neglected. It warrants, and would surely repay, much more attention than I can give here.

9.7 The Mental State Theory

According to the Mental State Theory (*MST*) of the classical utilitarians, *only conscious states have intrinsic value or disvalue*, and everything else has value

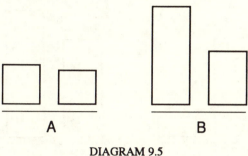

DIAGRAM 9.5

or disvalue only to the extent that it promotes positive or negative conscious states.[21]

At first, MST *seems* to support the Slogan.[22] Consider, for example, diagram 9.5. If the column heights represent the quality of people's conscious states (where the taller the column the higher the quality), then according to MST there would be *no* reason to regard the greater inequality in B as bad, since there is *no one* whose quality of conscious states it affects adversely, and hence no one for whom it is worse.[23] Here, MST seems not only to yield the Slogan's results, but to account for those results and, correspondingly, for the Slogan itself.

21. More particularly, the classical utilitarians were *hedonists*. They held that conscious mental states are intrinsically valuable or disvaluable to the extent they are pleasurable or painful. However, one could be a Mental State Theorist but not a hedonist. That is, one could hold that the value or disvalue of certain conscious states—for example, those related in relevant ways to truth, knowledge, or beauty—is not reducible to the value of those states' pleasure or pain. (It is arguable that Mill's "doctrine of higher pleasures" involves an important step away from simple or "pure" hedonism, toward a more robust Mental State Theory, but I shall not pursue this here. It is also arguable that Mill's doctrine involves a move toward a Subjective Desire Fulfillment Theory.) Having acknowledged that there may be different versions of a Mental State Theory, I shall ignore this fact in the ensuing discussion. This does not significantly affect my results. Also, let me emphasize that on the Mental State Theory only *conscious* states have intrinsic value or disvalue. I trust the text is clear about this, but given that many mental states are not conscious, I reiterate it here to avoid any chance of confusion about this point.

22. I emphasize the word "seems" here because some readers have been misled by my claims regarding the connection between MST and the Slogan. It is not my view that MST *actually* "supports" or "accounts" for the Slogan, only that it may *appear* to given the evaluations it yields to certain situations. The main point of this section is to show that however plausible it may seem, the appearance in question is illusory.

23. As the reader may note, I am here considering what MST would say about A and B considered *just by themselves*. I am ignoring the effects of A and B on the conscious states of us, as observers, who may care about equality. For our present purposes there are good reasons to do this, some of which are noted below in my discussion of proportional justice.

To insure that my example is relevant to the Slogan as I am interpreting it (that is, as shorthand for 1), I am assuming that the greater inequality in B hasn't by itself caused negative conscious states (envy?) that happen to be outweighed by other positive conscious states present in B but not in A. Perhaps the worse-off group is separated by an ocean and unaware of the better-off group. Perhaps this group is composed of mental state utilitarians who do not care about inequality *per se*, and hence are unequivocally pleased by what they take to be uniform improvement for the better.

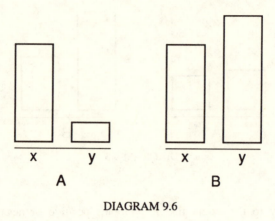

DIAGRAM 9.6

I believe MST represents a significant insight of the classical utilitarians. It is arguable, for example, that ice cream, tropical paradises, and Beethoven's symphonies, as well as rotten eggs, desert wastelands, and screeching brakes, only have their value or disvalue in virtue of their affects on conscious states. Indeed, it is arguable that *most* things only have value or disvalue in virtue of their affects on conscious states. Nevertheless, MST goes too far in claiming that *only* the quality of conscious states are intrinsically valuable. Surely, this position is implausible as a full theory about outcomes. If it were true it would undermine virtually *every* ideal.

Consider diagram 9.6, and the conception of *proportional justice* according to which there ought to be a proportion between faring well and doing well. Let A and B represent alternative afterlives, with the x columns representing the quality of the saints' conscious states, and the y columns that of the sinners'. Furthermore, assume A accurately reflects how the two groups "should" fare according to proportional justice and their earthly lives. Clearly, in accordance with proportional justice A would be better than B.

Is this implausible? Many, including Aristotle, Kant, and Ross, have thought not. Yet on MST not only would B be better, there would be *no* respect in which it was worse.

Most would find this hard to accept. They believe there would be *something* morally bad about the evilest mass murderers faring better than the most benign saints, even if there was *no one* for whom it was worse.[24]

It might be contended that there is someone for whom B is worse than A (at least in one respect), namely us, the observers who are bothered by B. Strictly

---

24. B isn't worse for the saints. By hypothesis they fare as well in B as in A. And it certainly isn't worse for the sinners! Hence there is no one for whom it is worse. (We may suppose, if we want, that the saints are blissfully unaware of how the sinners are faring, though if they are truly *saints* this supposition may be unnecessary. I leave God, and His feelings out of this discussion [perhaps He doesn't exist]; but notice, on the view being called into question, what reason could He have for preferring A to B, when there is no one for whom B is worse?)

speaking this is correct, but irrelevant. Our concern is with how A and B *themselves* compare. To assess this from the perspective of MST, we must restrict our attention to the quality of conscious states of those who are actually in A and B. To include our reactions as observers would not be to assess the situations themselves, but to assess another, wider, situation, one that merely included the original situations among its components. Of course, it might be claimed that there *is* no respect in which B is worse than A considered by themselves, and hence that the only reason B is worse than A (at least in one respect) is that we, the observers, are bothered by B. However, despite the claims of Hobbes and others,[25] many believe this gets things backward. Thus, most advocates of proportional justice would deny that B is worse than A because they find it objectionable. Rather, they would contend, the *reason* they find B objectionable is because injustice is bad. Thus, most who believe that B is worse than A in at least *one* respect would insist that this would be so even if there were no observers "offended" by the situation, or even if the only observers were indifferent to injustice or perhaps even relished it.[26]

These considerations suggest that unless one is willing to reject proportional justice entirely, and abandon the view that there is *some* respect in which B is worse than A (considered by themselves), one must reject the Slogan as supported by MST. To the question, How *could* one situation be worse than another if there is *no one* for whom it *is* worse? one might respond, It could be worse if it were worse regarding proportional justice. This would express the view that the quality of conscious states is *not* all that matters—proportional justice does too. Naturally, an egalitarian could make a similar response.

Analogous remarks could be made about freedom, autonomy, virtue, duty, or any other ideal. Consider diagram 9.7, where the column heights again represent the quality of conscious states. If in A people were free, autonomous, virtuous, or dutiful, and in B people were much less so, A might be preferred to B by those who value the ideals in question. Rejecting the Slogan as supported by MST, they would contend that in addition to the quality of conscious states we (should) also care about people's freedom, autonomy, virtue, or duty fulfillment.

Ironically, the Slogan as supported by MST would even be rejected by the classical utilitarians themselves, who would undoubtedly judge the "live for today" policy of section 9.5 worse than the "take care of tomorrow" policy, as it is worse in terms of both total and average utility. But of course this judgment cannot be made if one situation cannot be worse than another if there is *no one* for whom it *is* worse in terms of the quality of his conscious states.

So, among those who would reject the Slogan as (apparently) supported by MST

25. Recall Hobbes's famous claim "whatsoever is the object of any man's appetite or desire, that is it, which he for his part calleth good " (from the section "Good. Evil." in chapter 6 of *Leviathan* [1651]). This claim is endorsed by John Mackie (*Ethics: Inventing Right and Wrong* [Penguin, 1977]), and too many others to bother citing.

26. I have contended that, on MST, we should assess how situations compare considered by themselves. It is worth observing that the Slogan would lose its force—from which the central claims of this chapter would follow—if, in assessing situations, appeals were made to how observers would react or, for that matter, to what a rational impartial spectator would say. The reasons for this are (implicitly) given in sections 9.8 and 9.9, so I shall not duplicate them here.

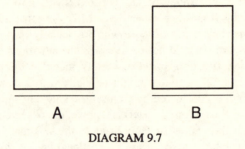

DIAGRAM 9.7

would be the proponents of proportional justice, equality, freedom, autonomy, virtue, duty, and even maximizing total or average utility. This does not mean, of course, that one *should* care about *each* of these ideals. No positive argument has been offered in support of them. But unless one is willing to reject them *all*, one cannot reject *any* merely because it entails that one situation could be worse than another though it is not worse for the quality of anyone's conscious states. *Other* reasons must be found to oppose the ideals one finds implausible.

Most agree that MST has serious shortcomings as a full theory of the good. But many would disagree on exactly where MST goes wrong. Though easily ignored, the source of this disagreement is important. To illustrate it, let us invoke the distinction noted at the end of section 9.6, between theories about self-interest and theories about outcomes. Recall that the former tell us what is good or bad *for* someone,[27] the latter what makes an *outcome* good or bad. Unfortunately, the precise relationship between these is not evident, and failure to distinguish them carefully has been the source of much confusion, as well as, perhaps, the Slogan's appeal.

Some who reject MST object to it as a theory about outcomes, though not as a theory about self-interest. They think it plausible that something can only be good or bad *for* someone insofar as it affects the quality of her conscious states, but deny that only the quality of conscious states is intrinsically good or bad. For example, advocates of proportional justice could agree that sinners faring better than saints needn't be worse *for* anyone, yet insist that such a situation might still be bad, because proportional justice has value beyond its being good *for* people.

On the other hand, some who reject MST object to it as a theory about outcomes *because* they think it inadequate as a theory about self-interest. For example, some believe that freedom is good *for* people, beyond its influence on the quality of conscious states. So, they might regard a world with a higher quality of conscious states but less freedom as worse than one with lower quality of conscious states but more freedom precisely *because* they believe people are better off in the latter than the former.

Naturally, one might reject MST for both reasons, thinking it goes wrong as a theory about self-interest *and* as a theory about outcomes, without the latter being due *only* to the former.

27. Which is, of course, very different from telling us what makes someone good or bad.

Each of these reasons may underlie Nozick's example of the experience machine. He writes:

> Suppose there were an experience machine that would give you any experience you desired . . . . Would you plug in? *What else can matter to us, other than how our lives feel from the inside?* First, we want to do certain things, and not just have the experience of doing them . . . . [Second,] we want to *be* a certain way, to be a certain sort of person. Someone floating in a tank is an indeterminate blob . . . . We learn that something matters to us in addition to experience by imagining an experience machine and then realizing that we would not use it . . . . Perhaps what we desire is to live (an active verb) ourselves, in contact with reality. (And this, machines cannot do *for* us.)[28]

Most agree with Nozick. Even if some would plug themselves in, most would think it bad if everyone were to do so, even if there was no one for whom it was worse in terms of the quality of their conscious states. However, is this because the quality of conscious states is not all that matters for (a) the "badness" of outcomes, or (b) what makes someone's life good or bad? Though this issue has largely been overlooked, I suspect some think the former, some the latter, and some both.

MST was first offered as a full theory of the good. Believing that only the quality of conscious states was relevant to the good for both individuals *and* outcomes, the classical utilitarians saw no need for different theories of the good. Regrettably, many have unwittingly followed their path, assuming the same theory would suffice for self-interest, outcomes, and the full theory of the good. Thus, convinced of MST's implausibility as a full theory of the good, many dismissed it without pursuing the source of its shortcomings. This is unfortunate, for on reflection I think some would agree that although MST is *not* an adequate theory about outcomes, it *is* an adequate theory about self-interest. That is, it is arguable that one of the great insights of the classical utilitarians was not only that *most* things are only good insofar as they promote positive mental states, but the further point that *nothing* is good *for* someone, that is, in her self-interest, except insofar as it positively affects the quality of her conscious states.

The foregoing is not only of general importance, it directly bears on our central issue. According to the Slogan, one situation *cannot* be worse than another in even one respect, if there is *no one* for whom it *is* worse in even one respect. This implies that one's theory of outcomes must be a direct function of (perhaps, in a sense, supervenient on) one's theory of self-interest. Clearly, however, to accept MST as a theory about self-interest, while rejecting it as a theory about outcomes is to deny the relation in question. More specifically, it is to insist that some factors can be relevant to the goodness of outcomes other than those relevant to what is good *for* people. Thus, on the view in question, one must reject the Slogan and the arguments invoking it, at least on its most natural and straightforward interpretation.[29]

Interestingly, once one distinguishes between theories about self-interest and theories about outcomes the Slogan may lose much of its plausibility. After all,

---

28. Nozick, *Anarchy, State, and Utopia,* pp. 42–45, his emphasis.
29. The reason for this tag will become clear in this chapter's final section.

while the quality of people's lives will certainly play a (and perhaps the) major role in the goodness of outcomes, why should the correct theory about outcomes be dependent on the correct theory about self-interest in the way the Slogan would have us believe?

Still, if one thinks MST fails as a theory about self-interest, one may yet believe that the correct theory about outcomes will involve an alternative to MST that does support the Slogan. Let us next consider if a Subjective Desire Fulfillment Theory yields this result.

9.8 The Subjective Desire Fulfillment Theory

In this section, I note many unresolved questions facing the Subjective Desire Fulfillment Theory (*SDFT*). Minimally, this shows that rhetorical appeals to the Slogan are (currently) unjustified insofar as they ultimately rest on SDFT. I next suggest that, even if its problems can be met, SDFT probably does not support the Slogan. I end by arguing that, even if some plausible version of SDFT supports the Slogan, it will not support the particular arguments that in fact invoke the Slogan.

Let me begin by considering SDFT as a theory about self-interest; that is, as a theory that tells us what is good or bad *for* someone. I shall later widen my discussion to include consideration of SDFT as a theory about outcomes.

As a theory about self-interest, SDFT holds that something will be good or bad for someone insofar, and only insofar, as it promotes or contravenes the fulfillment of her desires; where, roughly, the value of fulfilling an agent's desires is ultimately derivable from her desires themselves. So, on this view, the agent is, within certain limits to be discussed, the ultimate arbiter of her own good. What she desires is good for her and, importantly, it is her desiring it which makes it so.

Some are attracted to SDFT by the following sort of case.

> Suppose Jones was deeply committed to *his* helping eradicate world hunger. A leading agronomist, he devotes his life to developing high-yield grains that are resistant to known diseases and pests and that only require cheap, efficient, technologies. His genius and persistence produce phenomenal results, and toward the end of his life his biggest concern is to warn against the dangers of genetic homogeneity and exclusive reliance on his crops and their related technologies. At the time of his death Jones is a contented man, as world hunger has abated and its end is in sight. Unfortunately, Jones's crops and technologies are so efficient other agricultural methods are soon abandoned. When, thirty years later, a new crop disease evolves, the world's crops are destroyed, alternative farming technologies are no longer available, and the world is plunged into famine on an unprecedented scale.

Many believe Jones would have failed in the one way he most wanted to succeed. Although it is not his fault, his life's work brought about the very state of affairs he had devoted himself to preventing. Indeed, had he known what would come to pass, Jones never would have embarked on the path he did. Given this, some think the turn of events after his death would be worse for Jones, even though it would not affect his conscious states. Unlike MST, SDFT can capture this view, for although the later developments would have no bearing on the quality of Jones's conscious states, they would have a bearing—a powerfully negative one—on the fulfillment of his deepest (self-regarding) desires.

Similarly, some are attracted to SDFT because it can account for the view that even if no one's mental states are adversely affected, there would be something wrong with slandering another, deceiving another, making a promise to someone dying and then counting it as of no weight, and plugging everyone into Nozick's experience machine. This is because most have strong desires that would be contravened by such actions.

In addition, some are attracted to SDFT by theoretical considerations about the relationship between conscious states and desires. They believe conscious states are not *themselves* good or bad. Rather, they think, whether a conscious state is good or not depends on whether it plays a role in fulfilling some desire.

One important implication of SDFT follows directly from the Jones and dying promise cases, and indirectly from the others. One cannot ignore past desires merely because they are past or even because the desirer has died.[30]

Despite its attractions I have great reservations about SDFT as a theory about self-interest. I also have reservations about SDFT as a theory about outcomes, according to which, roughly, one outcome will be better than another if there is a greater fulfillment of people's desires in the one outcome than the other (where this, of course, must take account of both the number and strength of fulfilled [good] and unfulfilled [bad] desires). Let me next indicate some of my worries about SDFT, both as a theory about self-interest and as one about outcomes. Later I will argue

---

30. The reason for this is put nicely by Parfit. He writes, "These . . . Theorists count it as bad for me if my desire is not fulfilled, even if . . . I never know this. How then can it matter whether, when my desire is not fulfilled, I am dead? All that my death does is *ensure* that I will never know this. If we think it irrelevant that I never know about the non-fulfillment of my desire, we cannot defensibly claim that my death makes a difference" (*Reasons and Persons*, p. 495).

This position's implications extend well beyond this chapter's central concerns. It has long been thought an *essential* feature of utilitarianism that it is a forward-looking doctrine, and this has been counted among both its greatest strengths (accounting for some of its reformist implications and its independence from prevailing codes and norms) and its greatest weaknesses (because of its disregard for past histories, promises, contracts, and so on). But the forward-looking aspect of utilitarianism is not a function of its formal features either as a maximization doctrine or as one concerned solely with the consequences of actions.

So, *classical* utilitarianism was essentially forward looking, because it accepted MST, and because one cannot affect past states of consciousness. However, one can affect whether certain past desires are fulfilled, because even self-regarding desires can be about the future, and one's relation to it. So, combined with SDFT, utilitarianism *needn't* be essentially forward looking.

R. M. Hare was one of the first to both recognize and accept the implications in question. He writes "to frustrate a desire of mine is against my interest even if I do not know that it is being frustrated, or if I am dead." Later he adds, "for what it is worth I will record my opinion that the dying man's interests are harmed if promises are made to him and then broken, and even more that mine are harmed if people are cheating me without my knowing it." (From "Ethical Theory and Utilitarianism," in *Contemporary British Philosophy*, ed. by H. D. Lewis [Allen and Unwin, 1976], pp. 130–31.), Thomas Nagel has an interesting discussion of these issues in his essay "Death" (in *Mortal Questions* [Cambridge University Press, 1979], pp. 1–10).

that even if my worries can be allayed, SDFT probably will not support the Slogan or the way it has been invoked.

Some profess difficulty in understanding how something could be *intrinsically* good or bad without being good or bad *for* someone. Confronted with MST's shortcomings, they are driven to, and find comfort in, SDFT, according to which someone can be made worse off by the contravening of her desires even if she is never aware this has happened and it has *no* effect on the quality of her conscious states. For my own part, I confess the latter view seems no less mysterious than the former. Surely, in the clearest most straightforward sense, the person *herself* won't be harmed if, after she is dead, someone slanders her. *She* is no longer around *to be* harmed. Exactly where, when, and how is the damage done, such that *she* is now worse off than she was before?[31] The mystery is perhaps less gripping when the person is still alive, but it is not less puzzling.

Perhaps we are to understand such claims counterfactually. Slander is worse for someone if it is true that *had* she learned of it she would have been worse off. Yet how does the truth of that counterfactual actually *make* her worse off? If a tree had fallen on Sue, she would have been worse off, but that doesn't make her so.

A Subjective Desire Fulfillment Theorist might respond: "Granted, it may sound a *bit* odd to say someone can be harmed by events not affecting her conscious states. But this merely shows there is *some* force to MST. Having seen in section 9.7 that MST is implausible, the correct conclusion to draw is that there are *different* ways something can be worse for someone. And, on reflection, we see that something can be worse for someone by contravening her desires."

This may be the correct conclusion to draw from section 9.7, but it is neither obvious nor forced on us. Why not grant, with the Mental State Theorist, that something can only be worse *for* someone insofar as it adversely affects the quality of her conscious states, but reject the view that something can only be morally *bad* if it is bad *for* someone? Why shouldn't we say, for example, that contravening Sue's desires is bad, even if, because she is dead, it isn't worse *for her*? Notice, this would be consistent with holding that the action only is bad because Sue had the desires she did.

---

31. Note, I am not asking how death can be worse for someone than being alive, since once someone is dead there is no *someone* for whom the death is worse. Similarly, I am not suggesting that one cannot harm someone by killing him, since once he has been killed *he* is no longer around to be harmed by his death. You can harm someone by killing them, because you deprive him of a worthwhile life he would otherwise enjoy. The suggestion is that *once* someone is dead his life is *over*. It has already been *led*. You cannot continue to improve or worsen the quality of someone's life *after* he's led it. Consider this example. Suppose Bill kills John, thereby preventing him from enjoying a worldwide vacation he would otherwise have taken. Although it is true that at the time the trip would have taken place *John* is no longer around to benefit from the trip, by hypothesis this is only because Bill has killed John. Thus, among the respects in which Bill harmed John, by killing him, is by depriving him of his vacation. Bill is just as responsible for the loss to John of not being able to take the vacation as he would have been if he had merely embezzled funds from John's (uninsured) company so that John couldn't afford the vacation. Suppose, on the other hand, that John dies of a heart attack several months before taking his vacation. After he has died, Bill embezzles funds from John's company. In doing so, Bill does not harm John by depriving him of the vacation he would have taken had he not died of the heart attack. John is already dead. Bill's embezzlement harms John's estate, but it does not harm John.

Because all might agree that (1) acting against the desires of the dead isn't worse for them in terms of the quality of their conscious states, (2) nevertheless we ought not to so act, and (3) our so acting might only *be* bad because of desires they had while alive, it may seem inconsequential whether we describe such actions as bad because they contravene desires or because they are worse *for* people. There are two reasons to reject this. First, recognizing actions or outcomes as bad though not worse for anyone enables us to see the weakness of the Slogan and the arguments invoking it. Second, accepting the view that contravening desires is actually worse for people enables one to sidestep the explanation called for on the alternative view as to *why* contravening desires is bad.

When I slander the dead, is this bad because contravening desires is intrinsically bad,[32] slander is intrinsically bad, contravening desires and/or slandering fail(s) to show proper respect due someone with a moral personality, doing so fails to properly express my moral personality, or for some other reason? I don't know the full answer to this question, but it is not evident that the "badness" of my action lies in my harming the person whose desire I have contravened or, for that matter, in anyone's being left worse off than he or she was before.[33]

Another worry regarding SDFT is whether a plausible account can be given of *which* desires are to count as being better or worse for someone when they are fulfilled or contravened. Should it be her *actual* desires or her *conditional* ones— those she *would* have if she were unrushed, clear thinking, or fully informed. Similarly, should it be her *global* desires—that is, the deepest desires she has about her life as a whole—or her *local* desires, the particular desires one has at each moment of her life? Moreover, what are we to say when someone's desires are the result of "distorting" influences? What if the "distorting" influences are the factors usually involved in "normal" social conditioning? On SDFT it is crucial that one be able to identify those desires, the fulfillment of which promotes someone's good. But, on an SDFT—unlike an objective theory—it is unclear how one could plausibly do this.

The preceding worries mainly concern SDFT's plausibility as a theory about self-interest. Even if they could be allayed, SDFT seems implausible as a theory about outcomes.

According to SDFT as a theory about self-interest, someone will be worse off if, after she is dead, events conspire to undermine the ends she seriously pursued.[34] Yet throughout history people have earnestly promoted ends we do not share. Does this mean we *ought* to consider what would best promote the ends of, for example, the devoted Spartans, Monarchists, Jacobeans, and Pilgrims, in deciding what to do? This is what SDFT as a theory of outcomes would seem, implausibly, to require.

Interestingly, if we retain SDFT as a theory about self-interest yet reject is as a

32. Here, as elsewhere, I am assuming the person in question had a "self-regarding" desire that he not be slandered. The meaning and importance of this assumption will become clearer.

33. Here and later, see note 31 to clarify my meaning when I suggest that in some cases the "badness" of my action might not lie in "anyone's being left worse off than they were before." It is not an implication of my view that being killed cannot be bad for the person killed (since once someone has been killed *he* is no longer around to be worse off than he was before).

34. Assuming the person had a deep desire to make a lasting contribution toward those ends or ideals.

theory of outcomes, the result is a position almost the obverse of the Slogan. Instead of an outcome only being good or bad if it is good or bad *for* people, an outcome's being good or bad *for* people (such as the Spartans) need not be relevant to *its* being good or bad.

Many of my worries dovetail with standard worries about subjective theories. For example, many believe we need not count the desires of sadists and bigots—past or present—even if they are deeply committed to advancing pain or prejudice. Similarly, many think ignoring the starving's desire for food would be worse than ignoring an even stronger desire for money to build a telescope, even if the telescope builder were the one starving and would herself prefer money for the telescope to food.[35] It is unclear how SDFT can capture these sentiments without invoking an objective element. (Many of the worries raised here, and later, also apply to the Mental State Theory. Thus, many would claim that we need not count the pleasures of sadists and bigots, or that we need not give the telescope builder money rather than food even if she would get greater pleasure from the former than the latter.)

Notice, some would claim that there is no respect in which fulfilling the sadist's desires would even be better for the *sadist*. Others would claim that while it may be in the sadist's interest to fulfill her sadistic desires, there is no respect in which the fulfillment of such desires makes the *outcome* better. The former view challenges SDFT's plausibility as a theory about self-interest, the latter challenges its plausibility as a theory about outcomes. My own view is that the desires of sadists, bigots, telescope builders, and the like are more of a threat to SDFT's plausibility as a theory about outcomes than as a theory about self-interest. That is, I think it is harder to deny that there is any respect in which the fulfillment of the sadist's desires is better *for her*, than it is to deny that there is any respect in which it makes the *outcome* better.[36]

Perhaps most important, SDFT cannot accommodate many people's deepest views about the nature and foundations of moral value. This is not the place to rehash the arguments for or against objectivity in ethics. Suffice it to say, many would insist that if morality is not to be a vain and chimerical notion, it cannot be our desires for freedom, justice, or autonomy that *make* them good; otherwise if we came to desire slavery, injustice, and external controls, it would then be true that *those* were good.[37]

35.   This example is taken from Thomas Scanlon's "Preference and Urgency," *Journal of Philosophy* 72 (1975): 655–69.

36.   Of course, many in the history of philosophy would regard my remarks here as too weak. Some would claim that the fulfillment of the sadist's desires not only lacks positive value, it possesses negative value, or disvalue. Specifically, some would claim that the fulfillment of the sadist's desires is, in itself, worse for the sadist, and similarly, some would claim that, ceteris paribus, the fulfillment of the sadist's desires makes an outcome worse. Whatever the merits of these claims they are stronger than I need for my current purposes. Someone who accepts such claims will also accept my weaker claims.

37.   This parallels the view that many have toward the age-old Euthyphro question: Is what God commands good because He commands it, or does He command it because it is good? (See Plato's *Euthyphro*.) Many think that if morality is not to be a vain and chimerical notion, it must be the latter and not the former. Otherwise God could command us to murder and murder would then be good. Also, note that as suggested previously, many of this and the following paragraph's remarks would apply mutatis mutandis against the Mental State Theory, at least as a theory about outcomes.

This last point is worth special emphasis. People differ markedly in what they value. Where some would trade losses in freedom, autonomy, equality, or justice, for gains in the quality of their conscious states, others would not; where some would agree with Mill that the discontented genius is better off than the contented simpleton, others would not; where some would value freedom more than justice, others would not. On SDFT nothing precludes such disagreements. To the contrary, SDFT would support each side where disputes arose. But, of course, such disagreements *need* not occur. If, per chance, everyone preferred one alternative to another, then on SDFT as a theory about outcomes it would be *that* alternative which was better, *whichever* one it was. Indeed, an alternative that no one desired would be an alternative in no way good.

On an objective theory there is room for saying that everyone is mistaken in what they value. On a subjective theory, where what makes something good is that people desire it,[38] such a claim seems indefensible. The upshot of this is important, though not surprising. SDFT has room for whatever ideals people care about—for any desires people have based on their ideals. Yet, as a subjective theory, it leaves no room for the objectivity or intrinsic value of *any* ideal. Thus, even if SDFT supported the Slogan, one could not appeal to it to undermine the intrinsic value of certain ideals, without committing oneself to the ultimate subjectivity of *all* our ideals.

Of course, one might claim that an unrushed, clear thinking, fully informed person *must* rationally prefer some of the positions noted. But first, unless the good is objective there seems little to recommend this. In fact, if anything, it seems these issues are ones about which there *is* room for rational disagreement even though, on an objective theory, there may be one "best" answer. Second, in the absence of independent arguments for the rationality of certain positions, such a claim will be of no help in adjudicating between rival positions, as everyone can avail themselves of the claim that *their* positions would be preferred by unrushed, clear thinking, fully informed people (like themselves!). And third, once such independent arguments have been presented I suspect the boundary into objectivity will have been crossed and SDFT will have been left behind.

So far, I have merely raised serious questions about SDFT, both as a theory about self-interest and as one about outcomes. Still, I hope to have said enough to remind the reader that SDFT is hardly self-evident. It follows that even *if* SDFT supported the Slogan—a big "if"—this would not license the rhetorical appeals to the Slogan that abound in philosophy and economics. At best the Slogan would remain controversial, awaiting the resolution of the problems facing SDFT, or still another argument, independent of both MST and SDFT, which has yet to be given.

One question about which there is much dispute is whether SDFT should be *Restricted*—only attaching weight to the fulfillment of an agent's self-regarding desires, her desires about how *she* fares and how *her* life progresses; or *Unrestricted*—also attaching weight to an agent's other-regarding desires, her desires about how *others* fare and how *their* lives progress, as well as any desires she may have about the world

38. I use this as shorthand for the more cumbersome: "what makes something good is that it figures in the fulfillment of someone's desires."

per se.[39] Now in general any desire intimately connected with one's deepest projects and commitments will count as self-regarding in the relevant sense. Still, whether a particular desire is self-regarding is not simply a matter of the desire's strength. People can have strong desires about others (for example, that their children fare well) or weak desires about themselves (for example, that their meal be tasty).

The dispute between Restricted and Unrestricted SDFT's deserves separate attention for two reasons. First, its root may partly lie in a failure to distinguish between a theory's plausibility as a theory about self-interest or outcomes, and its plausibility as a full theory of the good. Second, reflection on the dispute suggests that, even setting aside its controversial nature, SDFT does not support the Slogan.

Consider two cases. Case I is put by Derek Parfit in *Reasons and Persons*. He writes:

> Suppose that I meet a stranger who has what is believed to be a fatal disease. My sympathy is aroused, and I strongly want this stranger to be cured. Much later, when I have forgotten our meeting, the stranger is cured. On the Unrestricted Desire-Fulfillment Theory, this event is good for me and makes my life go better. This is not plausible. We should reject this theory. (p. 494)

Case II may be put as follows.

> Suppose Jean has a strong other-regarding desire that certain graves be well tended. And suppose Liz could, with equal ease, fulfill either this strong desire or Jean's much weaker self-regarding desire for some suntan oil. Assuming Liz had no duty to do the latter, most would agree that *if* she were going to fulfill one of the desires, it would be better to fulfill the strong one.

Reflecting on case I, many are drawn to the conclusion that a Restricted SDFT is more plausible than an Unrestricted one. Reflecting on case II, many are drawn to the opposite conclusion. There is an element of truth to both positions, but its exact nature is easily (and too often) overlooked.

Case I illustrates that an Unrestricted SDFT is implausible as a theory about self-interest.[40] Case II illustrates that a Restricted SDFT is implausible as a theory about outcomes. Together, then, cases I and II suggest that neither a Restricted nor an Unrestricted SDFT is plausible as a *full* theory of the good. But this does not show that each should be rejected out of hand. It remains possible that a Restricted SDFT is plausible as a theory about self-interest, an Unrestricted SDFT is plausible as a theory about outcomes, and neither is more plausible than the other *simpliciter*.

An Unrestricted SDFT will count certain things as good or bad that we do not think are good or bad *for* anyone. This shows we must either reject the Unrestricted SDFT, even as a theory about outcomes, or reject the Slogan. Similarly, a Restricted SDFT fails to count as good for people certain factors we regard as good. This

---

39. The desire that the moon be made of green cheese is "other-regarding" in the sense it is being used here as is the desire that one's children fare well.

40. Parfit is clear about this. He does not claim for his example more than it shows. Others, I suspect, have been less careful in their thinking.

shows we must either reject the Restricted SDFT, even as a theory about self-interest, or reject the Slogan. Thus, once one gets clear about the strengths and weaknesses of the two views, one sees that neither a Restricted nor Unrestricted SDFT will plausibly support the Slogan.[41]

I have argued that SDFT is at best controversial. I have also argued that neither a Restricted nor Unrestricted SDFT will support the Slogan. Let me conclude this section by noting that even if some version of SDFT were both to ultimately prove true, and to support the Slogan, it would *not* support the numerous arguments implicitly invoking the Slogan.

On any plausible version of SDFT one will want to count as good *for* someone the satisfaction of those desires intimately connected with her deepest projects and commitments. Thus, recall how SDFT answers Nozick's challenge about the experience machine. On such a theory there would be good reason not to plug ourselves in because, as Nozick rightly observes, among our deepest desires are the desires to "do certain things . . . to *be* a certain way . . . and to live (an active verb) ourselves, in contact with reality." Well similarly, on SDFT there would be good reason to strive for freedom, justice, autonomy, and so on because those *too* count among (some) people's deepest desires.

Consider again Nozick's Wilt Chamberlain example. Although on SDFT it might be true that Chamberlain's receiving a million dollars could not be bad if there was no one for whom it was worse, the "if" clause would not be fulfilled. As long as there are (or have been) people for whom the advance of equality is among their deepest projects and commitments, there *will be* someone for whom the situation in question is worse in terms of the contravening of their relevant desires.[42]

41.   The argument regarding the Restricted SDFT might be put as follows. Suppose one accepts the view that a Restricted SDFT is plausible as a theory about self-interest, but believes, in case II, that Liz should fulfill Jean's other-regarding desire about the graves rather than her self-regarding desire about the suntan oil. One should then reject the Slogan, for while tending the graves would be better than getting the lotion there may be *no one* for whom it *is* better and, indeed, someone for whom it is worse—namely, Jean, whose self-regarding desire for the suntan oil goes unfulfilled. (For the sake of this example I am assuming that the people in the graves had no desires one way or the other about the tending of their graves. In other words, I take it that Liz might base her actions solely on the nature of Jean's desires without needing to appeal to the claim that tending the graves is really better *for* the people in the graves.)

This point is generalizable. Although a Restricted SDFT is more plausible than an Unrestricted one as a theory about self-interest, there are cases where we think the right way of respecting someone, or acting on her behalf, would be to do what she would most want us to do rather than what would be best *for her*. Often, this involves giving weight to some of her strong unrestricted desires (even in cases where she would never learn of our action). Thus, on a Restricted SDFT an element enters into our assessment of alternatives beyond what is best *for* the particular people in those alternatives. Hence, a Restricted SDFT will not support the Slogan.

I leave to the interested reader the construction of the analogous argument regarding the Unrestricted SDFT.

42.   The crucial point here is the one noted previously, that on any plausible version of SDFT one will want to count as good for someone the satisfaction of those desires intimately connected with her deepest projects and commitments. One might try to deny this, but I do not see how to distinguish in a non-ad hoc and non-question-begging way between, say, the deep projects and commitments of one who cares about advancing equality or justice and those of one committed to advancing science or writing a masterpiece to be read and admired for generations to come.

Hence, on SDFT, the Slogan would not support the kind of position Nozick has put forward. Similar remarks would apply to each of the arguments noted earlier that implicitly invoke the Slogan. One must look elsewhere for a position supporting both the Slogan and arguments invoking it.

9.9 The Objective List Theory

Let us next consider the Objective List Theory *(OLT)*. As a theory about self-interest, OLT would hold that some things are good or bad *for* people independent of the quality of their conscious states or the fulfillment of their desires. Similarly, as a theory about outcomes, OLT would hold that some things are intrinsically good or bad—that is, make an outcome good or bad—independent of the quality of people's conscious states or the fulfillment of people's desires. Since I think OLT is most compelling as a theory about outcomes, and since many of my considerations would apply, mutatis mutandis, to OLT as a theory about self-interest, I shall mainly address OLT as a theory about outcomes. However, during the course of my discussion, I shall also comment on OLT's implications as a theory about self-interest.

As a theory about outcomes, OLT can avoid most problems facing MST and SDFT while capturing much of their appeal. OLT can count as objectively good most of the pleasures MST counts, but it needn't count *all* pleasures as such. Thus, for example, it can avoid the unpalatable view that even the sadist's pleasures make an outcome better. Similarly, in ranking outcomes OLT can count as good the fulfillment of desires plausibly counted as such by SDFT, yet disregard the desires of sadists and bigots, discount the desires of past generations that are not independently binding, and accord weight to some, but not necessarily all, unrestricted desires.[43]

Most important, OLT reflects (or would if it could be adequately worked out) the view of moral values that many think must be correct if morality is not to be a vain and chimerical notion. After all, as noted earlier, many believe that unlike most other factors, the goodness of the moral ideals cannot be based on people's desires or the quality of their conscious states.

There are, then, powerful attractions to OLT as a theory about outcomes. But OLT also has problems—including the profoundly deep one of determining the *correct* Objective List. Rather than minimize this problem, I believe it is partly because well-meaning, conscientious, and seemingly rational people differ markedly on this issue that rhetorical appeals to the Slogan should be rejected. This will be developed further, but first let me suggest that once one moves to OLT there seems to be little, if any, reason to be wedded to the Slogan.

Once we recognize that some things are intrinsically valuable independent of people's desires or conscious states, it seems an open question what the full

---

43. Similarly, as a theory about self-interest, OLT could count as good for people any of the conscious states or fulfilled desires plausibly regarded as such by the Mental State or Subjective Desire Fulfillment Theories, but could regard some alternatives as better or worse for people independently of the quality of their conscious states or the fulfillment of their desires.

range of objective values would involve regarding their nature, content, or relation to sentient beings. Although presumably there will be some essential connection between our nature and the boundaries of moral value, why must it be one of *benefit*, for either us or others? Why *can't* the boundaries of the objectively good extend beyond what is good *for* someone—perhaps focusing on our capacity to *lead* a *morally* good life, as well as on our capacity to *have* a *prudentially* good life?

To be sure, an Objective List for outcomes would include many factors regarded as good on our theory about self-interest. For example, if my helping you gives me pleasure, or satisfies one of my desires, my doing so will count as good for me, and in this case the fact that it is good for me may count, on OLT, as a good feature of the outcome. Still, there seems to be plenty of room for our Objective List about outcomes to include some factors, like certain moral ideals, which are not necessarily good *for* anyone.

Consider a typical list of ideals some have thought objectively valuable: utility, autonomy, freedom, rights, virtue, duty, equality, justice. Cases can be constructed for each of these ideals where violation of the ideal would not be worse for anyone in terms of the fulfillment of their desires or the quality of their conscious states. Given this, how should one respond?

One might insist that in such cases there *is* no respect in which the frustration of the ideal is bad. This supports the Slogan, but in essence requires abandoning OLT. In particular, it requires leaving *every* moral ideal off the Objective List for outcomes. Few would accept this response. Certainly most who have invoked the Slogan have not, and would not, accept it as undermining the objectivity of virtually all moral ideals.

Alternatively, one might argue that some ideals are good *for* people even when they do not promote higher quality conscious states or greater desire fulfillment. For example, it might be urged that freedom and autonomy are objectively good *for* people in the sense imagined. This would involve adopting an Objective List Theory about self-interest that would enable one to retain the Slogan without rejecting the objectivity of *all* our ideals.

I am dubious of this position. I find it at least as plausible to claim that freedom and autonomy are objectively good beyond the respects in which they benefit people as to claim that they are good *for* someone even if she doesn't desire them and they are worse for the quality of her conscious states. Still, even granting the position in question, at most it shows that there is *some* reason—and not the best, I think—to include such ideals on our Objective List for outcomes. It assuredly does *not* show that the Slogan should be retained, and that ideals lacking this feature must, perforce, be left off. Moreover, once one grants that some ideals may appear on our correct Objective List for self-interest, even though they do not necessarily promote higher-quality conscious states or greater desire fulfillment, what is to prevent someone from claiming about any plausible ideal that it, too, belongs on our correct Objective List for self-interest?

Consider again our earlier example about the saints and sinners. Even if we don't believe with Kant and others that A, the situation where everyone "gets what they deserve," is better all things considered than B, the situation where the evilest mass murderers fare better than the most benign saints, is there *nothing* morally bad about the latter situation? *No* respect in which B is worse than A?

Or consider two societies, C and D. Society C is composed of equally deserving members where all are treated fairly and equally. Society D is composed of equally deserving members where most are treated as well as the people in C, but a few enjoy special rights and privileges as part of a hereditary aristocracy.[44] I, for one, am inclined to think C would be better than D all things considered. But even if this is too strong, is there *no* respect in which D is worse than C? Is there *nothing* morally bad about some equally deserving people being treated worse than others?[45]

If one believes there is *some* respect in which B is worse than A, or D is worse than C, even if there is no one for whom they are worse in terms of the quality of their conscious states or desire fulfillment, then one is faced with two alternatives. One can claim that justice and equality both belong on our Objective List about self-interest or that both belong on our Objective List about outcomes. Let me briefly comment on each of these positions.

Some people might argue that there are always some people for whom injustice and inequality are bad, namely the "victims" of injustice or inequality. That is, one might argue that injustice and inequality are always bad for those people who have a legitimate complaint regarding injustice or inequality, and this is so even if the injustice or inequality does not adversely affect the quality of their conscious states or desire fulfillment. So, for example, some people would claim that B's injustice *is* bad for the saints, and similarly that D's inequality *is* bad for those who do not enjoy the special rights and privileges of the hereditary aristocracy.[46] I do not myself find these claims particularly plausible.[47] But once one has moved to an

---

44. This need not cause envy or resentment among the others. I am assuming this to be the case in my example. The people may simply be indifferent to the practice or, as with many in England or Sweden, they may rather fancy it.

45. These remarks parallel Thomas Scanlon's in "Nozick on Rights, Liberty, and Property." He writes:

> If the evil of being relatively disadvantaged justifies eliminating inequalities by redistribution . . . . it may be asked whether it does not provide an equally strong reason for simply worsening the position of the better off when redistribution is not possible. This may sound irrational, but in the case of many social inequalities, for example, distinctions of rank or social caste, egalitarian demands for the elimination of non-redistributable advantages are not implausible. In other cases, where we think that non-redistributable advantages should not be eliminated, this is not because these advantages are consistent with pure egalitarianism, but because we temper the demands of equality with other considerations. Equality is not our only concern. (pp. 9–10)

46. John Broome has suggested both of these claims to me in correspondence, and defends the latter claim for certain versions of inequality in *Weighing Goods* (Basil Blackwell, 1991); see especially chaps. 8 and 9.

47. Consider, for example, a variation of my saints and sinners case, where there are no saints, only sinners. In A the sinners get what they deserve according to their life lived on earth. In B the sinners fare even better than they would have deserved to had they been saints. Kant would claim that B was worse than A all things considered. Ross, among others, would at least agree with Kant that there was one important respect—regarding justice—in which B was worse than A. Here one cannot claim that B's injustice is bad for the saints. There aren't any saints, or anyone else for that matter. Hence, if there must be someone for whom B's injustice is bad, it must be bad for the sinners themselves. I, myself, find this hard to accept. I think B's injustice is bad, but not because there is any respect in which it is bad *for the*

Objective List Theory about self-interest, it is unclear on what basis such claims could be ruled out.

Importantly, if one adopts an Objective List Theory about self-interest and includes on it ideals such as justice and equality, the Slogan may no longer seem implausible. Specifically, with a broad enough Objective List Theory, it may well be that any case in which one outcome is better or worse than another in any respect will also be a case in which there is someone for whom that outcome is better or worse in some respect. But such a move will save the Slogan only by robbing it of its teeth. In particular, if it is an open question what factors or ideals will appear on the correct Objective List about self-interest—as it surely must be, given the present state of argument about such issues—one cannot appeal to the Slogan to undermine any particular factors or ideals. After all, to do so would simply beg the question against whether the factors or ideals in question belong on the correct Objective List Theory about self-interest. Thus, even if the Slogan could be defended given a sufficiently broad Objective List Theory about self-interest, it would not yet serve any of the particular conclusions for which it has been invoked.

On the other hand, suppose one believes there is *some* respect in which B is worse than A, or D is worse than C, yet resists the claim that justice and equality belong on our Objective List about self-interest. It remains open for one to claim that justice and equality belong on our Objective List about outcomes, even though there is no intimate connection between the value of these ideals and their being good *for* people. To be sure, claiming this will require one to reject the Slogan. But why should this worry an advocate of the Objective List Theory about outcomes? How *could* one situation be worse than another if there is *no one* for whom it *is* worse? To the advocate of OLT, it could be worse if it is worse with respect to justice or equality.

Of course, it is one thing to believe the correct Objective List for outcomes will include ideals like justice and equality. It is quite another to *prove* this must be so. But in this respect ideals like justice and equality fare no worse than any other ideal. For example, that utility is always good *for* people, and hence would appear on the correct Objective List for self-interest, is certainly no *proof* that it must appear on the Objective List for outcomes. Indeed, this might be disputed by those mainly concerned with proportional justice.

Undoubtedly, then, it will be far from easy to construct and justify the correct Objective List for outcomes. But if this *can* be done, I suspect many ideals on the List will be there for Kantian reasons, because they express respect for moral

---

sinners—that is, not in their self-interest—to spend eternity at a saintly level, rather than at their vastly lower deserved level.

Hegel would disagree. He believes that by being punished the criminal is honored as a rational being and that the guilty have a *right* to be punished. Thus it seems that for Hegel punishment is good for the wicked. (See, for example, section 100 of *The Philosophy of Right* [1821].) Contrary to Hegel, I believe the right to be punished is one that clear thinking, rational, criminals could, and would, gladly, and without any reservations, forgo. Obviously, this is because I do not share Hegel's view about the nature of rational beings. (I am grateful to Derek Parfit for this variation of my saints and sinners example, which he discusses in chapter 3 of his manuscript "On Giving Priority.")

agents, whether ourselves or others, or perhaps for the moral law itself.[48] (To be indifferent between the sinners faring better than the saints and the saints faring better than the sinners is, in a deep and fundamental way, to fail to express a preference for good over evil.) Such Kantian notions are, of course, extremely elusive. All the more reason careful reflection and argument are needed in this area.

These remarks bear on my earlier suggestion that even if freedom and autonomy are, in a sense, objectively good for people, this is probably *not* the best reason for including them on the Objective List for outcomes. Several attempts have been made recently to argue for the objective value of freedom, autonomy, or rights.[49] It is telling that *none* of these attempts appeals to the supposed fact that these ideals are objectively good *for* people. Instead, the arguments have been couched almost exclusively in Kantian terms—of expressing respect for moral agents, or of treating people as ends in themselves. But then, if these are appropriate reasons for including an ideal on the Objective List for outcomes, it seems they might also warrant the inclusion of ideals like duty, justice, or equality, independent of the extent to which such ideals have the added feature of being objectively good *for* people.

It seems, then, the correct Objective List for outcomes (if there is one) may include ideals not justified by their being good *for* people. Correspondingly, it seems that like MST and SDFT, OLT will not support the Slogan.

Of course, as implied, one could always retain the Slogan by claiming that failure to show proper respect for moral agents or the moral law *is* bad *for* some-one—for example, the person to whom the respect is due or the agent herself whose wrongful action fails to respect her own worth as a moral agent. However, I believe this confuses issues, blurring an important distinction between harming someone and failing to respect someone. It also suggests that in acting wrongly we invariably harm ourselves,[50] which seems too easy a route to a conclusion so many great philosophers have tried, without success, at which to arrive. Still, as noted, even if we set these worries aside, this move saves the Slogan only by robbing it of its teeth. For the advocate of any plausible ideal could make such a move—that is,

---

48. I believe that on most plausible theories of self-interest to express respect for moral agents or the moral law in a Kantian sense will not *necessarily* be good *for* anyone (though it usually will). I briefly discuss the contrary view later.

49. See, for example, the writings of Nozick, *Anarchy, State, and Utopia*; Ronald Dworkin, *Taking Rights Seriously* (Harvard University Press, 1978); Charles Fried, *Right and Wrong* (Harvard University Press, 1978); and Alan Donagan, *The Theory of Morality* (University of Chicago Press, 1977).

50. Strictly speaking, this would only follow if failing to respect others, or the moral law, always involved failing to respect ourselves. But I think this is precisely what Kant and his followers would want to say. On a deontological, or agent-relative view, the focus is always on the agent, on what *I do*, rather than on the outcome, or what happens. For Kant, when I fail to respect others, this is wrong not because of the bad effects this has for them, but because I have failed to act in accordance with a good will, which means I have failed to act in accordance with the moral law that I prescribe to myself. Correspondingly, the wrongness of my action will be intimately bound up with my failing to respect my moral personality as a free and autonomous member of the realm of ends. On the view under discussion this would necessarily have to be regarded as being worse for me. (I take it a similar claim would need to be made about virtue theories. According to virtue theorists we are blameworthy whenever we evidence a bad character by [voluntarily] failing to act virtuously. Presumably, all such actions would have to be regarded as harmful to the agent. This is a conclusion Aristotle would embrace, but one that cannot simply be asserted.)

claim that there would always be *someone* for whom the violation of her ideal would be worse (the violator, if no one else). Thus, the Slogan could not be used to support any of the particular conclusions for which it has been invoked. This is, I think, the right conclusion, but not the most plausible way of arriving at it.

I have not argued that any particular ideals *must* appear on the correct Objective List for outcomes. (Though, admittedly, I would be surprised if ideals like justice and equality, which many have thought lie at the core of morality, were not to appear.) Rather, I have tried to show that, once one moves in the direction of an Objective List Theory, it becomes an open question which ideals really belong on such a list and why.

That there is substantial disagreement about the correct Objective List for outcomes, or even self-interest, underscores the importance of careful thought and argument about the nature of these Lists. Of course, one might simply *insist* that the Slogan *must* be right, that ideals like justice and equality are not intrinsically good *for* anyone, and hence that ideals like justice and equality must be rejected. But to do so would probably be wrong and certainly be unwarranted. Such an assertion begs the questions that most need addressing. Instead of advancing the level of moral argument it cuts off debate where it needs to begin. In sum, until significant reasoning about the nature and foundation of the correct Objective Lists establishes otherwise, arguments based on rhetorical appeal to the Slogan should be rejected.

9.10 Summary and Discussion

The Slogan has been appealed to without argument by philosophers and economists across the ideological spectrum. In this chapter, I have shown that despite, or perhaps because of, its widespread and uncritical acceptance, there is no single position represented by the claim that one situation *cannot* be worse than another if there is *no one* for whom it *is* worse. The most natural and straightforward interpretation of the Slogan asserts a significant but purely formal relationship between theories about self-interest and theories about outcomes. Thus, the substantive content of the Slogan will depend on these theories. But these are theories about which there is much disagreement. Correspondingly, many who *think* they agree in accepting the Slogan are in fact committing themselves to very different positions.

In this chapter, I have also assessed whether a Mental State Theory, a Subjective Desire Fulfillment Theory, or an Objective List Theory would plausibly support either the Slogan or the arguments invoking it. My arguments suggest, first, that none of these theories would justify rhetorical appeals to the Slogan; second, that the most plausible versions of these theories would probably not support the Slogan; and, third, even those versions of the theories that (might) support the Slogan would *not* support most of the particular arguments that have invoked the Slogan.

In sum, once one distinguishes between theories of the good pertaining to self-interest and theories of the good pertaining to outcomes, there is good reason to doubt the Slogan, and even better reason to reject the arguments rhetorically invoking it. Thus, in the absence of an argument for the Slogan yet to be given, one must seek other justification for the positions one finds plausible.

Sparked by the arguments of this chapter, several alternative principles have been offered as related to the Slogan.

P1:   If in situation Y there is no one who is worse off than he is in X, then in bringing about X, rather than Y, I have violated no one's rights.

P2:   Whether one situation is better or worse than another *for* someone is always relevant to whether that situation is better or worse.[51]

Several claims might be made regarding the relation between the Slogan and P1 or P2. It might be claimed that, despite my assertions to the contrary, few, if any, ever accepted the Slogan; what they accepted instead was P1 or P2. Alternatively, it might be claimed that P1 or P2 is what advocates of the Slogan understand it to mean, that is, that the correct interpretation of the Slogan just is P1 or P2. Finally, it might be claimed that while many in fact accepted the Slogan, what they *should* have accepted instead (and perhaps did accept as well) was P1 or P2.

For the purposes of this chapter let me simply state, without argument, my reaction to these claims. First, I deny the claim that few, if any, ever accepted the Slogan. Over the past years I have met many who think the Slogan expresses an important truth and who are loath to give it up, despite my arguments. Second, although there might be a connection for some between the Slogan and P1 or P2, I do not believe the Slogan is plausibly interpreted as P1 or P2. At the very least, the Slogan would be a *very* misleading way of expressing either P1 or P2. Third, to those who insist on interpreting the Slogan as P1 or P2, or who advocate P1 or P2 as preferable to the Slogan, I grant that P1 or P2 may be more plausible than (alternative interpretations of) the Slogan, but I point out that unless they are interpreted so as to be trivially true, and therefore uninteresting, neither P1 nor P2 justify rhetorical appeals to them.[52] Finally, and most important, P1 and P2 are much

---

51.   P1 was suggested by Bill Rowe, P2 by Thomas Hill, Sr.

52.   It may seem otherwise, particularly in the case of P2. But though I myself think P2 is probably true, its spirit is more controversial than first appears. Most who accept P2 believe utility is intrinsically good. Correspondingly, they use P2 to express their view that whatever *other* factors may *also* be relevant to a situation's being good, to the extent one situation is better than another for someone, it must be, to that extent, better. But I take it this is precisely what Kant, among others, would deny. (Recall Kant's claims that "the sight of a being adorned with no feature of a pure and good will, yet enjoying uninterrupted prosperity, can never give pleasure to a rational impartial spectator," and that the "good will seems to constitute the indispensable condition even of worthiness to be happy," from the first paragraph of the first section of the *Foundations of the Metaphysics of Morals*, trans. Lewis White Beck [Bobbs-Merrill, 1981], p. 9.) Thus, in the example of the saints and the sinners noted earlier, I think Kant would deny that the sinners faring well is in one respect good, though in another bad. Rather, I think Kant would insist that the situation in which the sinners fare better than the saints is *wholly and unequivocally* worse than the situation in which everybody receives what they deserve.

It is not only advocates of proportional justice who must deny the spirit of P2. Considering our obligations toward future generations, some believe that certain lives are so diseased or deprived that even if they are worth living, and so of value for the people whose lives they are, it would have been better in itself—even apart from their effects on others—if those lives had never been led. (See Gregory Kavka's "The Paradox of Future Individuals," *Philosophy and Public Affairs* 11 [1982]: 93–112.) Others believe that even if lives worth living are never intrinsically bad, many such lives are not intrinsically good—though they have subjective value for the possessors of such lives, they do not make the world better from the impersonal (objective) moral point of view. (See Parfit's

weaker than the interpretation of the Slogan I discussed, and whatever their ultimate plausibility, neither would support the particular conclusions for which the Slogan has been invoked.[53]

It is, I think, impressive testimony of the Slogan's seductive power that it seems to have tremendous force whenever it can be invoked to support one's position. Indeed, I suspect many who would be unmoved by the Slogan if it were employed against something they favor—perhaps justice, rights, or duty—nevertheless find it convincing when employed against something they reject, such as virtue, equality, or rule-utilitarianism.[54] Moreover, most who have read this chapter continue to assert that surely there must be some cases or some interpretation that makes invoking the Slogan appropriate. Therefore, let me close this section with two observations as to why people may have found the Slogan plausible. A third explanation for the Slogan's plausibility is discussed in the following section.

My first observation has already been touched on and can be dealt with briefly. It was an important step in moral philosophy when classical utilitarians emphasized the extent to which the value of things depended on their being good or bad *for* sentient beings. On reflection, it seems true of most everything that it only has the value it does because of the way it affects conscious states or the fulfillment of desires. Faced with this tremendous insight, it is easy to suppose that what is so of most things must be true of everything. Moreover, it may seem that only by accepting this view can one avoid the Pandora's box of intuitionism in ethics. It is only when one looks closely at the moral ideals and the different theories about self-interest and outcomes that one begins to doubt the legitimacy of this position and the range of its use.

Second, some of the Slogan's appeal may result from our drawing questionable conclusions from misleading cases. For example, all agree that putting out people's eyes would be wrong, even if that were the only way of achieving equality. Moreover, for most, this judgment is *so* firm, they might naturally conclude both that there is nothing to be said for the ideal of equality and that the truth of the Slogan accounts for this fact. But, natural or not, this conclusion is highly suspect.

In such examples our other ideals are either silent or line up squarely against equality. Our concerns about utility, perfectionism, humanitarianism, and rights combine to yield our strong unequivocal judgments. But these are *all-things-consid-*

"Future Generations," and part 4 of *Reasons and Persons*.) On reflection, I think advocates of both positions must reject P2.

53. In this respect, of course, they are no worse off than the interpretations I discussed. But neither are they better off. I suspect some people may have been partly attracted to the Slogan because they accepted both P1 *and*

P3: One situation cannot be worse than another if no one's rights would be violated in bringing the one situation about rather than the other.

However, P3 is not plausible. And in any event, insofar as P1 and P3 imply the Slogan, together they are subject to all the problems this chapter raises.

54. I confess, much to my chagrin, that only after working on this chapter did I realize that I had been implicitly invoking the Slogan against positions I rejected long after I had dismissed similar arguments made by others against equality. Of course, I did not then realize, as I now do, that an implicit appeal to the Slogan underlay both kinds of arguments. (My embarrassment is only slightly lessened by the fact that I suspect I have plenty of company in making this mistake.)

ered judgments; perfectly compatible with equality being one ideal, among others, deserving of value. And, in cases where our other ideals diverge, equality often seems to rightly make a difference.

9.11 Reconsidering the Slogan's Appeal: Individualism, Holism, and Egalitarianism

Is there *nothing* further to be said in support of the Slogan? I am unsure about this, but there *may* be a kernel of truth the Slogan awkwardly expresses which *is* both deep and important. However, this fact, if it is one, does not undermine my central claims.

The final reason I want to suggest for the Slogan's attraction is that some may be associating the Slogan with the *individualistic* approach to ethics, according to which individuals are the proper objects of moral concern, *not* groups or societies. On this view societies are merely human institutions. These institutions promote their members' interests, to a more or less satisfactory degree, and when they fail to do so it is up to their members to modify them, or perhaps to create entirely new societies or institutions. Thus, on the individualistic approach, unlike the *global* or *holistic* approach, it doesn't matter what happens to a group or society *per se*—whether it is left intact, slightly modified, or entirely transformed; what matters is what happens to the present and future individuals who are or would be affected by that group or society.

One prominent position that is individualistic in the sense described is Kantianism. Kant distinguished between two kinds of objects in the universe, "persons" and "things." "Persons" were rational individuals who possessed freedom, autonomy, and dignity. "Things" were objects lacking these characteristics. For Kant, "persons" were always to be treated as ends in themselves, and never merely as a means. "Things," on the other hand, could be used as we saw fit.

Clearly, in Kantian terminology, society would be a "thing" rather than a "person." *Society* isn't a rational individual. *It* doesn't have freedom, autonomy, and dignity in Kant's sense of those words. It is merely an artificial entity people construct to promote their ends. Thus, according to Kant, in deciding what we ought to do it is sufficient to insure our action's rightness that we treat each person as an end in himself; we don't have to further consider whether our action is good for *society*. After all, for Kant, *society* doesn't have to be treated as an end in itself, people in society have to be so treated.

I have a different view than Kant about the scope of morality—about *which* individuals merit moral consideration.[55] Still, as we have seen, I suspect that global or holistic approaches are usually mistaken in moral philosophy, whether embodied in a principle like Rawls's maximin principle, with its focus on the worst-off *group*, or in a principle like average utilitarianism, with its focus on society's average level. I think, then, there is much to be said for individualism in ethics. But if this is right, it may help to explain the Slogan's appeal and, more particularly, why some have thought the Slogan poses a special threat to egalitarianism.

---

55. Although Kant *may* be right that an individual's capacity to act freely and autonomously is required for moral *agency*, I believe, with the utilitarians, that an individual's capacity to feel pleasure or pain is sufficient to merit moral consideration.

Up to now, I think most people have thought about inequality holistically. It was thought the egalitarian arrived at his judgments by focusing on societies as a whole, and the patterns of distribution within them. Correspondingly, it was thought the egalitarian's judgments were fundamentally judgments about how *societies* fared regarding inequality, as if inequality was bad because it was bad for a *society* to be unequal. On the holistic approach, then, the egalitarian seems to be in a position analogous to that of someone who cares about what happens to *France*, over and above the extent to which sentient beings are affected by events involving France. This is because, on the holistic approach, the egalitarian's concern seems to extend *beyond* his concern for the individuals *in* society, to the society itself.

Naturally, the individualistic approach opposes such a view, and the Slogan can be used to express this opposition. Thus, the rhetorical question, How *could* one situation be worse than another if there is *no one* for whom it *is* worse? can be taken to express the individualist's position that *societies* are not the proper objects of moral concern—people *in* societies are.

I believe, then, that insofar as it is taken to express the individualistic approach, the Slogan does challenge views like average utilitarianism and *holistic* egalitarianism. I agree, therefore, that the Slogan presents a serious challenge to egalitarianism as it has normally been thought of. Clearly, however, even if the holistic egalitarian is unable to defend his position against individualism's force, this poses no threat to egalitarianism as it has been presented in this book. On my view egalitarianism is not holistic; it is individualistic. The egalitarian is not concerned with how *societies* fare relative to one another; he is concerned with how *individuals* fare relative to one another. Thus, on my view, the egalitarian cannot be accused of the mistake, if it is a mistake, of regarding *societies* as the proper objects of moral concern. Hence, one must look elsewhere for a criticism of egalitarianism.

More generally, I believe most ideals can be properly understood individualistically. So, for example, the utilitarian, the egalitarian, and the person who cares about proportional justice can all agree that sentient individuals are the proper objects of moral concern. Where they disagree is in their answer to the question, What is it *about* sentient individuals one should care about? Is it *only* their utility, or is it also their share in the distribution of goods, either relative to others or relative to what they deserve?

I conclude that, insofar as the Slogan is taken to express the individualistic approach, it *may* express (though no doubt misleadingly) an important truth about morality. So, in one respect, people's intuitive reactions to the Slogan may be justified after all. However, the truth the Slogan expresses is not uncontroversial. More important, it will not support the particular conclusions for which the Slogan has been invoked. Our main results stand.

9.12 Conclusion

Invoking the Slogan does serve one important function. It forces us to get clearer about the nature of, and relation between, theories of the good that are about self-interest, theories of the good that are about outcomes, and the full theory of the good. In particular, it forces those who would reject the Slogan to get clear about what they care about besides the quality of conscious states, or desire fulfillment, in order to give reasons as to *why* one situation is worse (or better) than another though there is no one for whom it is worse (or better). However, once they have done this, and their reasons have been given, the plausibility of those reasons must be assessed on their own merits, independently of the Slogan.[56] The mere fact that a position is incompatible with the Slogan is not *itself* a reason to reject that position.

Thus, I think the main argument of most antiegalitarians should be rejected, and hence that section 9.2's considerations do not force the egalitarian to a position like extended humanitarianism. As noted earlier, extended humanitarianism may be plausible in its own right, but if so, that only gives one reason to be an extended humanitarian *in addition* to an egalitarian. Of course, as indicated, nothing I have said represents a positive argument for why one *should* care about inequality. It is extremely difficult to *prove* to the nonegalitarian that it really *is* bad for someone to be worse off than another through no fault of his own. But, as observed earlier, in this respect the egalitarian has lots of company, for it is also difficult to *prove* that injustice, disutility, or lack of freedom is bad.

I, for one, believe that inequality is bad. But do I *really* think there is some respect in which a world where only some are blind is worse than one where all are? Yes. Does this mean I think it would be better if we blinded everybody? No. Equality is not all that matters.[57] Nor is equality the only ideal that would, if exclusively pursued, have terrible implications. The same is true of justice, freedom, utility, and virtually every other ideal. This is not a reflection of the implausibility of our ideals, it is a reflection of the fact that morality, like inequality, is extremely complex.

56. Unless, of course, the reason is holistic in nature, and the Slogan is being appealed to in virtue of its individualistic element. But even then one needs to *argue* the case against holism; one can't simply assume individualism is true and then beg the question against holism.

57. Scanlon makes a similar point in the passage cited previously (see note 45) from "Nozick on Rights, Liberty, and Property." But Scanlon is discussing social inequalities when he argues that in some cases "egalitarian demands for the elimination of non-redistributable advantages are not implausible . . . [because] equality is not our only concern" (pp. 9–10). Suffice it to say, I think Scanlon is right. But I think his remarks hold for natural inequalities as well.

10

Conclusion

Let me conclude this book by summarizing the first nine chapters; reconsidering the charge that the notion of inequality is inconsistent; discussing some possible practical implications; and commenting, a final time, on the plausibility of my individualistic approach to inequality.

10.1 Summary

Chapter 1 was mainly introductory. It provided an overview of the book and introduced a slew of preliminary comments. I acknowledged that in many cases my terminology, presuppositions, and methodology were controversial, but begged the reader's patience and indulgence. Moreover, I claimed that "since even mistaken views can be illuminating, there is reason to hope this book's approach will shed light on the nature of inequality even for those rejecting its central tenets." I trust I was not being unduly optimistic. Although this book is no doubt filled with questionable assumptions, shaky arguments, and controversial conclusions, I believe it raises and illuminates many issues about the notion of inequality.

Chapter 2 examined the question of how we judge one situation to be worse than another regarding inequality. I began by noting that our notion of inequality allows us to focus on particular individuals and make judgments about the extent to which those individuals have a complaint regarding inequality. I next showed that there is a division in our thinking regarding both the question of who has a complaint, and the question of how we determine the size of one's complaint. Specifically, I argued that one might plausibly maintain any of three views: the relative to the best-off person, the relative to the average, or the relative to all those better off view of complaints. I then considered various egalitarian judgments people make, together with judgments they might make about an artificially simple group of worlds—the Sequence. In doing this, I noted that there are three principles of equality—the additive, maximin, and weighted additive principles—each of which represents appealing intuitions that might plausibly combine with any of the three views of complaints to yield a judgment about how good a situation is regarding inequality. In addition, I illustrated that in accordance with certain other views, our egalitarian judgments would be based on how gratuitous the inequality appears to be, how much deviation there is from a state of absolute equality or, in the case of social inequality, society's principles and institutions responsible for inequality.

So by considering various judgments we make, together with others we would make, I showed that there are many different positions underlying and influencing our egalitarian judgments. I did not claim each of these positions is equally appealing, but I did maintain that each represents views not easily dismissed. Since these elements often conflict, I concluded that we may come to think that the notion of inequality is largely inconsistent and severely limited, or alternatively, that it is complex, multifaceted, and partially incomplete. I return to this issue in section 10.2.

Chapter 3 considered inequality in more complex situations. I began by presenting the results of an informal poll about how various situations compare regarding inequality. I noted a wide range of agreement in people's pretheoretical judgments regarding the situations and a striking correlation between the extent of agreement among respondents and the extent of agreement among chapter 2's aspects.

Our discussion confirmed inequality's complexity and illustrated that together chapter 2's aspects can accommodate and explain the pretheoretical judgments of most egalitarians across a large spectrum of cases. In addition, our discussion suggested one reason people may have failed to recognize inequality's complexity. This is because in comparing situations regarding inequality many have tended to focus on certain "paradigm" cases about which *each* of chapter 2's aspects agree. Since in such cases clear, firm, judgments were widely shared, it was easy to assume that inequality is a fairly simple notion and to fail to see that people may in fact have been responding to different features in assessing inequality.

I next considered how variations in the levels of homogeneous groups would affect inequality. We saw that here, too, chapter 2's aspects could account for people's pretheoretical judgments involving the raising or lowering of different groups. In addition, they could account for both our firm absolute judgments about such situations, such as that other things equal raising (or lowering) the level of the best- (or worst-) off group would clearly and unequivocally worsen inequality, and our firm relative judgments, such as that regarding inequality the worse off a group was the better (or worse) it would be to raise (or lower) that group.

Our discussion illustrated that aspects that disagree in their judgments of the Sequence might agree in other cases, and also that aspects that agree about the Sequence might disagree in other cases. In addition, our discussion showed the importance of not assessing an aspect's plausibility too quickly. As we saw, aspects that may seem most (or least) plausible in considering the Sequence may seem least (or most) plausible when considering other situations.

Another point our discussion implied is that while most people's pretheoretical egalitarian intuitions may be plausible, in the sense of being supported by various aspects of inequality, in many cases "discordant" intuitions will need revising once inequality's full scope and complexity are taken into account. Similarly, though in most cases our results confirm the "collective general sense," they do not simply rubber stamp the majority's view. To the contrary, our results suggest that in some cases even the pretheoretical judgments of the majority need revising.

I next considered how transfers affect inequality. I began by considering even transfers, and then addressed both efficient and inefficient transfers. We saw that in general egalitarians would want transfers to go from the "highest" to the "lowest" possible group and that chapter 2's aspects support this position. We also saw that chapter 2's aspects support the Pigou-Dalton condition (PD) in cases of the sort economists generally considered. However, we noted that PD's scope must be limited in ways having both theoretical and practical significance. Thus, whereas in accordance with PD it is true that any *even* transfer from worse- to better-off would worsen inequality, and from better- to worse-off would improve it (so long as the transfer merely served to reduce the gap between them), it is not true that *any* transfer from worse- to better-off would worsen inequality or from better- to worse-off would improve it. Certain efficient transfers from worse- to better-off would improve inequality, whereas certain inefficient transfers from better- to worse-off would worsen it.

In considering transfers we saw that there is no simple or general rule for whether a given transfer would improve inequality. Whether it does will depend on the levels of those involved, on the kind of transfer in question, and the extent to which the transfer raises and lowers those affected. Nevertheless, it appeared this book's theoretical considerations can plausibly account for both the much discussed cases of even transfers, and the less discussed but perhaps more common cases of efficient and inefficient transfers.

Chapter 4 considered two questions regarding the proper focus of egalitarian concern. I began by considering the average and proportional average principles of equality, both of which focus concern on reducing inequality between the average members of society's groups. I argued that both face profound difficulties, not the least being that each gives weight to small inequalities between groups while giving *no* weight to (even) large inequalities within groups. Our discussion reinforced one of the book's central tenets. Claims expressing concern about society's inequality, or about inequality between society's different groups, must ultimately be understood as expressing concern about the inequality between the society or groups' *members*. We have no special concern about society *per se*, or about the groups *themselves*, what we have is a concern for the *individuals* who compose society and its groups. Equality, like many other ideals, should be understood individualistically, not holistically.

I next addressed the plausibility of focusing on the very best-off person when measuring individual complaints, and considered whether the relative to the best-off person view of complaints (BOP) should be modified or rejected. Drawing on the results of chapters 2 and 3, I claimed BOP's spirit and underlying reasoning are important elements of inequality that must be accounted for, but acknowledged that BOP might need revising if it is not to seriously distort our judgment in cases where the best-off person's condition is anomalous. I considered several ways of revising BOP and argued against shifting our attention from the best-off person to either the average member or each of the members of the best-off group. I also suggested it would be mistaken simply to lessen BOP's weight when the best-off person's condition was anomalous. Instead, I suggested we may want to focus our attention mainly (though not wholly) on the best-off person whose condition was not "anomalous."

After considering BOP, I briefly discussed the maximin principle of equality (MPE). I noted one could not plausibly capture MPE's spirit and underlying reasoning either by focusing on the worst-off person or by adopting Rawls's solution of focusing on the "representative member of the worst-off group" (if that is understood as the average member of the worst-off group). Nor could one plausibly capture MPE along the lines of BOP. Rather, one needs an approach expressing our special concern for *each* of society's worst-off members, but in a way giving greatest weight to those faring poorest.

Chapter 5 considered various approaches to measuring inequality. I began by discussing the economists' statistical measures. I pointed out important similarities between these measures and chapter 2's theoretical considerations. In particular, I argued that the range gives expression to the positions underlying the relative to the best-off person view of complaints and the maximin principle of equality; the relative mean deviation gives expression to the positions underlying the relative to the average view of complaints and the additive principle of equality; the gini coefficient gives expression to the positions underlying the relative to all those better off view of complaints and the additive principle of equality; and the variance, the coefficient of variation, and the standard deviation of the logarithm each give expression to the relative to the average view of complaints and certain views corresponding to a weighted additive principle. More generally, I showed that between them the statistical measures reflect each of chapter 2's three ways of measuring individual complaints and each of the three principles of equality. Thus, I suggested, on the view that each way of measuring complaints might plausibly combine with each principle of equality, one might hold that between them the statistical measures *indirectly* support nine of chapter 2's aspects.

I noted, therefore, that the statistical measures represented a fine start toward elucidating inequality, but that unfortunately economists did not adequately pursue the source of their plausibility. Had they done so they might have been recognized that inequality is even *more* complex than had been realized, that some measures conflict at a very deep level—as the ultimate views underlying them seem fundamentally opposed—and that the statistical measures are best regarded as merely first approximations for capturing certain *aspects* of inequality.

I concluded my discussion of the statistical measures by observing that given the connection between the statistical measures and inequality's aspects, the fact that many economists responded to the statistical measures as they originally did lends further independent support to chapter 2's claims: we *do* have the egalitarian views I argued we have, they *are* plausible, and they *cannot* easily be dismissed.

I next considered Atkinson's measure, which seems to oppose this book's approach, since it inextricably links inequality to income, utility, and social welfare. I showed that Atkinson's measure has many features that make it attractive to economists, but argued that these features are not all desirable in a measure of inequality. Most important, I claimed that Atkinson's measure obscures what is distinctive about the egalitarian's concern. Specifically, I noted that while Atkinson's measure is *compatible* with egalitarianism, it is also compatible with nonegalitarian, and even antiegalitarian, positions. Nevertheless, I acknowledged that in general Atkinson's measure reflects many of the egalitarian's judgments, and I suggested that this is because in most cases Atkinson's measure reflects those intuitions underlying a relative to the average view of complaints and a weighted additive principle. Moreover, it does this in way that avoids some shortcomings of other approaches that also reflect the intuitions in question. Thus, I urged that Atkinson's measure, like the statistical measures, is best regarded not as a measure of the whole of inequality, but as a useful, though flawed, measure of one important aspect of inequality. I claimed, therefore, that Atkinson's measure does not pose a threat to this book's approach. To the contrary, I suggested that my approach helps illuminate both the strengths and weaknesses of Atkinson's measure, and is compatible with the former.

I then considered Amartya Sen's intersection approach, which compares worlds by taking an intersection of a selected subset of measures of inequality. I argued that an intersection approach is not the best way of capturing a complex and multifaceted notion. The intersection approach's main problem is that it does not allow trade-offs. It yields the judgment that A is better than B, if and only if A is better than B according to *each* of the selected measures. So, on the intersection approach there is no way of taking into account the number of, relative significance of, or degree of support provided by the aspects yielding different judgments. Thus, although an intersection approach's orderings may be uncontroversial (if its measures are selected carefully), they are likely to be extremely limited. In fact, the more complex and multifaceted a notion is, the more limited an intersection approach is likely to be as a measure of that notion.

I next proposed my own suggestion for how one might best proceed so as to capture (as) accurately (as possible) a complex and multifaceted notion like inequality. Bearing the intersection approach's shortcomings in mind, I suggested one should first try to get clear on what the notion's aspects are, next try to arrive at an accurate measure of each aspect, and then construct a measure of those measures so as to accord each aspect its "due weight." One point I emphasized is that according each aspect its "due weight" may require a complex, nonadditive, function whose weightings depend on the relative—and perhaps contextually determined—importance of each aspect in combination with the others. Specifically, I pointed out that my individualistic approach is not committed to the additive separability of inequality's aspects or, for that matter, of moral ideals. Thus I claimed that my approach is compatible with the fundamental hermeneutic and gestalt insight that the whole may be greater or less than the sum of its parts.

Chapter 6 considered whether inequality matters more in a poor society than a rich one. Though the answer to this has been a matter of some confusion, I suggested this is one of the few significant questions about inequality to which a (relatively) clear answer can be given: Yes. Specifically, I argued that in measuring inequality one cannot merely focus on the absolute size of the gaps between the better- and worse-off. One must also consider the relative position of the worse-off vis-à-vis the others in their world. When one does this, one sees that how bad a gap of n units is regarding inequality depends upon how well off the people are between whom that gap obtains: the worse off they are, the worse the inequality.[1]

In addition to my positive arguments supporting this position, I considered several arguments purporting to show that inequality matters less in a poor society than a rich one. I pointed out that despite their popularity, such arguments rest on a confusion of two separate questions: When is one situation worse than another regarding inequality? and When is one situation worse than another *all things considered*? Once one distinguishes between these questions it becomes evident that although such arguments *may* support the claim that only a relatively rich society can "afford the luxury" of worrying about inequality, they do not establish that inequality matters less in a poor society than a rich one. Instead, they merely remind us that inequality is not all that matters.

I next addressed how a measure of inequality should capture the view that inequality matters more at low levels than high ones. I considered four approaches. Ultimately, I argued that the most promising approach would measure the gaps between the better- and worse-off and weight the relevant numbers arrived by a certain amount, depending upon how well off the people were whose complaints were being measured. Such an approach would involve constructing and employing a scale of the sort shown in diagram 10.1, where the right-hand numbers represent people's levels and the left-hand numbers how much to weight each unit that someone at that level is worse off than another.

I claimed that such an approach plausibly captures the sensitivity we want, while avoiding the other approaches' shortcomings. More particularly, I noted that such an approach captures the view that inequality matters more at low levels than at high levels in a way that focuses on the levels of the individuals between whom inequality obtains, rather than society's average level; reflects the view that, ceteris paribus, an increase in the best-off person's level unequivocally worsens inequality; reflects the view that improving someone's position should lessen his complaint relative to those better off, not only because the gaps between them are smaller, but also because those gaps should count for less given his improved position; allows it to handle cases where people are near or below the zero level; and enables it to avoid giving too much weight to inequality at low levels relative to high levels, so as to reflect the fact that proportional increases in welfare worsen inequality.

While discussing the four approaches, I tried to clarify and resolve the debate between economists like Atkinson, who suggested that perhaps our inequality index I should increase with proportional increases, and hence that inequality matters more at high than at low levels, and those like Sen, who maintained that inequality matters less at high than at low levels, and hence that I should decrease with proportional increases. I suggested the dispute may have partly stemmed from an unfortunate terminological coincidence, which led both sides to assume that

---

1. At least this is so for most cases about which we are concerned. As noted, the question becomes more complicated in cases where the worse-off are *way* below the level at which life ceases to be worth living, and also in cases where even the better-off are below the zero level. My own view is that the generalization in question holds even for such cases. But I did not try to defend this claim, and some of chapter 6's arguments might have to be revised to accommodate it.

most well-off

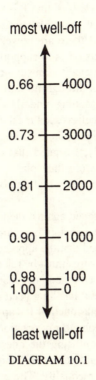

DIAGRAM 10.1

whether I should increase with proportional increases is ultimately the same issue as whether inequality matters more at high levels than low ones. These, I argued, are separate issues, and once that is kept clear, one sees that while Atkinson was right that I should increase with proportional increases, Sen was right that inequality matters less at high levels than low ones.

In addition, I pointed out that the first approach for capturing inequality's sensitivity—the one incorporated into most of the economists' measures of inequality—can be seen as attempting to capture inequality's sensitivity by focusing on the *society* in which inequality obtains, rather than on the *individuals* between whom inequality obtains. This, I argued, is mistaken or misleading in at least two respects. First, it seems to suggest, wrongly, that it makes sense to speak of a society as being *at* a given level of welfare. *Societies* aren't at given welfare levels; people in societies are. Second, it misconstrues the proper objects of our concern. The "badness" of inequality doesn't consist in *society* being in such a position, it consists in society's members being in such a position. They are the "victims" of inequality, not the artificial or abstract entity "society." My claim, then, was that ultimately our concern about inequality is not a concern about how societies fare relative to one another, but a concern about how the *individuals* in those societies fare relative to one another. I return to this claim in section 10.4.

Chapter 7 considered how variations in population size affect inequality. I began by considering the Standard View, P, according to which proportional size variations do not affect inequality. I acknowledged that P is very appealing and that a number of inequality's aspects support it. But I also showed that many of inequality's aspects oppose P and argued that there are powerful and important reasons not to revise or supplement those aspects so as to support P. My argument appealed to the fundamental intuition underlying egalitarianism—that it is bad, unfair or unjust, for some to be worse off than others through no fault of their own—as well as to the more specific intuitions and reasoning underlying those aspects opposing P. In addition, I suggested that if one believes, as most do, that in general numbers count for morality, one should also believe this regarding inequality, as similar considerations support both views. Finally, I argued that depending on one's view of the relation of moral ideals and the role they play in our all-things-considered judgments, one may have to accept the view that numbers count regarding inequality, if they count regarding utility.

In defending my position I argued against the plausibility of average views, and in particular argued that how bad a society is regarding inequality has *nothing* to do with its average level. This entailed that the approach to size variations incorporated into most of the economists' measures must be rejected. In addition, I urged that our notion of inequality is not so much essentially distributive as it is essentially comparative. This is significant, since it has long been assumed that inequality is essentially distributive, and since I think much of P's appeal is based on this assumption.

I next considered two objections to my position. I quickly rejected the first, the Shrinking World objection, as confusing the question of whether one situation is better than another all things considered, with the question of whether one situation is better than another regarding inequality. The second objection, that the cost of opposing P is the Repellant Conclusion (RC), required much more discussion. Ultimately, I agreed that the second objection is worrisome, but argued that one could respond to it in one of two ways. First, one might offer an explanation as to why RC *seems* so counterintuitive but in fact is acceptable. Alternatively, one might deny that opposing P entails RC by adopting a new way of thinking about moral ideals and their underlying aspects, which enables one to reject both P and RC.

Our discussion of the Repellant Conclusion raised deep questions about the nature and relation of moral ideals. In particular, I argued that the standard way of understanding the relation between moral ideals and the role they play in our all-things-considered judgments must be rejected whatever one's views about P and RC. As an alternative to the standard approach I proposed a gymnastics model for moral ideals—according to which there is an upper limit on how good a situation can be both with respect to any particular ideal and all things considered. I urged that the gymnastic model merits careful consideration, but acknowledged that it faces serious shortcomings, and that we may need another way of thinking about ideals.

Chapter 8 discussed whether the proper unit of egalitarian concern should be people's lives, taken as a whole, or selected portions of their lives. Following Dennis McKerlie I began by distinguishing between three possible views: *complete lives* egalitarianism, *simultaneous segments* egalitarianism, or *corresponding segments* egalitarianism. I argued that the most widely accepted view, complete lives egalitarianism, is deeply implausible in cases of what McKerlie calls "changing places egalitarianism"—cases in which there are gross and pervasive inequalities, but where the demographic composition of the better- and worse-off groups changes periodically so that each person, in turn, is both the beneficiary and victim of the inequalities.

I next showed that although simultaneous and corresponding segments egalitarianisms are more plausible than complete lives egalitarianism in cases of "changing places egalitarianism," the latter position is more plausible than the former two in other cases—for example, where the choice is between having the same or different people victimized by inequality over time. On both simultaneous and corresponding segments egalitarianism the nature of past inequalities between individuals is irrelevant to the nature of future inequalities between those individuals, but this seems implausible. This raised the obvious question of how an egalitarian *should* count past inequalities between contemporaries, to which I suggested there is no clear answer.

I next presented a test case that illustrated the difference between the simultaneous and corresponding segments views. I pointed out that one's reactions to the test case might reveal a great deal about which of the various views regarding the proper unit of egalitarian concern one found most plausible. The upshot of my remarks was to suggest that here, as elsewhere, several egalitarian views are possible, each of which seems plausible in some cases and implausible in others.

I concluded chapter 8 by pointing out that the considerations discussed have important practical implications regarding intergenerational inequality—both between overlapping (the young and the aged) generations, and nonoverlapping (past, present, and future) generations. I also observed that similar considerations would be relevant to other ideals besides inequality.

Chapter 9 argued against *the Slogan*, a position that I believe underlies the reasoning of most nonegalitarians. According to the Slogan, one situation *cannot* be worse (or better) than another if there is *no one* for whom it *is* worse (or better).

I introduced the Slogan via a discussion of *extended humanitarianism*, a view that wants each person to fare as well as possible, but gives special weight, or priority, to the worse-off. I argued that extended humanitarianism is completely implausible as a version of egalitarianism, but noted two examples that might seem to force an egalitarian toward a position like extended humanitarianism. I then pointed out that at the heart of the examples is the Slogan, a position with tremendous intuitive power.

I claimed that the Slogan enjoys widespread appeal, underlies numerous arguments in philosophy and economics, and is almost always invoked implicitly and rhetorically. Nevertheless, I contended that widespread agreement about the Slogan is more apparent than real, that substantive interpretations of the Slogan are neither obvious nor uncontroversial, and that the Slogan does not support most of the particular positions it has been thought to support.

In assessing the Slogan I distinguished between different theories of the good: specifically, between theories about *self-interest*, which tell us what is good or bad *for* someone; theories about *outcomes*, which tell us what makes an outcome good or bad; and *full* theories of the good, which will include everything that is relevant to an assessment of goodness. I next pointed out that the Slogan makes a claim about what is relevant to a situation's being good. In particular, it implies that one's theory of outcomes must be a direct function of one's theory about self-interest. I then argued at length that there is no reason to believe that the correct theory about outcomes is dependent on the correct theory about self-interest in the way the Slogan entails. Specifically, I argued that the Slogan is unlikely to be supported by any of the most plausible theories of the good—a Mental State Theory, a Subjective Desire Fulfillment Theory, or an Objective List Theory—and, more important, that even if some version of the theories did support the Slogan, it would *not* support most of the particular arguments for which the Slogan has been invoked.

In rejecting the Slogan I did not offer any positive arguments for why one *should* care about inequality, or any of the other positions against which the Slogan has been invoked. But I believe I undermined the view that lies at the heart of perhaps the most prevalent, and intuitively powerful, antiegalitarian arguments.

I concluded chapter 9 by noting that the Slogan *might* be used (albeit misleadingly) to express the individualistic view that individuals, not societies, are the proper objects of moral concern. And I acknowledged that so understood the Slogan may express a deep and important truth that challenges egalitarianism as it has normally been understood. But I observed that such a position does not threaten my view of egalitarianism.

10.2 Inequality: Complex or Inconsistent?

This book had raised many questions that, of necessity, have been left open. However, in this section I would like to return to an issue postponed from the end of chapter 2. The issue is whether it is defensible for the egalitarian to proceed as if inequality is complex and multifaceted. If not, then it may seem that much of my work, however interesting, is for naught.

So what should the egalitarian say to the nonegalitarian who might insist that many of inequality's so-called aspects are not merely *contingently* in conflict but *fundamentally incompatible*? Specifically, how might one respond to the claim that inequality is inconsistent and (hence?) incoherent, as it simply *cannot* be true *both* that everybody but the best-off person has a complaint *and* that only those below the average have a complaint, or that the size of someone's complaint should be measured by comparing her with the average *and* by comparing her with the best-off person *and* by comparing her with all those better off than she?

Perhaps the egalitarian's most natural and plausible response is simply to deny that inequality's aspects are *fundamentally* incompatible.[2] The egalitarian can claim that inequality's aspects represent *different*—but not *contrary*—positions, and in support of this she can point to cases where *all* the aspects would be in accord (see chapter 3). More generally, the egalitarian can reconcile apparently contradictory views regarding who has a complaint, and how one should measure complaints, by insisting that there are different *kinds* of egalitarian complaints. Thus, there is noth-

2. Shelly Kagan argued persuasively for this position in correspondence, and this paragraph and the following one are heavily indebted to his discussion.

ing inconsistent or incoherent about the view that there is *one* kind of egalitarian complaint that all but the best-off person have, and *another* kind that only those below the average have. Similarly, there is nothing inconsistent or incoherent about claiming that the size of *one* kind of complaint should be measured by comparing how someone fares relative to the average, the size of *another* kind of complaint should be measured by comparing how she fares relative to the best-off person, and the size of a *third* kind of complaint should be measured by comparing her to all those better off than she. Such a claim is merely another way of maintaining that there are different features of a situation that are legitimate cause for *genuine* egalitarian concern; that is, there are different sources of complaints—different ways in which people fare relative to others—that generate different reasons for reducing inequality in one way or another.

It would, of course, be inconsistent and incoherent for the egalitarian to hold that there is only one kind of egalitarian complaint and that it should be measured, say, by comparing how someone fares relative to the average, while at the same time holding that there is *another* kind of complaint as well, or that complaints should (also?) be measured some other (incompatible) way(s). But this needn't be the egalitarian's view. Her view may simply be that inequality's aspects represent different sources of egalitarian reasons, and hence different ways of reducing inequality, and while these may, and often do, conflict, they are not fundamentally incompatible.

The preceding considerations are powerful, and I believe they enable the egalitarian to avoid the charge of inconsistency. But I suspect some may find them unconvincing. Therefore, let me next consider three possible responses.

First, some nonegalitarians may challenge the claim that different features may be legitimate cause for egalitarian concern. They may deny that there are *any* genuinely egalitarian reasons for reducing inequality, much less that there are *many* such reasons corresponding to different kinds of egalitarian complaints. Whatever the ultimate merits of such a position—obviously I think it mistaken—it is irrelevant to our present concern. Such a view challenges the importance of inequality's aspects—by denying that they reflect anything of genuine moral significance—but it says nothing about their compatibility. The nonegalitarian view that inequality is an implausible, unimportant, or objectionable ideal does not entail that inequality is inconsistent or incoherent.

Second, some may hold that the egalitarian obtains consistency only by forsaking a unified notion of inequality in favor of a fragmented cluster of distinct notions. Instead of there being a *single* concept, *inequality*, there are really *different* concepts corresponding to different kinds of complaint or concern. Rather than misleadingly calling these different concepts *aspects* of inequality, we should at best regard them as different *senses* of "inequality" and refer to them accordingly, say, as inequality$_1$, inequality$_2$, inequality$_3$, and so on. Better yet, one might claim, we should junk the terminology of "inequality" (or, at most, retain it for *one* concept). Instead, each distinct concept should be given its own name and assessed in its own terms.

The foregoing raises interesting questions about the nature and criteria of multifaceted concepts. But at most it suggests that the notion of inequality may be ambiguous and misleading, it does not show it is inconsistent or incoherent. That is, whether we grant that inequality's "aspects" are best regarded as different *senses* of "inequality," or perhaps as distinct notions that should be given distinct names, is irrelevant to whether the positions in question are *compatible*. And that, after all, is our present concern.

Note, the egalitarian *could* accept the terminological points suggested already but deny that for reasons of consistency she has *forsaken* a unified notion of inequality in favor of a fragmented cluster of distinct notions. Instead, she might claim that *all along* she has had a set of compatible concerns that for various reasons have previously been grouped under the name "inequality" but which she now sees more accurately as a set of related but distinct notions.[3]

Naturally, I reject the second response. Though I have *some* sympathy for it, in the end I believe inequality *is* best regarded as a complex notion composed of many aspects rather than as an ambiguous name for a patchwork of distinct notions. Despite their differences, inequality's aspects express a common concern—about how people fare relative to others—in virtue of which it is appropriate to regard them as different aspects of one notion, inequality. Moreover, adopting the second response would have historical, cultural, practical, and stylistic disadvantages. In any event, I think the work of this book—in terms of identifying and elucidating the different elements underlying "inequality's aspects"—will enable us to assess the plausibility of the positions in question; what we *call* those positions is neither here nor there. But having said all that let me next suggest that the second response is terminological, and although there are many respects in which terminology matters, it does not matter for this book's substantive claims.

If we accepted the terminological view of the second response this book would require a new title, and a new term in virtually every sentence where "inequality" is used. This would be a great nuisance, but the content of my remarks would be unaffected. I have claimed there are many plausible views underlying and influencing the way situations are judged in terms of how people fare relative to others. Whether we call these views and the people they influence "aspects of inequality" and "egalitarians," or employ other names for the positions and people in question, does not affect the significance of my arguments and claims.

Let us next turn to the third response. The third response holds that while inequality's aspects *could* be compatible *if* one carefully interpreted their nature and scope, to do so would be artificial and ad hoc. On this view, the claim that inequality's aspects are compatible because they correspond to different *kinds* of concern amounts to little more than terminological chicanery; it implies that inequality's aspects really reflect *different* notions (whether we regard them as such or not), whereas in fact inequality's aspects have been offered, and are best understood, as genuine rivals for different ways of understanding the *same* notion, *inequality*.

I have serious doubts about the third response. It is little more than an assertion, and one might argue that it begs the question against the view it opposes. But suppose it could be defended. What would that imply about the nature of inequal-

---

3. Of course, were she to adopt such a position the "egalitarian" might also think it best to give herself a new, more appropriate, name.

ity? Would the nonegalitarian be vindicated in dismissing equality? Or could the egalitarian still advocate (some semblance of) her position?

Notice, even if one thought many of inequality's aspects were contradictory, one needn't reject *everything* about which the egalitarian cares. One could, for instance, always retain those elements one finds *most* compelling and reject the contradictory ones. But suppose this involved forsaking many of the egalitarian's concerns, as presumably it might if the third response were defensible. Would the egalitarian be forced to such a position, or could she still hang on to the "different aspects" view in the face of the third response? I find this a perplexing question, to which I offer the following tentative remarks.

Normally when we show someone that his position involves two contradictory elements, we expect him—not unreasonably I think—to give one up. Thus, on the third response the different aspects view would not be easy to defend. Nevertheless, I think there are some cases—probably more than most philosophers realize or care to admit—where it seems more plausible to (temporarily?) embrace a contradiction than any alternative that suggests itself.[4] This, I believe, would be one such case.

Let me mention two other cases that *may* fit this mold: one from ethics and one from the history of science. The first arises regarding the conflict between deontological and consequentialist theories. Most pluralists assume that deontological and consequentialist theories often conflict but are nonetheless compatible. Nevertheless, when one explores the foundations of such theories—for example, their competing views of the importance and nature of duty, the good, morality's scope, impartiality, autonomy, or maximization—one *may* come to the view that the two theories ultimately rest on fundamentally incompatible positions. Suppose one came to such a conclusion. I believe it would *still* be more plausible to maintain that each reflects significant aspects of morality than to give one or the other up. That is, I believe it would be more plausible to (continue to) allow each to play a role in our moral judgments than to only allow those judgments to be informed by one or the other.

The second case arose at the beginning of this century with Bohr's model of the atom. From the time of its initial publication Bohr's model was widely recognized to be internally inconsistent. Despite this Bohr's model prevailed as the reigning model of the atom for over a decade because of its successful predictions and its ability to explain certain phenomena better than any alternative model.[5] Eventually, of course, Bohr's model was replaced by the quantum mechanical one. However, it seems likely it was the greater predictive success and explanatory power of the quantum mechanical model, more than the inconsistency of Bohr's model, that led to the ascendancy of the former over the latter. Thus, in both ethics and science, it may seem appropriate to embrace a contradiction if that is necessary to explain or reflect our judgments or data.

Of course, it is one thing to accept *temporarily* an inconsistent theory, while we

---

4. I am reminded here of the remark often attributed to Benjamin Franklin, "Consistency is the hobgoblin of philosophers and people with little minds" (where I have often suspected that what was really *meant* was: consistency is the hobgoblin of philosophers—people with little minds!).

5. I am grateful to Richard Grandy for this example.

wait for an adequate consistent one to be developed; it is quite another to maintain that an inconsistent theory reflects the way things *really are*. My present remarks are only intended to suggest that although the different aspects view may be somewhat unsettling, until a more adequate alternative arises it may be more plausible to embrace its contradictory elements—if we assume, with the third response, that some of its elements are contradictory—than to give some of them up. A full defense of this claim lies beyond this book's scope, as do the interesting metaphysical and epistemological questions surrounding the issue of whether an inconsistent theory could be true.[6]

In sum, I think the egalitarian can plausibly deny that inequality's aspects are *fundamentally* incompatible, by stressing the fact that they reflect *different* concerns the egalitarian has. After all, why can't there be more than one genuinely egalitarian reason to care about how people fare relative to others? But even if this is not so, and one ultimately comes to the view that inequality's aspects *are* fundamentally incompatible, I think it may still be more plausible—at least for the time being—for one to proceed as if inequality is a complex, multifaceted notion than to only allow a consistent subset of aspects to inform one's egalitarian judgments.

10.3 Practical Implications

This book has been mainly theoretical in nature. I have attempted to clarify the notion of inequality, and considered how best to capture that notion. I have not attempted to construct a measure of inequality incorporating my results. Until that is done, this book's practical implications remain largely speculative. Still, let me briefly comment on some possible implications of my work—implications I find interesting, surprising, and frankly, a bit dismaying.

Consider again the Sequence, discussed in chapter 2. The Sequence, it will be recalled, consists of 1,000 worlds, each with a better- and worse-off group, such that in the first world there are 999 people better-off and 1 person worse-off, in the second there are 998 better-off and 2 worse-off, in the third there are 997 better-off and 3 worse-off, and so on. Its first, middle, and last worlds are represented in diagram 10.2 as f, m, and l, respectively.

In chapter 2, I argued that inequality's aspects support different orderings of the Sequence. I said nothing about what I think our final all-things-considered judgment should be about how the worlds compare regarding inequality. Let me partially rectify that now with two claims.

6. Many are unwilling to admit the possibility that an inconsistent theory might be true. Others, like W. V. O. Quine, think it is conceivable one might appropriately come to accept such a view, but believe our picture of the world would have to change radically before that would be the case (see, for example, *From A Logical Point of View* [Cambridge University Press, 1953]). I must confess (dare I?) that I am not sure our world picture would have to change all that much for us to accept *certain* inconsistencies as true. Interestingly, there is no question I would find some inconsistencies less objectionable than others. One wonders why this is so and what the criteria might be for the palatability of an inconsistency. Perhaps there is a simple correlation between an inconsistency's palatability (not to say its truth) and how necessary it seems to be to explain or maintain a position we need or want to defend.

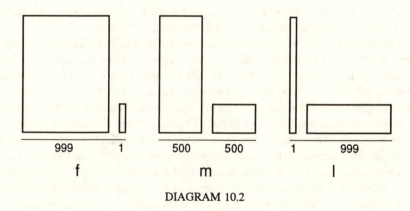

999   1   500   500   1   999

f   m   l

DIAGRAM 10.2

First, when all is said and done, and each of the aspects is properly considered, I think our final judgment will be that, regarding inequality, the Sequence first gets worse, then gets better. Second, for any two "reciprocal" worlds, that one will be worse whose better-off group is bigger. (Recall that the nth and nth last worlds of the Sequence are "reciprocal" worlds or, put differently, if a world has p better-off and q worse-off, its "reciprocal" world has q better-off and p worse-off.) Applied to diagram 10.2, my claims imply that, all things considered, m's inequality is worse than either f's or l's and, *regarding inequality*, l is better than f.

These judgments are not self-evident, especially the second. Ultimately, however, I think both are pretty uncontroversial, and I shall not argue for them. Instead, I shall assume they are correct, in order to proceed quickly to some interesting implications. The reader who denies these judgments may or may not face similar implications. Probably, his view will have its own interesting implications. But I shall not pursue this, since I think denying these judgments would be hard to defend.

Suppose, then, I am right—that, all things considered, the Sequence first gets worse, then better, regarding inequality. This implies that there may be cases where the only acceptable or feasible way of promoting equality is to first promote inequality. For example, imagine we are in a world, p, like the Sequence's 900th world (with 100 better-off and 900 worse-off). There are several ways of promoting a more equal world. First, we might transfer (some sources of) welfare from the better- to worse-off. Second, we might simply lower the quality of life of the better-off. Or third, we might leave the better-off alone and concentrate on improving the worse-off's lot.[7] Now there are times when each of these ways of promoting equality might be pursued. There are also times, however, when this is not the case for the first two ways; either because they are not practically realizable or, since equality is not all that matters, because they are morally unacceptable. Suppose this is the case for p, that is, that only the third alternative is available. Then, unless we

7. I do not claim these are the only ways of promoting equality. Nor do I claim that the three ways mentioned are mutually exclusive.

are able to raise the level of all, or most of the worse-off simultaneously, we may first have to worsen the inequality in order eventually to improve it.

Suppose, for example, that on average, we are able to raise 50 people every 10 years to the level of the better-off; but that we cannot raise more people a lesser amount that is still significant. (Perhaps the people suffer from different medical diseases, and our resources are such that if we pursue a cure for several diseases at once our efforts will be so diffuse as to be largely futile, whereas if we focus on one disease at a time, on average we will cure 50 people every 10 years.) If we pursued this strategy—which might be the only acceptable one available to us—the inequality would first worsen, before eventually improving, as the world moved further from a situation like 1 in diagram 10.2, toward the situations like m and f. Notice, it would take 160 years of such increases just to reach p's reciprocal situation— where there were 900 better-off and 100 worse-off. So, if my second claim is true—that between reciprocal worlds that one will be worse whose better-off group is smaller—it would take *more* than 160 years before we finally succeeded in improving p's inequality.

I have claimed that under certain circumstances we may have to first worsen inequality in order eventually to improve it. I believe this point is not just of theoretical interest. Although the world is not as neatly divided as the "haves" and "have nots" terminology suggests, a large portion of the world's population can be roughly divided into two groups such that the better-off group is both significantly smaller, and better off, than the worse-off group. This suggests that the world is not too unlike a later member of the Sequence. Moreover, in addition to whatever moral arguments might be mustered against them, it seems likely that at the global level social, political, and economic realities will severely limit the use and impact of the first two methods of improving inequality. Thus, there is reason to think that the egalitarian strategy most likely to affect seriously global inequality would be one that concentrated on improving the worse-off's lot. Practically, however, efforts to improve all or most of the worse-off at once would not be effective. Substantial and lasting progress is only likely to occur, if at all, over a long period of time, as development slowly spreads through cities, counties, provinces, countries, and eventually global regions.

These considerations suggest that effective efforts to reduce global inequality are likely to parallel closely those described previously for improving p's inequality. Thus, as we improve the lot of more and more of the worse-off, we may actually be *worsening* inequality as our world moves further from an l-like world toward an m-like world. Moreover, it may be a long time before the worsening trend reverses itself, and a very long time before the world approaches close enough to an f-like world for the net change in inequality to be for the better. Thus, we may have to endure worse inequality for a very long time if we hope to improve global inequality effectively. *Regarding inequality*, it may or may not be worth it.[8]

Contrary to the common view, then, we may, for a time, be *worsening* inequality

---

8. Whether it would be worth it from an egalitarian standpoint would depend on such factors as how long the worsened inequality lasted, how much worse it was, how much better the end state's inequality was than the initial state's, and how long the end state might last.

even as our programs to benefit the worse-off *succeed*. Moreover, this situation is not like many standard cases where the egalitarian embraces one kind of inequality for less of another. It is well known that if one cares about inequality of welfare, one may not only tolerate, but in fact require, inequalities of other kinds. For example, one may require an *unequal* division of resources between the healthy and the handicapped, or an unequal division of food between the starving and the sated. But in such cases sacrifices or trade-offs may not be an issue. One need not be embracing something bad for the sake of something good, for one's concern may simply be with inequality of welfare, and not about inequality of resources or food. The situation is different in the preceding case. Here, a significant trade-off *is* being made: not between two kinds of inequality, one of which matters, and one of which doesn't, but between situations that are genuinely worse in terms of the egalitarian's concerns and situations that are better.

Some people have suggested that due to factors such as incentive and trickle down effects, we might be able to reduce inequality faster by temporarily increasing it. (This is the professed view of certain conservatives, who maintain that giving extra short-term benefits to those who are already best-off will not only serve the interests of all, but will in fact serve to promote equality faster and more effectively than alternative policies.) If true, this would be one instance where the "freeway effect" holds. The "freeway effect" is the term some economists use to describe cases where the fastest way to achieve a desired end involves taking a route that at some point carries us away from our ultimate goal. It gets its name, of course, from the fact that often the fastest way to drive from A to B, involves leaving a local road that connects them directly, and perhaps even driving *away* from B, in order to hook up with a freeway that runs more or less between them.

The situation discussed earlier is similar to one where the "freeway effect" holds. But there is a difference. Where the "freeway effect" holds, the egalitarian can (generally) choose between different routes to his goal. He can take the local route, which slowly but steadily decreases inequality, or he can take the express route, which temporarily increases inequality, but ultimately decreases it faster than the local route. In the situation I described, speed is not the issue. The choice isn't between a slow direct route or a fast indirect one. The direct route is not available, and the indirect route may be slow. The issue, then, is whether to take the indirect route or stay put. Following the economists' lead, we might say that in such situations the "detour effect" holds. As I have already suggested, in some cases taking the detour won't be worth it, in others it will. The same holds true for taking the freeway.

Let me next suggest that analogous considerations yield similar results about discrimination and its consequences. Consider a world, q, like the Sequence's 750th world (where 250 people are better-off and 750 are worse-off). Suppose that while the population is 42% white male, 42% white female, and 16% minority, the better-off group is 90% white male, 8% white female, and 2% minority. Suppose, further, this is due to widespread and persistent discrimination interfering with the opportunities of women and minorities. We can imagine legislation introduced to end the discrimination. If such legislation was passed, and ultimately *successful*, would the world be significantly better regarding inequality? Unfortunately, it is by no means certain it would. To see this, let me first indicate two reasons others have thought not, and then add a third of my own.

Some believe equality of opportunity would do little to change a society's basic pattern of inequality. They maintain that while equality of opportunity might change the better- and worse-off groups' *composition*, it would have little effect on society's basic inequality-generating mechanisms, and hence would have little effect on the size or disparity of the better- and worse-off groups. A simplified version of their position might be put as follows. Egalitarians object to the inequality obtaining between, say, doctors and ditchdiggers. It seems grossly unfair that the latter should be so much worse off than the former through no fault of their own. But achieving equality of opportunity is not likely to affect substantially the number of doctors and ditchdiggers society requires. Nor is it likely to affect the inequality obtaining between them. What *will* change is the makeup of the two professions. More doctors will be women and minorities, while more ditchdiggers will be white males. Still, *the basic inequality between doctors and ditchdiggers will be largely unchanged*, and it is *that* the egalitarian (primarily) objects to, whatever the racial or sexual composition of the two groups.[9]

Others have argued that achieving equality of opportunity will in fact worsen inequality, as it will eventually increase the disparity between the better- and worse-off. John Schaar puts this point as follows:

> It is clear that the equal-opportunity policy will increase the inequalities among [people] . . . . In previous ages, when opportunities were restricted to those of the right birth and station, it is highly probable . . . that many of those who enjoyed abundant opportunities to develop their talents actually lacked the native ability to benefit from their advantages. Under the regime of equal opportunity, however . . . those who genuinely are superior in the desired attributes will enjoy rich opportunities to develop their qualities. This would produce, within a few generations, a social system where the members of the elites really were immensely superior in ability and attainment to the masses. We should then have a condition where the natural and social aristocracies would be identical.[10]

Together, these two positions raise serious doubts about the extent to which ending discrimination would significantly improve a society's inequality. Still, perhaps the factual claims underlying these positions are wrong. Perhaps an end to discrimination would not increase the disparity between the better- and worse-off groups and would do more than change their composition. Perhaps it would result in women and minorities faring just as well as white males always had, without the white male population being affected one way or another. This seems unlikely, but suppose it were so. Let us next consider its implications for q, which before discrimination ended resembled the Sequence's 750th world.

9. Thomas Nagel, among others, implies a similar view in "Equal Treatment and Compensatory Discrimination," *Philosophy and Public Affairs* 2 (1973): 348–63. Reprinted as "The Policy of Preference," in Nagel's *Mortal Questions* (Cambridge University Press, 1979), pp. 91–105.

10. John Schaar, "Equality of Opportunity and Beyond," in *Nomos IX: Equality*, ed. by R. Pennock and J. Chapman (Atherton Press, 1967), pp. 231–32.

Before discrimination ended, 90% of the 250 better-off were white males. This means that free from the discrimination hampering others, 225 of q's 429 white males had been able to "make good" in q. Thus, assuming that with discrimination's end a comparable percentage of women and minorities would fare equally well, its eradication would result in an increase of 205 white women and 35 minorities in the better-off group. There would then be 225 white men, 225 white women, and 40 minorities in the better-off group, and its composition would reflect that of the populace at large (42%, 42%, and 16%, respectively). Presumably, this is exactly the sort of result one would hope to achieve with antidiscrimination legislation. However, such a result would *not* be an improvement regarding inequality. To the contrary, in accordance with the judgment that the Sequence first gets worse, then better, q's change from a world where 250 are better-off and 750 worse-off, to one where 490 are better-off and 510 worse-off, would be a change for the worse regarding inequality.[11]

The practical implication of these remarks is that there may be many issues and programs about which we have to rethink our position. This is because most programs benefiting the worse-off are defended largely, if not wholly, in the name of equality. *Yet it may well be that the effect of some of these programs would be to worsen inequality, not improve it.* Thus, as my discussion suggests, if the benefits to all, or most, of the worse-off would be relatively minor compared with the benefits to those fortunate enough to take full advantage of their new opportunities, ending discrimination might actually worsen inequality by transforming our society from one resembling a later world of the Sequence into one resembling a middle world. Similarly, if the best we could realistically hope for would be for globalwide aid programs to improve the lot of 20, or 30, or even 50 percent of the worse-off, then although there are many respects in which such results would represent tremendous improvement, equality might not be one of them.

Three comments on the preceding remarks. First, it makes a great difference to my work's practical implications which worlds of the Sequence ours most resembles. The particular problems I have been describing only arise if, in the relevant respects, our world resembles the later, rather than the earlier, worlds. Unfortunately, data such as the following strongly suggest that it does, even if one bears in mind that there is no direct correlation between welfare, and income or wealth.[12]

---

11. I am assuming here, as I have throughout the book, that the egalitarian cares about equality of welfare and not equality of opportunity. In fact I incline toward this view myself, partly for the two reasons already noted; first, equality of opportunity does little to alleviate a society's basic pattern of inequality, and second, it may actually exacerbate undeserved inequalities—for example, between the intelligent and the stupid, or the healthy and the handicapped.

Naturally, someone might care about *both* kinds of inequality—or neither. Also, though I find them compelling, someone who cares about equality of opportunity but not equality of welfare will be unmoved by the above considerations. So, let me remind the reader that similar considerations would apply regarding inequality of opportunity, or any other kind of inequality. That is, if our concern is truly about *equality* of opportunity—rather than simply that each have as *much* opportunity as possible—we should find a situation where *half* have much more opportunity than the others *worse* than one where only a few have much more opportunity than the rest.

12. One can argue endlessly about the extent to which such data are misleading. For example, since $175 buys much more in a so-called third world country than in a so-called first world country, facts

1. In the early to middle 1960s, the percentage share of income of the bottom 40 percent of the population was 10 percent, 15 percent, and 15 percent, in France, the United Kingdom, and the United States, respectively. On the other hand, that of the top 5 percent was 25 percent, 19 percent and 19 percent, respectively.
2. On the international level the pattern is even more pronounced. In chapter 2 it was noted that in 1970 half of the world's population lived in countries with a national per capita income of less than $175, compared with the United States's $4,760. In terms of percentage income, the share of the bottom 60 percent of the international population was less than 10 percent, while that of the top 10 percent was nearly 40 percent.
3. The share of personal wealth is even more widely skewed than that of income. In Great Britain, the top 5 percent had 56 percent of personal wealth in 1968 (as opposed to only 19 percent of the income in 1964).[13]

Second, it might be argued that programs benefiting the worse-off should not be assessed on an individual basis. More specifically, it might be contended that while the particular effects of any one such program might be to worsen inequality, their combined effects would lessen inequality—especially, it might be added, if one bears in mind the long term effects of such programs. Without debating whether such a position could be successfully defended, let me simply observe that this is not how programs to benefit the worse-off have usually been defended. It represents a new position, one requiring an argument that has yet to be made.

Third, if we do ultimately decide that certain programs benefiting the worse-off cannot be justified in the name of equality, this does not mean we must oppose such programs. But it does mean other reasons must be found to support them. I believe such reasons can be found. However, what those reasons might be, and the conditions under which they will be strong enough to outweigh our egalitarian (and other) concerns is a large topic that must be left for another time. (Notice, as the first point implies, such reasons will only oppose our egalitarian concerns up to a certain point. Thus, if and when such programs, or other events, succeed in transforming our world into one resembling the Sequence's earlier worlds, our concern for equality will support rather than oppose the programs in question.)

Before going on, let me comment on the plausibility of the implication I have been discussing—that some programs benefiting the worse-off may worsen inequality. I realize that many readers will find this implication counterintuitive. I share this view. In fact, as already indicated, I find this implication both surprising and dismaying. Still, I believe this is one of those cases where our initial, pretheoretical, intuitions may need revision in the light of moral theory.

---

about the average per capita incomes of first and third world countries may seem to exaggerate the disparity between the average first and third world members. Even so, when all the mitigating factors and relevant qualifications are taken into account, it seems clear that it is the Sequence's later worlds, rather than its middle or earlier worlds, that our world most resembles.

13. These data were gleaned from A. B. Atkinson's book *The Economics of Inequality* (Clarendon Press, 1975). See pp. 134, 238-39, 241, and 244. Though this book, and the particular data cited, is now somewhat dated, the basic pattern of inequality it suggests is, unfortunately, not.

There are many reasons the implication in question seems counterintuitive. For example, in many cases raising some of the worse-off will improve inequality, so we may naturally, but mistakenly, assume this will be so in all cases. In addition, raising some of the worse-off will always improve inequality according to *some* important egalitarian aspects, and those may be the one's most naturally elicited, or given greatest intuitive weight, when considering such moves. Also, since raising *all* of the worse-off clearly and unequivocally improves inequality, it is natural to suppose that raising some of the worse-off—which seemingly brings us closer to that goal—must do so as well. Finally, raising some of the worse-off will improve an outcome in terms of many other respects, some of which—for example, extended humanitarianism—are easily and often confused with egalitarianism. In sum, I think there is good reason our pretheoretical intuitions regarding such cases may be at odds with our considered judgments. But I believe they are. That is, on reflection, I stand by the implication noted. Insofar as one cares about *inequality*, there may be cases where raising some, but not all, of the worse-off would be undesirable.

Let me conclude my discussion of practical implications with a point that may be less interesting than the others but is probably of wider significance. On reflection, it seems that many of our pretheoretical egalitarian judgments fail to take into consideration inequality's full complexity. Instead, they are based on one, or perhaps a few, particular aspects of inequality. Not surprisingly, I think many of these judgments will have to be revised, together with any ideas or policies founded on them.

For example, in chapter 2 I noted the strong tendency to judge that it is worse if a bully or tyrant discriminates against a single individual or small group than if he subjects half the population to such treatment. In addition, there is a strong tendency to judge that periods like the Middle Ages—where a few lived like kings, while many suffered—were among history's worst regarding inequality. These, and numerous judgments like them, will have to be amended if in fact our final judgment regarding inequality is that the Sequence first gets worse, then better.[14] We can, of course, continue to maintain that such situations are horrible in certain respects about which the egalitarian deeply cares. Nevertheless, when all is said and done, and each aspect is given its proper weight, I think we will have to admit that, however bad they may be regarding *other* ideals, their *inequality* isn't nearly as bad as we previously thought.

Most of this book's specific implications remain to be worked out. Still, I have given some reasons for believing that when they are worked out they may be far-reaching and perhaps, in some cases, surprising.

10.4 Individualism versus Holism: Final Thoughts

Among the many claims this work defends, perhaps the most significant concern the general nature of inequality—that inequality is a complex, essentially comparative,

14. Notice, *whatever* our final judgment of the Sequence turns out to be, those judgments based on aspects yielding a different ordering of the Sequence will have to be revised.

individualistic notion. Of particular interest, I believe, is this book's individualistic approach. The argument for this approach comprises virtually the entire book. It involves two elements, negative considerations against holistic egalitarianism and positive considerations for individualistic egalitarianism. Of these, the latter are more prevalent and by far the most important.

Of course holism is a notion that can be understood in many ways and identified with many views. I have not offered anything like a general refutation of holism. To the contrary, in chapter 5 I endorsed, and claimed my approach was compatible with, a position often identified with holism—namely, the hermeneutic and gestalt insight that the whole may be greater or less than the sum of its parts, a view that challenges additive separability and the notion that parts can be fully understood independently of the whole and each other. What I have expressed doubts about is a version of holism that would regard groups or societies as *themselves* proper objects of moral concern, over and above the extent to which they involve and affect the groups' or societies' *members*.

My negative considerations *against* holistic egalitarianism—understood in the sense described previously—have been scattered throughout this work. They range from chapter 2's defense of the most plausible version of a maximin principle of equality; to chapter 4's attack on the Average and Proportional Average Principles and its discussion of the most plausible version of BOP; to chapter 6's rejection of the economist's method of giving more weight to inequality at low levels than high levels, by relativizing inequality to society's average; to chapter 7's rejection of average views in general; to chapter 9's contention that the Slogan's plausibility could be partly due to the fact that it (misleadingly) expresses what may be a deep and important truth: namely, the individualistic view.

I believe chapter 4's considerations against an egalitarian view that focuses on average group levels are compelling, but I confess that most of my other considerations against holistic egalitarianism hardly constitute *arguments*. For the most part, they consist of variations of the bald assertion that *societies* aren't the proper objects of moral concern, individuals *in* societies are. Obviously I find that assertion intuitively powerful—or I wouldn't repeat it so many times!—but it doesn't establish the falsity of holistic egalitarianism. Rather, one might claim, it begs the question against it.

Given this book's approach some readers may be surprised that I have not mounted a more vigorous direct attack on holistic egalitarianism. But I am not sure what sort of argument one could offer to *prove* the falsity of holistic egalitarianism and, in truth, doing so has not been my main concern. My main concern has been to present and develop an alternative view, individualistic egalitarianism. And I have done this not because I have a philosophical ax to grind regarding the respective merits of individualism versus holism, but because I find an individualistic approach to inequality plausible and illuminating. Put crudely, I have advocated an individualistic approach to inequality because it works! In ethics, as in science, I think this is ultimately our criterion for assessing a theory's adequacy.

Some people might oppose a holistic approach to inequality based on considerations and questions of the following sort. On the holistic approach—which is concerned with *societies* and their distributions, rather than *individuals* and the comparisons between them—it is difficult to see exactly what the egalitarian cares about, and why. Moreover, it is difficult to see on what basis she makes her judgments. When the egalitarian looks at two societies, what is it she is looking for? Inequality, of course, but what is it that makes one society's inequality worse than another's? What features is she supposed to focus on in order to arrive at her decision? Does she simply "see" which is worse—perhaps in virtue of some special sense attuned to inequality? If so, how does she know that she hasn't got it wrong, that her special sense is functioning properly rather than leading her astray?

I do not wish to pursue these questions, which I suspect underlie the thinking of some nonegalitarians. Suffice it to say, I think most of the difficulties raised by such questions, if they are difficulties, do not apply to my approach. On the individualistic approach one can, I think, understand what the egalitarian cares about, why she makes the judgments she does (even some of those that are mistaken), and how she is supposed to determine when one situation is worse than another. There is nothing simple or obvious about inequality on the individualistic approach. But on the other hand there is nothing particularly mysterious about it either. In this respect, perhaps, individualism is preferable to holism.

To the considerations previously adduced in this book, let me add one more particular reason for favoring an individualistic approach. It was alluded to in chapter 9, and concerns the individualistic approach's ability to account for certain features of our moral psychology.[15]

Many egalitarians are affected by inequality in a highly personal way. When confronted by the poverty stricken or the severely handicapped, their reaction is not simply, "tsk, tsk, what a bad society we live in." Nor do they merely feel bad that their society isn't doing enough about inequality, or even, that *they* aren't doing as much as they should. Their feelings extend beyond that, to their own good fortune. Specifically, they feel a personal sense of guilt or shame that *they* fare so well, while others, no less deserving than they, fare so poorly.

Now many would claim such feelings of guilt or shame are unwarranted, and they may be right. But that is beside the point. The fact is many egalitarians *have* such feelings, and they are difficult to account for on the holistic approach. If the egalitarian's basic concern is with the pattern of distribution in society as a whole, what is it that gives rise to his feelings of guilt or shame about how well *he* fares? On the individualistic approach, one can easily account for these feelings. On that approach the egalitarian focuses on those who are worse off and compares them with *himself*, among others. Since he regards it as bad for some to be worse off than others through no fault of their own, this individualistic comparison naturally gives rise to the feelings in question.

Even if the difficulties facing a holistic approach are not insurmountable, I believe the individualistic approach is more plausible as an account of inequality. Mainly I believe this because of the individualistic approach's ability to account for the content of our egalitarian judgments. Thus, as we have seen, the individualistic approach can accommodate and explain the pretheoretical judgments of most egalitarians, and this is so not only in the "paradigm" cases about which there is near

15. The following point was brought to my attention by Thomas Nagel.

unanimity of agreement, but in many other cases where there is a wide range of agreement or lack thereof. Moreover, the individualistic approach provides a principled method and perspective from which to assess and in some cases revise people's pretheoretical judgments. In addition, the individualistic approach can account for the considered moral judgments of most egalitarians whether those judgments are absolute or relative in nature. In sum, there is reason to hope that the individualistic approach may eventually lead to a theory of inequality that is coherent, systematic, illuminating, and plausible.

The challenge to the holist is to develop an account of inequality that is equally promising. Although this book does not rule out such a possibility, nothing remotely resembling such an account has yet to be offered.

In conclusion, there are good reasons for adopting this book's individualistic approach. In fact, once one adopts the individualistic approach, it is hard—for me, anyway—to see how people could have thought about inequality in any other way.

I began this book by raising a question that has received little attention from philosophers: when is one situation worse than another regarding inequality? In addressing this question, I presented and developed a new way of understanding our notion of inequality.

This book's implications extend far beyond the topic of inequality. This is perhaps most obvious in chapters 7 and 9, where I argue that our moral ideals may have to share certain formal, or structural, features—so, for example, if numbers count for utility they may also have to count for inequality; that the natural and standard way of understanding utility and its relation to our all-things-considered judgments must be rejected; that we need a new model for understanding our moral ideals, perhaps one like my gymnastics model where there is an upper limit on how good a situation can be regarding both any particular ideal and all things considered; that the Slogan, an intuitively powerful position that underlies numerous arguments in philosophy and economics, does not support the conclusions for which it has been invoked; and that we need a much better understanding of our theory, or theories, of the good, one that, among other things, distinguishes and reassesses the relationship between a theory about self-interest, a theory about outcomes, and a full theory of the good. Though sometimes less obvious, this book's other chapters also have many wide-ranging implications. Too many to enumerate here.[16]

Of course, whatever its implications for other aspects of morality, this is a book about inequality. I have argued that the common view of inequality—as a simple, holistic, and essentially distributive notion—is thoroughly misguided. Instead, I

16. These observations have some bearing on an issue discussed in chapter 1. Throughout this book I have assumed that one can meaningfully, and usefully, address the question, When is one situation worse than another *regarding inequality*? keeping that question separate from the question of how situations compare regarding other ideals. Many are initially skeptical of this claim. They believe ideals cannot be treated in isolation from each other in the way such a question suggests. I believe this book's results represent a partial vindication of both views. I believe my results demonstrate that one *can* focus on my question, and substantially illuminate the notion of inequality. But in so doing we must inevitably consider broader issues and topics, such that making progress on the "restricted" front of inequality requires progress on the "wider" front of morality.

have suggested that inequality is complex, individualistic, and essentially compara-tive. I have also argued that there is great confusion about whether inequality matters more at low levels than high levels; that the standard view that proportional size increases do not affect inequality needs serious revision; that we need a differ-ent approach to measuring inequality than those that have been suggested; that the common view about the proper unit of egalitarian concern is inadequate; that many of our commonsense egalitarian judgments will need to be revised; and that what is perhaps the most important and influencial antiegalitarian position should be re-jected.

Inequality is a topic that has generated volumes of intense debate; not only within the secluded walls of the academy, but in countless social, political, and personal arenas of policy and conscience. If our results are even remotely on target, it is a debate that has been shrouded in error and confusion. Few, if any, moral ideals have been more widely discussed, yet less well understood.

Appendix A: New Aspects
of Inequality Considered

Although I refer to this appendix at various places earlier, it would be best not to read it before completing chapter 4.

In this book I have argued that, suitably modified, chapter 2's aspects are capable of accommodating and explaining both the pretheoretical intuitions and firm considered judgments of most egalitarians. Naturally, one wonders whether our catalog of inequality's aspects is complete,[1] or whether there may still be other aspects with a role to play in our egalitarian judgments. In this appendix I shall consider five suggestions for new aspects or factors relevant to judging inequality. They may be presented with the aid of diagram A.1.[2]

---

1. Where this is separate from the question of whether the aspects may still need to be revised in certain ways—for example, along the lines considered in chapters 6 and 7.

2. The reader may note that A.1 is a variation of an earlier diagram. The variation is simply that of representing B in the second manner depicted here rather than the first, and similarly for C and D.

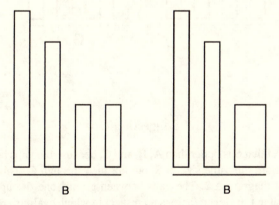

When one group is raised or lowered to another's level, one might accurately look at the resulting situation as having either two groups of the same original size at the same level, or as having one group twice the original size at that level. In the ensuing discussion it will generally be most helpful to look at such a change the latter way, although it will sometimes be useful to look at it the former way. Here, as elsewhere, we shall let context determine our usage.

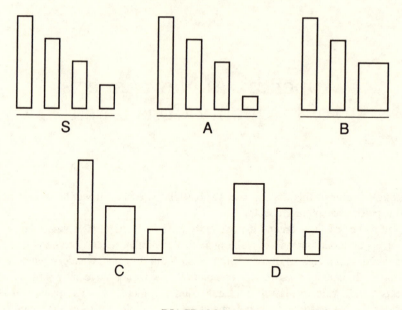

DIAGRAM A.1

DIAGRAM A.2

A.1 Suggestion One

One might suggest that S is better than A, B, and C, because the gaps between groups one through four are the same size in S, but not in A through C. This suggestion is absurd. Consider diagram A.2. The gaps between groups one through four are the same size in F, but not in G. But there is no respect in which egalitarians would prefer F to G. Egalitarians think it is bad for some to be worse off than others through no fault of their own. They are concerned with how people fare relative to others. In every respect G's people fare better relative to others than F's do.

True, the size of the gaps in F are equal, whereas those in G are not. So F has a *kind* of equality G lacks. But this kind of equality is purely mathematical. It has no *moral* significance. Thus, ultimately, suggestion one is no more plausible than the claim that egalitarians should regard it as bad that there are more real numbers than natural numbers, or more electrons than protons.

No one, to my knowledge, has endorsed suggestion one. I mention it because its absurdity is readily seen, and because it is not too unlike a second suggestion to which some have been drawn.

A.2 Suggestion Two

One might suggest that S is better than B, C, and D in diagram A.1, because the sizes of the better- and worse-off groups are equal in S, but not in B, C, and D. This suggestion is no more plausible than the last one, though in discussion it is clear some are attracted to it. Consider again diagrams A.1 and A.2. Like S, F is evenly divided into four groups. Like B, G *can* be regarded as unevenly divided into three.[3] Notwithstanding this, there is no reason to regard F's inequality as better than G's. Equality in the numerical sizes of the better- and worse-off groups is, by itself, no more relevant to the egalitarian's concern than equality in the numerical sizes of the gaps between those groups. Both are purely mathematical. Neither is itself relevant to how people fare relative to others.

The foregoing helps explain why, in chapter 2, I noted that I am unaware of any plausible positions supporting the judgment that the Sequence first gets better, then worse. Looking at the Sequence, some are tempted to judge the middle worlds better than the end worlds because their populations are more evenly divided. On reflection, however, this fact clearly gives us no reason to prefer the middle worlds. It merely corresponds to the degree of equality in the numerical sizes of the better- and worse-off groups, which, as we have just seen, is not among the egalitarian's (moral) concerns. Thus, while there is a *sense* in which the Sequence's middle world is perfectly equal—having the same *number* in the better- and worse-off groups—the relevant sense is purely mathematical, akin to the kind of perfect equality that would obtain if everyone had the same number of hairs, or there were the same number of protons as electrons. Again, the egalitarian's concern is with how people fare relative to others, and in this respect the Sequence's middle world is decidedly *not* perfect.

A.3 Suggestion Three

One might claim that S is better than A through D because S's population comes closer to lying along a straight line than A through D's. Suggestion three is best illustrated by diagram A.3, which removes the space between A.1's groups, adds a

3. I have not bothered to redraw G, but I am here assuming G could equally well be represented and viewed as containing three groups of which the worst-off would be twice the size of the other two. See the previous note.

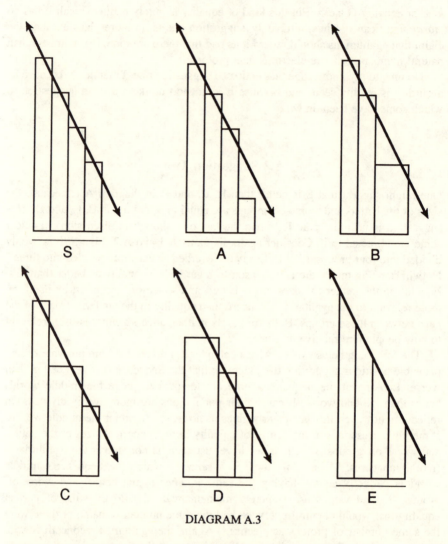

DIAGRAM A.3

new situation, E, and superimposes a line upon each figure. On this view, E would be even better than S. Several factors might subtly combine to make this view attractive. First, straight lines possess a kind of visual, structural, or geometrical equality that may influence our reactions. Second, a perfectly equal situation's diagram *will* lie along a straight line, so one may think that in general the closer a diagram comes to lying along a straight line the better it is regarding inequality. Third, a *person* who is "straight" is consistent, rule-governed, fair, and just, notions often associated with equality. Correspondingly, there may be a subliminal tendency to associate the "straighter" diagrams with situations that are more consistent, rule-governed, fair, and just, and, hence, by further association, more equal. For these, and perhaps other reasons, some may be drawn to suggestion three. Nevertheless, suggestion three is not plausible.

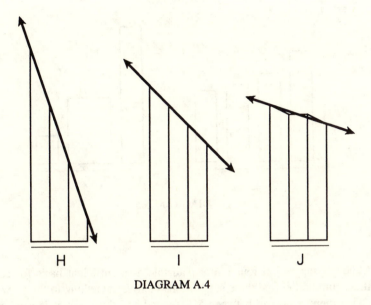

DIAGRAM A.4

Morally, the kind of visual, structural, or geometrical equality that E possesses, and that S approximates more than A through D is no more relevant than the kinds of arithmetical equality considered in suggestions one and two. Similarly, while a perfectly equal situation's diagram *will* lie along a straight line, not just any line will do. It must be horizontal. What makes a situation perfect regarding equality is that each is as well off as every other, *not* that its diagram lies along a straight line. And, of course, while a "straight" *person* may be fair and just, there is no more reason to attribute such properties to a straight diagram than there would be to think boxes must somehow be fairer or more just than balls.

Consider diagram A.4. Is there *any* reason to regard H's inequality as *good* as I's? Is there any respect it is better than J's? Surely, not. Again, the egalitarian's concern is with how people fare relative to others. That H and I lie along straight lines, while J does not, is completely irrelevant to this concern.

Psychologically, bold, sharp, gaps in diagrams may accentuate inequality, while smooth, continuous, lines may soften it. Suggestion three's implausibility helps remind us to guard against such factors—to bear in mind what our diagrams represent and to not be misled by their visual features.

A.4 Suggestion Four

One might suggest that B, C, and D are better than S in diagram A.1, because more people are (exactly) equal to each other in the former worlds than the latter one. Although some have been drawn to this view, it is implausible as stated. Consider diagram A.5. More people are (exactly) equal to each other in M than in L. Nevertheless, M is *not* better than L.

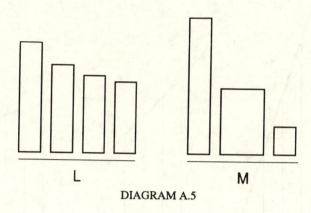

DIAGRAM A.5

Although suggestion four is not plausible as a sufficient basis for comparing situations, unlike the first three suggestions there *is* something to the view in question. That there is no gap between M's second and third groups is *some* reason to prefer M to L, but not *enough* reason to outweigh M's other, much bigger, gaps. Still, saying there is one respect in which M is better than L, because more people are (exactly) equal in M, is misleading. The significant fact is that some fare better relative to each other in M than in L—that is, groups two and three—and this is adequately captured by chapter 2's aspects, specifically by either of the additive principles when combined with the relative to all those better off view of complaints. Thus suggestion four turns out to be a red herring. No new aspect is needed to capture what is plausible about it.

A.5 Suggestion Five

One might suggest that S is better than C and D, since everybody in S is at least as well off as everybody in C and D, and some are better-off. Suggestion five may seem plausible "all things considered." Moreover, if we assume the better-off are not responsible for the worse-off's plight, it may seem there is no morally permissible way of transforming S into C or D—for example, it may seem such a move would necessarily involve unacceptable interference with individual rights, freedom, or autonomy. Whether or not these claims are right, they are irrelevant to our present concerns. Our concern is *not* with how situations compare all things considered, or with the moral permissibility of transforming one situation into another. Our concern is with how situations compare *regarding inequality*.

As I note elsewhere and argue in chapter 9, many would defend suggestion five. They would insist there is *no* respect in which one situation could be worse than another if there is *no one* for whom it *is* worse. For reasons presented in chapter 9, which I shall not repeat here, I think this important and prevalent position should be rejected—along with suggestion five which is ultimately based on it.

A.6 Final Remark

Over the years I have heard many suggestions about how inequality should be assessed. Some simply turn out to be nonegalitarian positions in disguise. Of the others, the only ones involving significant new alternatives to chapter 2's aspects were presented as suggestions two through five. And as we have seen, those suggestions should be rejected. Of course there may still be other aspects involved in the notion of inequality than those uncovered in this book. It would be wildly premature and presumptuous to assume otherwise. However, if there are other aspects of inequality that withstand philosophical scrutiny I am not aware of them. Perhaps this book's shortcomings will aid in their discovery.

Appendix B: How Variations in Complex Heterogeneous Situations Affect Inequality

In sections 3.2–3.5 we considered how variation in group levels affects inequality, and noted how transfers between groups will have different effects depending on the groups' relative positions and the degree and kind of transfers involved. To facilitate discussion we assumed perfect homogeneity within each group. Our assumption did not affect our results but was, of course, unrealistic. As useful as it often is, both practically and theoretically, to divide situations neatly into groups—for example, the upper, middle, and lower classes, or the first, second, and third worlds—there remains significant diversity within these groups. In this appendix I illustrate how considerations analogous to those already presented would apply to variations both within and between heterogeneous groups. As we shall see, virtually the entire argument of sections 3.2–3.5 could be straightforwardly applied, mutatis mutandis, to cases involving heterogeneous groups.

The topic of how inequality would be affected by variations within heterogeneous groups was first broached in chapter 4, where I considered the average and proportional average principles of equality. With that chapter as background, including its introduction of sloped diagrams, let us consider what chapter 2's aspects imply about variations involving heterogeneous groups.

Note, the ensuing discussion contains no major surprises, which is why it is presented in an appendix rather than in the main body of the text. Readers prepared to trust my judgment, and not independently interested in reviewing the familiar details underlying my claims, need not work through this material. Instead, they may want to skip directly to this appendix's concluding section, "B.5 Summary and Assessment."

B.1 Variations in Heterogeneous Group Levels

In sections 3.2 and 3.3, we considered how variations in group levels affect inequality for cases involving homogeneous groups. We saw that chapter 2's aspects support the relative judgment that regarding inequality the worse off a group was, the better it would be to improve its situation and the more objectionable it would be to

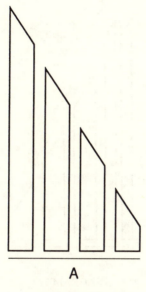

A

DIAGRAM B.1

worsen it. Specifically, we saw that, ceteris paribus, raising the worst-off group to the next group's level clearly and unequivocally improved inequality according to each of chapter 2's aspects. Also, that similar improvements in increasingly better-off groups involved a shift in both the number of aspects supporting such a move and the strength of their support (or opposition), to the point that raising the best-off group clearly and unequivocally worsened inequality according to each aspect. Analogously, lowering the best-off group to the next group's level clearly and unequivocally improved inequality according to each aspect, with similar reductions in increasingly worse-off groups involving a shift in both the number of aspects supporting such a move and the strength of their support (or opposition), to the point that lowering the worst-off group would clearly and unequivocally worsen inequality according to each aspect.

Without repeating section 3.2 and 3.3's lengthy arguments, let me simply note that analogous arguments and results could be given and reached for cases involving the raising and lowering of heterogeneous groups. For example, considering diagram B.1, lowering the best-off group to the second best-off group's level (or alternatively raising them even higher) would improve (or worsen) A's inequality according to each of chapter 2's aspects. Similarly, raising the worst-off group to the third group's level (or lowering them even further) would improve (or worsen) A's inequality according to each aspect. Moreover, as with homogeneous groups, for intermediate groups there will be a shift both in the number of aspects supporting or condemning a given increase or decrease, and (for some aspects) in the strength of support or condemnation the aspects give.

Note, chapter 2's aspects directly yield the preceding result. No emendations are

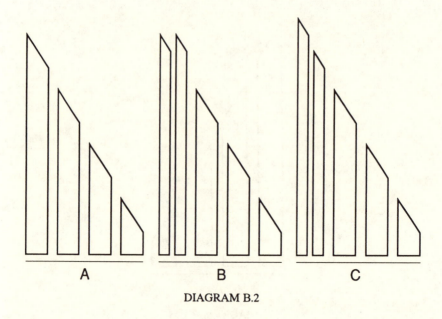

DIAGRAM B.2

necessary to get the "correct fit" for heterogeneous groups.[1] Likewise, chapter 2's aspects directly yield similar results when applied to the raising and lowering of different individuals within heterogeneous groups. For example, raising B.1's very best-off individuals a certain amount will worsen A's inequality according to every aspect. By the same token, raising an intermediate person the same amount may either worsen or improve A's inequality depending on whether her situation is closer to that of the best- or worst-off person but, importantly, it will neither worsen it as much as raising the best-off person nor improve it as much as raising the worst-off person.

B.2 Variations within Heterogeneous Groups

To illustrate how altering individuals within a heterogeneous group may differentially affect inequality, consider diagram B.2. A contains four heterogeneous groups such that within each group people are evenly spread from best- to worst-off. B would result from A if the worse-off half of A's best-off group were raised n units so that as a group their situation paralleled that of the better-off half. C would result from A if the better-off half of A's best-off group were raised n units.

Moving from A to C involves the kind of change described previously, where a situation's best-off individuals are made even better off. Even to the eye, C's inequality seems worse than A's, and as observed already C will be worse than A

1. But see part 2 of chapter 4 for ways one might want to revise or interpret the relative to the best-off person view of complaints and the maximin principle of equality.

according to each of chapter 2's aspects. Moving from A to B involves an improvement for some who are already better off than most, but not for the very best-off. Here, too, I think B's inequality seems worse than A's "even to the eye," but this comparison is less obvious than the other. Indeed, comparing B with C it seems clear, even to the eye, that C's inequality is worse than B's. These intuitive "eyeball" reactions can be supported by the combined judgments of chapter 2's aspects. B will be worse than A according to each aspect not involving BOP: MP & AVE, MP & ATBO, AP & AVE, AP & ATBO, WAP & AVE, WAP & ATBO, Deviation, and Gratuitousness. However, B will be better than A according to AP & BOP and WAP & BOP, and roughly equivalent to A according to MP & BOP.[2] Comparing B with C, B will obviously be better than C according to each of BOP's three aspects. It will also be better according to AP & ATBO, WAP & AVE, and WAP & ATBO. It will be equivalent according MP & AVE, AP & AVE, Deviation, and Gratuitousness, and roughly equivalent according to MP & ATBO. None of the aspects judge B worse than C.

The foregoing illustrates how raising different people within a heterogeneous group can differentially affect inequality and suggests how raising (or lowering) people at different levels can involve a shift both in the number of aspects supporting or condemning a given increase or decrease and, for some aspects, in the strength of support or condemnation the aspects give. We have seen that in terms of some aspects—MP & AVE, AP & AVE, Deviation, Gratuitousness, and, for practical purposes, MP & ATBO—raising the best-off group's worse-off half may worsen inequality, and to the same extent that raising the better-off half would. In terms of other aspects—AP & ATBO, WAP & AVE, and WAP & ATBO—raising the best-off group's worse-off half may worsen inequality, but to a lesser extent than raising the better-off half would. In terms of one aspect, at least—MP & BOP—raising the best-off group's worse-off half may not significantly affect inequality, whereas raising the better-off half would worsen it. In terms of still other aspects—AP & BOP and WAP & BOP—raising the best-off group's worse-off half may improve inequality, whereas raising the better-off half would worsen it. Finally, we observed that no aspects would favor raising the best-off group's better-off half over similarly raising its worse-off half.

The particular results noted here are not generalizable. If we considered increases of different sizes or within different groups or for different people within the same group, we would find variations in both the aspects' particular judgments and the extent of agreement among them. Still, the foregoing illustrates the type and direction of shifts in our egalitarian judgments associated with varying different people within heterogeneous groups.

Considerations like the foregoing suggest that our results about the effect of increases or decreases in a homogeneous group's level can be extended to increases or decreases of people within heterogeneous groups. Indeed, as remarks in chapter

---

2. B will probably be slightly better than A in virtue of maximin's tie-breaking clause. But the difference between the two situations that the tie-breaking clause captures will be pretty insignificant— that is, insofar as we are concerned with how a situation's worst-off members fare relative to the best-off person, there will be little to choose between A and B.

4 anticipate, they can in fact be extended to apply to increases or decreases of particular individuals not only within heterogeneous groups but between heterogeneous groups. For any two people, p and q, if p is better off than q then, ceteris paribus, raising p (or lowering q) will never be preferable to raising q (or lowering p) according to any aspects, whereas raising q (or lowering p) will always be preferable to raising p (or lowering q) according to at least one aspect. Thus, together chapter 2's aspects not only capture our firm absolute judgments that, other things equal, increases (decreases) in the best- (worst-)off person will clearly and unequivocally worsen inequality, and that limited decreases (increases) in the best- (worst-)off person will clearly and unequivocally improve it, they also capture our firm relative judgment that regarding inequality the worse off someone is the better it would be to improve her situation and the worse it would be to worsen it. (I have tried to give the reader a sense, without fully arguing, for the accuracy of these claims. Relevant arguments could be produced, but would involve many cases and tedious calculations. If the reader accepts our earlier arguments regarding homogeneous groups, I trust he or she will see how those arguments might be extended to heterogeneous groups. Skeptical readers are cordially invited to confirm our claims for themselves.)

In section 3.4 I claimed that in general egalitarians want transfers to go from the "highest" possible group to the "lowest" possible group, and in section 3.5 I showed how together chapter 2's aspects would capture this notion for any transfer of any size or kind.[3] In chapter 4 I observed that a "more perspicuous" version of the egalitarian's view would be that other things equal transfers should go from the best- to the worst-off individuals. One desirable implication of the foregoing discussion is that together chapter 2's aspects capture the "more perspicuous" version of the egalitarian's view in a way straightforwardly applying to individual transfers both within and between heterogeneous groups—specifically, the relative judgment that, regarding inequality, the worse off someone is the better it would be to improve her situation and the worse it would be to worsen it entails the view in question.

B.3 The Pigou-Dalton Condition and Even Transfers Involving Heterogeneous Groups

The preceding discussion has another desirable implication. Together chapter 2's aspects capture the most plausible version of the Pigou-Dalton condition (PD) for individual transfers both within and between heterogeneous groups, where, roughly, according to PD even transfers between better- and worse-off should be favored or opposed depending on whether they reduce or increase the gaps between them.

Let A involve heterogeneous groups and two people, p and q, with p better off than q. Let A* and A** be alternatives to A such that moving from A to A* involves an even transfer of 2n units from p to q reducing their gap, whereas moving from

3. The different kinds of transfers—efficient, even, and inefficient—are introduced and defined in section 3.5.

A to A** involves an even transfer of 2n from q to p increasing their gap. Then the choice between A* and A** involves two elements at the same time: a choice between raising either q or p 2n, and a choice between either lowering p or q 2n. Since p is better off than q, our preceding results imply it would be better to raise q than p, and also better to lower p than q. Hence, A*'s inequality will be better than A**'s as the former is better than the latter in terms of both elements involved in the choice between them.

The foregoing result is quite general, since A might be any society, p and q any two people such that the one is better off than the other, and n any size. It tells us that for any even transfer involving better- and worse-off it will be better if the transfer goes from the better- to worse-off than from the worse- to better-off.

So far the argument only yields a relative ranking. We know A** is worse than A* but not yet how either compares with A. Still, given that in A p and q occupy intermediate positions between those they occupy in A* and A** one would expect A should be worse than A* and better than A**, and in fact there are many ways to show this. For example, letting A*** and A**** be alternatives where p and q occupy the intermediate positions between those they occupy in A and A* and A and A**, respectively, one could give arguments analogous to the preceding to show that A is worse than A*, and better than A**.

Thus, as claimed previously, our earlier results imply that together chapter 2's aspects will capture the most plausible version of PD. They also imply, plausibly, that according to chapter 2's aspects the extent to which an even transfer from better- to worse-off improves inequality depends on both the levels of those involved and the size of the transfer.

The point about levels follows immediately from the fact that together the aspects imply that the better off someone is relative to others the better (or less bad) it will be for her to be lowered by transfers from her to another, and similarly that the worse off someone is relative to others the better (or less bad) it will be for her to be raised by transfers to her from another.[4] Likewise, the point about transfer sizes follows immediately from PD. (Let p and q be any two in A such that p is better off than q. Suppose one could either bring about B, by transferring n from p to q, or C, by transferring n + k from p to q, where n and k are both positive and where p will still be at least as well off as q in C. The Pigou-Dalton condition directly entails not only that B and C are better than A, but that C is better than B, since one could bring about C from B by an even transfer [of k] from a better- to worse-off person (p to q) reducing their gap. Hence, our earlier results—which imply that together chapter 2's aspects capture PD—also imply that according to chapter 2's aspects the extent to which even transfers from better- to worse-off improve inequality [partly] depends on the transfers' sizes.)

---

4. Not every aspect will be directly sensitive to the levels of those between whom transfers occur. For example, in many cases Deviation will be indifferent between a transfer from p to q and one from r to s even if r were better off than p and s were worse off than q. The point is that *together* chapter 2's aspects imply that the extent to which an even transfer improves inequality will depend, among other things, on the levels of those involved.

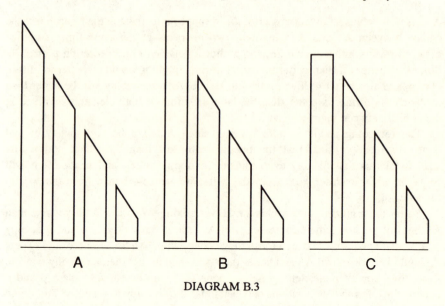

DIAGRAM B.3

B.4 Heterogeneous Groups and Different Kinds of Transfers

In section 3.5, we discussed how different kinds of transfers between homogeneous groups would affect inequality. Distinguishing between efficient, even, and inefficient transfers, we saw that while in accordance with PD egalitarians would approve even transfers from better- to worse-off, whether they would approve other transfers would depend on the relative levels of the groups involved, on the kinds of transfers in question, and in some cases, at least, on the *extent* to which the transfers were efficient or inefficient. As the reader has probably surmised by now, considerations and conclusions analogous to section 3.5's could be given for different kinds of transfers both within and between heterogeneous groups. Consider diagram B.3. As usual, A contains four unequal heterogeneous groups where the population is evenly spread within each group. B would result from A if the best-off group's members were raised to the level of the best-off person. C would result from A if the best-off group's members were lowered to the level of the group's worst-off person.

Considering diagram B.3, I think most would intuitively judge B's inequality worst and C's best. One might arrive at this conclusion via direct pairwise comparisons between the alternatives, or via the combined influence of one firm pairwise judgment that B is worse than C, A worse than C, or B worse than A, together with the recognition that since A is intermediate between B and C in the only respect in which the situations differ, A's inequality will be intermediate between the others.

The moves from A to B and A to C are similar to others this book considered. Moving from A to B improves some already better off than most in a way that removes the gaps within the best-off group but increases the gaps between those whose positions were improved and all those (already) worse off than they. In terms of chapter 2's aspects, the net effect of this is B will be better than A on AP & BOP and WAP & BOP, and roughly equivalent to A on MP & BOP, however, B will be worse than A on MP & AVE, MP & ATBO, AP & AVE, AP & ATBO, WAP & AVE, WAP & ATBO, Deviation, and Gratuitousness. On the other hand, moving from A to C not only removes the gaps within the best-off group, it decreases the gaps between those whose positions were lowered and everyone else. Such a move would be approved by each of chapter 2's aspects. And, of course, moving from C to B would improve the best-off, further increasing the gaps between them and everyone else. As we have seen, regarding inequality such a move would be clearly and unequivocally condemned by each of chapter 2's aspects.

Not surprisingly, the foregoing suggests that together chapter two's aspects will likely yield the intuitively plausible ranking of B worse than A and A worse than C. But notice, as with a similar example in section 3.5, moving from A to B can be seen as a limiting case of a set of efficient transfers between each of the best-off group's members and the best-off person. Although strictly speaking there have been no *transfers*, given that an efficient transfer increases the lot of those benefited by more than it decreases the lot of those worsened, one might say such a case involves "perfectly efficient" transfers as the "gainers" not only gain more than the best-off person loses, they gain some without the best-off person losing anything. Similarly, moving from A to C can be seen as a limiting case of a set of inefficient transfers. This suggests egalitarians will approve transfers within the best-off group if they are "sufficiently" inefficient but condemn them if they are "sufficiently" efficient.

This point may be developed still further along the lines presented in section 3.5. We have seen[5] that, overall, lowering a member of A's best-off group in diagram B.3 toward the group's worst-off member will improve A's inequality and raising a member of the best-off group toward the best-off person will worsen A's inequality. We have also seen that even transfers reducing the gap between better- and worse-off will improve A's inequality. From this we may infer that *any* inefficient transfer reducing the gap between two individuals within the best-off group will improve A's inequality. After all, one can view the inefficient transfer as a two step process. First, for every unit gained by the worse-off person a unit is lost by the better-off person. This constitutes an even exchange improving A's inequality. Second, because the transfer is inefficient there would be an additional lowering of the better-off person toward the best-off group's worst-off member. Overall this would further improve A's inequality. Hence, the inefficient transfer's net effect would be to improve A's inequality.

On the other hand, it seems some but not all efficient transfers within the best-off group would worsen A's inequality. Suppose that within the best-off group, p was 300 units better off than q. It is very likely A's inequality would be worsened by an *extremely* efficient transfer whereby p lost 1 and q gained 299, as the extent to which lowering p 1 improves A's inequality is likely to be significantly outweighed by the extent to which raising q 299 worsens it. By the same token, given that an even transfer of 150 from p to q would clearly improve A's inequality (such a move would be approved by some of chapter 2's aspects and condemned by

5. Or can infer from the considerations presented in this appendix and elsewhere.

none), it is highly unlikely that a *slightly* efficient transfer, say, where p lost 149 units and q gained 151, would worsen it. It appears, then, the judgments yielded by chapter 2's aspects about efficient transfers within A's best-off group will shift depending on just how efficient the transfers are. Naturally, the general range where the shift occurs (there is unlikely to be a precise point) will be a function both of changing judgments yielded by the aspects and the weight each aspect is given.

Similar considerations could be presented to assess the effect of different kinds of transfers within and between other groups. As in section 3.5, I shall not pursue the many possibilities. However, let me add two observations to the foregoing.

First, the case of transfers within A's worst-off group mirrors the one just presented. Transfers reducing the gaps between better- and worse-off members will improve A's inequality if they are even or efficient. If they are inefficient, whether they improve A's inequality will depend on just how inefficient they are. Underlying these judgments is the fact that, overall, insofar as a transfer lowers a member of the worst-off group toward the initial level of the worst-off person, it will worsen A's inequality, but the extent to which it does this is not as significant, proportionally, as the extent to which raising a worse-off person toward the initial level of the group's best-off member improves it.[6]

Second, throughout the foregoing discussion I made two simplifying assumptions. I assumed transfers went from better- to worse-off, and I assumed transfers merely reduced the gaps between the individuals concerned. Some of my particular conclusions need revision if these simplifying assumptions are dropped, but the book's general considerations still hold and apply equally well to such cases. For example, in accordance with PD any even transfer from a worse- to a better-off person in A's best-off group will worsen A's inequality, as will any efficient transfer. On the other hand, an inefficient transfer from a worse- to a better-off person in A's best-off group may or may not improve A's inequality depending on the extent to which it is inefficient.[7]

Notice, if one drops the assumption that transfers merely reduce the gaps between the individuals concerned, it will no longer be true that chapter 2's aspects will approve *any* inefficient transfer from better- to worse-off within the best-off group, or *any* efficient transfer from better- to worse-off within the worst-off group. But this is both expected and desirable. For example, suppose p and q, were both initially in the best-off group, with p better off than q. Suppose next there was a transfer from p to q *so* inefficient that q was only raised a little, while p was made worse off than everyone else—to the extent that overall the gaps between p and A's other members were now much worse than before. In such a case, together chapter 2's aspects would rightly condemn the inefficient transfer from p to q.

6. As we saw in section 3.5, this is implied by the fact that—in accordance with the Pigou-Dalton condition's most plausible version—even transfers from better- to worse-off persons within the worst-off group will improve inequality.

7. Interestingly, it is likely a transfer will worsen A's inequality if it is only "slightly" inefficient, will improve A's inequality if it is "moderately" inefficient, and will worsen A's inequality again if it is "extremely" inefficient. The following paragraph in the text illustrates why the last shift in judgment may occur.

B.5 Summary and Discussion

To sum up: The considerations relevant to assessing variations of homogeneous group levels can be extended to assessing variations of individual levels within and between heterogeneous groups. For example, we have learned that according to chapter 2's aspects, the overall effect on inequality of raising or lowering someone will depend on her initial position relative to others and the extent to which she is raised or lowered. Raising (lowering) someone very well (poorly) off relative to others will tend to worsen inequality, whereas lowering (raising) her will, at least to a certain extent, improve inequality. Moreover, the worse-off someone is relative to others, the better it will be for her to be raised and the worse it will be for her to be lowered.

Additionally, we have seen that according to chapter 2's aspects a transfer between p and q may or may not improve inequality, depending on the levels of p and q, and both the kind and extent of the transfer. For example, a transfer from a better- to worse-off person within the best-off group might be approved if it was even, inefficient, or not "too" efficient, but condemned if "too" efficient, whereas the same kind and size of transfer that would be objectionable within the best-off group would be desirable within the worst-off group, and even more desirable between the best- and worst-off groups.

Though we have once again focused on (relatively) simple examples this does not affect our general results. Analogous considerations could be presented for cases involving different numbers of groups, different numbers within the groups, and different patterns of distribution within and between the groups. So, for any population involving better- and worse-off individuals, together chapter 2's aspects will capture the most plausible version of the Pigou-Dalton condition, will condemn raising the best-off person or lowering the worst-off person, and will imply that the worse off someone is relative to others the better it will be to raise her and the worse it will be to lower her. In addition, for any transfer from p to q, such that p loses n and q gains k, the extent to which chapter 2's aspects approve or disapprove of the transfer will depend on p and q's levels (how they fare relative to others as well as to each other), on the kind of transfer in question (whether $n > k$, $n = k$, or $n < k$—and the sizes of n and k—which will determine both the extent to which the transfer will be efficient or inefficient when $n \neq k$, and how much p and q's positions change relative to others).

In this appendix I have mainly discussed how our earlier results about variations in homogeneous group levels could be extended to variations of individuals within heterogeneous situations. I have not emphasized how our results accord with the egalitarian's pretheoretical and considered judgments. Still, at various points I noted our conclusions seemed desirable or capable of capturing our all-things-considered egalitarian judgments, and I think most egalitarians would, on reflection, endorse our conclusions. Hence, as with the simpler cases involving homogeneous groups, I think chapter 2's aspects can accommodate and explain what many egalitarians would say about complex heterogeneous cases. Thus, as one might hope, this appendix's results further suggest that a unified account of inequality might be given such that, however obscure the egalitarian's judgments might be in cases of great complexity, the basic sentiments and principles underlying them remain essentially the same.

Finally, the reader will have noticed that, as promised, this appendix contains no major surprises. (The reason it is an appendix!) In fact, I suspect most readers will have found the arguments familiar, and the results predictable and unexciting. This is unfortunate from the reader's standpoint but desirable from ours. That our results (by now) seem obvious and uncontroversial is, I believe, testimony to the plausibility of chapter 2's aspects when applied to complex heterogeneous cases.

Appendix C:
Variations in Population Size—
Different Aspects, Different Views

In this appendix, I show how chapter 2's aspects would yield various answers to the following question, N, if those aspects are not to be supplemented to support the Standard View, P, or avoid the Repellant Conclusion, RC.

N: How, if at all, do size variations affect inequality?

C.1 Size Variations and Maximin

Consider first the maximin principle of equality. On this principle, how bad a world's inequality is, is determined by how the worst-off group fares regarding inequality—where, if the worst-off group fares the same in two worlds, the best world is the one whose worst-off group is smallest (if they are the same size, the second worst-off groups are similarly compared and so on).[1] Combined with the relative to the best-off person view of complaints, the maximin principle suggests the following answer to N: variation in the number of people who are best-off does not affect how bad a world's inequality is, while variation in the number of people who are not best-off does, but only to the relatively insignificant extent of breaking ties between otherwise equivalent worlds.

So, for example, in a world with four groups (1) variation in the worst-off group's size will be insignificant relative to a change in its level or the best-off group's level; (2) variation in the second worst-off group's size will be insignificant relative to a change in its level or the worst-off group's size (or, of course, those changes even more fundamental than the worst-off group's size); (3) variation in the second best-off group's size will be insignificant relative to a change in its level or the second worst-off group's size (or those changes even more fundamental); and (4) variation in the best-off group's size will be insignificant. To the limited extent that variation in a group's size does affect inequality, increases worsen it and decreases lessen it.

1. This is the version of the maximin principle I presented and defended in chapter 2. Those who believe another version is more plausible—perhaps because they accept a person-affecting or deontological version of egalitarianism—would have to amend the following remarks accordingly.

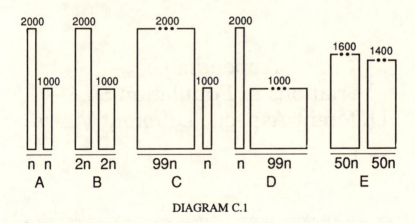

DIAGRAM C.1

Thus, applied to the worlds of diagram C.1, the combination of the maximin principle and the relative to the best-off person view of complaints yields the judgments that A is worse than E, equivalent to C, and better than B and D. More generally, one can see that in most realistic cases, size variations will have little or no effect on which of two situations is worse.

The picture changes when the maximin principle is combined with the relative to the average view of complaints. On that combination of views, varying the number of better- and worse-off affects inequality as follows: increasing those below the initial average will improve inequality, since it lowers the average, and hence decreases the size of the worst-off group's complaint. Correspondingly, increasing those who are at the average level will leave inequality unaffected, and increasing those who are better off than the initial average will worsen inequality. Thus, the most drastic changes affected by size variations will occur either when groups above the average increase and groups below the average decrease, in which case the inequality will worsen markedly, or when groups above the average decrease and groups below the average increase, in which case the inequality will improve markedly. Increases or decreases on both sides of the average will tend to offset each other, as will increases and decreases on the same side of the average. Naturally, the extent to which such increases and/or decreases offset each other will be a function of the group's levels and the amounts of variation involved.

Thus, applied to diagram C.1, the combination of the maximin principle and the relative to the average view of complaints yields the judgment that A is worse than D and E, and better than B and C. More generally, on this combination of views size variations affect inequality not only in the tie-breaking manner of the last combination of views, but also to the extent that such variations alter the average and, hence, the magnitude of the worst-off's complaints.

Combined with the relative to all those better off view of complaints, the maximin principle yields yet another answer to N. On this combination of views, varying the worst-off group's size will only have the relatively insignificant effect of breaking ties between otherwise equivalent worlds; but varying other groups' sizes will worsen inequality, since the worst-off group's members will then fare worse relative to all those better off than they. Analogously, decreases in the size of such groups will lessen inequality. Thus, insofar as we are influenced by this combination of views, A will be better than B, C, D, and E. (In claiming that A is better than E, I am not forgetting that we will want to count a gap of k units more at level 1,000 than at level 1,400. Still, a gap of k units will not count ten times as much at level 1,000 as at level 1,400).

C.2 Size Variations and the Additive and Weighted Additive Principles

Other answers to N are suggested by the additive and weighted additive principles, both of which reflect the view that if it is bad for one person to be worse off than another, it is worse for two people to be in such a position. So, for example, when combined with the relative to the best-off person view of complaints, these principles suggest that for all but the very best-off there will be a significant and direct correlation between the number of better- and worse-off and how bad inequality is. That is, increases in those who are not best-off will worsen inequality, decreases will improve it. On these views, then, A will be better than B, D, and E, and equivalent to C.

As we saw in chapter 2, when combined with the relative to the average view of complaints, both the additive and weighted additive principles measure inequality as a function of how much deviation there is from the average. Of course, on the weighted additive principle, extra weight will be attached to deviations furthest below the average; and, on both views, large deviations below the average will be weighted more than small ones when, in accordance with chapter 6's results, people's levels are taken into account. Still, one can see that, on either combination of views, size variations will affect a world's inequality to the extent that they affect the variations from the average.

Unfortunately, the effect of size variation is more complicated on these combinations of views than on the others we have discussed. So, for example, an increase in the size of a group below the initial average will lower the average, with the following results: those at or below the new average will deviate less from the average than previously; those at or above the old average will deviate more from the average than previously; those between the old average and the new one will go from deviating below to deviating above the average, with those closest to the old average deviating more, and those closest to the new average deviating less, than they did before; and the new members of the increased group will deviate below the average by a certain amount.

However, despite such complications a bit of reflection and arithmetical manipulation reveals that the overall affect of increases in a group size below the initial average is to increase deviation from the average and worsen the inequality. This is also the overall effect of increases in the population above the initial average. Correspondingly, decreases in the population above or below the initial average will lessen the overall deviation from the average and improve the inequality. (Interestingly, decreasing a group's size improves inequality [slightly] more than increasing it by the same amount worsens it.) Naturally, size variation in those at the average will leave both the average level and the deviation from the average unchanged. So, on the views in question such variation will not affect inequality. Also, as one would expect, size variations in those near the average will have less effect on the overall deviation from the average, and hence less effect on the inequality, than size variations in those further from the average. Thus, the views in question suggest a different answer to N than the other views discussed; though when applied to diagram C.1, there is some agreement with the other views in the particular judgments it yields. To wit: A is better than B, C, D, and E.

Combined with the relative to all those better off view of complaints, the additive and weighted additive principles suggest still another answer to N. On such views, there would be a direct and unambiguous correlation between size variations and inequality. Increases in the population at any level would worsen inequality, decreases would lessen it. Specifically, increases in those worst-off would worsen inequality by increasing the number who have a complaint; increases in those best-off would worsen inequality by increasing the size of people's complaints; and increases in those at other levels would worsen inequality in both respects, by increasing the number who have a complaint, and the size of the complaints of those even worse off than they. Naturally, decreases in the population would have the opposite effect for parallel reasons. So, as indicated already, the effect of size variations is different on these views than on the others discussed. As it happens, however, these views, like the last ones, yield the judgment that A's inequality is better than B's, C's, D's, and E's.

C.3 Size Variations and Inequality's Other Aspects

There were three other aspects of inequality noted in chapter 2. According to one, how bad inequality is depends upon how much deviation there is from a state of absolute equality, where this is determined by measuring the deviations from the median. According to another, how bad inequality is depends upon how gratuitous it is, where roughly this is determined by considering how much redistribution would "cost" the better-off relative to how much it would "benefit" the worse-off. According to the third, how bad a society's inequality is depends upon that society's principles and institutions and the extent to which they are responsible for the kind of inequality obtaining.

As one might expect by now, each of these ways of judging inequality suggests a different answer to N. The first suggests an answer similar to that suggested by the additive principle and the relative to the average view of complaints; except, as noted, it focuses on deviations from the median rather than deviations from the mean. So, on this view, size variations will affect inequality to the extent they affect deviations from the median. Increases in deviations worsen inequality, decreases lessen it. Applied to diagram C.1, this view implies that A is better than B and E, while equivalent to C and D.

Regarding inequality's "gratuitousness," increases in those at or near the worst-off's level would tend to improve inequality, as it would tend to increase the "costs" of redistribution to the better-off and decrease the "benefits" to the worse-off. On the other hand, increases in the number of people at or near the level of the best-off would tend to worsen inequality, as it would tend to decrease the "costs" of the redistribution to the better-off and increase the "benefits" to the worse-off. As usual, decreases would have the opposite effect of increases.

On this view, A and B would be equivalent, as the ratio of "costs" to "benefits" from redistribution would be equally gratuitous. Meanwhile, A would be better than C, and worse than D. As for the comparison between A and E, on the plausible assumption that there is a decreasing marginal utility of the sources of welfare, A would (probably) be worse than E, as the ratio of gains to losses from a redistribution of the sources of welfare would (probably) be larger in A than E.

Finally, one can see that yet another answer to N is suggested on the view that how bad a society's inequality is depends on its principles and institutions, and the extent to which they are responsible for the inequality obtaining. On such a view variations in population size will not affect how bad a society is regarding inequality unless accompanied by variations in the relevant principles and institutions. Size variation *itself* has no effect. On this view, then, we could not judge, as yet, how A compares to the other worlds of diagram C.1. Such a judgment would be about, and hence would need to be based on, information that has not been given: information about the relevant principles and institutions of the worlds in question. And, of course, as noted in chapter 2, such a judgment would only concern those worlds' social justice; it would not be plausible as a judgment concerning their natural justice.

C.4 Summary and Discussion

I have been examining the answers to N suggested by chapter 2's aspects of inequality. The results of this examination can be summed up as follows. First, there are various judgments of how A compares with diagram C.1's other worlds, and no two worlds for which each aspect yields the same ordering. Second, depending on the different aspects, size variations will have no effect, a relatively insignificant effect, a relatively significant and direct effect (increases worsening inequality, decreases lessening it), or a relatively significant and inverse effect (increases lessening inequality, decreases worsening it), depending on whether the group is best-off, worst-off, at the average level, at the median level, or at some other level. Third, chapter 2's twelve aspects suggest nine answers to N. Each aspect suggests a distinct answer except for those involving the additive and weighted additive principles. Those aspects yield similar answers when (and only when) they involve similar views of complaints. Finally, as will be discussed next, the twelve aspects fall into four general groups in the way they measure inequality.

The first, and by far the largest, group, measures inequality solely as a function of the better- and worse-off's levels and the *number* of people at those levels. Although there may be one level where size variation is not a factor,[2] for all other levels there will be a significant correlation between the numbers and the inequality. Specifically, increases in the number of better- or worse-off will significantly worsen inequality, and decreases will significantly improve it. A fortiori, proportional increases in the population will significantly worsen inequality and proportional decreases will significantly improve it. The first group includes the aspect of inequality combining the maximin principle with the relative to all those better off view of complaints, the aspect measuring deviations from the median, and each of the six aspects involving the additive or the weighted additive principles.

The second group measures inequality primarily as a function of the better- or worse-off's levels, and the *ratios* between them. Variations in the size of the better- and worse-off groups significantly affect inequality *only* to the extent that they alter the ratios between the better- and worse-off. As such, the numbers in the better- and worse-off groups are largely insignificant. (It may not be completely insignificant, as it may break ties between otherwise equivalent worlds.) Accordingly, proportional increases in the better- and worse-off groups will not significantly affect inequality, as the ratios between those groups would not be altered by such a change. Correspondingly, if A is significantly worse than B to begin with—that is, no tie-breaking clause is needed to rank them—no amount of proportional increases in B's population would render it worse than A. The second group includes the aspect of inequality combining the maximin principle and the relative to the average view of complaints, as well as the aspect focusing on inequality's gratuitousness.

The third "group" consists of one member: the aspect combining the maximin principle with the relative to the best-off person view of complaints. On this view, only the *levels* of the best- and worst-off are significant. The ratios between the better- and worse-off groups make no difference, while the numbers in the better- and worse-off groups, and the levels of those between the best- and worst-off only have the relatively insignificant effect of breaking ties between otherwise equivalent worlds. Thus, on this view, too, proportional increases in the better- and worse-off will not significantly affect inequality. Moreover, if A is significantly worse than B, no amount of increases in B's groups—proportional or otherwise—will render it worse than A.

The fourth "group" consists of the remaining aspect. According to that aspect, neither the number of people in, nor the ratios between, nor even the levels of the better- and worse-off groups affect how bad a society is regarding inequality. What matters on that view is solely the society's principles and institutions, and the extent to which they affect the kind of inequality obtaining. Thus, on that view, increases in the better- and worse-off groups—proportional or otherwise— will not itself make a later stage worse than an earlier one, or one society worse than another.

---

2. Depending on the aspect, this may be the level of the best-off person, the average person, or the median.

Thus, the issue of whether size variations affect inequality is almost as complicated as inequality itself. A full resolution of it must await the determination of how much to weight inequality's different aspects, although I think such a determination will itself partly depend on the answer it yields to this issue.[3] Of course, a full resolution of the issue may not be possible. By the same token, a resolution may be incomplete without being inaccurate.

3. Here, as elsewhere, I think one must engage in the sort of "back and forth" process Rawls describes in order to ultimately arrive at our "considered" judgments in a state of "reflective equilibrium." Our pretheoretical intuitions about which aspects seem most plausible will influence our judgments about how different-sized societies compare regarding inequality. But by the same token, our pretheoretical intuitions about how different-sized societies compare regarding inequality will influence our judgments about which aspects are most plausible. (See pp. 20-21 and 48-53 of John Rawls's *A Theory of Justice* [Harvard University Press, 1971]; Norman Daniels's "Wide Reflective Equilibrium," *Journal of Philosophy* 5 [1979]: 256-82; and Henry Sidgwick's *The Methods Of Ethics*, 7th ed. [Macmillan, 1907].)

Bibliography

No editions of classic texts have been specified; however, when available, the original publication dates of such texts have been noted.

Ake, Christopher. "Justice as Equality." *Philosophy and Public Affairs* 5 (1975): 69-89.

Anscombe, G. E. M. "Modern Moral Philosophy." *Philosophy* 33 (1958): 1-19. Reprinted in Judith J. Thomson and Gerald Dworkin, eds., *Ethics.* Harper and Row, 1968.

_____."Who is Wronged?" *Oxford Review,* no. 5 (1967): 16-17.

Aristotle. *Nicomachean Ethics.*

Atkinson, A. B. "On the Measurement of Inequality." *Journal of Economic Theory* 2 (1970): 244-63.

_____.*The Economics of Inequality.* Clarendon Press, 1975.

Ayer, A. J. *Language, Truth and Logic.* Gollancz, 1936.

Barry, Brian. "Circumstances of Justice and Future Generations." In *Obligations to Future Generations,* edited by R. I. Sikora and Brian Barry, pp. 204-48. Temple University Press, 1978.

Bedau, Hugo A. "Radical Egalitarianism." In *Nomos IX: Equality,* edited by R. Pennock and J. Chapman, pp. 3-27. Atherton Press, 1967.

Benn, Stanley I. "Egalitarianism and the Equal Consideration of Interests." In *Nomos IX: Equality,* edited by R. Pennock and J. Chapman, pp. 61-78. Atherton Press, 1967.

Bentham, Jeremy. *An Introduction to the Principles of Morals and Legislation.* 1789.

Berlin, Isaiah. "Equality." *Proceedings of the Aristotelian Society* 56 (1955-56): 300-26.

Blackorby, C., and D. Donaldson. "Measures of Relative Equality and Their Meaning in Terms of Social Welfare." *Journal of Economic Theory* 18 (1978): 59-80.

_____."A Theoretical Treatment of Indices of Absolute Inequality." *International Economic Review* 21 (1980): 107-36.

Bourguignon, F. "Decomposable Income Inequality Measures." *Econmetrica* 47 (1979): 901-20.

Bowie, N. E. "Equality and Distributive Justice." *Philosophy* 45 (1970): 255-80.

Brandt, Richard B. *A Theory of the Good and the Right.* Clarendon Press, 1979.

Broome, John. "Uncertainty and Fairness." *Economic Journal* 94 (1984): 624-32.

_____."Utilitarianism and Expected Utility." *Journal of Philosophy* 84 (1987): 405-22.

_____."What's the Good of Equality?" In *Current Issues in Microeconomics,* edited by John D. Hey, pp. 236-62. Macmillan, 1989.

_____."Rationality and the Sure Thing Principle." In *Thoughtful Economic Man,* edited by Gay Meeks, pp. 74-102. Cambridge University Press, 1991.

_____.*Weighing Goods.* Basil Blackwell, 1991.

Browne, D. E. "The Presumption of Equality." *Australasian Journal of Philosophy* 53 (1975): 46-53.

_____."Nonegalitarian Justice." *Australian Journal of Philosophy* 56 (1978): 48-60.

Buchanan, James M. "Equality as Fact and Norm." *Ethics* 81 (1970-71): 228-42.

Catlin, George E. G. "Equality and What We Mean By It." In *Nomos IX: Equality,* edited by R. Pennock and J. Chapman, pp. 99-111. Atherton Press, 1967.

Cohen, Marshall, Thomas Nagel, and Thomas Scanlon, eds. *Equality and Preferential Treatment.* Princeton University Press, 1977.

Cowell, Frank. "On the Structure of Additive Inequality Measures." *Review of Economic Studies* 47 (1980): 521-31.

Cowell, F., and K. Kuga. "Additivity and the Entropy Concept: An Axiomatic Approach to Inequality Measurement." *Journal of Economic Theory* 25 (1981): 131-43.

_____."Inequality Measurement: An Axiomatic Approach." *European Economic Review* 15 (1981): 287-305.

Cowen, Tyler. "Distribution in Fixed and Variable Numbers Problems." *Social Choice and Welfare* 7 (1990): 47-56.

Cowen, Tyler, and Jack High. "Time, Bounded Utility, and the St. Petersburg Paradox." *Theory and Decision* 25 (1988): 219-23.

Crocker, Lawrence. "Equality, Solidarity, and Rawls' Maximin." *Philosophy and Public Affairs* 6 (1977): 226-39.

Dalton, Hugh. "The Measurement of the Inequality of Incomes." *Economic Journal* 30 (1920): 348-61.

Dancy, Jonathan. *Reading Parfit.* Basil Blackwell, forthcoming.

Daniels, Norman. "Wide Reflective Equilibrium." *Journal of Philosophy* 5 (1979): 256-82.

_____.*Am I My Parents' Keeper? An Essay on Justice between the Young and Old.* Oxford University Press, 1988.

_____."Equality of What: Welfare, Resources, or Capabilities?" *Philosophy and Phenomenological Research* 50 (1990): 273-96.

Dasgupta, P., A. Sen, and D. Starrett. "Notes on the Measurement of Inequality." *Journal of Economic Theory* 6 (1973): 180-87.

Donagan, Alan. *The Theory of Morality.* University of Chicago Press, 1977.

Donaldson, David, and John Weymark. "A Single Parameter Generalization of the Gini Indices of Inequality." *Journal of Economic Theory* 22 (1980): 67-87.

Dorsen, Norman. "A Lawyer's Look at Egalitarianism and Equality." In *Nomos IX: Equality*, edited by R. Pennock and J. Chapman, pp. 28-38. Atherton Press, 1967.

Dworkin, Ronald. *Taking Rights Seriously.* Harvard University Press, 1978.

_____."What is Equality? Part 1: Equality of Welfare." *Philosophy and Public Affairs* 10 (1981): 185-246.

_____."What is Equality? Part 2: Equality of Resources." *Philosophy and Public Affairs* 10 (1981): 283-345.

Fiske, S. T., S. E. Taylor, N. Etcoff, and J. Laufer. "Imaging, Empathy and Causal Attribution." *Journal of Experimental Social Psychology* 15 (1979): 356-77.

Flew, Antony. "Equality or Justice?" *Midwest Studies in Philosophy* 3 (1978): 176-94.

_____.*The Politics of Procrustes: Contradictions of Enforced Equality.* Prometheus Books, 1981.

_____."Equality, Yes Surely; But Justice?" *Philosophical Papers* 15 (1986): 197-204.

Frankel, Charles. "Equality of Opportunity." *Ethics* 81 (1970-71): 191-211.

Frankena, William. "The Concept of Social Justice." In *Social Justice*, edited by Richard Brandt, pp. 1-29. Prentice-Hall, 1962.

Frankfurt, Harry. "Equality as a Moral Ideal." *Ethics* 98 (1987): 21-43.

Fried, Charles. *Right and Wrong.* Harvard University Press, 1978.

Gauthier, David. "Justified Inequality?" *Dialogue* (Canada) 21 (1982): 431-43.

Gibbard, Alan. "Preference Strength and Two Kinds of Ordinalism." *Philosophia* 7 (1978): 255-64.

Griffin, James. "Equality: On Sen's Weak Equity Axiom." *Mind* 90 (1982): 280-86.

_____.*Well-Being: Its Meaning, Measurement, and Moral Importance.* Oxford University Press, 1987.

Hare, R. M. "Ethical Theory and Utilitarianism." In *Contemporary British Philosophers*, edited by H. D. Lewis, pp. 113-31. Allen and Unwin Press, 1976.

Harmon, Gilbert. "Moral Relativism Defended." *Philosophical Review* 84 (1975): 3-22.

_____. *The Nature of Morality*. Oxford University Press, 1977.

_____. "Relativistic Ethics: Morality as Politics." *Midwest Studies in Philosophy* 3 (1978): 109-21.

Hartkamp, Steven. *Social Inequality: Preliminary Remarks Towards a Measurement of Inequality*. March, 1991, unpublished.

Hegel, G. W. F. *Philosophy of Right*. 1821.

_____. *Logic: Being Part One of the Encyclopedia of the Philosophical Sciences*. 1830.

Held, Virginia. "Egalitarianism and Relevance." *Ethics* 81 (1971): 359.

Hobbes, Thomas. *Leviathan: or the Matter, Forme and Power of a Commonwealth Ecclesiasticall and Civil*. 1651.

Honderich, Ted. "The Question of Well-being and the Principle of Equality." *Mind* 90 (1981): 481-504.

Internal Revenue Code of 1986, as Amended.

Kagan, Shelly. "The Additive Fallacy." *Ethics* 99 (1988): 5-31.

Kant, Immanuel. *Foundations of the Metaphysics of Morals*. 1785.

_____. *The Metaphysical Elements of Justice*. 1797.

_____. *Metaphysical Principles of Virtue*. 1797.

Kavka, Gregory. "The Paradox of Future Individuals." *Philosophy and Public Affairs* 11 (1982): 93-112.

Kohler, Wolfgang. "Gestalt Theory: Foundations and Current Problems." In *The Selected Papers of Wolfgang Kohler*, edited by Mary Henle, pp. 13-122. Liveright Press, 1971. Originally published in 1913.

_____. *The Place of Value in a World of Facts*. Live Right, 1966. Originally published 1938.

Kolm, S. Ch. "Unequal Inequalities." *Journal of Economic Theory* 12 (1976): 416-42.

Lock, Grahame. "Self-ownership, Equality of Resources and the Case of the Indolent Indigent." *Rechtsfilosofie en Rechtstheorie* 1 (1989): 35-46.

Locke, John. *Two Treatises of Government*. 1684.

Lucas, J. R. "Against Equality." *Philosophy* 40 (1965): 296-307.

_____. "Against Equality Again." *Philosophy* 52 (1977): 255-80.

Lucash, Frank S. *Justice and Equality Here and Now*. Cornell University Press, 1986.

Lyons, Daniel. "The Ethics of Redistribution." *Mind* 78 (1969): 427-33.

Mack, Eric. "Distributionism versus Justice." *Ethics* 86 (1975-76): 145-53.

Mackie, J. L. *Ethics: Inventing Right and Wrong*. Penguin, 1977.

Malthus, T. R. *An Essay on Population*. 1802.

Marx, Karl. *Capital*. Vol. 1. 1867.

_____. *Capital*. Vols. 2 and 3, edited by Frederick Engels. 1885 and 1894.

McArthur, L. Z., and L. K. Solomon. "Perceptions of an Aggressive Encounter as a Function of the Victim's Salience and the Perceiver's Arousal." *Journal of Personality and Social Psychology* 36 (1978): 1278-90.

McCloskey, H. J. "Egalitarianism, Equality, and Justice." *Australasian Journal of Philosophy* 44 (1966): 50-69.

_____. "A Right to Equality?" *Canadian Journal of Philosophy* 6 (1976): 625-42.

McKerlie, Dennis. "Equality and Time." *Ethics* 99 (1989): 475-91.

Meade, J. E. *The Just Economy*. Allen and Unwin, 1976.

Mill, John Stuart. *Utilitarianism*. 1859.

Moore, G. E. *Principia Ethica*. 1903.

Mortimore, G. W. "An Ideal of Equality." *Mind* 77 (1968): 222-42.

Nagel, Thomas. *The Possibility of Altruism.* Clarendon Press, 1970.

_____."Equal Treatment and Compensatory Discrimination." *Philosophy and Public Affairs* 2 (1973): 348–63. Reprinted as "The Policy of Preference," in Thomas Nagel, *Mortal Questions.* Cambridge University Press, 1979.

_____."The Justification of Equality." *Critica* 10 (1978): 3–31. Reprinted as "Equality," in Thomas Nagel, *Mortal Questions.* Cambridge University Press, 1979.

_____.*Mortal Questions.* Cambridge University Press, 1979.

_____."The Limits of Objectivity." In *The Tanner Lectures on Human Values,* I, edited by S. McMurrin, pp. 77–139. University of Utah Press and Cambridge University Press, 1980.

_____.*The View from Nowhere.* Oxford University Press, 1986.

_____.*Equality and Partiality.* Oxford University Press, 1991.

Narveson, Jan. "Utilitarianism and New Generations." *Mind* 76 (1967): 62–72.

_____."Moral Problems of Population." *The Monist* 57 (1973): 62–86.

_____."Future People and Us." In *Obligations to Future Generations,* edited by R.I Sikora and Brian Barry, pp. 38–60. Temple University Press, 1978.

Nelson, William. "Equal Opportunity." *Social Theory and Practice* 10 (1984): 157–84.

Newbury, David. "A Theorem on the Measurement of Inequality." *Journal of Economic Theory* 2 (1970): 264–66.

Newfield, J.G.H. "Equality in Society." *Proceedings of the Aristotelian Society* 66 (1965–66): 193–210.

Nielsen, Kai. *Equality and Liberty: A Defense of Radical Egalitarianism.* Rowman Littlefield, 1986.

Nisbett, R., and L. Ross. *Human Inference: Strategies and Shortcomings of Social Judgment.* Prentice-Hall, 1981.

Nozick, Robert. *Anarchy, State, and Utopia.* Basic Books, 1974.

Oppenheim, Felix. "Egalitarianism as a Descriptive Concept." *American Philosophical Quarterly* 7 (1970): 143–52.

_____."Egalitarianism and Moral Judgements." *Ethics* 82 (1971–72): 171–72.

Parfit, Derek. "Overpopulation." Unpublished manuscript, 1976.

_____."Innumerate Ethics." *Philosophy and Public Affairs* 7 (1978): 285–301.

_____."Future Generations: Further Problems." *Philosophy and Public Affairs* 11 (1982): 113–72.

_____.*Reasons and Persons.* Oxford University Press, 1984.

_____."Comments." *Ethics* 96 (1986): 832–72.

_____."On Giving Priority to the Worse-off." Unpublished manuscript, 1989.

Paul, Ellen Frankel, Fred D. Miller, and Jeffrey Paul, eds. *Liberty and Equality.* Basil Blackwell, 1985.

_____.*Equal Opportunity.* Basil Blackwell, 1987.

Pen, J. *Income Distribution.* Allen Lane, 1971.

Pigou, A. C. *Wealth and Welfare.* Macmillan, 1912.

_____.*The Economics of Welfare.* 4th ed. Macmillan, 1932.

Plamenatz, John. "Diversity of Rights and Kinds of Equality." In *Nomos IX: Equality,* edited by R. Pennock and J. Chapman, pp. 79–98. Atherton Press, 1967.

Plato. *Euthyphro.*

_____.*Protagoras.*

Quest, Edward. "Whatever Arises from a Just Distribution by Just Steps Is Itself Just." *Analysis* 37 (1976–77): 204–08.

Quine, W. V. O. *From a Logical Point of View.* Cambridge University Press, 1953.

Rae, Douglas, et al. *Equalities.* Harvard University Press, 1981.

Rawls, John. *A Theory of Justice*. Harvard University Press, 1971.

Raz, J. "Principles of Equality." *Mind* 87 (1978): 321–42.

Rescher, N. *Distributive Justice*. Bobbs-Merrill, 1967.

Roemer, John. "Equality of Resources Implies Equality of Welfare." *Quarterly Journal of Economics* (1986): 751–84.

Ross, L. "The Intuitive Psychologist and His Shortcomings: Distortions in the Attribution Process." In Advances in Experimental Social Psychology 10, edited by L. Berkowitz, pp. 174–77. Academic Press, 1978.

Ross, L., T. M. Amabile, and J. L. Steinmetz. "Social Roles, Social Control, and Biases in Social Perception Processes." *Journal of Personality and Social Psychology* 35 (1977): 485–94.

Ross, W. D. *The Right and the Good*. Clarendon Press, 1930.

Rothschild, Michael, and Joseph Stiglitz. "Some Further Results on the Measurement of Inequality." *Journal of Economic Theory* 6 (1973): 188–204.

Rousseau, Jean J. *Discourse on the Origin of Inequality*. 1755.

_____.*The Social Contract*. 1762.

Runciman, W. G. *Relative Deprivation and Social Justice*. Routledge and Kegan Paul, 1966.

_____."Processes, End States, and Social Justice." *Philosophical Quarterly* 28 (1978): 37–45.

Scanlon, Thomas. "Preference and Urgency." *Journal of Philosophy* 72 (1975): 655–69.

_____."Nozick on Rights, Liberty, and Property." *Philosophy and Public Affairs* 6 (1976): 3–25.

_____."Rights, Goals, and Fairness." *Erkenntnis* 11 (1977): 81–95. Reprinted in Stuart Hampshire, ed., *Public and Private Morality*. Cambridge University Press, 1978.

_____."Equality of Resources and Equality of Welfare: A Forced Marriage?" *Ethics* 97 (1986): 111–18.

Schaar, John H. "Equality of Opportunity and Beyond." In *Nomos IX: Equality*, edited by R. Pennock and J. Chapman, pp. 228–49. Atherton Press, 1967.

Schwartz, Thomas. "Obligations to Posterity." In *Obligations to Future Generations*, edited by R. I. Sikora and Brian Barry, pp. 3–13. Temple University Press, 1978.

Sen, A. K. *Collective Choice and Social Welfare*. Holden Day, 1970.

_____.*On Economic Inequality*. Clarendon Press, 1973.

_____."Equality of What?" In *Tanner Lectures on Human Values*, Vol. I. University of Utah Press and Cambridge University Press, 1980. Reprinted in Amartya Sen, *Choice, Welfare and Measurement*, pp. 353–69. Basil Blackwell and MIT Press, 1982.

_____."Well-being, Agency and Freedom: The Dewey Lectures 1984." *Journal of Philosophy* 82 (1985): 169–220.

Sen, A. K. and B. Williams, eds. *Utilitarianism and Beyond*. Cambridge University Press, 1982.

Shorrocks, A. "The Class of Additively Decomposable Inequality Measures." *Econometrica* 48 (1980): 613–25.

_____."Inequality Decomposition by Factor Components." *Econometrica* 50 (1982): 193–211.

_____."On the Distance between Income Distributions." *Econometrica* 50 (1982): 1337–39.

Sidgwick, Henry. *The Methods Of Ethics*. 7th ed. Macmillan, 1907.

Slote, Michael A. "Desert, Consent, and Justice." *Philosophy and Public Affairs* 2 (1973): 323–47.

Smart, J. J. C. and Bernard Williams. *Utilitarianism: For and Against*. Cambridge University Press, 1973.

Taurek, John. "Should the Numbers Count?" *Philosophy and Public Affairs* 6 (1977): 293–316.

Taylor, Shelley. "The Availability Bias in Social Perception and Interaction." In *Judgment Under Uncertainty: Heuristics and Biases*, edited by D. Kahneman, P. Slovic, and A. Tversky, pp. 190–200. Cambridge University Press, 1982.

Taylor, S. E., S. T. Fiske, N. Etcoff, and A. Ruderman. "The Categorial and Contextual Bases of Person Memory and Stereotyping." *Journal of Personality and Social Psychology* 36 (1978): 778–93.

Temkin, Larry S. "Inequality." *Philosophy and Public Affairs* 15 (1986): 99–121.

_____."Intransitivity and the Mere Addition Paradox." *Philosophy and Public Affairs* 16 (1987): 138–87.

_____."Additivity." In *Encyclopedia of Ethics*, edited by Lawrence Becker and Charlotte Becker, pp. 15–18. Garland Press, 1992.

_____."Intergenerational Inequality." In *Philosophy, Politics, and Society*, 6th ser., edited by Peter Laslett and James Fishkin, pp. 169–205. Yale University Press, 1992.

_____."Harmful Goods, Harmless Bads." In *Value, Welfare and Morality*, edited by R. G. Frey and Christopher Morris. Cambridge University Press, forthcoming.

Thomson, J. J. "Preferential Hiring." *Philosophy and Public Affairs* 2 (1973): 364–84.

Tversky, A., and D. Kahneman. "Availability: A Heuristic for Judging Frequency and Probability." *Cognitive Psychology* 5 (1973): 207–32.

_____."Judgment under Uncertainty: Heuristics and Biases." *Science* 185 (1974): 1124–31.

Varian, Hal. "Equity, Envy, and Efficiency." *Journal of Economic Theory* 9 (1974): 63–91.

_____."Distributive Justice, Welfare Economics, and the Theory of Fairness." *Philosophy and Public Affairs* 4 (1975): 223–49.

_____."Dworkin on Equality of Resources." *Economics and Philosophy* 1 (1985): 110–25.

Vlastos, Gregory. "Justice and Equality." In *Social Justice*, edited by Richard Brandt, pp. 31–72. Prentice Hall, 1962.

Weale, Albert. *Equality and Social Policy*. Routledge and Kegan Paul, 1978.

Westermarck, Edward. *Ethical Relativity*. Harcourt, Brace and Company, 1932.

Williams, Bernard. "The Idea of Equality." In *Philosophy, Politics, and Society*, 2nd ser., edited by Peter Laslett and W. G. Runciman, pp. 110–31. Basil Blackwell, 1962.

Wittgenstein, Ludwig. *Philosophical Investigations*. Translated by G. E. M. Anscombe. Macmillan, 1953.

Wolheim, Richard. "Equality." *Proceedings of the Aristotelian Society* 56 (1955-56): 281–300.

Young, Michael. *The Rise of the Meritocracy*. Penguin Books, 1961.

Index